Shaping the Future of IoT with Edge Intelligence

How Edge Computing Enables the Next Generation of IoT Applications

RIVER PUBLISHERS SERIES IN COMMUNICATIONS AND NETWORKING

Series Editors:

Abbas Jamalipour
The University of Sydney, Australia

Marina Ruggieri
University of Rome Tor Vergata, Italy

The "River Publishers Series in Communications and Networking" is a series of comprehensive academic and professional books which focus on communication and network systems. Topics range from the theory and use of systems involving all terminals, computers, and information processors to wired and wireless networks and network layouts, protocols, architectures, and implementations. Also covered are developments stemming from new market demands in systems, products, and technologies such as personal communications services, multimedia systems, enterprise networks, and optical communications.

The series includes research monographs, edited volumes, handbooks and textbooks, providing professionals, researchers, educators, and advanced students in the field with an invaluable insight into the latest research and developments.

Topics included in this series include:-

- Communication theory
- Multimedia systems
- Network architecture
- Optical communications
- Personal communication services
- Telecoms networks
- Wifi network protocols

For a list of other books in this series, visit www.riverpublishers.com

Shaping the Future of IoT with Edge Intelligence

How Edge Computing Enables the Next Generation of IoT Applications

Editors

Rute C. Sofia

fortiss GmbH, Germany

John Soldatos

Netcompany-Intrasoft, Luxembourg

River Publishers

Routledge
Taylor & Francis Group

NEW YORK AND LONDON

Published 2024 by River Publishers
River Publishers
Alsbjergvej 10, 9260 Gistrup, Denmark
www.riverpublishers.com

Distributed exclusively by Routledge
605 Third Avenue, New York, NY 10017, USA
4 Park Square, Milton Park, Abingdon, Oxon OX14 4RN

Shaping the Future of IoT with Edge Intelligence / by Rute C. Sofia, John Soldatos.

ISBN: 978-87-7004-027-3 (hardback)
    978-10-0381-215-9 (online)
    978-10-3263-240-7 (master ebook)

DOI: 10.1201/9788770040273

Printed on acid-free paper.

This book has received funding from the European Union's Horizon 2020 research and innovation programme under grant agreements No. 956671 and No. 825075.

Contents

II Artificial Intelligence of Things (AIoT) and AI at the Edge

4 Machine Learning (ML) as a Service (MLaaS): Enhancing IoT with Intelligence, Adaptive Online Deep and Reinforcement Learning, Model Sharing, and Zero-knowledge Model Verification

Jorge Mira, Iván Moreno, Hervé Bardisbanian, and
Jesús Gorroñogoitia

5 Federated Learning Models in Decentralized Critical Infrastructure

Ilias Siniosoglou, Stamatia Bibi, Konstantinos-Filippos Kollias,
George Fragulis, Panagiotis Radoglou-Grammatikis,
Thomas Lagkas, Vasileios Argyriou, Vasileios Vitsas,
and Panagiotis Sarigiannidis

III Blockchain Solutions for Trusted Edge Intelligence in IoT Systems

11 Decentralized Strategy for Artificial Intelligence in Distributed IoT Ecosystems: Federation in ASSIST-IoT

Eduardo Garro, Ignacio Lacalle, Karolina Bogacka,
Anastasiya Danilenka, Katarzyna Wasielewska-Michniewska,
Charalambos Tassakos, Anastasia Theodouli, Anastasia
Kassiani Blitsi, Konstantinos Votis, Dimitrios Tzovaras, Marcin
Paprzycki, and Carlos E. Palau

12 Achieving Security and Privacy in NG-IoT using Blockchain Techniques 251
Vasiliki Kelli, Anna Triantafyllou, Panagiotis Radoglou-Grammatikis,
Thomas Lagkas, Vasileios Vitsas, Panagiotis Fouliras, Igor Kotsiuba,
and Panagiotis Sarigiannidis

IV   Novel IoT Applications at the Cloud, Edge, and "Far-Edge" 267

13 Enabling Remote-controlled Factory Robots via Smart IoT Application Programming Interface 269
Ivo Bizon Franco de Almeida, Rania Rojbi, Nuria Molner,
and Carsten Weinhold

14 A Practical Deployment of Tactile IoT: 3D Models and Mixed Reality to Increase Safety at Construction Sites   **285**
Piotr Sowiński, Tina Katika, Fotios K. Konstantinidis,
Anna Dabrowska, Ignacio Lacalle, Angelos Amditis,
Carlos E. Palau, and Marcin Paprzycki

15 Haptic and Mixed Reality Enabled Immersive Cockpits for Tele-operated Driving   **301**
Raul Lozano, Miguel Cantero, Manuel Fuentes, Jaime Ruiz,
Ignacio Benito, and David Gomez-Barquero

16 The EFPF Approach to Manufacturing Applications Across Edge-cloud Architectures   **319**

Rute C. Sofia, Carlos Coutinho, Gabriele Scivoletto,
Gianluca Insolvibile, Rohit A. Deshmukh, A. Schneider,
Violeta Damjanovic-Behrendt, Fernando Gigante, Usman Wajid,
Alexandros Nizamis, Dimosthenis Ioannidis, and Theofilos Mastos

V   IoT Skills and Business Models   **349**

17 The EU-IoT Skills Framework for IoT Training and Career Development Processes   **351**

J. Soldatos

18 Digital Business IoT Maturity Patterns from EU-IoT Ecosystem 377

Parwinder Singh, Michail Beliatis, Emilie Mathilde Jakobsen,
and Mirko Presser

Preface

J. Soldatos[1] and R. Sofia[2]

[1]Netcompany-Intrasoft, Luxembourg
[2]fortiss GmbH, Germany
Email: john.soldatos@netcompany-intrasoft.com, sofia@fortiss.org,
rute.sofia@ieee.org

The Book

In recent years, there is an on-going shift of data and applications from the cloud to edge computing data centers and devices. Edge computing expands conventional centralized hyperscale models to enable real-time, ultra-low-latency applications, privacy-preserving, and energy- efficient applications. Internet of Things (IoT) devices are the heart of the edge computing paradigm serving as producers, consumers, and processors of large amounts of data. Specifically, IoT devices are among the main data sources of non-trivial cloud/edge applications such as lifestyle management applications in health-care, predictive maintenance applications in industry, and connected car applications in transport. Moreover, IoT devices are commonly deployed as edge devices, i.e., they deal with data collection and data processing close to the field. There are also cases where IoT devices, cyber−physical systems, and smart objects (e.g., robotic cells, unmanned aerial vehicles, etc.) implement actuation functionalities that drive edge intelligence. Overall, a wide range of IoT applications are nowadays based on cloud/edge architectures and related deployment paradigms.

The development, deployment, and operation of IoT applications at the edge are currently enabled by a rich set of cutting-edge digital technologies. For instance, 5G/6G networks are commonly used to ensure high-bandwidth and ultra-low-latency operations in an edge computing environment. Such operations are key for supporting a host of emerging applications such as autonomous driving and metaverse applications involving Tactile Internet interactions. As another example, embedded machine learning and federated machine learning technologies enable the implementation of artificial intelligence (AI) functionalities at the edge (edge AI). Edge AI functionalities facilitate the implementation of a rich set of real-time, power-efficient, and privacy-friendly IoT applications. There are also cases where IoT solution integrators integrate distributed ledger technologies (DLTs) (i.e., blockchain infrastructures) in the cloud/edge computing continuum to implement decentralized intelligence use cases. The latter are usually characterized by strong security and are particularly handy in scenarios where centralized control is hardly possible (e.g., due to the lack of a trusted third party).

Based on the above-listed technologies, IoT developers and solution integrators are offered with many possibilities to implement IoT applications in-line with the cloud/edge paradigm. Specifically, they are provided with the means for implementing different deployment edge computing configurations that vary in terms of latency, energy efficiency, levels of data protection, degree of decentralization, real-time performance, and other characteristics. In this context, IoT researchers, developers, and engineers must be able to understand the characteristics and functionalities of the various edge intelligence technologies, along with their implications on the functional and non-functional properties of IoT solutions.

This book presents the technologies that empower edge intelligence, along with their use in novel IoT solutions. Specifically, it presents how 5G/6G, edge AI, and blockchain solutions enable novel IoT-based decentralized intelligence use cases at the cloud/edge computing continuum. Emphasis is to be paid on how these technologies support a wide array of functional and non-functional requirements spanning latency, performance, cybersecurity, data protection, real-time performance, energy efficiency, and more. The chapters of the book are contributed by six EU-funded projects (H2020 ASSIST-IoT, H2020 EFPF, H2020 iNGENIOUS, H2020 IoT-NGIN, H2020 TERMINET, and H2020 VEDLIoT), which have recently developed novel IoT platforms that enable the development and deployment of edge intelligence solutions. Each one of the projects employs its own approach and uses a different mix of networking, middleware, and IoT technologies. Therefore, each of the chapters of the book contributes a unique perspective about the capabilities of the enabling technologies and their integration in practical real-life applications in different sectors. The editing of the book has been coordinated by the H2020 EU-IoT project, which is an EU-funded coordination and support action (CSA) that is destined to support the European IoT community and to foster the development of a strong European IoT ecosystem. Apart from the editing of the book, EU-IoT has also contributed chapters about two of the ever important complementary assets that empower the development and deployment of successful edge intelligence applications, namely IoT business models and IoT skills. The book includes a dedicated part that discusses these resources that complement the research and scientific solutions.

Book Structure and Contents

The book is structured in five distinct parts. The first four focus on four different sets of enabling technologies for edge intelligence and smart IoT applications in the cloud/edge/IoT continuum. The fifth and final part is devoted to business models and skills frameworks for edge intelligence applications. Specifically, the five parts of the book and the chapters that they comprise are as follows:

The first part of the book (Part 1) is titled "**Edge Intelligence with 5G/6G Networks**." It provides insights on how the capabilities of 5G and 6G networks boost edge intelligence and related next generation IoT applications in the cloud/edge continuum. The first part of the book includes the following chapters:

- **Chapter 1 is titled "Edge Networking Technology Drivers for Next-generation Internet of Things in TERMINET Project."** It provides an overview of novel technological building blocks of future networks that empower next-generation IoT applications. The chapter is based on work carried out in the scope of the H2020 TERMINET project.
- **Chapter 2 is titled "AI-driven service and slice orchestration."** It is contributed to the book by the H2020 INGENIOUS project. The chapter illustrates how AI/ML techniques can help in augmenting the network slicing and service orchestration logic towards improving automation and intelligence. The chapter also illustrates how AI/ML boosts self-adaptation to satisfy the dynamics of next-generation IoT services.
- **Chapter 3 is titled "Tactile IoT Architecture for the IoT-Edge-Cloud Continuum: The ASSIST-IoT Approach"** and is contributed to the book by the H2020 ASSIST-IoT project. The chapter illustrates an approach for the development and deployment of tactile IoT systems, which is grounded on a reference architecture that is built on cloud-native concepts and several enabling technologies such as AI, cloud/edge computing, 5G, DLT, and AR/VR interfaces.

The second part of the book (Part 2) is titled "**Artificial Intelligence of Things (AIoT) and AI at the Edge**." It focuses on solutions for developing and deploying AI systems at the edge of the network toward achieving latency, privacy, and power-efficiency benefits. This second part of the book includes the following chapters:

- **Chapter 4 is titled "ML as a Service (MLaaS): Enhancing IoT with Intelligence with Adaptive Online Deep and Reinforcement Learning, Model Sharing, and Zero-Knowledge Model Verification."** The chapter describes work carried out in the scope of the H2020 IoT-NGIN project. It presents an MLOps that leverages MLOps platform for the delivery of intelligent IoT.
- **Chapter 5 is titled "Federated Learning Models in Decentralized Critical Infrastructure."** It focuses on federated learning solutions for decentralized critical infrastructures (CI). The chapter highlights the advantages and disadvantages of federated learning for CI applications and presents practical examples of federated learning for CI protections in different settings like power production facilities, agricultural sensor networks, smart homes, and more. The chapter is contributed to the book by the H2020 TERMINET project.
- **Chapter 6 is titled "Analysis of Privacy Preservation Enhancements in Federated Learning Frameworks"** and reflects work carried out in the scope of the H2020 IoT-NGIN project. It introduces privacy-preserving techniques for federated learning systems, notably techniques that enable fully private machine learning model sharing and training.
- **Chapter 7 is titled "Intelligent Management at the Edge."** It is contributed by the H2020 IoT-NGIN project. The chapter presents different cloud-native technologies enabling scalable, cost-efficient, and reliable IoT solutions. It also details various distributed and hierarchical monitoring frameworks and metrics collection schemes that can be used as inputs to AI engines. Moreover, the chapter discusses application placement problems focused on delay minimization in geographically distributed single-cluster environments.
- **Chapter 8 is titled "IoT Thing to Service ML-based Semantic Matchmaking at the Edge."** It is based on work partially carried out in the scope of the H2020 EU-IoT and H2020 EFPF projects. The chapter discusses the use of ML to support edge-based semantic matchmaking toward handling large-scale integration of IoT data sources with IoT

platforms. Emphasis is paid on how to alleviate the interoperability challenges of this integration.

- **Chapter 9 is titled "A Scalable, Heterogenous Hardware Platform for Accelerated AIoT based on Microservers."** It presents a modular microserver-based approach that enables the integration of different, heterogeneous accelerators into one platform. The work benchmarks the various accelerators considering their performance, energy efficiency, and accuracy. It is based on work carried out in the scope of the H2020 VEDLIoT project.
- **Chapter 10 is titled "Methods for Requirements Engineering, Verification, Security, Safety, and Robustness in AIoT Systems"** and is also contributed by the H2020 VEDLIoT project. The chapter presents a scalable, heterogenous hardware platform for accelerated AIoT based on microserver technology.

The third part of the book (Part 3) is titled "**Blockchain Solutions for Trusted Edge Intelligence in IoT Systems**." It unveils the potential benefit of using DLT technologies for edge intelligence in IoT systems. This part of the book comprises the following chapters:

- **Chapter 11 is titled "Decentralized Strategy for Artificial Intelligence in Distributed IoT Ecosystems: Federation in ASSIST-IoT"** and comprises work that has been carried out in the scope of the H2020 ASSIST-IoT project. It presents a decentralized learning solution for automotive and fleet management settings. The solution leverages distributed ledger technology among other solutions to improve the efficiency of the distributed learning paradigm, while preserving privacy.
- **Chapter 12 is titled "Achieving Security and Privacy in NG-IoT using Blockchain Techniques"** and presents work carried out in the context of the H2020 TERMINET project. It provides an overview of blockchain's security and privacy benefits for next-generation IoT applications. Moreover, the chapter discusses how blockchain technology can be used in conjunction with other technologies of the cloud/edge continuum.

The fourth part of the book (Part 4) is titled "**Novel IoT Applications at the Cloud, Edge, and Far-Edge**" and focuses on the presentation of novel IoT applications in the cloud/edge continuum, notably applications that exhibit edge intelligence among other characteristics. This part of the book comprises the following chapters:

- **Chapter 13 is titled "Enabling Remote Controlled Factory Robots via Smart IoT Application Programming Interface"** and reflects work that has been carried out in the H2020 iNGENIOUS project. The chapter provides an overview of IoT applications that comprise real-time control, touch, and sensing/actuation. The applications are put in the context of various industrial sectors.
- **Chapter 14 is titled "A Practical Deployment of Tactile IoT: 3D Models and Mixed Reality to Increase Safety at Construction Sites"** and is contributed by H2020 ASSIST-IoT. This chapter presents a mixed reality application that leverages cloud/edge middleware of the ASSIST-IoT project to enhance the safety and health of blue-collar workers at a construction site.
- **Chapter 15 is titled "Haptic and Mixed Reality Enabled Immersive Cockpits for Tele-operated Driving"** and is contributed by the H2020 iNGENIOUS project. It illustrates an approach for solving some of the autonomous operation challenges of autonomous mobile robots and of unmanned aerial vehicles in dynamic settings. The approach is based on the combination of low-latency 5G-IoT networks and immersive cockpits equipped with haptic and mixed reality devices. The chapter explains how such devices provide intuitive feedback toward facilitating context-aware decision making.
- **Chapter 16 is titled "The EFPF Approach to Manufacturing Applications Across Edge−Cloud Architectures."** It is contributed by the H2020 EFPF project and describes how industrial IoT systems and technologies enable a manufacturing as a service (MaaS) paradigm. The chapter provides insights on the integration of a diverse set of services such as data analytics, factory connectors, and interoperable data spines toward a high level of automation across different shopfloors.

The fifth part of the book (Part 5) is titled "**IoT Skills and Business Models**." It describes complementary assets and resources for deploying and operating modern IoT applications. This part of the book comprises two chapters:

- **Chapter 17 is titled "The EU-IoT Skills Framework for IoT Training and Career Development Processes"** and is based on work that has been carried out in the H2020 EU-IoT project. It introduces a skills framework that can facilitate IoT-related upskilling and reskilling processes. Moreover, it illustrates how the framework can be used to drive the specification of learning paths for popular IoT skills profiles.

- **Chapter 18 is titled "Digital Business IoT Maturity Patterns from EU-IoT Ecosystem."** It presents novel and disruptive IoT business model practices, along with trends and patterns in different industries. The presented patterns and best practices suggest an appropriate toolbox for stimulating a higher degree of innovation-driven thinking and exploitation for next-generation IoT applications. The chapter has been authored based on work carried out in the H2020 EU-IoT project.

The target audience of the book includes:

- IoT researchers that focus on novel technologies in the cloud/edge/IoT continuum and have a special interest in edge intelligence applications.
- Practitioners and providers of IoT solutions, which have an interest in the development, deployment, and operation of novel next-generation IoT use cases.
- Managers of IoT projects that need to gain insights on novel technology enablers of IoT applications in the cloud/edge/IoT continuum.

The book is provided in an Open Access publication, which makes it broadly and freely available to the cloud/edge computing and IoT communities. We would like to thank River Publishers for their collaboration and support in making this Open Access publication a reality. We would also like to thank the contributing projects for their research and scientific contributions. Moreover, we would like to acknowledge funding and support from the European Commission as part of the seven projects that contributed to this edited volume. We really hope that the IoT community will find this Open Access publication useful and interesting.

John Soldatos

Route Sofia

Acknowledgements

The editing of this book has been funded by the European Commission (EC) in the scope of its H2020 program, via projects EU-IoT (Grant number 956671) and EFPF (grant number 825075).

List of Figures

List of Tables

List of Contributors

Amditis, Angelos, *Institute of Communication and Computer Systems, Greece*

Anastasakis, Z., *Synelixis Solutions S.A., Greece*

Argyriou, Vasileios, *Kingston University, England*

Bardisbanian, Hervé, *Capgemini, France*

Barragan, Juan Sebastian Camargo, *i2CAT Foundation, Spain*

Beliatis, Michail, *BTECH, Aarhus University, Denmark*

Benito, Ignacio, *Nokia Spain S.A., Spain*

Bernini, G., *Nextworks, Italy*

Bibi, Stamatia, *University of Western Macedonia, Greece*

Blitsi, Anastasia Kassiani, *The Centre for Research Technology, Hellas, Greece*

Bnouhanna, Nisrine, *Technical University of Munich, Germany*

Bogacka, Karolina, *Systems Research Institute, Polish Academy of Sciences, Poland; Warsaw University of Technology, Poland*

Bourou, S., *Synelixis Solutions S.A., Greece*

Cantero, Miguel, *5G Communications for Future Industry Verticals S.L. (Fivecomm), Spain*

Carmona-Cejudo, Estela, *i2CAT Foundation, Spain*

Córdova, Andrés Cárdenas, *i2CAT Foundation, Spain*

Coronado, Estefanía, *i2CAT Foundation, Spain; Universidad de Castilla-La Mancha, Spain*

Coutinho, Carlos, *Caixa Mágica Software, Portugal*

Dabrowska, Anna, *Central Institute for Labour Protection – National Research Institute, Poland*

Damjanovic-Behrendt, Violeta, *Salzburg Research Institute, Austria*

Danilenka, Anastasiya, *Systems Research Institute, Polish Academy of Sciences, Poland; Warsaw University of Technology, Poland*

Deshmukh, Rohit A., *Fraunhofer Institute for Applied Information Technology FIT, Germany*

Felber, Pascal, *University of Neuchâtel, Switzerland*

Flottmann, M., *Osnabrück University, Germany*

Fornes-Leal, A., *Universitat Politècnica de València, Spain*

Fouliras, Panagiotis, *University of Macedonia, Greece*

Fragulis, Georgios, *University of Western Macedonia, Greece*

Franco de Almeida, Ivo Bizon, *Vodafone Chair Mobile Communication Systems, Technische Universität Dresden, Germany*

Fuentes, Manuel, *5G Communications for Future Industry Verticals S.L. (Fivecomm), Spain*

Ganzha, M., *Institute of Communications and Computer Systems, National Technical University of Athens, Greece*

Garro, Eduardo, *Prodevelop S.L., Spain*

Gigante, Fernando, *AIDIMME, Spain*

Gomez-Barquero, David, *iTEAM Research Institute of Universitat Politècnica de València, Spain*

Gorroñogoitia, Jesús, *Atos Spain, Spain*

Goudos, Sotirios, *Aristotle University of Thessaloniki, Greece*

Griessl, R., *Bielefeld University, Germany*

Gugala, K., *Antmicro, Poland*

Hagemeyer, J., *Bielefeld University, Germany*

Heyn, Hans-Martin, *Gothenburg University, Sweden*

Insolvibile, Gianluca, *Nextworks, Italy*

Ioannidis, Dimosthenis, *Centre for Research and Technology Hellas (CERTH), Greece*

Jakobsen, Emilie Mathilde, *BTECH, Aarhus University, Denmark*

Kaiser, M., *Bielefeld University, Germany*

Katertsidis, Nikolaos, *University of Western Macedonia, Greece*

Katika, Tina, *Institute of Communication and Computer Systems, Greece*

Kelli, Vasiliki, *University of Western Macedonia, Greece*

Khurshid, Anum, *Research Institutes of Sweden AB, Sweden*

Knauss, Eric, *Gothenburg University, Sweden*

Kollias, Konstantinos-Filippos, *University of Western Macedonia, Greece*

Konstantinidis, F., *Institute of Communications and Computer Systems, National Technical University of Athens, Greece*

Konstantinidis, Fotios K., *Institute of Communication and Computer Systems, Greece*

Kotsiuba, Igor, *iSolutions Lab, Ukraine*

Kucza, N., *Bielefeld University, Germany*

Lacalle, I., *Universitat Politècnica de València, Spain*

Lacalle, Ignacio, *Communications Department of Universitat Polit'ecnica de Val'encia, Spain*

Lacalle, Ignacio, *Communications Department of Universitat Polit'ecnica de Val'encia, Spain*

Lagkas, Thomas, *International Hellenic University, Greece*

Latosinski, G., *Antmicro, Poland*

Liatifis, Athanasios, *University of Western Macedonia, Greece*

Lozano, Raul, *iTEAM Research Institute of Universitat Politècnica de València, Spain*

Martínez, Adrián Pino, *i2CAT Foundation, Spain*

Mastos, Theofilos, *KLEEMANN HELLAS S.A., Kilkis Industrial Area, Greece*

Ménétrey, Jämes, *University of Neuchâtel, Switzerland*

Mika, K., *Bielefeld University, Germany*

Mira, Jorge, *Atos Spain, Spain*

Molner, Nuria, *iTEAM Research Institute of Universitat Politècnica de València, Spain*

Moreno, Iván, *Atos Spain, Spain*

Mosahebfard, Mohammadreza, *i2CAT Foundation, Spain*

Moscholios, Ioannis, *University of Peloponnese, Greece*

Nizamis, Alexandros, *Centre for Research and Technology Hellas (CERTH), Greece*

Ödman, D., *EMBEDL AB, Sweden*

Palau, C. E., *Universitat Politècnica de València, Spain*

Palau, Carlos E., *Communications Department of Universitat Polit'ecnica de Val'encia, Spain*

Palau, Carlos E., *Communications Department of Universitat Polit'ecnica de Val'encia, Spain*

Paprzycki, Marcin, *Systems Research Institute, Polish Academy of Sciences, Poland*

Paprzycki, Marcin, *Systems Research Institute, Polish Academy of Sciences, Poland; Warsaw University of Technology, Poland*

Pasin, Marcelo, *University of Neuchâtel, Switzerland*

Piscione, P., *Nextworks, Italy*

Pliatsios, Dimitrios, *University of Western Macedonia, Greece*

Porrmann, F., *Bielefeld University, Germany*

Porrmann, M., *Osnabrück University, Germany*

Presser, Mirko, *BTECH, Aarhus University, Denmark*

Qararyah, F., *Chalmers University of Technology, Sweden*

Radoglou-Grammatikis, Panagiotis, *University of Western Macedonia, Greece*

Raza, Shahid, *Research Institutes of Sweden AB, Sweden*

Rojbi, Rania, *Vodafone Chair Mobile Communication Systems, Technische Universität Dresden, Germany*

Ruiz, Jaime, *Nokia Spain S.A., Spain*

Sarigiannidis, Panagiotis, *University of Western Macedonia, Greece*

Schiavoni, Valerio, *University of Neuchâtel, Switzerland*

Schneider, A., *Fraunhofer Institute for Applied Information Technology FIT, Germany*

Scivoletto, Gabriele, *Nextworks, Italy*

Seder, E., *Nextworks, Italy*

Siddiqui, Muhammad Shuaib, *i2CAT Foundation, Spain*

Singh, Parwinder, *BTECH, Aarhus University, Denmark*

Siniosoglou, Ilias, *University of Western Macedonia, Greece*

Skias, D., *Netcompany-Intrasoft S.A., Greece*

Sofia, Rute C., *fortiss Research Institute of the Free State of Bavaria for Software Intensive Systems and Services – affiliated with the Technical University of Munich, Germany*

Soldatos, J., *Netcompany-Intrasoft S.A, Luxembourg*

Sowiński, Piotr, *Systems Research Institute, Polish Academy of Sciences, Poland; Warsaw University of Technology, Poland*

Szmeja, P., *Systems Research Institute Polish Academy of Sciences, Poland*

Tassakos, Charalambos, *TwoTronics GmbH, Germany*

Tassemeier, M., *Osnabrück University, Germany*

Theodou, Anastasia, *The Centre for Research Technology, Hellas, Greece*

Torres-Pérez, Claudia, *i2CAT Foundation, Spain*

Trancoso, P., *Chalmers University of Technology, Sweden*

Triantafyllou, Anna, *University of Western Macedonia, Greece*

Tzovaras, Dimitrios, *The Centre for Research Technology, Hellas, Greece*

Velivasaki, T. H., *Synelixis Solutions S.A., Greece*

Vitsas, Vasileios, *International Hellenic University, Greece*

Votis, Konstantinos, *The Centre for Research Technology, Hellas, Greece*

Voulkidis, A., *Synelixis Solutions S.A., Greece*

Wajid, Usman, *Information Catalyst, UK*

Waqar, M., *Chalmers University of Technology, Sweden*

Wasielewska-Michniewska, Katarzyna, *Systems Research Institute, Polish Academy of Sciences, Poland*

Weinhold, Carsten, *Barkhausen-Institut gGmbH, Germany*

List of Abbreviations

3GPP	3rd generation partnership project
5GAA	5G automotive association
5GC	5G core
5QI	5G quality of service indicators
AAI	Authentication and authorization interface
ACK	Acknowledgement
AF	Architecture framework
AGV	Automated guided vehicle
AI	Artificial intelligence
AIoT	Artificial intelligence of things
AIOTI	Alliance for IoT innovation
HLA	High level architecture
AIOTI	Alliance for the internet of things innovation
AMQP	Advanced message queuing protocol
AMR	Autonomous mobile robot
AN	Access network
AOT	Ahead-of-time
API	Application programming interface
AR	Augmented reality
ASIC	Application-specific integrated circuit
AWS	Amazon web services
B5G	Beyond 5G
BKPI	Business key performance indicator
BLE	Bluetooth low energy
BMP	Business model pattern
BMs	Business models
BPMN	Business process modelling notation
BSS	Business support system
CA	Certification authority
CAB	Conformity assessment body

CCC	Confidential computing consortium
CD	Continuous delivery
CD	Continuous development
CDN	Content delivery network
CDP	Career development paths
CE	Community edition
cGAN	Conditional generative adversarial network
CI	Continuous integration
CI	Critical infrastructure
CN	Core network
CNCF	Cloud native computing foundation
CNN	Convolution neural network
CoAP	Constrained application protocol
COB	Core ontology for biology and biomedicine
COCO	Common objects in context
COM	Computer on module
CPPS	Cyber−physical production systems
CPS	Cyber−physical systems
CPU	Central processing unit
CRD	Kubernetes resource definition
CS	Communication services
CSA	Coordination and support action
CSMF	Communication service management function
D2D	Device-to-device
DataOps	Data operations
DBSCAN	Density-based spatial clustering of applications with noise
DDS	Data distribution service
DeepLIFT	Deep learning important features
DevOps	Development and operations
DL	Deep learning
DLT	Distributed ledger technology
DMAT	Digital maturity assessment tool
DP	Differential privacy
DPDK	Data plane development kit
DPU	Deep-learning processing unit
DSP	Digital signal processor

E2E	End-to-end
eBPF	extended Berkeley filter packer
EC	European commission
EDBE	Edge data broker enabler
EFPF	European connected factory platform for agile manufacturing
EG	Electric grid
EM	Element manager
eMBB	Enhanced mobile broadband
EMR	Electronic medical records
ETSI	European telecommunications standardisation institute
EU	European union
EU-IoT	European union internet of things
EV	Electric vehicle
EVM	Ethereum virtual machine
FATE	Federated AI technology enabler
FL	Federated learning
FLS	Federated learning system
FoF	Factories of the future
FP16	16-bit floating-point precision
FP32	32-bit floating-point precision
FPGA	Field programmable gate array
GAN	Generative adversarial network
Gbit/s	Giga bit per second
GCP	Google cloud platform
GDPR	General data protection regulation
GF	Grant-free
GitsOps	Git operations
GOPS	Giga-operations per second
GPGPU	General purpose GPU
GPS	Global positioning system
GPU	Graphics processing unit
GRU	Gated recurrent unit
GSMA	GSM association
GST	Generalized network slice template
GUI	Graphical user interface

GWEN	Gateway/edge node
H2020	Horizon 2020
HARA	Hazard identification and risk assessment
HARQ	Hybrid automatic repeat request
HDP	Hybrid differentially private
HE	Homomorphic encryption
HEU	Horizon Europe
HIS	Hyperspectral imaging
HMD	Head mounted display
HMI	Human−machine interface
HP	High performance
HPC	High performance computing
HR	Human resources
HSLL	High speed low latency
HTTP	Hypertext transfer protocol
I/O	Input/output
IaC	Infrastructure as a code
IAI	Innovint aircraft interior GmbH
IAM	Identify access management
IDE	Integrated development environment
IdM	Identity manager
IDS	Intrusion detection systems
IIC	Industrial internet consortium
IICF	Industrial internet connectivity framework
IID	Independent and identically distributed
IIoT	Industrial internet of things
ILSVRC	ImageNet large-scale visual recognition challenge
IMU	Inertial measurement unit
INT8	8-bit integer precision
IOF	Industrial ontology foundation
IoT	Internet of things
IoT-NGIN	IoT engine to the next generation IoT
IoU	Intersection over union
IP	Intellectual property
IP	Internet protocol
IPv6	Internet protocol version 6

ITU-T	International telecommunication union standardization sector
JIT	Just-in-time
JSON	JavaScript object notation
KPI	Key performance indicator
LCM	Lifecycle management
LiDAR	Light detection and ranging
LoRa	Long range
LP	Low power
LPWAN	Low power wireless network technologies
LRA	Linear resonant actuator
LSP	Large scale pilot
LSTM	Long short-term memory
LTSE	Long-term storage enabler
M2M	Machine-to-machine
MANO	Management and orchestration
mAP	Mean average precision
MD-5	Message-digest 5
MEC	Multi-access edge computing
mIoT	Massive internet of things
ML	Machine learning
MLaaS	ML as a service
MLOps	Machine learning operations
mMTC	Massive machine-type communications
mmWave	Millimeter wave
MQTT	Message queuing telemetry transport
MR	Mixed reality
MSE	Mean square error
MVP	Minimum viable product
NAT	Network address translation
NBI	Northbound interface
NF	Network function
NFV	Network functions virtualization
NFVI	NFV infrastructure
NFVO	NFV orchestrator
NG-IoT	Next-generation IoT
NG-SDN	Next-generation SDN

NIST	National institute of standards and technology
NM	Network manager
NOMA	Non-orthogonal multiple access
NR	New radio
NRM	Network slice resource model
NSD	Network service descriptor
NSI	Network slice instance
NSMF	Network slice management function
NSSI	Network slice subnet instance
NSSMF	Network slice subnet management function
NSST	NSS template
NST	Network slice template
NWDAF	Network data analytics function
OBO	Open biological and biomedical ontology
OEM	Original equipment manufacturer
OEO	Open energy ontology
OL	Online learning
ONNX	Open neural network exchange
OPC	UA Open platform communications unified architecture
OPC-UA	OPC Unified architecture
OPEX	Operational expenditure
OPI	Open programmable infrastructure
OS	Operating system
OSH	Occupational safety and health
OSS	Open source software
OSS	Operations support system
OWL	Ontology web language
P4	Programming protocol independent packet processors
PaaS	Platform as a service
PCB	Printed circuit board
PCIe	Peripheral component interconnect express
PDU	Protocol data unit
PLC	Programmable logic controller
PNF	Physical network function
PoC	Proof of concept

PoS	Proof of stake
POSIX	Portable operating system interface
PoW	Proof of work
PPFL	Privacy preserving federated learning
PRNG	Pseudo random number generator
Pub/Sub	Publish/subscribe
PUD	Performance and usage diagnosis
PV	Power-voltage
PVC	Persistent volume claim
QoE	Quality of experience
QoS	Quality of service
R&D	Research and development
RA	Reference architecture
RAN	Radio access network
RATS	Remote attestation procedures
RECS	Resource efficient cluster server
REST	Representational state transfer
RF	Radio frequency
RFID	Radio frequency identification
RIC	RAN intelligent controller
RIS	Reconfigurable intelligent surfaces
RML	RDF mapping language
RNN	Recurrent neural network
ROAM	Risk, opportunity, analysis, and monitoring
ROS	Robot operating system
RSA	Rivest–Shamir–Adleman
RTT	Round trip time
SaaS	Software as a service
SAREF	Smart applications reference
SBA	Service-based architecture
SCADA	Supervisory control and data acquisition
SDK	Software development kit
SDN	Software-defined networking
SFP	Small form-factor pluggable
SGX	Secure guard extensions
SHA-256	Secure hash algorithm 256
SLA	Service level agreement

SLAM	Simultaneous location and mapping
SMC	Secure multiparty computation
SME	Small and medium enterprise
SOA	Service-oriented architectures
SoC	System on chip
SON	Self-organizing networks
SQL	Structured query language
SSO	Single sign-on
SST	Slice/service type
TAM	Technology acceptance model
TD	Things description
TEE	Trusted execution environment
TFF	Tensorflow federated
THz	Terahertz
TN	Transport network
TOCTOU	Time-of-check to time-of-use
ToD	Tele-operated driving
TOPS	Tera operations per second
ToR	Top of rack
TPM	Trusted platform module
TSDB	Time series databases
TSMatch	Thing to service matching
UAV	Unmanned aerial vehicle
UC	Use case
UDP	User datagram protocol
UE	User equipment
UI	User interface
UID	Unique identifier
UPF	User plane function
URLLC	Ultra-reliable and low-latency communications
USB	Universal serial bus
UWB	Ultrawideband
V2X	Vehicle-to-everything
VEDLIoT	Very efficient deep learning in IoT
VIM	Virtual infrastructure manager
VNF	Virtual network function
VNFM	VNF manager

VPN	Virtual private network
VR	Virtual reality
VSB	Vertical service blueprint
VSD	Vertical service descriptor
VSMF	Vertical service management function
WAN	Wide area network
WASI	WebAssembly system interface
WaTZ	A trusted WebAssembly runtime environment with remote attestation for TrustZone
WEF	World economic forum
WMF	World manufacturing forum
WOM	Walter Otto Müller
WoT	Web of things
WoTSE	Web of things search engine (WoTSE)
WSDL	Web services description language
WSN	Wireless sensor network
XAI	Explainable artificial intelligence
XDP	Express data path
ZSM	Zero-touch network and service management

Part I

Edge Intelligence with 5G/6G Networks

1

Edge Networking Technology Drivers for Next-generation Internet of Things in the TERMINET Project

Athanasios Liatifis[1], Dimitrios Pliatsios[1], Panagiotis Radoglou-Grammatikis[1], Thomas Lagkas[2], Vasileios Vitsas[2], Nikolaos Katertsidis[1], Ioannis Moscholios[3], Sotirios Goudos[4], and Panagiotis Sarigiannidis[1]

[1]University of Western Macedonia, Greece
[2]International Hellenic University, Greece
[3]University of Peloponnese, Greece
[4]Aristotle University of Thessaloniki, Greece
E-mail: aliatifis@uowm.gr; dpliatsios@uowm.gr; pradoglou@uowm.gr; tlagkas@cs.ihu.gr; vitsas@it.teithe.gr; n.katertsidis@uowm.gr; idm@uop.gr; sgoudo@physics.auth.gr; psarigiannidis@uowm.gr

Abstract

The rapid growth of the Internet of Things has shaped the design and deployment of mobile networks to accommodate the need for ubiquitous connectivity and novel applications. The recent advancements in wireless communications and computing technologies allow the connection of a wider range and number of devices and systems, thereby enabling the design and development of next-generation Internet of Things applications. However, current networking technologies cannot accommodate the increasing number of IoT devices as well as satisfy the heterogeneous and stringent requirements in terms of bandwidth, connectivity, latency, and reliability. Motivated by these remarks, this chapter aims to provide an overview of key novel technologies, which are expected to be integral components of future networks

DOI: 10.1201/9781032632407-2

and can effectively address the challenges associated with satisfying the aforementioned requirements.

Keywords: Next-generation Internet of Things, software-defined networking, network function virtualization mobile edge computing, digital twins, radio access network.

1.1 Introduction

The past couple of years have seen an increased interest in the Internet of Things (IoT) [1]. IoT is one of the fastest evolving technologies and it is being increasingly adopted and shaped by various industries and organizations to push their vision. As a result, IoT is expected to be a core component of the future Internet and has received much attention from both industry and academia due to its great potential to deliver customer services in many aspects of modern life. IoT enables the interconnection of various appliances and devices to the internet, enabling them to communicate and exchange data. This interconnected network of devices is expected to introduce substantial changes to the ways people live and work.

The main advantage of IoT is the ability to collect, aggregate, and analyze large volumes of data, enabling the automation of various processes or generating useful insights that assist in the decision-making process. IoT is being integrated into various application verticals, including smart healthcare, smart industry, autonomous vehicles, smart agriculture, and smart cities.

The latest advancements in wireless communications and computing technologies integrate enhanced connectivity, increased bandwidth and data rates, and ultra-low-latency communications, making it feasible to connect a wider range of systems and devices and enabling the realization of next-generation IoT (NG-IoT) applications [2]. To this end, researchers have identified a number of key challenges that have to be addressed:

1. **Large data volumes and number of devices:** A distinct characteristic of IoT is the dense deployment of massive numbers of devices. These devices generate a large volume of data that have to be efficiently transferred and processed. The Big Data concept is concerned with how these data are collected, stored, and processed.
2. **Ubiquitous wireless connectivity:** Mobile networks provide ubiquitous wireless connectivity, enabling reliable communications between humans. Consequently, they are promising candidates for the

communications infrastructure. However, the traffic generated by IoT devices features some special characteristics and has considerable differences compared to traffic generated by human-to-human communications. Therefore, these attributes have to be considered during the design and deployment of future mobile networks.

3. **Interoperability:** Interoperability refers to the ability of devices and applications from different vendors to work together seamlessly. It is considered one of the most important aspects of the IoT, as it enables the communication and sharing of data among devices, regardless of the manufacturer or technology they use. Key challenges in achieving interoperability in the IoT domain include the diversity of devices and protocols, as well as the lack of standardization in the field.

4. **Energy efficiency:** Energy efficiency is concerned with the minimization of energy consumption while ensuring the provisioning of a minimum quality of service (QoS). It is a critical factor in IoT, as most of the devices have limited energy reserves. Therefore, the reduction of the consumed energy assists in extending their operating time. Moreover, achieving a high energy efficiency level can effectively reduce the total network energy consumption.

5. **Cybersecurity considerations:** Cybersecurity considerations include the measures adopted to protect the devices, data, and networks from unauthorized access and cyberattacks, such as man-in-the-middle attacks, device spoofing, and denial-of-service attacks. Cybersecurity has become a major concern due to the increasing number of IoT devices. Furthermore, the limited processing capabilities of IoT devices make the deployment of advanced cybersecurity countermeasures challenging.

To address the aforementioned challenges, several technologies have emerged. This chapter aims to provide an overview of these technologies, describe their key features, and outline potential applications. An illustration of the technology drivers for NG-IoT is presented in Figure 1.1.

1.2 Technology Drivers

1.2.1 Software defined networking and network function virtualization

Software defined networking (SDN) and network function virtualization (NFV) have revolutionized the way networks are designed, deployed, and

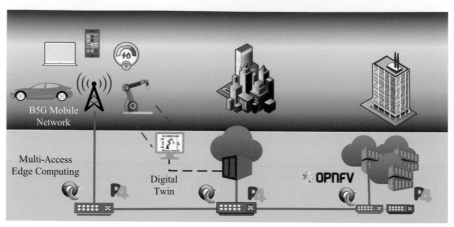

Software Defined Networking - Network Function Virtualization

Figure 1.1   NG-IoT technology drivers.

operated [3]. Traditionally, data forwarding and control mechanisms were intertwined in every forwarding device (e.g., switch, router, firewall, etc.) resulting in limited flexibility in terms of new functionality and freedom of choice of hardware solutions. Each vendor offered specific tools and frameworks rendering multi-vendor deployment a hard task for large organizations (operational expenditure – OPEX). SDN, and, notably, OpenFlow [4], are promising technologies that can address the challenges associated with managing and operating complex networks. Consequently, service providers can focus on developing novel and customized solutions suitable for the size, needs, and customer profiles while maximizing the usage of networking infrastructure.

Networking functionalities, such as firewalls and load-balancing processes, were implemented by dedicated and expensive hardware solutions. Also, network scalability was not particularly considered, resulting in higher capital expenditures [5]. Moreover, the support for new protocol demands required the replacement of existing infrastructure and time-consuming processes. By leveraging the advancements of virtualization technologies, NFV offers dynamic network scaling and allows for placing network functionalities in the appropriate location, thereby minimizing network downtime.

The combination of SDN and NFV allows for realizing a dynamic, efficient, and customized networking infrastructure. Network services can be deployed easily in any part of the network and combined to form a chain of services [6]. Furthermore, SDN complements NFV offering a standardized mechanism to manipulate the behavior of forwarding devices through well-defined interfaces. The control plane can identify abnormal behavior in the data plane and re-adjust the path flows traverse to avoid cascading effects.

Despite the fact that SDN and NFV have acted as catalysts for many network services, current solutions are accompanied by several limitations. The next generation of computer networks, also referred to as next-generation SDN (NG-SDN), is characterized by fully programmable data planes offering packet-based monitoring solutions, whereas SDN and NFV will be tightly coupled further complementing each other. Programming languages and frameworks like P4, eBPF/XDP, and DPDK enable end-to-end programmability and experimentation with new protocols following a continuous integration/continuous development (CI/CD) approach [7]. Additionally, network functions can be, fully or partially, offloaded to programmable targets alleviating the control plane from continuous monitoring of the data plane state. Advances to artificial intelligence and machine learning (AI/ML) are also reflected in the control plane through intelligent applications that utilize the enriched statistics collected from the data plane [8], while existing SDN controllers are updated or new ones are developed to take full advantage of what programmable targets have to offer [9]. Frameworks like open programmable infrastructure (OPI) aim to unify programmability across infrastructure components (computing, AI/ML, networking, storage, etc.) granting developers standardized mechanisms of programming the entire infrastructure [10].

1.2.2 Beyond 5G mobile networks

5G mobile networks facilitate the design and development of applications with highly heterogeneous communication requirements by defining specific application classes such as enhanced mobile broadband (eMBB), ultra-reliable and low-latency communications (URLLC), and massive machine-type communications (mMTC). Nevertheless, the rapid growth of intelligent and autonomous IoT networks is likely to exceed the capabilities of 5G mobile networks.

As a result, researchers from academia and industry are focusing on the beyond 5G (B5G) mobile networks and their accompanying technological advances in order to prepare the way for NG-IoT development [11]. Due to its superior features over previous network generations, such as extremely high throughput, ultra-low-latency communications, and intelligent network capabilities, B5G networks are expected to deliver a new level of service and user experience in IoT networks.

- **Support for massive IoT:** B5G networks will enable the deployment of a massive number of IoT devices, with the ability to deploy millions of devices in a square kilometer. This will allow IoT applications to be deployed in domains such as smart cities, industrial automation, and agriculture [12].
- **Ultra-reliability and low-latency communications:** B5G networks facilitate the realization of IoT-based application scenarios that require ultra-reliability and low latency. Such application scenarios include remote surgery, virtual and augmented reality applications, autonomous vehicles, and intelligent industrial robotics [13].
- **Seamless wireless protocol integration:** The integration of various wireless protocols will assist in achieving the stringent requirements of NG-IoT. For example, the integration of Wi-Fi and B5G protocols will enable the leverage of the high-capacity links of Wi-Fi and the enhanced coverage of mobile networks. Moreover, additional wireless protocols can be integrated, with each one introducing different advantages, such as Bluetooth low energy (BLE), LoRa, etc.
- **High-frequency communication:** High-frequency communication refers to the use of higher frequency bands in wireless communications, such as millimeter wave (mmWave) and terahertz (THz) frequencies [14], [15]. The mmWave range includes frequencies in the range of 30–300 GHz, while the THz range includes frequencies between 100 GHz and 10 THz. These frequencies offer a much larger bandwidth compared to traditional mobile network frequencies. As a result, larger numbers of devices can be accommodated and very high data rates can be achieved. However, these signals are more susceptible to obstacles such as trees and buildings, making the deployment of such high-frequency networks more challenging.
- **Novel radio access schemes:** Radio access schemes are a key component of wireless communication systems, as they manage the use of the limited radio frequency (RF) spectrum. Due to the massive connectivity and low-latency requirements, several radio access schemes have emerged, such as the non-orthogonal multiple access (NOMA) and grant-free (GF) access schemes. NOMA schemes aim to schedule multiple devices over the same radio resources, while GF schemes allow

devices to transmit their data without having to request radio access beforehand, effectively reducing latency [16].

- **Reconfigurable intelligent surfaces:** Reconfigurable intelligent surfaces (RIS) enable the manipulation of electromagnetic signals through a large number of passive, programmable, and low-cost elements [17]. These elements are able to control the absorption, refraction, and reflection of the signals, therefore reducing the signal fading, reducing the required transmission power, and enhancing the spatial spectrum reuse. Moreover, RIS reduce network expansion costs, as they mitigate the need to deploy more base stations for providing coverage to devices located at the network edge or behind obstacles.

1.2.3 Digital twin

The digital twin concept enables the digital representation of a physical object or system. A digital twin is generated by accumulating data from sensors on the physical device or system and utilizing that data to construct a virtual model of the real device or system [18]. The digital system coexists with the physical one as the two systems are interconnected through reliable and low-latency links. Real-time data transfers between physical and digital systems provide synchronized and coherent operation of the physical and virtual counterparts [19].

This enables the implementation of various simulation scenarios and analyses using this model for evaluating the possible outcomes, prior to their actual application in the real world. Consequently, digital twins can be used to construct digital representations of IoT devices and/or networks, in order to monitor, control, and assess the performance of the device/system in real time. Digital twins can be used in a variety of applications and scenarios including the following:

- **Virtual prototyping:** The digital twin of a device can be used for testing and assessing various design options, leading to an optimal design of the final product before its construction. This can effectively reduce the overall manufacturing time, as well as the associated testing costs.
- **Predictive maintenance:** By monitoring the performance of a device or system over time, the digital twin can be used to predict when maintenance is needed and to schedule maintenance at the most optimal time. Moreover, "what-if" scenarios can be simulated in order to find the best course of action with respect to the object's maintenance.

- **Building automation:** Typically, buildings consist of various components from different domains, including ventilation, heating, energy, mechanics, and plumbing. The digital twin of a building, a building complex, or a whole city can effectively facilitate building/city management and mitigate the environmental footprint (i.e., realizing a green building).

1.2.4 Multiple-access edge computing

Multi-access edge computing (MEC) is an emerging paradigm that attempts to converge telecommunication and IT services by delivering a cloud computing platform at the network edge [20]. MEC provides storage and computing resources at the network's edge, therefore lowering latency for mobile end users and maximizing the utilization of mobile backhaul and core networks. Consequently, MEC enables the development of a wide range of novel applications and services and the introduction of new business models. Key applications enabled by the MEC include the following:

- **Computation offloading:** Computationally intensive applications such as augmented and virtual reality applications require large data volumes to be transmitted and processed in real time. As a result, the conventional approach of transmitting and routing the data to datacenters with ample computing resources cannot ensure the real-time constraint. Computation offloading enables resource-constrained devices to partially or fully offload computationally intensive tasks to the computation resources offered by MEC, thereby reducing the processing time, increasing battery lifetime, and enhancing the network's energy efficiency [21], [22]. Additionally, as the processing takes place at the network edge, the communication and latency overheads are mitigated.
- **Next-generation Internet of Things:** Traditional IoT application scenarios involve aggregating large data volumes and forwarding them to a cloud environment for further processing. However, emerging next-generation IoT applications have increased constraints in terms of latency and reliability (e.g., autonomous vehicle scenarios). MEC can facilitate the deployment of storage and computing resources in close proximity to the devices, ensuring both redundancy and fast responses to device requests [23]. For instance, MEC is a key enabler for vehicle-to-infrastructure and vehicle-to-vehicle communications. Vehicles connected through the distributed MEC nodes can send and receive

real-time information, such as traffic congestion and warnings from other vehicles.

- **Content delivery and caching:** Image and video sharing constitute a large portion of mobile traffic. Such content is stored in datacenters and is distributed to the users through content delivery networks (CDNs). Nevertheless, there may be a lack of content in the proximity of the users, resulting in increased buffering time and lower quality of experience (QoE). To this end, MEC can effectively assist in realizing a distributed CDN by also taking into consideration information and context about the users in the proximity [24], [25].

1.3 Conclusion

The rapid expansion of the IoT considerably affects the planning of networks in order to satisfy the need for ubiquitous connectivity, increased data rates, and low-latency communications. NG-IoT is considered an evolution of the conventional IoT paradigm that is enabled by the latest advancements in wireless communications and computing technologies. NG-IoT allows the design and development of innovative services and applications.

NG-IoT applications feature heterogeneous and stringent requirements in terms of latency, reliability, and connectivity. To this end, various technologies and frameworks have emerged, aiming to address these requirements and the associated challenges. This chapter provided an overview of key technology drivers, namely the NG-SDN, NFV, B5G mobile networks, digital twins, and MEC, by presenting the main principles and outlining several application scenarios. These technologies are expected to be core components of future networks and facilitate the development of novel applications and services.

Acknowledgements

This work has received funding from the European Union's Horizon 2020 research and innovation program under grant agreement No. 957406 (TER-MINET).

References

[1] H. Cao, M. Wachowicz, C. Renso, and E. Carlini, "Analytics everywhere: Generating insights from the internet of things," *IEEE Access*, vol. 7, pp. 71749–71769, 2019, doi: 10.1109/ACCESS.2019.2919514.

[2] NG-IoT Consortium, "Building a roadmap for the next generation internet of things: Research, innovation and implementation 2021-2027." Sep. 2019.

[3] D. Kreutz, F. M. V. Ramos, P. E. Veríssimo, C. E. Rothenberg, S. Azodolmolky, and S. Uhlig, "Software-defined networking: A comprehensive survey," *Proceedings of the IEEE*, vol. 103, no. 1, pp. 14–76, 2015, doi: 10.1109/JPROC.2014.2371999.

[4] N. McKeown *et al.*, "OpenFlow: Enabling innovation in campus networks," *SIGCOMM Comput. Commun. Rev.*, vol. 38, no. 2, pp. 69–74, Mar. 2008, doi: 10.1145/1355734.1355746.

[5] Z. Latif, K. Sharif, F. Li, M. M. Karim, S. Biswas, and Y. Wang, "A comprehensive survey of interface protocols for software defined networks," *Journal of Network and Computer Applications*, vol. 156, p. 102563, 2020, doi: https://doi.org/10.1016/j.jnca.2020.102563.

[6] K. Kaur, V. Mangat, and K. Kumar, "A comprehensive survey of service function chain provisioning approaches in SDN and NFV architecture," *Computer Science Review*, vol. 38, p. 100298, 2020, doi: https://doi.org/10.1016/j.cosrev.2020.100298.

[7] A. Liatifis, P. Sarigiannidis, V. Argyriou, and T. Lagkas, "Advancing SDN: From OpenFlow to P4, a survey," *ACM Computing Surveys*, Aug. 2022, doi: 10.1145/3556973.

[8] R. Amin, E. Rojas, A. Aqdus, S. Ramzan, D. Casillas-Perez, and J. M. Arco, "A survey on machine learning techniques for routing optimization in SDN," *IEEE Access*, vol. 9, pp. 104582–104611, 2021, doi: 10.1109/ACCESS.2021.3099092.

[9] R. Vilalta *et al.*, "Cloud-native SDN network management for beyond 5G networks with TeraFlow." virtual event, Jun. 2021. Available: https://zenodo.org/record/5089908

[10] Linux Foundation, "Open programmable infrastructure project." Sep. 2022. [Online]. Available: http://www.opiproject.org/

[11] Z. Zhang *et al.*, "6G wireless networks: Vision, requirements, architecture, and key technologies," *IEEE Vehicular Technology Magazine*, vol. 14, no. 3, pp. 28–41, 2019, doi: 10.1109/MVT.2019.2921208.

[12] X. Chen, D. W. K. Ng, W. Yu, E. G. Larsson, N. Al-Dhahir, and R. Schober, "Massive access for 5G and beyond," *IEEE Journal on Selected Areas in Communications*, vol. 39, no. 3, pp. 615–637, 2021, doi: 10.1109/JSAC.2020.3019724.

[13] B. S. Khan, S. Jangsher, A. Ahmed, and A. Al-Dweik, "URLLC and eMBB in 5G industrial IoT: A survey," *IEEE Open Journal*

of the Communications Society, vol. 3, pp. 1134–1163, 2022, doi: 10.1109/OJCOMS.2022.3189013.

[14] L. Zhang *et al.*, "A survey on 5G millimeter wave communications for UAV-assisted wireless networks," *IEEE Access*, vol. 7, pp. 117460–117504, 2019, doi: 10.1109/ACCESS.2019.2929241.

[15] K. M. S. Huq, S. A. Busari, J. Rodriguez, V. Frascolla, W. Bazzi, and D. C. Sicker, "Terahertz-enabled wireless system for beyond-5G ultra-fast networks: A brief survey," *IEEE Network*, vol. 33, no. 4, pp. 89–95, 2019, doi: 10.1109/MNET.2019.1800430.

[16] D. Pliatsios, A.-A. A. Boulogeorgos, T. Lagkas, V. Argyriou, I. D. Moscholios, and P. Sarigiannidis, "Semi-grant-free non-orthogonal multiple access for tactile internet of things," in *2021 IEEE 32nd annual international symposium on personal, indoor and mobile radio communications (PIMRC)*, 2021, pp. 1389–1394. doi: 10.1109/PIMRC50174.2021.9569640.

[17] M. A. ElMossallamy, H. Zhang, L. Song, K. G. Seddik, Z. Han, and G. Y. Li, "Reconfigurable intelligent surfaces for wireless communications: Principles, challenges, and opportunities," *IEEE Transactions on Cognitive Communications and Networking*, vol. 6, no. 3, pp. 990–1002, 2020, doi: 10.1109/TCCN.2020.2992604.

[18] R. Minerva, G. M. Lee, and N. Crespi, "Digital twin in the IoT context: A survey on technical features, scenarios, and architectural models," *Proceedings of the IEEE*, vol. 108, no. 10, pp. 1785–1824, 2020, doi: 10.1109/JPROC.2020.2998530.

[19] S. Mihai *et al.*, "Digital twins: A survey on enabling technologies, challenges, trends and future prospects," *IEEE Communications Surveys & Tutorials*, vol. 24, no. 4, pp. 2255–2291, 2022, doi: 10.1109/COMST.2022.3208773.

[20] T. Taleb, K. Samdanis, B. Mada, H. Flinck, S. Dutta, and D. Sabella, "On multi-access edge computing: A survey of the emerging 5G network edge cloud architecture and orchestration," *IEEE Communications Surveys & Tutorials*, vol. 19, no. 3, pp. 1657–1681, 2017, doi: 10.1109/COMST.2017.2705720.

[21] S. Thananjeyan, C. A. Chan, E. Wong, and A. Nirmalathas, "Mobility-aware energy optimization in hosts selection for computation offloading in multi-access edge computing," *IEEE Open Journal of the Communications Society*, vol. 1, pp. 1056–1065, 2020, doi: 10.1109/OJCOMS.2020.3008485.

[22] D. Pliatsios, P. Sarigiannidis, T. D. Lagkas, V. Argyriou, A.-A. A. Boulogeorgos, and P. Baziana, "Joint wireless resource and computation offloading optimization for energy efficient internet of vehicles," *IEEE Transactions on Green Communications and Networking*, vol. 6, no. 3, pp. 1468–1480, 2022, doi: 10.1109/TGCN.2022.3189413.

[23] S. Hamdan, M. Ayyash, and S. Almajali, "Edge-computing architectures for internet of things applications: A survey," *Sensors*, vol. 20, no. 22, p. 6441, Nov. 2020, doi: 10.3390/s20226441.

[24] E. F. Maleki, W. Ma, L. Mashayekhy, and H. La Roche, "QoS-aware 5G component selection for content delivery in multi-access edge computing," 2021. doi: 10.1145/3468737.3494101.

[25] X. Jiang, F. R. Yu, T. Song, and V. C. M. Leung, "A survey on multi-access edge computing applied to video streaming: Some research issues and challenges," *IEEE Communications Surveys & Tutorials*, vol. 23, no. 2, pp. 871–903, 2021, doi: 10.1109/COMST.2021.3065237.

2

AI-driven Service and Slice Orchestration

G. Bernini, P. Piscione, and E. Seder

Nextworks, Italy
E-mail: g.bernini@nextworks.it; p.piscione@nextworks.it; e.seder@nextworks.it

Abstract

Current MANO solutions and existing tools for network slicing and service orchestration are still implemented as silo-based control and orchestration tools, mostly addressing the coordination of monolithic pipelined services that cannot be easily and transparently adapted to dynamic NG-IoT network and service conditions. Lack of agility and flexibility in the service and slice lifecycle management, as well as in the runtime operation, is indeed still an evident limitation. A tight integration of AI/ML techniques can help in augmenting the slice and service orchestration logics automation and intelligence, as well as their self-adaptation capabilities to satisfy NG-IoT service dynamics.

Keywords: NG-IoT, 5G, network slicing, orchestration, 3GPP, artificial intelligence, machine learning.

2.1 Introduction

In general, a 5G network infrastructure that provides an end-to-end connectivity service in the form of a network slice to the end users requires proper resource allocation and management. The allocation and the management of these resources become critical, especially when the number of user equipment (UE) starts to increase. To this end, the next-generation IoT (NG-IoT)

15   DOI: 10.1201/9781032632407-3

network slice orchestration supported by an artificial intelligence/machine learning (AI/ML) platform plays a crucial role, performing semi-automated decisions on resource allocation and management.

With 5G, the telecommunication industry is more and more looking at comprehensive management and orchestration (MANO) solutions to ease the deployment of heterogeneous vertical services and network slices across several technology domains. The concept of network slicing allows to jointly orchestrate resources (network, computing, and storage) and network functions (NFs) (virtualized or physical), which are managed and delivered together to instantiate and compose network services over a shared infrastructure. Network slices can be dynamically created and customized according to the requirements of the services that will run on top of them, for example, in terms of resource or function isolation and quality of service (QoS) guarantees. This has been considered in the iNGENIOUS project [1], where heterogeneous IoT network technologies and devices are required to interoperate with the 5G network to provide smart and innovative supply chain and industrial IoT services.

Current MANO framework solutions and existing tools for network slicing and NFV network service orchestration are still implemented as silo-based control and orchestration tools, mostly addressing the coordination of monolithic pipelined services that cannot be easily and transparently adapted to changing network and service conditions. Lack of agility and flexibility in the service and slice lifecycle management is still an evident limitation, thus requiring *ad-hoc* solutions and customizations for addressing the challenging NG-IoT time sensitive networking and ultra-low-latency requirements. Moreover, a full integration of 5G new radio (NR), NG-IoT, and edge computing technology domains is not yet achieved when it comes to deploying end-to-end network slices. Moreover, the overall capability of such orchestration approaches to fulfill heterogeneous service constraints and requirements still needs to be proved, as it often requires per-service customizations and human-driven adjustments to support end-to-end deployments. In addition, the adoption of AI/ML technologies for cognition-based optimizations, including their interaction across the different technological domains (e.g., network related, edge computing related, cloud computing related, etc.) and their tight integration with the service and slice lifecycle management is still at its early stages.

The current MANO coordination functionalities are highly linked to static internal coordination and orchestration logic. The management operations at different levels follow the workflows, which MANO is responsible for implementing. This results in lack of flexibility because when either minor adjustments are needed or unplanned events occur, MANO remains strict to its static coordination and orchestration logic. In this context, a tight integration with AI/ML techniques could address this kind of problem. AI/ML algorithms generally do not follow the if−then approach, but they are able to "learn" from past experience and, in some cases, take decisions. For the aforementioned reasons, in the iNGENIOUS project, one key innovation for what concerns the orchestration aspects is the intelligent management and orchestration of network resources for the NG-IoT ecosystem. In this context, since the resource demand could be fluctuating during a time period and at the same time the high-level requirements must be satisfied, a semi-automated decision-based approach comes into place.

2.2 Related Work

2.2.1 Management and orchestration of 5G networks

The 3GPP TSG-SA WG 5, responsible for the aspects related to management, orchestration, and charging of 5G networks, has defined a generalized mobile network management architecture in the 3GPP TS 28.500 specification [2]. The architecture, depicted in Figure 2.1, involves a 3GPP management system with a network manager (NM) and element manager (EM) that control the elements composing a 5G network, where each of them can be deployed as a physical network function (PNF) or a virtual network function (VNF). The presence of VNFs in the 5G mobile network introduces the need of a management and orchestration (MANO) framework responsible for their provisioning, configuration, and, more in general, for their lifecycle management (LCM), in cooperation with the 3GPP management system.

The MANO framework is based on the architecture defined by the ETSI NFV ISG for the NFV-MANO [3] and includes the three elements of the NFV orchestrator (NFVO), VNF manager (VNFM), and virtual infrastructure manager (VIM). In this scenario, the NM of the 3GPP management system is part of the operations support system/business support system (OSS/BSS) and interacts with the NFVO to request the provisioning and drive the management of the NFV network services composed of the VNFs that build the mobile communication network.

The adoption of virtualized functions as elements of the mobile network brings higher degrees of dynamicity and flexibility in the 5G network deployment. It also enables a number of features in its management and

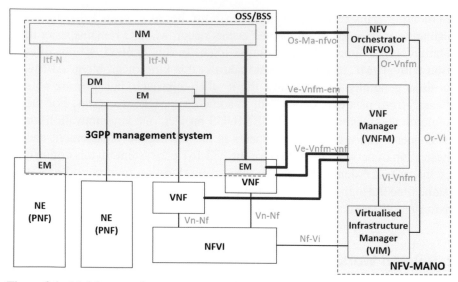

Figure 2.1   Mobile network management architecture – interaction between 3GPP management system and NFV-MANO framework [2].

operation, including dynamic instantiation, automated scaling, optimization, and healing. Such functionalities can be driven by an external management logic and actuated through the NFV orchestrator, with the cooperation of VNFM and VIM for the configuration of virtual functions and the control of the virtual resource allocation, respectively.

2.2.2 5G network slices

The network slicing concept has been introduced in 5G networks to allow the operators to effectively share their own infrastructure, creating multiple concurrent logical partitions, i.e., the network slices. Network slices can be easily customized according to the business requirements of their customers or the technical requirements of their services. Network slices can be differentiated and updated independently, offering various degrees of isolation, and they can be adapted in terms of mobile connectivity, virtual functions, or computing and storage resources.

Network slices can be easily configured to offer dedicated communication services to the verticals, e.g., customized on the basis of their production requirements. For example, ultra-reliable and low-latency communications

(URLLCs) meet the requirements of the production lines automated control in Industry 4.0 and smart factory scenarios. Massive Internet of Things (mIoT) communications are particularly suitable to manage huge amounts and high density of IoT sensors and actuators. Enhanced mobile broadband (eMBB) communications are the enablers for video producing and broadcasting, offering high data rates in both uplink and downlink directions. Vehicle-to-everything (V2X) communications support high-bandwidth, low-latency, and high-reliable interactions among moving (autonomous) vehicles and different entities such as other vehicles, pedestrians, etc.

The concept of network slicing is introduced in the 3GPP TS 23.501 [4] specification, where a network slice is defined like a logical network that provides specific network capabilities and characteristics. A network slice instance (NSI) consists of a set of network functions (NFs), with their own computing, storage, and networking resources. An NF can be implemented within an NSI as a PNF running on dedicated hardware or as a VNF instantiated over a computing shared infrastructure, e.g., on the cloud. In a 5G network, an end-to-end NSI includes the NFs related to control and user planes of the 5G core network, as well as next-generation RAN (NG-RAN) functions for the 3GPP mobile access network.

Network slices can be differentiated in terms of network functions and network capabilities, according to a number of major categories defined through a slice/service type (SST) including eMBB, URLLC, mIoT, and V2X. A network operator can thus instantiate multiple NSIs with their specific SST to differentiate the business offer toward its own customers. Moreover, multiple NSIs with the same SST can be instantiated and reserved to different customers to better guarantee their traffic QoS, isolation, and security.

The 3GPP TS 28.530 specification [5] defines the major concepts related to the management of a network slice to support specific types of communication services (CS), or vertical services. The network slice is presented as a logic network, including the related pool of resources, which enables the delivery of a CS on the basis of its characteristics and requirements (e.g., maximum latency and jitter, minimum data rates, density of UEs, coverage area, etc. Different types of CS can be supported through dedicated NSIs. An NSI can support one or more instances of CS. Moreover, an NSI is formally modeled as an end-to-end network slice subnet instance (NSSI), which in turn can include multiple NSSIs (see the network slice information model in Section 2.2.1 for further details). In particular, the figure shows a common pattern of network slice modeling, with the end-to-end NSSI composed of two lower level NSSIs: the former related to the 5G core network (CN) and the latter related to the access network (AN). Each of them includes the related NFs, which communicate through the underlying connectivity provided by the transport network (TN). In other terms, an NSSI represents a group of NF instances (together with their own resources) that implement a part of the NSI. Through this concept, it is possible to manage the set of NF and related resources as an atomic element, independently on the rest of the NSI.

2.2.3 Information models for 5G network slices

The information model of an NSI is defined in the 3GPP TS 28.541 [6], as part of the 5G network slice resource model (NRM). The model, represented in Figure 2.2, highlights how an end-to-end network slice, composed of several network slice subnets, can be deployed through a number of NFV network services and (virtual) network functions.

A network slice is associated with an end-to-end network slice subnet that defines the slice's internal elements and their interconnectivity, together with a set of service profiles describing the service requirements. Example of service profile parameters includes maximum number of UEs, service coverage

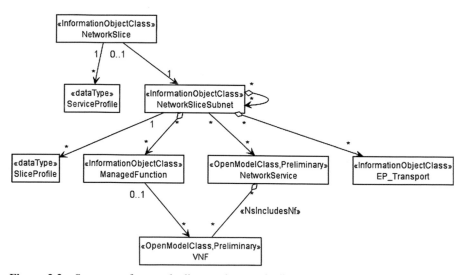

Figure 2.2   Structure of network slices and network slice subnets in network services and virtual network functions [6].

area, maximum latency, per-slice and per-UE throughput in uplink and down-link, maximum number of allowed connections, jitter, UEs' maximum speed, etc.

On the other hand, an NSD represents the topology of a network service, identifying its internal network functions (through references to the VNF and/or PNF descriptors) and describing how they are interconnected through the virtual links. Moreover, the NSD also defines the logic of the communications among the network functions, describing how the traffic should be forwarded through the sequence of functions. This aspect is defined through the "VNF forwarding graph," which indicates the sequence of VNFs, and the related "network forwarding path," which describe the traffic flows and their L2/L3 classifiers.

The 3GPP information model reported in Figure 2.2 captures the internal technical details of a network slice instance, identifying its components and their connectivity. However, when exposing the generic characteristics of a network slice toward external entities (for example, in case of network slice offers to potential customers), it is useful to refer to a "network slice template" that describes the slice capabilities through a more abstract model that hides its internal details and the operator implementation choices. In this case, the slice can be defined through the "generalized network slice template" (GST) [7] defined by the GSM association (GSMA).

2.2.4 Management of 5G network slices

The 3GPP TR 28.801 specification [8] defines the high-level functional archi-tecture for the management of network slices in support of communication services, identifying the three functional elements of the communication service management function (CSMF), network slice management function (NSMF), and network slice subnet management function (NSSMF).

At the upper layer, the CSMF is responsible of processing the requests for new CS and manages the CS instances provided by a network opera-tor. The CSMF translates the CS requirements into a set of network slice characteristics, e.g., defining the SST, the required capacity of the mobile connectivity, the QoS requirements, etc., and interacts with the NSMF to request the creation of the related NSI.

The NSMF is responsible for the management and end-to-end orches-tration of NSIs, on the basis of the requests received from the CSMF. The NSMF splits the NSI into its internal NSSIs, according to the NEST, and manages their lifecycle. Therefore, the NSMF is the entity that takes decisions about the composition of a NSI, including the re-usage of pre-existing NSSIs that can be shared among multiple NSIs, and the coordination of their provisioning, scaling, and/or configuration. The actuation of these decisions is then related to the NSSMFs, which are finally responsible for the management and orchestration of each NSSI.

As analyzed in the 3GPP TS 28.533 specification [9], which defines an architecture of the 3GPP management system designed following the service-based architecture (SBA) pattern, a typical deployment of the 3GPP management system is structured with domain-specific NSSMFs, related to the RAN, the CN, or TN domains. Such NSSMFs are customized according to the specific requirements and technologies adopted in their own target domain. As detailed in Section 2.4, the iNGENIOUS end-to-end network slice orchestration architecture follows a similar approach introducing dedicated NSSMF to handle the RAN, 5G core, and transport domains, as shown in Figure 2.3.

3GPP standards do not mandate any specific implementation of the NSMF and NSSMF components. However, the 3GPP TR 28.533 specification [9] proposes a deployment option, widely used in production infrastructures, where the management of the network slices and slice subnets lifecycle

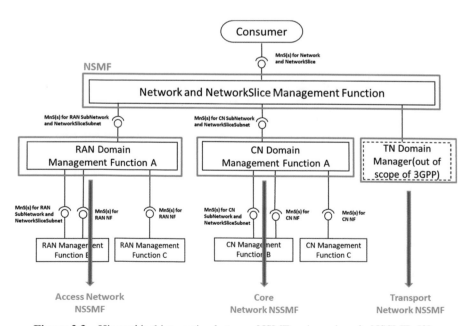

Figure 2.3 Hierarchical interaction between NSMF and per-domain NSSMFs [9].

is handled through an interaction with the NFV MANO system, where the NFV orchestrator is responsible for the lifecycle of the NFV network services associated with the NSSIs. The orchestration solution proposed by iNGENIOUS is aligned with this approach and relies on the NFV MANO for the instantiation and lifecycle management of the virtual functions related to the 5G core network and to the application services within the end-to-end network slices.

2.3 Architectural Principles

The end-to-end network slice orchestration framework solution proposed by the iNGENIOUS project has been conceived to satisfy the following architectural principles:

- *Principle #1*: The end-to-end network slice orchestration architecture should follow the global structure of the 5G system defined in the 3GPP specifications and make use of the latest technologies and architectures in the area of network function virtualization.
- *Principle #2*: The end-to-end network slice orchestration architecture should be aligned with the major 3GPP and ETSI standards in terms of functional architecture and interfaces with the aim of facilitating interoperability and integration with 5G infrastructure deployments.
- *Principle #3*: The design of the end-to-end network slice orchestration framework should maximize the re-use of existing architectural components from 3GPP and ETSI NFV specifications, e.g., in terms of management functionalities, MANO components, etc. When new functions or components are required, their interfaces should be designed to facilitate their integration with the existing standard frameworks.
- *Principle #4*: The end-to-end network slice orchestration should be augmented with closed-loop functionalities to achieve a high degree of automation in service and network slice operation. The integration of AI/ML solutions and technologies should be considered to go beyond current reactive closed-loop approaches in favor of proactive optimization solutions.
- *Principle #5*: The end-to-end network slice orchestration architecture should enable the implementations of its components as cloud-native services, easing the deployment in edge and cloud environments, in a modular, dynamic, and orchestrated way.

- *Principle #6*: The end-to-end network slice orchestration framework should make use of open interfaces and APIs to facilitate its integration with third-party systems and avoid vendor lock-ins.
- *Principle #7*: The design of the end-to-end network slice orchestration architecture should follow a modular pattern that enables its applicability to multiple use cases and deployment scenarios. It should facilitate composition and customization of the functional blocks according to accommodate specific requirements of the target use-case domains and required features.

2.4 Functional Architecture

The main principles and motivations described in the previous section led to the specification of the end-to-end network slice orchestration framework. In Figure 2.4 is available a mapping between the functional architecture described in the 3GPP TR 28.801 specification (Figure 2.4(a)) and the proposed high-level architecture of the end-to-end network slice framework, which is assisted by cross-layer AI/ML functionalities in support of the network slice operations (Figure 2.4(b)).

Figure 2.4(b) shows the three main functional blocks, namely vertical service management function (VSMF), network slice management function (NSMF), and network slice subnet management function (NSSMF), which play a specific and crucial role in the proposed orchestration framework. In particular, the VSMF layer is in charge of the lifecycle of vertical service instances, i.e., a service with high-level requirements. The VSMF translates the vertical service requirements into end-to-end network slice requirements. The NSMF layer is in charge of the lifecycle of end-to-end network slices. Furthermore, the NSMF interacts with different NSSMFs. The NSSMF layer is in charge of managing the specific lifecycle of the network slices subnet. This layer can include multiple instances of NSSMFs, one specific for each network domain (e.g., RAN, transport, core, etc.).

The number and type of end-to-end network slices applicable and suitable for a given vertical service strictly depend on its high-level requirements and application scenario. For instance, a URLLC and eMBB end-to-end slices can coexist on the same physical network infrastructure. The former can be referred to as an industry 4.0 scenario (e.g., robot communication service), while the latter as a video streaming communication service with a fixed QoS (e.g., video resolution).

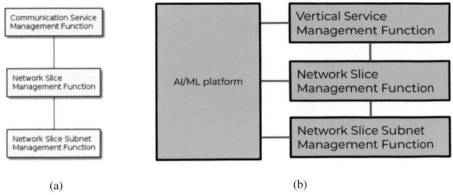

(a)   (b)

Figure 2.4 End-to-end network slice orchestration high-level architecture supported by AI/ML platform.

From an architectural perspective, the orchestration framework uses a cross-layer approach, meaning that each functional component described above is dedicated to manage and coordinate specific service, network slice, and resource operations, with tight cooperation to fulfill end-to-end and cross-layer consistency. The information available at the VSMF level is kept at the service level only, with abstraction in terms of network slice and resource details. On the other hand, at the NSSMF level, the information managed is technology- and vendor-specific. Therefore, the end-to-end network slice orchestration framework implements different mechanisms for translating the high-level requirements into technology- and vendor-specific requirements. The end-to-end orchestration framework is also supported by an AI/ML platform to execute some automatic decisions in the operation of vertical services and network slices.

In the following sections, the main components of the proposed architecture (already briefly described above) are detailed. In particular, for each component, the related functional decomposition is presented, including the information managed and the interaction with other layers.

2.4.1 Orchestration components

This section describes the internal components of the end-to-end network slice orchestration framework. Figure 2.5 depicts the functional architecture of the end-to-end network orchestration framework, derived from the high-level view of Figure 2.4. In particular, the 3GPP CSMF functionalities are realized by the vertical service management function (VSMF), the 3GPP

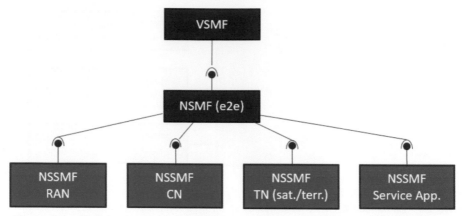

Figure 2.5   High-level software architecture end-to-end network orchestration framework.

NSMF functionalities are realized by the end-to-end NSMF, and finally the 3GPP NSSMF layer is mapped into multiple specific technology-tailored NSSMFs.

After a brief description of the network slice related data models supported by the end-to-end orchestration framework (which is key to capture how the various entities managed are modeled), the following sub-sections detail the functional decomposition and internal design of the VSMF, NSMF, and NSSMF components.

Data models:

The end-to-end network slice orchestration stack introduced above supports a multi-layered data model. This is used by each orchestration component to drive the lifecycle management operations and derive any requirement concerning services and network slices, and thus enforce the proper actions and invoke primitives in the lower layer components.

At the upper layer of the orchestration stack, the VSMF implements two different data models: the vertical service blueprint (VSB) and the vertical service descriptor (VSD). Both data models are based on a nonstandard information model defined as part of the vertical slicer (the baseline Nextworks software stack used for the end-to-end network slice orchestrator [10]) and represent respectively a class of vertical services (VSB) and a specific vertical service belonging to a certain class (VSD). The VSB describes a vertical service through service parameters defined according to digital/communication service providers' knowledge. Indeed, it provides a high-level description of the service that does not include infrastructure-related information. The VSD is obtained from a VSB, when a vertical consumer selects a class of service (i.e., a VSB) and produces a vertical service description by specifying certain value of the VSB parameters, which may include resource specifications, QoS and geographical constraints, number of users consuming the service, and also reference to specific vertical functions.

As anticipated above, at the NSMF and NSSMF levels, two different network slice data models are supported: the 3GPP network slice template (NST) and the GSMA GST. The latter is then called network slice type (NEST) once its attributes have been assigned proper values for a given service. The GSMA NEST allows the description of a network slice through value assignment according to the GSMA GST (GSMA, 2020). The main requirements expressed through the NEST consist of a list of 5G quality of service (QoS) indicators (5QI), which are subsequently mapped into NST's parameters that determine the type of the network slice. In particular, such 5QIs are used in the GST-to-NST translation process to determine the 3GPP-based service profile specified in the NST.

The 3GPP NST describes a network slice according to the attributes defined by the 3GPP network slice NRM [6], which provides network requirements and related resources' configuration. In particular, the NST, whose simplified class diagram is shown in Figure 2.6, contains a list of service profiles, each of them specifying the network slice type and the related

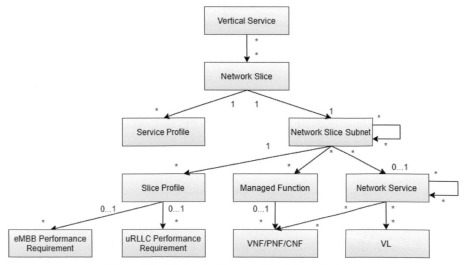

Figure 2.6 Network slice simplified class diagram.

QoS and service attributes (e.g., the latency, the maximum number of UE, the maximum supported packet size, etc.). In addition to the list of service profiles, the NST contains a reference to a network slice subnet (NSS) that can be represented through a NSS template (NSST) as part of the overall NST data model. The NSST contains a list of slice profiles, each of them representing the required properties of the NSS. The slice profile contains QoS attributes, similar to the service profile, and a list of performance requirements. The attributes included in the performance requirements depends on the type of the NSS. For instance, if the network slice type is URLLC, the list of performance requirements will contain parameters like the E2E latency, the jitter, the message size byte, and the communication service availability target. For eMBB network slices, the list of performance requirements can contain attributes like the experienced data rate, the area traffic capacity downlink, and the area traffic capacity uplink. Finally, two other attributes contained inside the NSST are a reference to a list of NSSTs and a network service descriptor (NSD) info field, which refers to the NFV network services that may be included into the NSS.

Vertical service management function:

As already mentioned, the VSMF is in charge of managing the requests of vertical service lifecycle management exploiting the related data model, i.e., the vertical service blueprint (VSB) and vertical service descriptor (VSD). Specifically, the VSB is a template used for representing a class of services. It contains parameters like the number of users, covered geographical area by the service, and so on. VSD is the parametrization of the defined VSB, specifying for instance the actual number of users the service, the actual geographical area where the service would be deployed, and so on.

In general, each vertical service is associated with a tenant that represents the vertical consumer/customer of the orchestration platform. However, each tenant has a maximum amount of resources for the vertical service provisioning defined within a service level agreement (SLA). Therefore, the VSMF implements operations to manage the tenant according to its specific SLAs information.

In general, the main aim of the VSMF is to manage the lifecycle of multiple vertical services in a seamless way. For this reason, different functionalities are supported by its internal components. The two main entities that interact with the VSMF at its northbound are: the network/admin operator for managing the onboarding of VSBs, and the configuration of the tenants and related SLAs; the vertical consumer/customer (i.e., the tenant) for requesting lifecycle operations of vertical services (e.g., instantiation, modification, termination, etc.).

Network service management function:

The NSMF is mainly responsible for managing the lifecycle of end-to-end network slices, according to the requirements and capabilities expressed in the generalized network slice template (GST) and network service template (NST).

As already described, the GST defined by GSM Association (GSMA) contains a set of attributes for defining a generic network slice regardless of the technology used for the network slice provisioning itself. The GST results in a NEST when GST's attributes are associated with a specific value [7]. Similarly, the NST and NSST, in compliance with the 5G NRM [6] (also detailed in Section 2.2.1), describe through an abstract model the slices' capability, without explicitly stating the internal technical details of the network slice itself. GSTs, NSTs, and NSSTs drive the whole lifecycle management of end-to-end network slices, implemented by the different components available within the NSMF.

Network slice subnet management function:

The NSSMF layer is a collection of different NSSMFs. Depending on the specific deployment scenario and specific 5G network infrastructure where the orchestration framework operates, the number and the type of NSSMFs can change. In the case of iNGENIOUS, the high-level architecture of the NSSMF layer is depicted in Figure 2.7.

Each specific network domain implements its own mechanisms, data models, REST APIs, and workflows for allocating computing and network

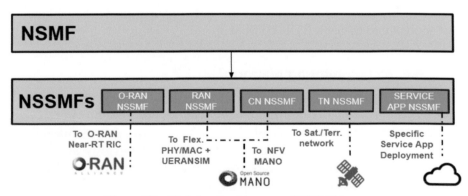

Figure 2.7 High-level architecture of NSSMF layer.

resources. For this reason, a tailored NSSMF implementation is needed to deal with the domain-specific controllers or local orchestrators, such as NFVOs, RAN controllers, SDN controllers, etc. Furthermore, the technical details of the domain are hidden by an abstraction layer each NSSMF provide: this approach allows the NSMF to deal transparently and uniformly with all the NSSMFs, providing flexibility to the NSMF perspective.

All NSSMFs follow a generic and unified functional decomposition, which aims at providing a set of common functionalities, which include: a northbound interface (NBI) for exploiting the NSSMF functionalities and for receiving subnet slice related requests (e.g., REST APIs), a core NSSMF service for validating and dispatching the requests into an event bus, publishing them as events, an event bus to allow communications among components using a topic-based and publish–subscribe mechanisms, an NSSMF handler to receive and process multiple requests and realizes the internal logic of the NSSMF.

From a software implementation perspective, each specialized NSSMF has its tailored realization: internal logic of NSSI provisioning, payload information model, and workflow interactions with the corresponding network domain controllers/orchestrators strictly depend on the technology, vendor, and interfaces supported. Some examples of NSSMFs developed in the context of the iNGENIOUS project are: O-RAN NSSMF, providing the translation of slice profiles into O-RAN A1 policies and A1 policy management operations in the O-RAN near real-time RAN intelligent controller (RIC); 5G Core network NSSMF, providing automated LCM, and configuration of 5G Core NFV network services through ETSI OSM [11]. The network service contains a 5G Core instance consisting of the control plane and user plane network functions of a 5G Core; service application NSSM, providing automated LCM and configuration of NFV network services modeling service virtual applications through ETSI OSM [11].

2.4.2 AI/ML and monitoring platform

As anticipated above, beyond the pure orchestration features, the iNGENIOUS end-to-end orchestration framework will provide closed-loop functionalities through the integration of a dedicated AI/ML and monitoring platform. First, the implementation of a closed-loop concept to fully automate the runtime optimization and adaptation of network slices requires knowledge on status and performance of (at least) the various involved NFs, network and computing resources. For this, specific monitoring capabilities have to be considered as key to collect and store relevant data on how the provisioned network slice instances (and the related resources) behave. Moreover, with the aim of going beyond the traditional reactive approach in fault and performance management, iNGENIOUS targets the implementation of predictive, proactive, and automated network slice runtime operation. For this, the end-to-end network slice orchestration framework makes use of AI/ML techniques to assist the decision-making processes mostly at the network slice management (and thus NSMF) level.

Therefore, the end-to-end network slice orchestration framework relies on an AI/ML and monitoring platform that is designed with the main purpose of supporting automated lifecycle management procedures for the optimization of network slices related resources (both network and computing). In practice, it aims at collecting metrics and information from heterogeneous resources, providing a variety of data inputs to AI/ML-based analytics and decision algorithms that can feed and assist the NSMF. The proposed platform is kept agnostic with respect to the specific algorithms consuming the monitoring data and provides two ways for accessing the data. First, it offers query-based access to retrieve historical or periodical data, for example, for the training of ML models. Second, it implements a subscribe/notify mechanism that allows to access streams of real-time data and can be used for real-time inference.

Figure 2.8 shows the high-level functional architecture of the AI/ML and monitoring platform. It is implemented through the integration of different data management open-source tools, augmented with additional *ad-hoc* components (such as the configuration manager and the adaptation layer) to ease the integration with the network slice orchestration components. As shown in the figure, the AI/ML and monitoring platform is built by the interaction of two building blocks: the monitoring platform and the AI/ML engine.

The monitoring platform provides both data storing and streaming functionalities, with proper interfaces exposed toward the AI/ML engine to consume the monitoring data. The data can be collected from different and heterogeneous data sources through the adaptation layer, which provides the necessary interfaces and logic to map the data from the sources to proper messages topics on the internal data bus. In particular, the adaptation layer is designed to be plug-in oriented, where each plug-in (or data-collection driver) collects data from a specific data source. This approach provides a high level of flexibility since the composition of the active plug-ins may vary with respect to the different network slices to be monitored or during the different phases of a network slice lifetime. A configurable Alert Manager (which is a built-in component of Prometheus) sends alarms to the bus when specific data

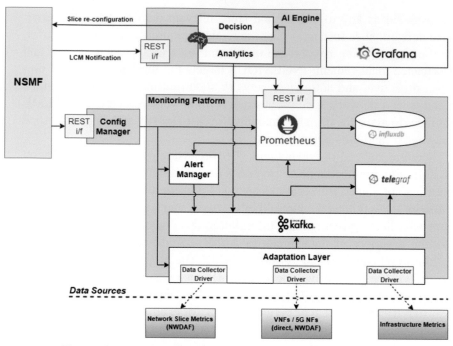

Figure 2.8   AI/ML and monitoring platform functional architecture.

exceeds certain thresholds, so that the alarm notification can be captured and stored in the Data Lake. The alarms and the data, both historical and near-real time, are therefore immediately available to the AI/ML engine that can access both the Data Lake and the message bus through dedicated interfaces. The whole monitoring platform is configured by the NSMF through the Config Manager, which for each network slice instance can tailor the behavior of the monitoring platform to properly collect, manage, and store the required data. Indeed, the Config Manager provides the logic for configuring Prometheus to properly aggregate the data collected through the message bus. Similarly, the Alert Manager is configured to produce different types of alerts when a given metric is exceeding a specific threshold. Moreover, the Config Manager is also responsible for the configuration of the different Data Collector Drivers to tailor the data collection from the various available sources according to the given network slice requirements.

The AI Engine is divided into two functional blocks, analytics and decision. The live data inputs are obtained by the analytics block through the monitoring platform, with analytics performance and results reported in

Grafana. The decision block passes the determined slice adaptations to the network slice orchestration components.

The analytics block can be subdivided into four stages designed for robust functionality on real-world data:

- Stage 1. Data pre-processing – real-time data contains many irregularities (e.g., null values) unrelated to the useful information derived from the target analysis. This noise can directly affect the ability of models to reliably infer behaviors in the incoming data. The data pre-processor cleans and normalizes the incoming dataset to avoid misbehavior of the model on real-world data.
- Stage 2. Feature detection – correlated time series data is analyzed with respect to long term behaviors that create unique features that can be used to predict future trends in network behavior. Selection of these features is achieved through the use of trained models capable of discriminating target behaviors.
- Stage 3. Inference engine – inference of future trends is performed using the identified features of the incoming dataset that are used as inputs in AI/ML algorithms to determine the most probable future state of the system. These predictions are then sent to the scaling logic to determine the most appropriate system adaptation.
- Stage 4. Logic – the predictions of the state of the system are combined with operational parameters to decide if, how, and when an adaptation will optimize the resources of the system. The logic interacts with the NSMF to accept any changes to the slice reconfiguration.

For what concerns the interaction with the network slice orchestration components, the AI/ML and monitoring platform offers a set RESTful APIs on top of the Config Manager and the AI/ML Engine. The purpose of the Config Manager API is to enable the automated configuration of specific monitoring jobs from the NSMF. Indeed, during the provisioning of the end-to-end network slice instances, through this API, the NSMF can trigger the monitoring of specific service and network-related metrics, to be then stored in the Data Lake, visualized in customized dashboards, and consumed by the AI/ML Engine. On the other hand, the AI/ML Engine offers an API that is exploited by the NSMF to notify the analytics and decision functionalities about the evolution of network slices lifecycle (e.g., instantiation, scaling, termination, etc.) as well as on the result of the related lifecycle operations (i.e., success or failure) to help in the contextualization of data retrieved from the monitoring platform.

2.5 Example of AI/ML-based Network Slice Optimization

AI/ML techniques are being adopted into 5G networks to support full automation in closed loops related to the management and runtime operation of 5G services and network slices. In practice, the target is to improve the optimization of network performances, while enhancing the users perceived experience. At the same time, AI/ML techniques can help in solving network management complexities brought by 5G, where several technologies and domains coexist for the provisioning of end-to-end services and slices. Currently, this requires *ad-hoc* integrations and knowledge of heterogeneous per-domain control and management solutions. Exploiting data that can be easily collected from the 5G infrastructure, network functions, and applications, AI/ML techniques can therefore help in fully automating 5G network services and slices runtime operations with a truly closed-loop approach.

In particular, the concept of network self-X (self-healing, self-optimization, etc.) based on the continuous monitoring of service attributes and performance parameters (data-driven) is a well-known approach in the context of 5G management platforms. The iNGENIOUS end-to-end network slice orchestration framework implements such automation mechanism by involving all the components building the platform: the orchestration stack, the monitoring platform, and the AI/ML engine. Indeed, when an end-to-end network slice is deployed, the orchestration platform (i.e., through the NSMF), as final step, configures the monitoring platform in order to continuously collect data that are relevant to determine the current status of the slice itself and the related services. The collected data are related to the different network subnet slices and their resources (e.g., 5G Core NFs, virtual applications, etc.). The monitoring platform collects and stores the data and make them available for the AI/ML engine that continuously takes decisions based on the monitored status, which can be a simple "do nothing" or slice optimization requests to be enforced toward the slice re-configuration interface offered by the NSMF. At this point, the NSMF translates such requests to real actions on the target (monitored) end-to-end slice.

The AI/ML innovation scenario considered in iNGENIOUS for the end-to-end network slice optimization targets the trigger of a pre-emptive auto-scaling of local-edge and central user plane functions (UPFs), in support of low-latency communication services, as shown in Figure 2.9. A single UPF instance can handle multiple protocol data unit (PDU) sessions; however,

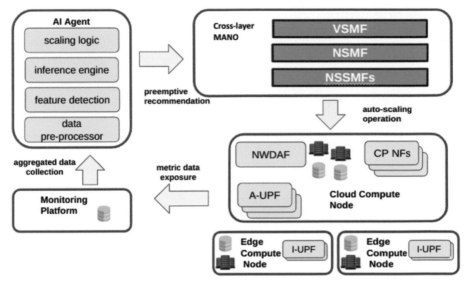

Figure 2.9 Closed-loop pre-emptive auto-scaling of UPF.

the resources of a UPF instance are finite. As traffic load increases, to avoid degradations in service caused by finite resources, more UPF instances can be deployed and started, and likewise, an idle UPF instance can be terminated when the traffic is low. This process can be achieved in a closed-loop continuous fashion that monitors, measures, and assesses real-time network data, and then automatically acts to optimize according to the SLA. It is important to note that human operators configure the automated actions and can manually modify them at any point within the loop.

The information used in pre-emptive auto-scaling, collected from the 5G infrastructure, and applications, can be related to specific UEs (mobility, communication pattern, etc.), NFs, network slices, or the network as a whole. UPF load information available from the NWDAF, including CPU, memory, and disk usage, can be supplemented with user plane data like bandwidth, latency, packet loss, etc., as well as UE-related information (mobility, position, etc.) to get accurate predictions of future network conditions. Within an edge compute node, a local NWDAF collects data from the UPF and exposes it to the monitoring platform. The platform collects the data from the NWDAF as well as other sources that are ingested after a pre-processing by the AI agent that performs a decision about the pre-emptive auto-scaling operation on UPF itself.

Acknowledgements

This work has been partially supported by the European Union's Horizon 2020 research and innovation program through the project iNGENIOUS under grant agreement No. 957216.

References

[1] H2020 iNGENIOUS, https://ingenious-iot.eu/web/

[2] 3GPP TS 28.500, "Management concepts, architecture and requirements for mobile networks that include virtualized network functions (Release 16)", v16.0.0, July 2020

[3] ETSI GS NFV-MAN 001, "Network Function Virtualisation (NFV); Management and Orchestration", v1.1.1, December 2014

[4] 3GPP TS 23.501, "System architecture for the 5G System (5GS); Stage 2 (Release 17)", v17.1.1, June 2021

[5] 3GPP TS 28.530, "Management and Orchestration; Concepts, use cases and requirements (Release 17)", v17.1.0, March 2021

[6] 3GPP TS 28.541, "Management and Orchestration; 5G Network Resource Model (NRM); Stage 2 and stage 3 (Release 17)", v17.3.0, June 2021

[7] GSMA, "Generic Network Slice Template", v5.0, June 2021

[8] 3GPP TR 28.801, "Study on management and orchestration of network slicing for next generation network (Release 15)", v15.1.0, January 2018

[9] 3GPP TS 28.533, "Management and Orchestration; Architecture framework (Release 16)", v16.7.0, March 2021

[10] Nextworks Slicer Open-source repository - https://github.com/nextworks-it/slicer

[11] ETSI Open Source MANO (OSM), https://osm.etsi.org/

3

Tactile IoT Architecture for the IoT–Edge–Cloud Continuum: The ASSIST-IoT Approach

A. Fornes-Leal[1], I. Lacalle[1], C. E. Palau[1], P. Szmeja[2], M. Ganzha[2], F. Konstantinidis[3], and E. Garro[4]

[1]Universitat Politècnica de València, Spain
[2]Systems Research Institute Polish Academy of Sciences, Poland
[3]Institute of Communications and Computer Systems, National Technical University of Athens, Greece
[4]Prodevelop SL, València, Spain
E-mail: cpalau@dcom.upv.es; alforlea@upv.es; iglaub@upv.es; Pawel.Szmeja@ibspan.waw.pl; maria.ganzha@ibspan.waw.pl; fotios.konstantinidis@iccs.gr; egarro@prodevelop.es

Abstract

This chapter describes the ASSIST-IoT approach for tactile IoT, proposing a reference architecture built on cloud-native concepts in which several enabling technologies (AI, cloud/edge computing, 5G, DLT, AR/VR interfaces, etc.) are integrated to implement advanced tactile IoT use cases, providing a set of guidelines, best practices, and recommendations toward this end.

Keywords: Reference architecture, next-generation IoT, cloud-native, Tactile Internet, enablers.

3.1 Introduction

With IoT consolidated in several application domains, the next-generation IoT (NG-IoT) has emerged, aiming at addressing more ambitious and complex use cases. Different enabling technologies have been identified as key toward this evolution, such as edge computing, 5G, artificial intelligence (AI) and advanced analytics, augmented reality (AR), digital twins, and distributed ledger technologies (DLTs). Still, there is not available any reference architecture (RA) that provides (technical and non-technical) requirements, guidelines, best practices, and recommendations that serve as blueprint for developing and implementing such systems, that being one of the main objectives of the ASSIST-IoT project.

Developing such RA thinking on its further adoption is crucial, and hence it tries to avoid a very high level of abstraction, selecting a set of design principles that consider current and expected trends in the IoT and enabling technologies communities. In this sense, the cloud-native paradigm (based on microservices, containerization, and DevOps practices) is embraced, adapted to the edge-cloud computing continuum as a baseline for its conception. Because of it, the RA will strive to bring flexibility, scalability, and ease of integration, which are crucial for coping with the continuous and fast evolution of the NG-IoT ecosystem as well as to help consolidate the implementation of tactile IoT across different business sectors, which are needed by the industry [1].

3.2 Concepts and Approach

Reference architectures are usually intended to be generic; so they can be applicable to different sectors or application domains. The RA developed in ASSIST-IoT follows the approaches and vocabulary specified in the standard ISO/IEC/IEEE 42010 [2], which is widely used in many modern RAs. Among the vocabulary used, the following terms are key in the conception of the presented architecture:

- **Stakeholder**: Individual, team, organization, or classes thereof, having an interest in a system [2]. They might be technology-focused or not, ranging from developers to testers, maintainers, administrators, and end users, among others [3].
- **Concern**: Topic of interest of one or more stakeholders to the architecture [4]. It includes needs, goals, expectations, requirements, design constraints, risks, assumptions, or other issues belonging to the system-of-interest [2].
- **View**: Work product representing the architecture from the perspective of specific system concerns [2], depicting how the architecture tackles them.

- **Perspective**: Collection of tactics, activities, and guidelines to ensure that a system displays a specific property, which should be considered across the views [3]. Perspectives are also referred to as system characteristics, although in ASSIST-IoT, the term **vertical** is used instead, representing not just properties but also functional blocks solving specific cross-cutting concerns.

IoT applications can be simple, composed of a less number of devices, with a basic frontend−backend-database schema and relaxed communication requirements in terms of latency and bandwidth. However, as IoT systems grow in size and complexity and NG-IoT requirements come to play, software architectures are highly recommended as a starting point to design them as well as to solve the specific needs or issues that may arise. There are different software architecture patterns [5], which could be combined in some cases: layered, event-driven, space-based, serverless, based on services, etc., and among the latter, monolithic, service-oriented architectures (SOA), and microservices. The ASSIST-IoT RA will consist in a layered architecture based on services, which is a result of the influence of cloud-native approaches over typical IoT representations.

3.2.1 Design principles

NG-IoT enables more appealing applications at the expense of complexity. Complementary technologies should be integrated depending on the use case addressed, and hence modularity and agile adaptation cycles must be ensured. The principles that govern the ASSIST-IoT RA are:

1. **Microservices**: The RA, apart from following a layered, multi-dimensional approach (see the next sub-section), proposes following a microservices pattern, allowing independent, self-contained services to be deployed and scaled while specifying boundaries and allowing coding freedom. All services should declare their own, well-defined communication interfaces.

2. **Containerization**: Virtualization, specifically in the form of containers, is key for deploying the services and decoupling them from the underlying hardware resources. They have much larger community support than alternatives such as unikernels or serverless, while being lighter, faster, and more flexible than virtual machines (VMs), and thus they are fostered in the cloud-native paradigm.

3. **Enablers**: An enabler is a collection of software, running on computation nodes, which delivers a particular functionality to the system. It is formed by a set of interconnected components, realized as containers, and exposing a set of well-defined interfaces (internals are not exposed or accessible). They can be essential (needed at all or most deployments), optional, or relevant only for certain use cases. Some features, due to containerization inconvenience or unfeasibility, should be implemented directly as a host operating system's (OS) service.

4. **Kubernetes**: A container orchestration framework provides many benefits, as automation of rollouts/rollbacks, error handling, and resource optimization (upscaling/downscaling) and, most importantly, bridges the gap from development to the market. K8s, although not mandated, is selected for being the *de facto* standard, and some decisions have been made considering it.

3.2.2 Conceptual approach

The conceptual architecture has been envisioned considering not only previous IoT schemas and cloud-native concepts but also the advancements in enabling technologies (e.g., edge computing, AI, SDN/NFV paradigm), outcomes from previous and concurrent projects, partners' expertise, and extensive research, being influenced primarily by the LSP programme [6], the OpenFog consortium [7], and AIOTI HLA [8]. The conceptual architecture is two-dimensional, primarily focused on the functional features, grouped in four layers or **planes** (device and edge, smart network and control, data management, and application and services), representing collections of features that can be logically layered on top of each other, intersected by cross-cutting properties, or **verticals** (self-*, interoperability, scalability, manageability, and security, privacy, and trust), as seen in Figure 3.1.

3.3 Architecture Views

The views described in the following sections compose, altogether, the whole scope of the architecture; separately, they represent an observation prism of the whole specification fit to the wills of a group of stakeholders. Five views have been developed: functional, development, node, deployment, and data, following a customized Kruchten's model [9], coined "$4\frac{1}{2}+1$," after splitting its development view into two (development and deployment). The relation among them can be seen in Figure 3.2.

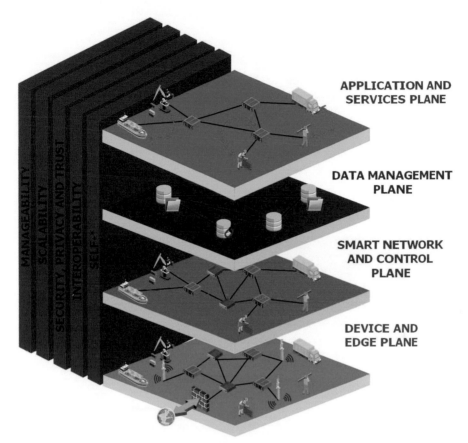

Figure 3.1 ASSIST-IoT conceptual architecture.

3.3.1 Functional view

This view, sometimes referred to as logical, represents the functionalities provided by a system, which is crucial for developers and maintainers as well as users and acquirers of the solution. A set of enablers are introduced for each of the planes (Figure 3.3), always considering that a system realization could require only a subset of them and/or include additional ones tailored to it.

3.3.1.1 Device and edge plane

This plane is in charge of (i) providing the infrastructure elements (e.g., computing nodes, networking elements, etc.) needed for interacting with end

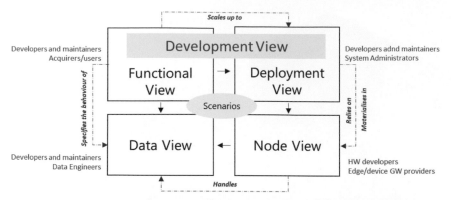

Figure 3.2 Custom $4\frac{1}{2}+1$ model of relation among views in ASSIST-IoT RA.

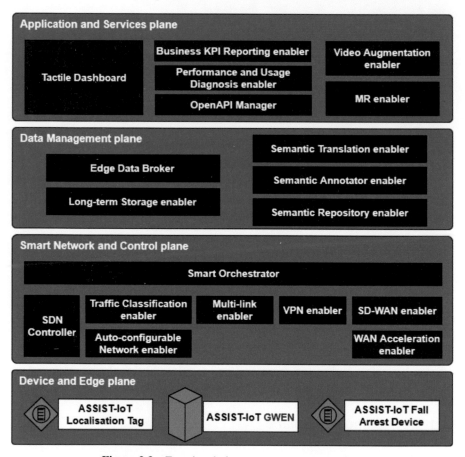

Figure 3.3 Functional view summary representation.

Figure 3.4 ASSIST-IoT's GWEN (left); infrastructure elements and functional blocks of the device and edge plane (right).

devices, sensors, and actuators, and integrating them with the rest of the architecture, and (ii) offering a set of (hardware/software/firmware) features that help realizing intelligence, pre-processing, and communication operations at the edge (e.g., from GPUs/FPGAs to AI frameworks, local processing functions, protocol adapters, specific extensions for communication protocols like LoRa, and ZigBee; whatever needed for a specific system realization). As a matter of fact, the project has designed (and developed) its own gateway/edge node (GWEN), which, apart from the required processing and storage resources, implements common interfaces and baseline functions needed for the RA to perform (firmware, OS, container engine, K8s, and pre-installed plugins). It is modular, meaning that features can be extended via expansion boards and SD slots. Regarding actual enablers, none has been defined in advance, as they are expected to be tightly coupled to the actual needs of the use cases addressed by a given system realization. Figure 3.4 presents a high-level schema of the GWEN, as well as the infrastructure and functional blocks of the plane.

3.3.1.2 Smart network and control plane

This plane hosts different communication and orchestration features, for deploying and connecting virtualized functions. A set of enablers have been selected as relevant (or, at least, interesting) for NG-IoT system realizations, grouped into four functional blocks: "orchestration," "software-defined networks," "self-contained networks realization," and "access networks management," as depicted in Figure 3.5. The smart orchestrator, designed considering ETSI MANO specifications [10], is the main enabler of the plane. It is in charge of controlling the lifecycle of other enablers (network and non-network-related) to be deployed on top of the virtualized infrastructure, managed by K8s, selected for being *de facto* standard toward cloud-native

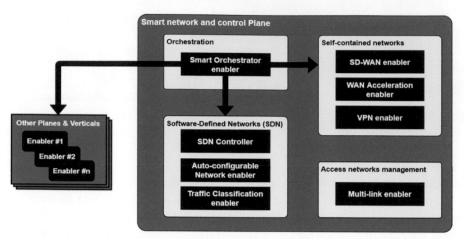

Figure 3.5 Enablers and functional blocks of the smart network and control plane.

paradigm [11]. Additionally, it performs intelligent resource scheduling operations (i.e., selecting the optimal place of the continuum for deploying an enabler) and applies communication rules and encryption among enablers.

Different adoption strategies for SDN in NG-IoT have been studied [12]. This RA presents a block devoted to it, consisting of (i) a controller, which manages the underlying SDN-enabled network; (ii) an auto-configurable network enabler, which acts over the controller to set policies optimally; and (iii) a traffic classification enabler, which identifies the type of traffic so networking rules are applied properly. This functional block is complemented by the programmatic rules that the orchestrator applies over the virtualized network.

The functional block related to self-contained networks includes enablers that provision secured channels over public or non-trusted networks. Three enablers are envisioned: one for establishing VPN tunnels for connecting isolated devices to a managed network and two for implementing SD-WAN, which follows a controller-agent schema to connect delocalized networks and to enable firewalling or application-level prioritization functions. Finally, within the access network management block, a multi-link enabler has been formalized, providing mechanisms for bonding different access networks to work as a logical, single one, thus bringing redundancy and reliability features.

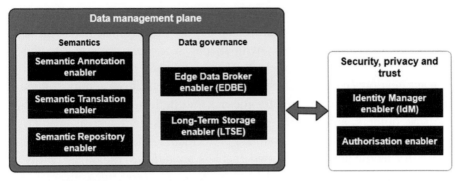

Figure 3.6 Enablers and functional blocks of the data management plane.

3.3.1.3 Data management plane

Traveling over the network layer, data will be shared, processed, and stored to be later on consumed by business/administrator applications and services. Five enablers are defined in this plane, separated into semantics and data governance blocks as one can see in Figure 3.6, supported by security, privacy, and trust mechanisms provided by enablers of such verticals. Data governance enablers include (i) a long-term storage enabler (LTSE), offering a dynamic, distributed space for highly available data persistence, accessible via API; and (ii) an edge data broker enabler (EDBE), key element for realizing data pipelines (Section 3.3.5), providing mechanisms for distributing data, filtering, and alerting, following scalable publication–subscription schemas aligned with current IoT trends.

Complementary to the data storage and transportation, a semantic framework is proposed to process (streaming and bulk), share, and present data. This framework includes (i) semantic annotation, for lifting data to fit a specific semantic format; (ii) semantic translation, for mediating between data that follow different ontologies or data models; and (iii) semantic repository, as a "hub" of data models, schemas, and ontologies, complemented with relevant documentation.

3.3.1.4 Applications and services plane

The upper plane is devoted to provide human-centric, user-friendly access to data, for both administrators and end users, including externals to a system realization. Three functional blocks have been identified (see Figure 3.7), with a set of enablers that, as occurs with the rest of the planes, could be extended.

The enablers allocated within the dashboards functional block are (i) the tactile dashboard, i.e., the main entry point to the system that will be used by administrators and users, with spaces accessible according to the provided credentials. It can provide mechanisms to add graphical interfaces to such application; (ii) the business KPI enabler, which allows administrators to prepare representation figures for metrics and indicators to be consumed by the stakeholders; and (iii) the performance and usage diagnosis enabler, which collects both system and enablers performance-related metrics.

Then, for tactile applications, two enablers are defined: the mixed reality and the video augmentation enabler. The former offers mechanisms for human-centric interaction, based on real-time and visual feedback and data from/to the system and the environment. It works jointly with hardware equipment; so the provided features and representations are largely influenced by it. The latter performs real-time computing vision functionalities over images or video streams (particularly, object detection and recognition), with recommended support from acceleration hardware. It should be highlighted that these enablers focus on particular augmentation capabilities, and additional ones could be thought for providing additional features from tactile and/or haptic interfaces.

Lastly, the OpenAPI manager allows exposing and monitoring API interfaces so that users and third-party systems can consume deployed enablers of the system. This enabler should be properly integrated with security enablers (i.e., identity manager and authorization server) to ensure that only rightful users/systems have access and to expose documentation to ease their respective usage.

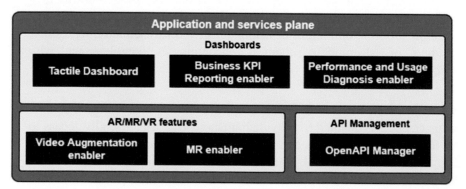

Figure 3.7 Enablers and functional blocks of the applications and services plane.

3.3.2 Node view

This view presents structural guidelines and recommendations to provision nodes that can be later on leveraged in NG-IoT systems. The provided data can be useful for stakeholders like hardware developers, edge devices, or gateway providers, as well as developers and maintainers of an ASSIST-IoT system. Nodes should not be understood as physical equipment but as a virtualized resource (e.g., a powerful physical server might host several virtual nodes); they can be placed on different tiers of the continuum (edge, fog, and cloud) and will likely have varying computing capabilities. Thus, to be ready as a node, a set of pre-requisites must be fulfilled:

- A K8s distribution must be installed (kubeadm and K3s encouraged), with a compatible container runtime (Docker recommended) and a Linux OS (the latter is not needed if K8s on bare metal is installed).
- A set of plugins for managing packages (Helm), storage classes (OpenEBS), and local and multi-cluster networking (Cilium). These specific plugins mentioned are not mandated but are compatible with the enablers developed in ASSIST-IoT.

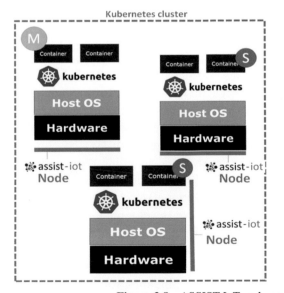 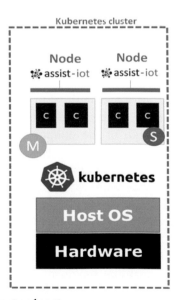

Figure 3.8 ASSIST-IoT node concept and spots.

3.3.3 Development view

This view aims at offering some guidelines and recommendations to ease the design and development of enablers, useful for developers and maintainers. Despite the project developing enablers for the different planes and verticals, it is possible that future systems rooting from ASSIST-IoT might require additional features. Enablers are to be designed respecting the principles of the RA, following some common conventions and considering the DevSecOps methodology [13] from the project. In particular, we have the following:

- **Virtualization**: Enablers should be deployable independently, and each of its components (inner functions) should be delivered in containers.
- **Encapsulation**: Enablers can communicate between each other, and with external clients, via explicitly defined and exposed interfaces (typically but not limited to REST APIs). Enablers' internal components are not exposed by default.
- **Manageability**: Enablers should expose a set of basic endpoints and logs (through **stderr** and **stdout** interfaces), following standard conventions for providing their status (e.g., with HTTP response codes and considering all the inner components), version (considering SemVer specifications), API documentation (Open API specifications), and relevant metrics (Prometheus-compatible format encouraged).

The process for designing and developing enablers is depicted in Figure 3.9, consisting in six main steps: (i) definition and formalization of requirements, considering its key features, main (software and hardware) constrains, and applicable use cases; (ii) breakdown of internal components, including its exposed interfaces and its internal communication; (iii) initial design of the endpoints to expose, including the manageability ones previously mentioned (i.e., /health, /version, /api, /metrics); (iv) baseline technologies and programming languages to leverage, avoiding reinventing the wheel while focusing on decentralization and resource optimization; (v) if data are involved, (sector, regional, and national) privacy regulations and ethical aspects should be considered; and once development starts, (vi) DevSecOps methodology should be followed [13], ensuring that the final result is secure by design. As additional tips, the use of verified container images, initial proofs of concept considering Docker compose tool before moving to K8s, and the provisioning of CI/CD pipelines for automating DevSecOps processes, including unit, functional, and security testing, are encouraged.

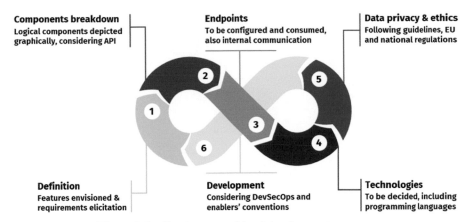

Components breakdown
Logical components depicted
graphically, considering API

Endpoints
To be configured and consumed,
also internal communication

Data privacy & ethics
Following guidelines, EU
and national regulations

Definition
Features envisioned &
requirements elicitation

Development
Considering DevSecOps and
enablers' conventions

Technologies
To be decided, including
programming languages

Figure 3.9 Continuous enablers' development process.

3.3.4 Deployment view

The deployment view addresses different concerns that can be useful, especially for network and system administrators (as well as developers and maintainers), such as hardware provisioning (computation nodes and networking elements), K8s setup, and the deployment of enablers and their integration to address a use case or business scenario.

3.3.4.1 Infrastructure and Kubernetes considerations

The computing continuum can be decomposed into tiers, each of them consisting of a set of nodes, extending from end devices (smart IoT devices, and MR/AR/VR interfaces) to edge (with one or multiple levels) and cloud, if needed. Being K8s strongly encouraged as virtualized infrastructure manager, the underlying connection among nodes must be IP-based (with the exception of the access network, as interfaces between end devices and edge gateways might involve other forms of communication, e.g., LPWAN and BLE). A generic topology is presented in Figure 3.10. A system topology design will strongly depend on the business scenario, security, and decentralization aspects, as well as economic reasons.

Regarding K8s, computing nodes are grouped into clusters, where at least one acts as **master**, in charge of control plane actions, and the rest as **workers** (which execute workloads). Some aspects that should be considered for a proper implementation include: (i) clusters should consist of nodes with similar performance; (ii) a multi-tier topology suggests having a master in control, rather than a master in charge of different tiers; (iii) if new nodes are

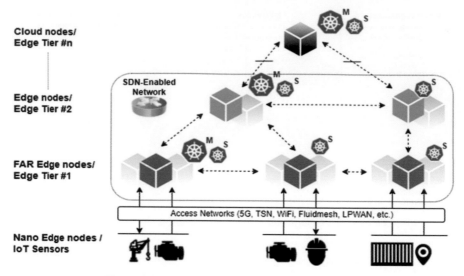

Figure 3.10   Generic topology of an NG-IoT system.

added to an existing tier, better to do it as workers to avoid devoting more resources to control plane tasks (unless done for high availability strategies); and (iv) K8s management is outside the scope of the architecture, despite requiring some minimum requirements (e.g., plugins and add-ons) that should be provisioned by network administrators. In any case, best practices for K8s security are encouraged [14] for any system realization.

3.3.4.2 Enablers deployment

The main and recommended tool for instantiating enablers over the managed computing continuum is the smart orchestrator, considered an essential enabler of the system. After provisioning the infrastructure, network, and K8s clusters, the latter must be registered in the orchestrator (individually, or as part of a group of clusters), and from this moment, a platform administrator can deploy enablers over them, either manually or automatically based on a desired policy. The orchestrator developed within ASSIST-IoT considers Helm as the packaging technology, but other formats (custom-made based on K8s manifests, Juju, or Kustomize) could have been used (and thus an orchestrator designed based on the selected one/s).

It is perfectly possible to deploy enablers directly over the managed continuum via Helm commands or utilizing third-party management software like Rancher Fleet. However, some of the additional features provided by the orchestrator, such as automatic application of networking rules, policy-based automatic scheduling, and mobility mechanisms for clusters without public or/nor fixed IP addresses are no longer supported.

Regarding enablers integration, ASSIST-IoT does not force that every expected or possible integration be realized, as there are just many artifacts, data schemas, technologies, etc. Still, when deemed necessary, some enablers' implementations made within the scope of the project have been integrated. On the one hand, some cases were evident, like the semantic suite (Section 3.3.1.3), the federated learning enablers (Section 3.4.3.2), or the security enablers (Section 3.4.3.1) related to identity management and authorization. On the other hand, other interactions were evaluated and, in some cases, integrated requiring higher or lower effort, like the OpenAPI manager with identity management, the manageability enablers with the smart orchestrator, or the tactile dashboard with BKPI and PUD enablers, among others. Besides, manageability enablers provide some mechanisms to provision agents within the right spot of the continuum as "integration bridges," providing translation of transport protocols (e.g., MQTT to MQTT) and basic data formatting capabilities.

3.3.5 Data view

This view, useful for data engineers as well as developers and maintainers, provides an overview of the flow of data within a system, with respect to their collection, processing, and consumption, specifying the actions made by the enablers (and other artifacts) over them. ASSIST-IoT introduces **data pipelines** as an abstraction design that represents such flows, avoiding information related to the underlying hardware infrastructure or network-related enablers. In essence, these pipelines present a linear sequence of steps where data are transmitted between data processing elements, from a given source/s (e.g., services, endpoints, devices, sensors, and outputs from another pipeline/s) to an output/s or sink/s (e.g., database, dashboard, log gatherer, source of following data pipeline/s, or simply deleted). Data travel as messages, through different paths, and having a specific format and content. An example of data pipeline is presented in Figure 3.11. In such representations, data sources, protocols and payload types, as well as enablers and services involved should be easily identifiable, accompanied with dedicated textual explanation when needed but trying to keeping them readable (i.e., avoiding gratuitous details). In any case, these representations do not aim to substitute other typical, dedicated UML or similar diagrams, but rather complement them.

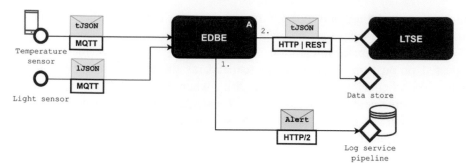

Figure 3.11   Data pipeline example.

3.4 Verticals

Verticals represent or provide NG-IoT properties and capabilities that (should) exist on different planes, either in an independent way or requiring cooperation from them. Five verticals have been identified as crucial for the development of NG-IoT systems, namely self-*, interoperability, scalability, manageability, and security, privacy, and trust. In some cases, capabilities are implemented through dedicated enablers (see Figure 3.12), while in others, they are the result of the design principles embraced. As with planes, some of them might not be needed for addressing certain use cases, and

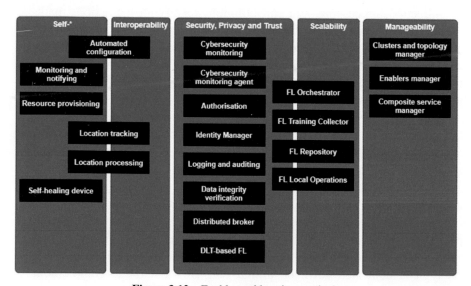

Figure 3.12   Enablers addressing verticals.

envisioning additional ones for bringing unavailable capabilities to a system is not precluded.

3.4.1 Self-*

This vertical refers to enablers implementing system autonomy capabilities, able to make intelligent decisions, where humans just manage them by policies (or just installing them) rather that manually acting over the involved mechanisms. According to IBM, eight conditions should be fulfilled to consider a mechanism as self-* [15].

Particularly, five enablers have been identified to extend the capabilities already present due to architecture design choices. (i) Self-healing enabler: considering K8s provides a set of healing mechanisms over managed services, this enabler extends them to the node itself, collecting data (e.g., battery and CPU usage, memory access, and network state), evaluating them, determining, and applying the optimal healthy remediation process. (ii) Self-resource provisioning: K8s also provides resource autoscaling mechanisms for services – still, these are static, meaning that once their behavior is set, they can only be changed manually. This enabler develops models of other deployed enablers to forecast their behavior, modifying the performance of these scaling mechanisms on-the-fly, without human intervention. (iii) Location tracking and (iv) processing enablers: these enablers work together for bringing contextual location data, with dedicated hardware and firmware extensions, and providing configurable and flexible geofencing capabilities based on such data, using either batch or streaming approaches. (v) Monitoring and notifying enabler: responsible for monitoring devices and notifying malfunctioning incidents, ensuring that telemetry data are sent and presented while validating its own performance. (vi) Automated configuration enabler: it allows users to define requirements (resources) needed to meet specific functionalities, and reactions over external actions or change of the pool of resources, all in an abstract way. In case of limited resources, the system will automatically decide which functionalities are kept, modifying existing configurations and emitting related messages and logs.

3.4.2 Interoperability

This vertical represents the ability of systems, devices, and/or applications to communicate together on the same infrastructure or on another while roaming. The IoT field, and by extension, NG-IoT systems, are heterogeneous in terms of hardware, data, and applications, and, hence, mechanisms that ease devices connection, data sharing, and service communication are needed to facilitate the adaptation of novel technologies and services. Interoperability is present at different levels, rather than addressed as enablers: (i) technical, when two or more information and communication technologies are able to accept data from each other; (ii) syntactic or structural, when two systems communicate and exchange data using compatible formats and protocols; and (iii) semantic, which entails applications and systems sharing the same understanding of the exchanged data.

Although any enabler has been directly assigned to this vertical, it is present through different enablers of the architecture. For instance, SDN-related enablers allow governing a networking infrastructure with hardware from different vendors autonomously, based on policies; the semantic suite brings processing and translation capabilities to store data and share them following specific ontologies or data models, enabling effective cooperation among IoT artifacts; also, the use of smart contracts coming from DLT-related enablers of the next vertical, allowing metadata management and non-repudiation from different sources or systems; in self-* localization tracking, various geospatial data sources can be combined (UWB and GPS); in federated learning (FL) suite (Section 3.4.3.2), enablers provide mechanisms to run on different clients and to accommodate training data from different formats, etc. Besides, although an interoperability suite like that in [16] could have been defined, its usage would require extensive knowledge of the several available mechanisms, and, hence, implementing them as independent enablers when needed is preferred instead.

3.4.3 Security, privacy, and trust

This vertical should be considered meticulously, as perceiving a system as unsecure, untrusted, or privacy-disrespectful would destine it to fail. Many mechanisms can be grouped under this vertical; the provided content is extended in [17].

3.4.3.1 Security

This pillar involves several aspects, from good practices for development and data access by design (e.g., DevSecOps) to enablers that provide confidentiality, integrity, availability, authentication, and authorization. Here, the following enablers have been defined:

- **Identity manager (IdM) and authorization enablers**: They offer (i) access control based on user/devices/system identity, and (ii) authorization over protected resources. The ASSIST-IoT RA depicts a decentralized approach, where decision-making features can be moved from a central point to distributed endpoints, sharing security policies (previously set by an administrator) to apply.
- **Cybersecurity monitoring enabler, and monitoring agents**: The central enabler consolidates the data collected by the agents distributed through the continuum to provide cybersecurity awareness, visibility, and response against detected threats.

Besides, additional considerations are presented. First, the OpenAPI management enabler from the applications and services plane includes a gateway, envisioned as primary access mechanism for (HTTP) third-party access. In this way, a single point should be exposed, secured, and documented, reducing the number of attack surfaces; and hence the IdM and authorization enablers must be integrated with this one. Second, when MQTT is the main communication protocol, different security mechanisms should be assessed, especially when the network is not considered secured or trusted. These include protection at (i) network level, providing tunnels between clients and brokers; (ii) transport level, encrypting data using SSL/SSL and certificates; and (iii) application level, considering user-password credentials (or Access Control List files) to grant or deny access, including the possibility of allowing nodes to publish or be subscribed only to specific topics.

3.4.3.2 Privacy

Privacy aims at protecting the information of individuals or private data from exposure in NG-IoT environments. In ASSIST-IoT, a set of rules for preserving it during development has been made, and, in addition, an FL suite for training ML algorithms in a decentralized environment has been designed, in which actual data is not exchanged but only the trained models. This suite is composed of (i) the central orchestrator, responsible for declaring the FL pipeline and control the overall lifecycle, including job scheduling and error handling; (ii) a repository, providing storage for ML algorithms, aggregation approaches, and trained models, supporting the rest of the enablers; (iii) local operations component, installed in the distributed nodes to perform data format verification and transformation, local model training, and inference, among other tasks; and (iv) training collector, which aggregates the models updated by the managed nodes and redistributes the combined model.

3.4.3.3 Trust

Trusts represents the level of confidence of the devices, data, or system of an ecosystem [18]. The RA does not delve on best practices and recommendations related to this, as there exist dedicated projects focusing on it [19]; still, it defines a set of enablers, based on DLT, for easing the implementation of trusted decentralized ecosystems: (i) logging and auditing, for storing critical actions and having a trusted source of truth; (ii) data integrity verification, based on hashed data; (iii) distributed broker, to facilitate data sharing of devices from different edge domains; and (iv) DLT-based FL enabler, an auxiliary component of the FL suite to manage ML contextual information, preventing any data alteration. Before using them, it is important to decide which events and data are critical, as data are replicated on the ledgers, and storing many data can cause performance issues.

3.4.4 Scalability

The RA pretends enabling elastic implementations, where hardware (node and system level), software, and services can be scaled up/down as seamlessly for adopters as possible. In ASSIST-IoT, this vertical does not result from the action of specific enablers, but rather due to design choices made and the use of K8s (or any similar container orchestrator framework), primarily. In this RA, we can find first hardware scalability, contemplating (i) processing, having nodes with constrained resources, like PLCs, to high-performance servers with large GPU arrays; (ii) storage, from simply flash chips to large arrays of storage clusters; (iii) network interfaces, with nodes having a single (wired and wireless) interface to others having several of them, with aggregation capabilities; and (iv) system, considering small-size to large-size, decentralized topologies, including possible business scenarios with thousands of clusters. The GWEN also incorporates mechanisms fostering this scalability dimension, through the expansion boards and modules through which storage, access networks, and computation capabilities could be expanded, if needed.

Besides, software scalability is also crucial, involving not just the deployment of services and applications but also the optimal scheduling of the managed resources. Regarding the latter, the use of K8s distributions, along with the smart orchestrator and resource provisioning enabler, guarantees that once a (software) feature is deployed over the infrastructure as an enabler, it (i) has its required resources, and (ii) can be scaled up/down automatically based on current and forecasted usage. Besides, being a microservices-based

RA and using containers as virtualization paradigm, features are decoupled by nature and can be developed and integrated quite easily, thanks to their respectively exposed interfaces. Additional guidelines and best practices can be found in [17].

3.4.5 Manageability

The last vertical responds to concerns related to the management of the overall system and the required enablers. Tools are needed to register and manage (large volume of) K8s clusters and enablers, including mechanisms to (i) detect and inform about faults, (ii) allow configuration options of the enablers to be deployed, (iii) enabling processes for storing and sharing logs and metrics of enablers and clusters, and everything (iv) in a secure and user-friendly manner. Along with the implementation of common endpoints for enablers depicted in Section 3.3.3, the following manageability enablers have been defined:

- **Clusters and topology manager**: It allows to register/delete clusters to the system, ensuring that they are working properly and providing graphical data of their distribution and hosted enablers.
- **Enabler manager**: Eases the management of enablers, in a graphical way, from the registration of enabler repositories to their instantiation (also configuration), logs consumption, and deletion.
- **Composite services manager**: It eases the flow of data between enablers, by provisioning interoperability agents that provide protocol (e.g., MQTT-HTTP) and basic payload translations. It includes a graphical interface to configure these agents, which are then deployed optimally within the continuum.

3.5 Conclusion

This chapter describes the reference architecture developed within the framework of H2020 ASSIST-IoT project, following cloud-native principles adapted to the edge–cloud computing continuum for next-generation, tactile IoT, providing a set of guidelines, best practices, and recommendations. It is based on microservices, using containers and Kubernetes as main virtualization technologies, as well as coining the concept of an enabler. Functionalities will be delivered in the form of these, which will belong to one of the planes (device and edge, smart network and control, data management, and application and services) or verticals (self-*, interoperability, scalability, manageability, and security, privacy, and trust) of the multi-dimensional approach of the architecture.

Since providing such information in an all-encompassing model would hinder its comprehension, the architecture has been divided in five separated views, namely functional, node, development, deployment, and data, each of them of utility for a particular group of stakeholders. It should be highlighted that this document, as well as the outcomes presented as the project's deliverables and code, is a reference for building tactile IoT systems, and, thus, it should be taken as such, rather than a platform ready to be deployed and used without performing any tailoring to the targeted business scenario.

Acknowledgements

This work is part of the ASSIST-IoT project, which has received funding from the European Union's Horizon 2020 research and innovation program under Grant Agreement No. 957258.

References

[1] I. Lacalle et al., "Tactile Internet in Internet of Things Ecosystems," in International Conference on Paradigms of Communication, Computing and Data Sciences (PCCDS 2021), 2021, pp. 794–807.

[2] ISO/IEC/IEEE 42010, "ISO/IEC/IEEE 42010 - Systems and software engineering - Architecture description," 2011.

[3] N. Rozanski and E. Woods, Software Systems Architecture: Working With Stakeholders Using Viewpoints and Perspectives. Addison Wesley, 2011.

[4] M. W. Maier, D. Emery, and R. Hilliard, "Software architecture: Introducing IEEE standard 1471," Computer (Long. Beach. Calif)., vol. 34, no. 4, pp. 107–109, 2001.

[5] M. Richards, Software Architecture Patterns. O'Reilly Media, 2015.

[6] CREATE-IoT Project, "D6.3. Assessment of convergence and interoperability in LSP platforms," 2020.

[7] OpenFog Consortium, "OpenFog Reference Architecture for Fog Computing," 2017.

[8] AIOTI WG Standardisation, "High Level Architecture (HLA) Release 5.0," 2020.

[9] P. B. Kruchten, "The 4+1 View Model of Architecture," IEEE Softw., vol. 12, no. 6, pp. 42–50, 1995.

[10] ETSI, "GS NFV-MAN 001 Network Functions Virtualisation (NFV); Management and Orchestration," 2014.

[11] A. Fornes-Leal et al., "Evolution of MANO Towards the Cloud-Native Paradigm for the Edge Computing," in International conference on Advanced Computing and Intelligent Technologies (ICACIT 2022), 2022, vol. 914, pp. 1–16.

[12] C. Lopez et al., "Reviewing SDN Adoption Strategies for Next Generation Internet of Things Networks," in International Conference on Smart Systems: Innovations in Computing (SSIC), 2021, vol. 235, pp. 619–631.

[13] O. López et al., "DevSecOps Methodology for NG-IoT Ecosystem Development Lifecycle - ASSIST-IoT Perspective," J. Comput. Sci. Cybern., vol. 37, no. 3, pp. 321–337, 2021.

[14] The Kubernetes Authors, "Kubernetes documentation - Security." Online: https://kubernetes.io/docs/conccpts/security/.

[15] IBM, "An architectural blueprint for autonomic computing," 2005.

[16] C. I. Valero et al., "INTER-Framework: An Interoperability Framework to Support IoT Platform Interoperability," Interoperability of Heterogeneous IoT Platforms. Springer, pp. 167–193, 2021.

[17] ASSIST-IoT Project, "D3.7 - ASSIST-IoT Architecture Definition – Final," 2022.

[18] NIST, "Internet of Things (IoT) Trust Concerns," 2018.

[19] TIoTA Alliance, "Trusted IoT Alliance Reference Architecture," 2019.

Part II

Artificial Intelligence of Things (AIoT) and AI at the Edge

4

Machine Learning (ML) as a Service (MLaaS): Enhancing IoT with Intelligence, Adaptive Online Deep and Reinforcement Learning, Model Sharing, and Zero-knowledge Model Verification

Jorge Mira[1], Iván Moreno[1], Hervé Bardisbanian[2], and Jesús Gorroñogoitia[1]

[1]Atos Spain, Spain
[2]Capgemini, France
E-mail: jorge.mira@atos.net; ivan.moreno@atos.net; herve.bardisbanian@capgemini.com; jesus.gorronogoitia@atos.net

Abstract

AI has changed our lives in many aspects, including the way we (as humans) interact with internet and computational devices, but also on way devices interact with us, and among them, in most of the processes of the industry and other socioeconomic domains, where machine learning (ML) based applications are getting increasing influence. Internet of Things (IoT) plays a key role in these process interactions, by providing contextual information that requires to be processed for extracting intelligence that would largely improve them. However, the delivery of ML-based applications for IoT domains faces the intrinsic complexity of ML operations, and the online interoperability with IoT devices. In this chapter, we present the IoT-NGIN ML as a service (MLaaS) platform, an MLOps platform devised for the delivery of intelligent applications for IoT. Its services for online deep learning (DL) training and inference, ML model conversion and sharing, and zero-knowledge model verification based on blockchain technology are also presented.

Keywords: MLOps, deep learning, online learning, model translation, zero-knowledge model verification.

4.1 Introduction

Internet of Things (IoT) facilitates the extraction of information from systems, through devices and sensors connected to them. Companies owning those systems can infer knowledge about their behavior and performance, with the aim of improving their understanding of diverse aspects. As an example, metrics gathered from sensors can be immediately used to trigger an alert on the situation where a concrete metric value overpasses a predetermined threshold. However, the increasing number of devices and sensors is generating a huge volume of information that companies need to face, a challenge identified by the Big Data 5 Vs [1]. As a result, a simple system service could not be capable anymore to cope with the data intricateness. Therefore, new solutions are required to face this complexity and effectively and purposely infer valuable information from it. With the development of new AI information extraction and ML-based inference techniques and algorithms and the advent of increasing computation power, notably based on GPUs and TPUs, it is now achievable to extract value from huge volumes of data and even predict the future behavior of systems. These breakthroughs will enable systems' stakeholders to better comprehend their company activities and improve future planning, leading to increase business value.

Primary users of these ML-based techniques are data scientists and ML engineers, who require a ML platform that can provide all the necessary services to process data, train ML models, share, and deploy them. Implementing and maintaining such an ML platform is a complex, time-consuming, and costly endeavor, requiring expertise that most of the companies lack. Therefore, a leading industry trend is addressing the provisioning of this kind of ML platforms, by offering all the services required to build and execute ready-to-use ML models. In addition, these ML platforms support the development of custom-tailored ML systems for some specific use cases. Such ML platforms are commonly referred to as machine learning as a service (MLaaS).

Companies leverage MLaaS to reduce the time and cost of integrating their ML modeling and delivery procedures into their development and CI/CD environments. By using MLaaS, data scientists can procure and preprocess the data and train the model, by focusing on their core competency, that is, in the ML development, rather than on the burden of taking care of the underlying procedures and infrastructure, which are provided and managed by the MLaaS.

Several MLaaS platforms are commercially available, either provided by big Cloud service providers, such as AWS ML, Microsoft Azure ML Studio, and Google Cloud Platform (GCP) ML Studio, or by specialized companies (e.g., BigML, Domino, Arimo, etc.). On the contrary, there are few MLaaS frameworks built around open-source services that support ML development and delivery, such as Kubeflow, MLFlow, and AirFlow, although they do not constitute a complete MLaaS platform. Building such a platform is challenging because:

- Lots of different functions are required to build up a complete MLaaS.
- For the same function, there could be several open-source projects to choose from. Determining the right one could require a long and complex evaluation.
- Projects are envisioned, designed, and implemented for a particular purpose, but scarcely concerned with their requirements of integration with other external services.
- The complexity to install, configure, maintain, manage, and use integrated services could be high.
- Further customizations and adaptations may be needed on the integrated services to fit the functional and non-functional requirements of the MLaaS.

The IoT-NGIN project has envisaged a holistic view for a complete MLaaS platform, supporting ML development and delivery in the domain of IoT, addressing the functional and non-functional requirements expressed in the project, and its high-level architecture. This task has been realized by seeking open-source projects, by selecting suitable components for specific purposes, and by determining the procedures to integrate them together in order to constitute a comprehensive framework. Besides, IoT-NGIN has adopted GitOps technologies, such as IaC and ArgoCD to automate the platform building and delivery.

The IoT-NGIN has implemented and delivered a minimum viable product (MVP) of the MLaaS platform, aimed to validate the platform function itself, and provide support for the use cases of the project Living Labs and the external projects that are adopting the IoT-NGIN technology.

The remainder of the chapter is organized as follows. Section 4.2 introduces the functional and technical specification of the IoT-NGIN MLaaS platform and its MVP implementation. The following sections describe additional ML services developed for MLaaS. In particular, Section 4.3 provides the functional and technical specification, implementation details, and validation results of the adaptive online deep learning service, while Section 4.4 does the same for model sharing, model translation, and zero-knowledge model verification services. Section 4.5 concludes the chapter.

4.2 MLaaS

4.2.1 MLaaS features

The functional view of the IoT-NGIN MLaaS platform is shown in Figure 4.1. In a high-level functional view, the platform is structured into i) the infrastructure hosting the platform and ii) the MLaaS services. This approach avoids binding MLaaS to a specific hosting environment, so permitting MLaaS to be delivered into diverse cloud infrastructures, including public, private, or even in bare-metal ones.

As the MLaaS platform aims to offer complete support for the ML development and delivery lifecycle, it includes the following functions:

- Data functions, including data acquisition, analysis, transformation, and storage;
- ML modeling, including ML model training, evaluation, and model transfer;
- ML deployment, including model sharing and translation;
- ML prediction, including model serving, batch, and real-time prediction.

Hosting infrastructure and monitoring/management tools are not part of the MLaaS platform. Nonetheless, the infrastructure must provide network access, computing resources, including CPUs/GPUs, and storage services. IoT MLaaS adopts a container-based microservice architecture compatible with Kubernetes clusters on bare-metal infrastructures.

As shown in Figure 4.1, the MLaaS platform consists of the following functional blocks:

- IoT gateway: Includes services to receive data from IoT devices, either through message queue brokers or HTTP/S REST API.

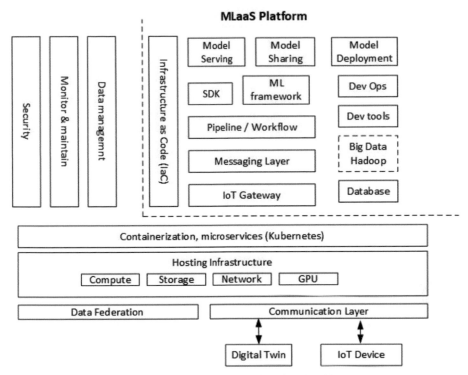

Figure 4.1 MLaaS framework functional architecture.

- Messaging layer: Includes components that interface the IoT gateway with other MLaaS upper services, by streaming the data events they consume.
- Database: Includes services providing data storage capabilities, including SQL and NoSQL databases, and time series services.
- Pipeline/workflow: Supports the building and deployment of portable, scalable ML workflows.
- ML framework: Provides ML frameworks and libraries required to build and train an ML model, including Tensorflow, Keras, PyTorch, scikit-learn, etc.
- SDK: Provides the development and testing environment to build and test ML models. A simple development environment supporting Python and Rust (as future work) is provided, but not a state-of-the-art IDE.
- Model serving: Offers services to deliver ML models through a REST API for prediction requests.

- Model sharing: Offers services to share ML models, to be used for model prediction, or for transfer learning. MLaaS also supports model translation across several popular ML frameworks. An external DLT system can be used to verify the model integrity by leveraging blockchain technology.
- Model deployment: Offers services to deliver ML models into the edge computing or into IoT devices; so they can infer predictions.
- Dev tools: Includes services aiming at assisting ML modeling, including notebook support and ML monitoring tools.
- DevOps: Includes CI/CD services to deploy new MLaaS services and ML models.
- Infrastructure as a Code (IaC): Contains the manifests required to configure the MLaaS platform.

4.2.2 MLaaS architecture, services, and delivery

The technical architecture of the reference implementation of the MLaaS platform is shown in Figure 4.2.

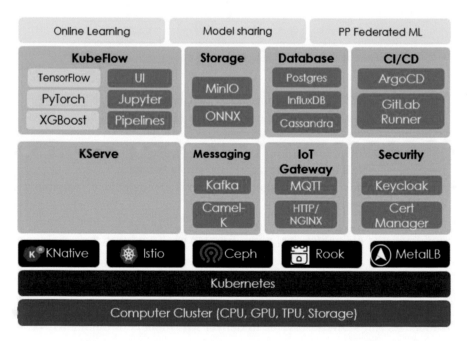

Figure 4.2   MLaaS framework reference technical architecture.

IoT-NGIN MLaaS uses Kubernetes as the main framework for the container-based instantiation of the MLaaS microservice architecture. Kubernetes is complemented with other services, including:

- Istio: A service mesh used by MLaaS components, such as Kubeflow and the Ingress gateway.
- Ceph: A unified storage service with an object block, being the default storage class.
- Rook: A cloud-native orchestrator for Kubernetes, used to manage Ceph storage.
- MetalLB: A load-balancer for metal Kubernetes clusters, used to allocate external load-balancer IP addresses to the Istio and the Nginx gateways.

MLaaS consists of several services hosted by the Kubernetes cluster. Current IoT-NGIN MLaaS platform does not include them all, although most of them, as some few services have not been required yet by the use cases; so its inclusion is left for future work. Kubeflow is the main component of the MLaaS platform. It offers ML frameworks (e.g., Tensorflow, Keras, PyTorch, MXNet, MPI, XGBoost, etc.) for model training, tools for pipelines/workflows implementation, and development tools such as Jupyter notebooks. Complementing Kubleflow, MLaaS includes KServe, a model inference service, for model serving. The IoT gateway is supported by i) Mosquitto MQTT, a message broker and ii) NGINX-based HTTP/S access to REST APIs. NGINX is a web server, also used as a reverse proxy and ingress gateway. These IoT gateway services are used to ingest data coming from IoT devices or digital twins. The messaging block, which exchange data messages between the IoT gateway and the Kubeflow/KServe services, is supported by i) Kafka, a distributed stream processing system with real-time data pipelines and integration and ii) Apache Camel-K, a lightweight integration framework for microservices. The storage block, which offers services for model sharing, is mainly supported by MinIO, a Kubernetes object storage, which can host ML models and other artifacts. The database block is supported by several SQL and non-SQL databases, including i) Postgres, an SQL object-relational database, ii) InfluxDB, a time-series platform with querying, monitoring, alerting, and visualization features, and ii) Casandra, a non-SQL distributed database. These services can be used for storing structured data and time series for ML model training. The CI/CD block is supported by i) ArgoCD, a declarative GitOps continuous delivery tool for Kubernetes and ii) GitLab Runner, a CI/CD GitLab pipeline runner. ArgoCD is used to deploy and maintain the MLaaS platform from the IoT-NGIN Git repository. GitLab Runner is used to upload ML models into IoT devices. Secure access to MLaaS is supported by Keycloak, an AAI/IAM service with SSO authentication for external services. The access to the MLaaS platform is done either via an Istio Ingress gateway for some components such as the Kubeflow dashboard and the KServe prediction services, or via the Nginx ingress gateways for other components such as MinIO.

On top of the MLaaS platform, several services, developed by IoT-NGIN, offer IoT-oriented ML features, including adaptive online deep learning, model sharing and translation, and zero-knowledge model verification. These services are introduced in the following sections.

The IoT-NGIN MVP reference implementation of the MLaaS platform has been installed and configured by ArgoCD from service IaC manifests hosted in the IoT-NGIN GitLab repository [2] following a GitOps approach [3].

4.3 Adaptive Online Deep Learning

4.3.1 Introduction

IoT ecosystems consist of a large number of devices (sensors, processors, and communications hardware) that are capable of collecting information about a specific environment, processing that information and sending it without any kind of human interaction. Hence, IoT devices generate dynamic data flows resulting in a non-feasible way to train an ML or deep learning (DL) algorithm in the traditional way (i.e., with a fixed dataset). Online learning (OL) technique allows to train ML models with datasets obtained from dynamic data flows. Thus, models can be retrained every time new data gets available; so the model knowledge is extended continuously. Another advantage of this technique is that models trained with OL can be adapted in real time to changes in the data distribution, minimizing the impact of the data drift problem. Therefore, OL technique can enable the adoption of AI in scenarios where it was not feasible before.

4.3.2 Features

An OL service must offer at least two features based on the characteristics of this AI approach: i) the dynamic training of ML models, as data become available, and ii) the inference provision when requested, by using the latest trained ML model. The dynamic training feature trains the model associated, by configuration, with the OL service, with datasets continuously fed into the OL service through streaming. The inference provision feature offers predictions generated by the current trained associated model. Model snapshots can be eventually stored in the MLaaS storage when significant performance gains are achieved, regulated by some configurable policies.

To offer the abovementioned main features, OL service supports real-time communication in order to receive the incoming data (see Figure 4.3). Among the communication protocols that are most used in the IoT domain, the Pub/Sub [9] pattern stands out, which allows different services to communicate asynchronously with very low latency. Pub/Sub is made up of producers and consumers. Producers communicate with consumers by broadcasting events. A consumer must be subscribed to a specific topic where the publisher is broadcasting on. The OL service supports real-time communication by integrating Kafka and MQTT. Kafka is an event-based platform that supports Pub/Sub as well as allows event streams to be stored and processed. In addition to real-time data, the OL service also processes data that comes through REST APIs.

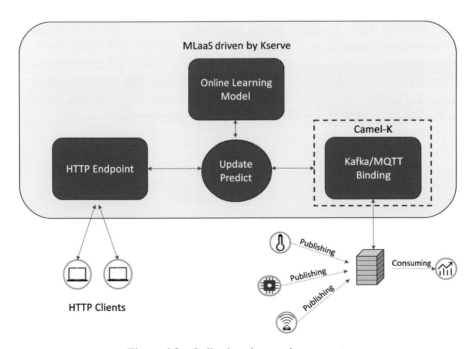

Figure 4.3 Online learning service concept.

Once the OL service receives the data, it uses an ML model to either i) perform a new training or ii) provide inference based on the input data. For this, the OL service supports some of the most popular frameworks for the development of ML models, such as TensorFlow, Keras, PyTorch, Sklearn, and Vowpal Wabbit. The OL service is deployed through the MLaaS KServe framework, which enables serverless model inference, through an HTTP-based REST API. However, as mentioned above, in IoT-NGIN applications, the data is commonly transmitted using protocols other than HTTP. For this reason, the deployment of the OL service requires an MQTT/Kafka-HTTP binding in order to receive the data. The Camel-K framework offers some integrators that perfectly fit this need.

4.3.3 Technical solution

This section describes the technical architecture details of the OL service. Figure 4.4 depicts all components present in the OL service.

As commented in a previous section, data is often sent through streaming flows in IoT scenarios, and the OL service instance only offers an HTTP endpoint; so it does not support, by default, PUB/SUB protocols such as MQTT or Kafka. Thus, a binding acting as a mediator between PUB/SUB and HTTP is needed. The binding is implemented using Camel-K. Whenever new data is published in the broker, the Camel-K binding receives it and redirects it to the HTTP REST API endpoint of the OL service. The binding can be seen as a Kafka/MQTT consumer, which is subscribed to a specific topic and when it receives new data, it redirects it to the OL service.

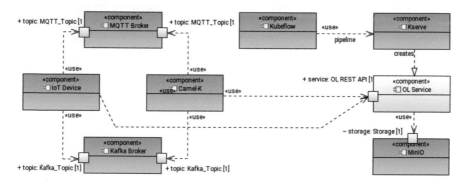

Figure 4.4   Online learning architecture.

When new data is published to retrain the model, the OL service processes this data and performs a training step. It analyzes the model losses and validation metrics and only in case the overall model performance is improved this model version is updated in the MLaaS storage (in this case, in MinIO), replacing the previous one.

Online model training is triggered on demand, by IoT devices, applications, or users, either by directly accessing the HTTP endpoint or by streaming through PUB/SUB on concrete topics. In the former case, a dataset is provided in batches, while in the latter case, dataset is provided in streaming, so that the dataset batch is created by the OL service once enough data is received. Next, data is pre-processed. The pre-processing procedure depends on the ML model architecture and the data structure, and it is use-case specific. KServe allows injecting into the OL workflow a module specialized in the dataset pre-processing stage, known as Transformer. Thus, the Predictor module for training and performing predictions remains independent of the use case and can be reused in any scenario. The only module that needs to be customized to each use case is the Transformer.

In the model inference scenario, predictions are requested by the IoT device, application, or user. The request can include an array with either i) some input data or ii) an empty array. After processing the request, OL returns the prediction when input data is provided, or it returns last available prediction when it is empty. This is useful when working for use cases requiring the forecasting of time series forecasting.

Another module optionally included in the OL service is the Explainer, powered by KServe. This module incorporates, to the OL workflow, an XAI layer that provides an explanation for the prediction performed by the ML model. It consists of a REST API endpoint that is waiting for the input data of the inference request. This module is optional and must be implemented by the ML model developer. If included, the OL offers an explanation to the prediction.

The OL service is deployed using KServe framework through Kubeflow. Kubeflow is utilized to deploy and execute ML workflows and KServe allows to serve ML models on arbitrary AI frameworks. The ML workflow contains the KServe implementation for deploying the OL service, and it is declared within a Kubeflow pipeline. The execution of this pipeline creates an OL service instance in MLaaS, exposed through an HTTP API REST endpoint. This instance encloses an ML model, waiting for incoming data in JSON format, either to be updated (i.e., retrained) or to perform an inference (i.e., prediction).

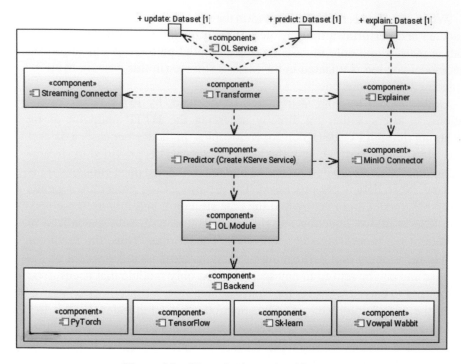

Figure 4.5 OL service internal architecture.

OL service modules have been implemented in Python since it offers a large ecosystem of libraries for AI. OL service is composed of the following modules (see Figure 4.5).

- Predictor (Create KServe service). It is responsible for deploying the REST API service within the OL service. It creates an HTTP endpoint that exposes the OL API for model update or prediction. The main library used in this module is KServe.
- Transformer. It receives a raw dataset and performs the data pre-processing stage. Therefore, it contains all functions needed to prepare the data for the ML model. This module is use case dependent; so it changes for each scenario.
- Explainer. It receives the pre-processed inference input data and returns the significance of each feature in the prediction. It is powered by KServe and must be implemented by the ML model developer.

- Online learning module. This API links the previous module to the backend module. It is responsible for choosing the correct backend and transmitting the model update or prediction requests.
- Streaming connector. This module provides tools to support real-time protocols. This module is not being used because KServe only supports HTTP connections, but it is implemented in case future versions of KServe start working with streaming data. The main libraries that have been used for its implementation and testing are Kafka and Paho-MQTT.
- MinIO connector. It provides the required tools to download and upload the ML models. This version stores the trained ML model in MinIO storage each time the model performance gain overpasses a given threshold. This module is based on the MinIO library.
- Backend. Modules are responsible for including required functions to perform ML model updates or predictions in each framework. The first version includes the following frameworks: Sklearn, Vowpal Wabbit, TensorFlow, and Pytorch.

Apart from the main OL service implementation, additional developments are also required for having the service deployed. They are listed below along with a brief description.

- OL service adaptation: This is the initial step and consists of configuring the OL service to set different parameters such as the MinIO host and the buckets where the ML models are stored, the backend (framework that was used to implement the model) to use in order to perform the model update or the prediction.
- Create the Docker image: Once the OL service is configured, it is required to wrap it within a Docker image that will be uploaded in a Docker registry so that Kubeflow can include it into the pipeline.
- Define KServe YAML manifest: This manifest defines the configuration of the OL service when deployed. It defines the name of the inference service, the number of replicas, the CPU limits, or the Docker image to use, among others.
- Create Kubeflow pipeline: At this point, we have the Docker image ready to use and the KServe YAML manifest that defines the OL service. The next step is to create a Kubeflow pipeline to incorporate the KServe YAML manifest and thus be able to run it.
- Run Kubeflow pipeline: This step deploys the OL service as an HTTP inference service.

- Define Camel-K binding: Camel-K binding consists of a YAML file that defines the broker and topics in which data is being dumped and the prediction service deployed in the previous step in order to resend the data.

4.3.4 Evaluation

This section describes a customized implementation of the MLaaS OL service and its evaluation on a smart energy forecasting scenario, which is depicted in Figure 4.6.

This smart energy scenario consists of a power-voltage (PV) electric grid (EG), whose status metrics are monitored by attached IoT devices. These metrics are published into a MQTT broker in specific topics and consumed by the OL service. The OL service hosts a specific ML model that is continuously trained as soon as new data is available.

The objective of the OL service is to forecast the EG power generation within the next 24 hours, giving a training dataset representing generation in the last 24/36 hours, published in the MQTT topic for power generation. This OL service faces the problem of time series forecasting, where the data becomes available as time goes by, which is a common use case for OL.

Once new data arrives at the OL service, it proceeds with the pre-processing step so that the data is prepared to be processed by the ML model

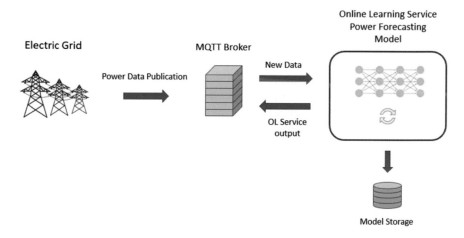

Figure 4.6   Smart energy forecasting scenario.

either for training the model or for inferencing the model in order to obtain forecasting. The following steps summarize the pre-processing stage (see Figure 4.7).

- Extraction of power value: The IoT devices transmit three-phase electric voltage and current data; hence, it is required to extract power value from these data.
- Resampling of the power data: Since the sampling rate in the smart energy scenario is too low, around 1 second, it is needed to resample the power data by aggregating all the values received within 1 hour and computing its average power. For this purpose, the Pandas library is used.
- Data scalation: ML presents higher performance and stability when all values are scaled between 0 and 1. Therefore, the power data is scaled by using the max−min scale strategy with pre-processing functions from the scikit-learn library.
- Time series windowing: The univariate time series forecasting algorithms take vectors as input. This step creates an input vector that contains the scaled averaged power per hour that is used to update the model or perform a prediction. The vectors are created by using different tools from Pandas and Numpy.

After the pre-processing stage, data is ready to train the ML model. However, so far, we have not provided any information about the architecture of the ML model hosted by OL service. The selected model architecture is based in recurrent neural networks (RNNs) [6] since we are facing time series forecasting problems. RRNs have demonstrated to work well when facing time series data, although they present some disadvantages such as the vanishing gradient problem [8]. After some evaluation, the selected layer is the gated recurrent unit (GRU) [7] because it solves the vanishing gradient problem suffered by the original RNN and presents faster convergence rate than other types of RNN such as long short-term memory (LSTM) variant. After the recurrent layers, we add two fully connected layers to apply a

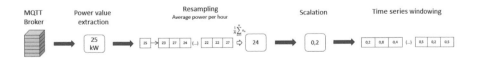

Figure 4.7   OL pre-processing stage.

linear transformation to the outputs of the GRU layers. Figure 4.8 depicts the architecture scheme.

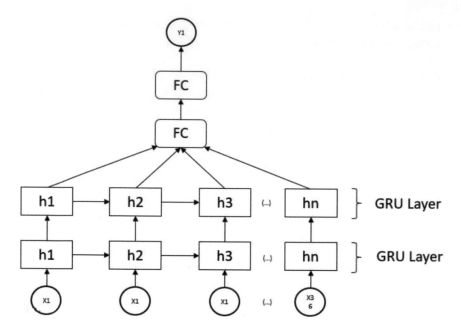

Figure 4.8   DL architecture for smart energy forecasting OL service.

Most of the time series forecasting problems faced with DL use the mean square error (MSE) between real values and model outputs as the loss function since it is one of the simplest to use. The neural network and the training procedure are implemented using the Pytorch library. This library is one of the most extended DL libraries, thanks to its easy-to-use framework with a large number of tools for DL.

To validate that the selected DL model architecture is a valid solution for this power forecasting scenario and deliver a ready-to-use OL forecasting service based on the trained DL model, we started by collecting power dataset for a time frame of 20 days. A data analysis was carried out to find out trends, seasonality, and correlation between power samples. After the analysis, we found out a daily seasonal component; so we could assume a period of 24 hours. After performing a slight experimentation, the OL service uses the training hyper-parameters shown in Table 4.1.

Table 4.1   Hyper-parameters for the OL service.

Hyper-parameter	Value
Epochs	50
Learning rate	0.005
β1	0.9
β2	0.99
Optimizer	Adam
Loss function	Mean squared error
Batch size	128

We train the DL architecture during 50 epochs with a batch size of 128 samples. We also use Adam optimizer [14] with a learning rate of 0.005 and β1 and β2 coefficients present values of 0.9 and 0.99, respectively.

Figure 4.9 shows the actual power data (orange line), inferences performed by the DL model (blue points) and the forecasting intervals with a 90% of confidence interval (blue area). It is important to note that the forecasting intervals can be computed since the errors between the actual data and the model predictions present a distribution that can be considered as Gaussian.

To assume errors that come from the Gaussian distribution, they have been subjected to normality tests: Shapiro−Wilk [10], Anderson−Darling [11], and D'Agostino−Pearson [12]. These tests consist of statistical hypothesis tests and allow checking whether the data contains certain property. Thus, two hypotheses are defined: the null hypothesis and the alternative hypothesis. The null hypothesis supports that the data probably comes from a normal distribution while the alternative hypothesis defends that the data present a different distribution. The statistical test returns a probability known as p-value. If this result presents a value lower than the defined significance level (0.05 in this case), the null hypothesis must be rejected; so the data distribution cannot be assumed as normal. Table 4.2 shows the p-values obtained. These normality tests have been implemented by using the Statsmodels and Scipy libraries.

Table 4.2   Normality test p-values.

Normality test	Power generation forecasting
Shapiro−Wilk	0.47
Anderson−Darling	0.76
Agostino−Pearson	0.10

The model can learn the seasonal variations that the generated power seems to have. Moreover, the inferences performed using the validation subset (data not included during training) offer significant good performance since the MSE obtained is 0.009 (see Figure 4.9).

OL solution includes an optional component to add an XAI dedicated REST API endpoint to provide explanations to the model output and obtain model predictions transparency. For this purpose, we have used the Captum library, which is an open-source Python library specialized in model interpretation methods built on Pytorch.

Captum allows to use different XAI methods to compute the importance of each input feature in the model prediction. Among several methods tested, DeepLIFT (deep learning important features) [13] provided best results; so it is the selected XAI method. This method belongs to the XAI backpropagation-based approach. This approach tries to highlight the input features that are easily predictable from the output.

DeepLIFT consists of on decomposing the output prediction of a neural network on a specific input by backpropagating the contribution of all neurons in the network to every feature of the input. It compares the activation of each neuron to its reference activation (a default or neutral input) and assigns contribution scores according to the difference. DeepLIFT also can separate positive from negative contributions; therefore, the features that have a positive impact on the prediction can be discriminated from the ones with a negative impact.

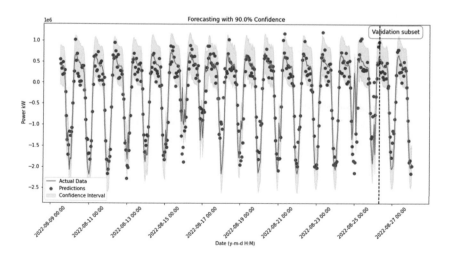

Figure 4.9　Power generation forecasting.

To verify whether DeepLIFT provides reasonable explanations, we have carried out a small evaluation of the power generation forecasting model. For this purpose, we have selected 1 input vector with 36 power measurements. We use DeepLIFT to obtain information about the features that have shown the highest relevance to return the prediction and we represent the contribution scores of each of the samples, as shown in Figure 4.10. Those features with high positive contribution are represented with green points, those that do not present an impact on the prediction are in yellow, and features that present negative contribution are in red. Therefore, DeepLIFT conclusion is the more recent the power sample, the more relevant it is.

At this point, both DL model and DeepLIFT methods have been validated and the OL service deployment can be carried out. The DL model is stored in MinIO so that the OL service can update it or can use it to perform predictions.

The deployment works in the same way described in the previous section. OL service implementation is configured so that the service loads and saves the model in the specific MinIO bucket and uses the Pytorch backend to train or predict, since the model has been defined by using this library. Furthermore, the XAI module script is added to the OL implementation. Then the OL service is wrapped in a Docker image, which is uploaded to a Docker registry. Later, the KServe YAML file is created for the service. The next step consists of creating the Kubeflow pipeline and executing it; so the OL service

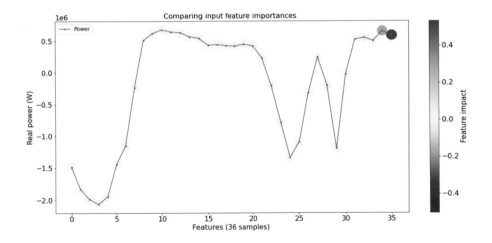

Figure 4.10 XAI analysis of power generation forecasting.

is deployed with an HTTP endpoint. Finally, the Camel-K binding is created indicating the MQTT broker address with the specific topic.

MLaaS online learning service code is available at the IoT-NGIN GitLab repository [4].

4.4 Model Sharing, Model Translation, and Zero-knowledge Model Verification

4.4.1 Introduction

The main motivation for the zero-knowledge verification framework is to provide a mechanism for ensuring the following:

1. The training phase of a machine learning model exclusively involves the inputs declared by the model owners.
2. Replicability of the training phase.
3. Immutability of the results of the training phase (i.e., trained model).
4. Ability to create an intermediate representation of the trained model in a common machine learning framework.

Since the training phase of an ML model is a deterministic process (provided the required initial conditions, including the seeds for any operation involving PRNG, e.g., batch normalization, and excluding non-deterministic models, i.e., VAE), by having full control of the datasets involved, the model architecture and hyper-parameter values, we can ensure that the model weights resulting from the training are the direct result from the inputs provided [18]. For this reason, to ensure that the resulting weights of a trained model exclusively involve the provided datasets, the training phase must be carried out in the premises of the system. To provide the ability for verifying and tracing the lineage of all inputs of the models, a platform for storing all relevant metadata and datasets involved is required. Additionally, the possibility for creating an intermediate representation of the model maximizes the compatibility of the registered models across a wide range of execution platforms, avoiding lock-in of the models in their original machine learning frameworks.

4.4.2 Features

In this section, we will introduce the services that make up the architecture of the system, and their responsibilities.

Model sharing service – features overview:

The model sharing service oversees the model training phase and storage of the results, given a model implemented in one of the supported ML backends, a set of hyper-parameter values, and the datasets involved. In addition to this, it is also in charge of providing access to, and enforcing access rules for the registered datasets and models.

The model registration process depends on the following inputs:

- model architecture implemented in one of the supported ML backends;
- an existing dataset in the system, for which the company and model developer are granted access to;
- hyper-parameter values for the model.

For each registered model, and all its associated inputs, a smart contract containing all the relevant metadata to ensure the reproducibility of the results of the training phase is deployed in the blockchain via the zero-knowledge verification service (see next subsection). The static files for the model architectures, resulting model weights and training metadata, as well as the datasets involved are stored in an object storage repository, to enforce control over the full storage lifecycle. To ensure the isolation of company resources in the shared object storage instance, each company resources are stored in independent buckets, with access credentials scoped to the company's resources. These credentials are obscured away from the end users and are generated and used exclusively in a programmatic manner by the system

Model training service – features overview:

The model training service oversees the training phase for each model registered via the model sharing service. To perform the training phase for a registered model, it first validates all the necessary inputs (as described in the introduction of the model sharing service).

Zero-knowledge model verification service – features overview:

The zero-knowledge model verification service provides a framework for end-to-end verification of stored models, and dataset identification. The blockchain is based on the Quorum blockchain service [16], which is an open source private blockchain platform with a fully capable implementation of the Ethereum virtual machine. For each model and dataset stored, there is a corresponding smart contract deployed in the blockchain. When deploying an Ethereum smart contract, the Ethereum virtual machine (EVM) stores internal bits of information, which are accessible when transacting with the contract. In this manner, we use smart contracts as sources of truth for all the relevant metadata for datasets and models. The metadata stored in the blockchain differs for models and datasets. As mentioned before, the objective is to store all the necessary metadata to verify and ensure the traceability and replicability of trained models. For this reason, one of the key pieces of stored metadata for trained models is a hash of the model weights, which allows the model sharing service to ensure the integrity of the artifact in the object storage repository. For datasets, as computing the hash of large files is a computationally intensive task, we store relevant statistics (unidimensional, matrix), as well as sample sizes, and total samples. By storing the hash of the model representation in the deployed smart contract, we can ensure the integrity of the stored models. We also store other model metadata, such as input and output vector sizes, and other relevant information regarding the datasets involved in the training phase.

Model translation service – features overview:

The model translation service provides a framework for generating an inter-mediate representation for machine learning models implemented in several frameworks. It leverages ONNX [17], a machine learning framework used as an intermediate compatibility layer between other popular machine learning frameworks, by providing an open format for representing machine learning models. One of the main use cases for needing an intermediate representation is due to hardware optimization concerns. Depending on the framework in which a machine learning model has been developed, the framework's back-end implementation may apply different optimizations to different hardware. The goal of using ONNX is to be able to access the implemented hardware-specific optimizations avoiding the lock-in of the implementation in a par-ticular framework, allowing the development of machine learning models in an open format that can be used to leverage the hardware optimizations implemented by other frameworks regardless of the original implementation's backend. There exist implementations for providing compatibility layers with ONNX for the most popular machine learning frameworks, e.g., PyTorch, Tensorflow, and scikit-learn. Some of these implementations are community efforts (i.e., open-source implementations), and in other cases such as in PyTorch, support is built in the framework.

4.4.3 Technical implementation

In this section, we will provide further details about the technical implementation of the services, and further insight into their interactions, as shown in Figure 4.11. Before further introducing the services individually, we will mention some guiding architectural and engineering practices followed in the development phase. We have followed a microservices approach for the design and development of the services. All the introduced services are implemented in Python, using the FastAPI framework. The OpenAPI specification for the services is generated dynamically by FastAPI. Documentation for the services is offered via Swagger, provided by FastAPI. Clients for the services APIs are programmatically generated with the OpenAPI generator library by using the OpenAPI specifications provided by FastAPI. For deployment, we followed a container-based approach, using Kubernetes as the container orchestration framework of choice.

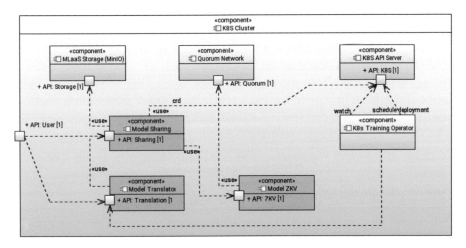

Figure 4.11   Internal architecture.

Model sharing service – technical details of implementation:

The access to the MLaaS block storage (powered by a MinIO instance) layer is handled exclusively by this service. Abstractions are provided for storage and retrieval of any size datasets and model architecture artifacts, as well as the results of the training processes. When storing datasets, and depending on the nature of each dataset, relevant statistics are collected and stored in the blockchain, in addition to storing the dataset in the block storage. Equivalently for model registration petitions, relevant metadata is extracted from the user's uploaded file and stored in the blockchain service in the form of an Ethereum smart contract. Each dataset and model is provided with a unique ID that is exposed to the user, and stored in an internal MLaaS relational database. For authorization purposes, each entry of this database registers the developer and its company in order to restrict the access of these assets. Authentication and authorization for storing and accessing models is implemented with MLaaS Keycloak. The JWT tokens provided by Keycloak provide with all necessary information for the model sharing service to enforce access rules for the tenants.

Upon model registration requests, the model sharing service will initiate a model training job, by means of the model training's HTTP API using its Python client implementation. Equivalently, communication with the blockchain service is achieved by means of the blockchain service's API Python client. For models for which their training jobs have finished successfully, the model sharing API allows for the download of the training results, after verifying the integrity of its associated artifacts by means of comparison of the hash stored in the blockchain contract, and the hash of the artifact upon download from the object storage layer. This service relies on a relational database in which, for each registered model, information about the company, developer, and smart contract address is stored.

The following operations are implemented in the HTTP REST API:

1. dataset and model registration (contract and storage in block storage layer);
2. dataset and model download.

Zero-knowledge model verification service – technical details of implementation:

The blockchain is powered by an instance of Quorum (MLaaS DLT), a private distributed ledger technology (DLT) implemented as a fork of the Ethereum blockchain. In our use case, a single member runs all the nodes that make up the network. Quorum supports private transactions (supported by Tessera, a component for private transaction management), in which encrypted data can be transferred between network participants and stored in a way such that only the involved participants can see the data. It is fully compatible with the Ethereum APIs and implements full support for smart contracts. To interact with the blockchain, we use the Web3.py Python library, and use the Solidity language specification for developing the smart contract code. The service uses separate addresses for each company to interact with the blockchain. These addresses' private keys are never shared with the end users. Using separate addresses for each company reduces the surface attack, limiting the exposure of any leaked private key to the scope of the company. Smart contracts are therefore deployed to the accounts issued for each of the companies.

The Ethereum virtual machine (EVM) runs contract code to completion or up to transaction gas (currency for covering transaction costs) exhaustion. However, Quorum allows for free-gas networks, and since it is a single member network, there exist no incentives for requiring gas for transacting in the network. In addition to the deployment of smart contracts for models and datasets, the service also implements the ability to fetch all stored metadata for already deployed contracts.

The following operations are implemented in the HTTP REST API:

1. deploying of smart contracts for datasets in the blockchain;
2. deployment of smart contracts for models in the blockchain;
3. fetching all metadata stored in a contract address.

Model translation service – technical details of implementation:

The model translation service provides a compatibility layer between three of the most widely spread ML frameworks (Pytorch, Tensorflow, and scikit-learn) by providing a managed service on top of ONNX [17]. Requests for model translation are allowed for all models already registered and for which their training jobs have finished successfully.

The following operations are implemented in the HTTP REST API:

1. generate intermediate representation in ONNX for an existing model.

Model training service – technical details of implementation:

The model training service is implemented as a Kubernetes custom operator, using the framework Kopf. Model training jobs are modeled as custom Kubernetes resource definitions (CRD), which include all the relevant information for the operator to process the training job.

On model registry, model developers must also specify a Docker image to be used as the environment for the model training. This requirement is set in order to provide model developers with maximum flexibility as well as allowing model developers to share the same environment across their local model development and training, and the training procedure performed in the model training cluster, essentially abstracting end users from any possible overhead introduced by the zero-knowledge verification process.

The results of the training are treated as output artifacts and must be stored in a specific output directory. This output directory is a mount of a Kubernetes persistent volume claim (PVC), and the contents of the PVC will be stored as a result of the model training job in the block storage upon an exit code that is received from the training container.

The custom resources are processed by the implemented Kubernetes operator in a queue-like manner and can be processed in either a sequential or parallel manner, depending on the availability and scalability of the hardware.

The model sharing service, upon the reception of a model registration request, will create an instance of the custom resource definition in the training Kubernetes cluster, with all the relevant input for the cluster to schedule the training job. This input contains:

- pointer to the UID of target model architecture;
- pointer to the UID of the target datasets;
- image registry link for the Docker training image;
- all relevant model starting conditions (e.g., PRNG seeds), exposed as environment variables to the containers running the specified Docker image.

The following operations are implemented in the HTTP REST API:

1. register model training jobs (creates the CRD in the target Kubernetes cluster);
2. check processing status for model training jobs.

The implementation code of the MLaaS services model sharing, model translator, and zero-knowledge verification service is available at the IoT-NGIN GitLab repository [15].

4.4.4 Evaluation

To exemplify the usage of the zero-knowledge verification framework, we will introduce the following test case, in which we register the Pix2Pix generative model [19] and the CMP facade dataset [20] and, after its training, generate the intermediate representation of the trained model in the ONNX framework (see Figure 4.12).

The Pix2Pix model implements a cGAN (conditional generative adversarial network), which is able to map input images to output images of a learned distribution from the training samples. For our use case, we will use building facades as the training input, and we expect the trained model to produce artificial facades, based on the learned latent distribution from the CMP facade dataset.

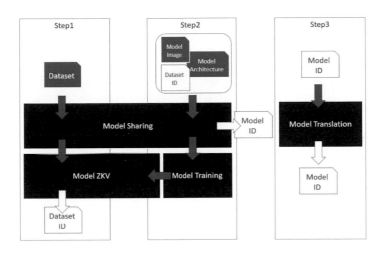

Figure 4.12 Evaluation process.

Before being able to register the model in the system, it is necessary to register all its associated datasets in the model sharing service (in our case, the CMP facade dataset). To do that, we make an HTTP POST request to the datasets endpoint in the model sharing service. The HTTP POST request is a multipart request, including the model architecture file and the initial metadata for the model (e.g., sample number, sample dimension, etc.).

curl --request POST\

--url http://<mlaas_model_sharing> /dataset/\

--header 'Content-Type: multipart/form-data'\

--form model=@model\

--form 'metadata={ ''sample_dimension'': ''(500,500)'', ''sample_num'' : 606}}'

Once the dataset is successfully registered in the system, we proceed with the registration of the model. In a similar way to the dataset registration process, to register the model in the system, we make an HTTP POST request to the model registration endpoint in the model sharing service. This POST request is also a multipart request, with the file containing the model architecture developed in the original machine learning framework, and the required model metadata (e.g., ID of the training dataset, input sample dimensions, total number of parameters, and initial conditions for all the hyper-parameters of the model, and link to the registry hosting the training Docker image).

curl --request POST\

--url http://<mlaas_model_sharing>/model/\

--header 'Content-Type: multipart/form-data'\

--form model=@model\

--form 'metadata={ ''model_params'': { ''sample_dimension'': ''(500, 500)'', ''params'': ''<json_params_initial_cond>''}, ''data_params'': { ''dataset_id'': ''<dataset_id>''}}'

In the model registration step, the model sharing service, upon verifying all necessary inputs, will trigger a new job in the model training service to schedule the training of the model and its associated datasets using the specified Docker image.

The model training service will then execute the training job, scheduling the Kubernetes deployment, and executing until an exit code is received from the container. Upon receiving a graceful exit code, it will then copy all the contents of the persistent volume attached to the container into the block storage layer, via the model sharing service. In this step, the model sharing service will also update the smart contract associated with the model with the metadata of the final trained model (e.g., model weights hash). We can verify the updated metadata by making a GET request to the model sharing service metadata endpoint:

curl --request GET\

--url http://<mlaas_model_sharing> /metadata/<model_id>

From this step onwards, the model is ready to be used for inference, being able to download it securely using the model sharing service, or to create an intermediate representation of the trained model in ONNX via the model translation service.

curl --request GET\

--url http://<mlaas_model_sharing>/model/<model_id>

To create an intermediate representation of the model, the developer must perform an HTTP POST request to the model translation service, specifying the ID of the trained model:

curl --request POST\

--url http://<mlaas_model_translation> /translate /<model_id>

Note that the service will reject any petitions for registered models for which its training jobs are not completed. Upon receiving the request, the model translation service will then perform the conversion of the model from the initial framework to ONNX and will store the results of this operation under a new ID (i.e., a new model). This new model will have all the invariant metadata of the original model, except for the changing metadata, e.g., backend (i.e., framework) of the model, model hash. Note that there was no training step involved in the model translation step. This is since ONNX allows for model conversion without the need of re-training the model.

Therefore, the model is now available in the original backend under the ID associated upon its registration in the system, and the ONNX version of the same model is also available under a newly assigned ID (as received in the response of the model translation service API call). It is necessary to assign different IDs as the zero-knowledge verification framework treats models as individual, independent units, due to the uniqueness of the metadata involved in the verification process.

4.5 Conclusion

This chapter has introduced the IoT-NGIN concept of MLaaS, its main features, and the implementation details of the MVP instantiated in the IoT-NGIN cluster. It has also provided the functional and technical specification of additional MLOps services incorporated into MLaaS: services required for MLOps in the IoT domain, such as the adaptive online learning service, intended for the ML model training and inference from streaming datasets, or other services that extend the MLOps functionality, such as the model sharing, model translator, and zero-knowledge model verification, which are not part of the MLOps frameworks available in the open-source community.

MLaaS is being used by IoT-NGIN use cases for the MLOps management of ML-based applications in the IoT domain. In particular, the usage of MLaaS for online model training and inference for smart energy forecasting has been used in the evaluation of the online learning services. The adoption of MLaaS in the other IoT-NGIN use cases will be the focus of development in the rest of the IoT-NGIN project.

Acknowledgements

The work presented in this chapter has been funded by the IoT-NGIN project, contract no. 957246, within the H2020 Framework Program of the European Commission.

References

[1] "The 5 V's of big data". Watson Health Perspectives. 17 September 2016.

[2] MLaaS platform. IoT-NGIN Gitlab repository: https://gitlab.com/h2020 -iot-ngin/enhancing_iot_intelligence/ml-as-a-service

[3] Beetz, F., & Harrer, S. (2021). GitOps: The Evolution of DevOps?. IEEE Software.

[4] MLaaS Online Learning repository at IoT-NGIN Gitlab: https://gitlab.c om/h2020-iot-ngin/enhancing_iot_intelligence/t3_2/online_learning

[5] Sayan Putatunda (2021), Practical Machine Learning for Streaming Data with Python: Design, Develop, and Validate Online Learning Models. ISBN: 9781484268674. Appress.

[6] D. E. Rumelhart, G. E. Hinton and R. J. Williams, "Learning internal representations by error propagation," San Diego, California: Institute for Cognitive Science, University of California., 1985.

[7] Rahul Dey, Fathi M. Salem, "Gate-Variants of Gated Recurrent Unit (GRU) Neural Networks", Department of Electrical and Computer Engineering Michigan State University, 2017

[8] Razvan Pascanu, Tomas Mikolov, Yoshua Bangio, "On the difficulty of training Recurrent Neural Networks," 2012.

[9] Jonathan Matsson, "The Publish-Subscribe Pattern", 2018

[10] S. S. Shapiro, M. B. Wilk, "An analysis of Variance Test for Normality (Complete Samples)", 1965

[11] T. W. Anderson. D. A. Darling, "Asymptotic Theory of Certain 'Goodness of Fit' Criteria Based on Sthocastic Processes", 1952

[12] Ralph D'Agostino and E. S. Pearson, "Tests for Departure from Normality. Empirical Results for the Distributions of b2 and $\sqrt{b1}$", 1973, p.613-622.

[13] Avanti Shrikumar, Peyton Greeside, Anshul Kubdaje, "Learning Important Features Through Propagating Activation Differences", 2019

[14] Diederik P. Kingman, Jimmy Lei Ba, "ADAM: A method for stochastic optimization," 2014

[15] MLaaS Model Sharing, Model Translator and Zero Knowledge Verification repository at IoT-NGIN Gitlab: https://gitlab.com/h2020 -iot-ngin/enhancing_iot_intelligence/t3_4/ml-model-sharing

[16] Quorum Blockchain Service: https://consensys.net/quorum/qbs/

[17] ONNX: https://onnx.ai/

[18] Chen, Boyuan, et al. "Towards Training Reproducible Deep Learning Models." Proceedings of the 44th International Conference on Software Engineering, 2022, https://doi.org/10.1145/3510003.3510163.

[19] Pix2Pix model: examples/tensorflow_examples/models/pix2pix at master ů tensorflow/examples ů GitHub

[20] CMP Facade Dataset: CMP Facade Database (cvut.cz)

5

Federated Learning Models in Decentralized Critical Infrastructure

Ilias Siniosoglou[1], Stamatia Bibi[1], Konstantinos-Filippos Kollias[1], George Fragulis[1], Panagiotis Radoglou-Grammatikis[1], Thomas Lagkas[2], Vasileios Argyriou[3], Vasileios Vitsas[2], and Panagiotis Sarigiannidis[1]

[1]University of Western Macedonia, Greece
[2]International Hellenic University, Greece
[3]Kingston University, England
E-mail: isiniosoglou@uowm.gr; sbibi@uowm.gr; dece00063@uowm.gr; gfragulis@uowm.gr; pradoglou@uowm.gr; tlagkas@cs.ihu.gr; vasileios.argyriou@kingston.ac.uk; vitsas@it.teithe.gr; psarigiannidis@uowm.gr

Abstract

Federated learning (FL) is a novel methodology aiming at training machine learning (ML) and deep learning (DL) models in a decentralized manner in order to solve three main problems seen in the artificial intelligence (AI) sector, namely, (a) model optimization, (b) data security and privacy, and (c) resource optimization. FL has been established as the "status quo" in today's AI applications especially in the industrial and critical infrastructure (CI) domain, as the three aforementioned pillars are invaluable in assuring their integrity. CIs include important facilities such as industrial infrastructures (smart grids, manufacturing, powerlines, etc.), medical facilities, agriculture, supply chains, and more. Deploying AI applications in these infrastructures is an arduous task that can compromise the CI's security and production procedures, requiring meticulous integration and testing. Even a slight mistake leading to the disruption of operations in these infrastructures can have dire consequences, economical, functional, and even loss of life. FL offers the needed functionalities to galvanize the integration and optimization of artificial intelligence in critical infrastructures. In this chapter, we will outline the application of federated learning in decentralized critical infrastructures, its advantages and disadvantages, as well as the different state-of-the-art techniques used in the CI domain. We will showcase how the centralized ML approach transitions into the federated domain while we will show practical examples and practices of deploying the federated learning example in representative CIs, like, power production facilities, agricultural sensor networks, smart homes, and more.

Keywords: Federated learning, artificial intelligence, data security, critical infrastructures, model optimization, resource optimization.

5.1 Introduction

5.1.1 Definition and motivation

Federated learning (FL) is a distributed machine learning technique that allows multiple devices or entities to collaboratively train a model while keeping their data on-device. In federated learning, the data is distributed across a large corpus of devices or entities. This approach trains an AI model on the remote device using the local data and then sends only the model to a specified aggregation unit. There, a new and optimized global model is created by aggregating the model updates from all the devices. This approach allows for the training of models on large amounts of data without the need to transmit or centralize it, thus addressing the challenges of data privacy, security, and resource allocation.

The methodology was first introduced by the Google Research team in a 2016 paper titled "Communication-Efficient Learning of Deep Networks from Decentralized Data" [1]. It represents an advancement from traditional distributed machine learning and is designed to address the challenges of training AI models without the need to transfer data, for reasons related to computation, allocation, and privacy.

The motivation behind FL is to enable machine learning in scenarios where data is distributed across devices or is sensitive and cannot be centralized. For example, in the case of personalized healthcare, data may be collected from multiple devices such as wearables, smartphones, and hospitals. In these scenarios, it is not practical or secure to centralize the data and allows for the training of models without compromising the privacy and security of the data. Additionally, this approach can be applied in mobile computing, where data is distributed across millions of mobile devices [2],

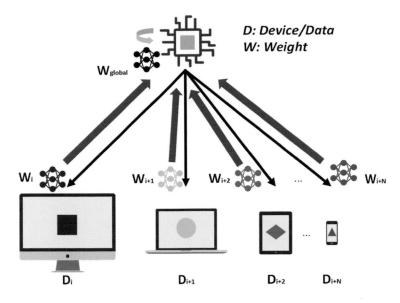

Figure 5.1 Federated learning concept.

and it allows training models on this data without the need to transmit large amounts of data over the network.

Federated learning also has the potential to democratize machine learning by enabling the participation of a large number of devices and entities in the training process. This can lead to more diverse and representative datasets, and also allows for training models in remote or underserved areas where data may not be easily accessible.

Federated learning can also be used to improve the performance of models in edge computing applications. By allowing devices to train models locally, federated learning can reduce the need for transmitting large amounts of data over the network, which can be beneficial in low-bandwidth or high-latency environments. Additionally, federated learning can enable the training of models that can be deployed on resource-constrained devices, such as IoT sensors or mobile phones.

5.1.2 Federated learning domains

Federated learning is an approach that aims to leverage the benefits of distributed AI model training. This approach is centered around three main pillars:

- **Model optimization:** Improves the model optimization process [3], [4] for the local node by providing an aggregated (global) model that contains knowledge accumulated by the aggregated models from all the devices.
- **Data privacy:** Preserves the integrity, security, and privacy of the data by keeping it at the edge nodes, rather than transferring it to a central infrastructure.
- **Resource optimization:** Designed to optimize [3], [5] the use of resources by communicating only the model parameters and some metadata between the federated server and the federated clients, instead of transferring the entire dataset. This conserves network resources and avoids possible bottlenecks, leads to lower latency, and allows for the distribution of the computing power needed for the AI model training among various nodes. Additionally, it enables to use the remote machines for the training process only when they are not used for other purposes, are connected to a steady power supply, and/or when there is a stable internet connection, which reduces the energy consumption of the federated process.

5.1.3 Use cases and applications

Federated learning has a wide range of use cases and applications, including but not limited to the following:

- **Personalized healthcare** can be used to train models that can predict a patient's health status or risk of developing a certain condition. This can be done by aggregating data from multiple devices such as wearables, smartphones, and hospitals. FL allows for the training of models without compromising the privacy and security of the patient's data, which is particularly important in the healthcare industry.
- **Mobile computing** can be used to train models on the large amounts of data generated by mobile devices such as smartphones and tablets. This can be used to improve the performance of mobile applications, such as natural language processing, image recognition, and more. For example, federated learning can be used to train models that can predict the battery life of a mobile device based on usage patterns.
- **Internet of Things** can be used to train models on data collected from IoT devices such as sensors and cameras. This can be used to improve the performance of edge computing applications, such as image and video processing, anomaly detection, and more.

- **Banking and finance** can be used to train models that can predict fraudulent transactions, by leveraging data from multiple banking institutions to train AI model, without actually transferring any data.
- **Natural language processing** can also be used to train language models by aggregating data from multiple sources without compromising the privacy of the data.

These are some examples of the utilization of the federated learning methodology in a variety of different popular domains. However, FL is continuously being adapted and tested to new applications as it is slowly becoming the baseline for machine learning in modern distributed infrastructures.

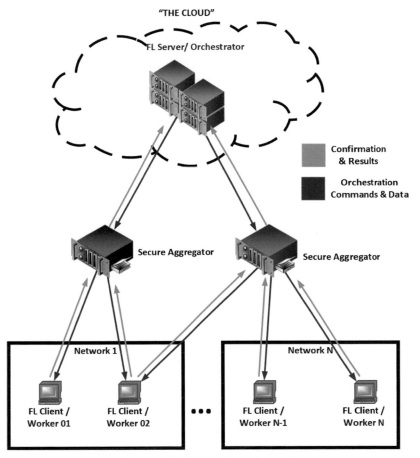

Figure 5.2 Simple federated learning architecture.

5.2 How Federated Learning Works

5.2.1 Overview of the architecture and process

Federated learning is a distributed machine learning methodology that allows for the training of deep learning models on a large corpus of edge devices. In this approach, models are trained locally on the edge devices, and their weights are sent to a central server where they are combined to form a global model using an algorithm such as federated averaging. The global model is then sent back to the remote devices for use. The central server distributes an initial global model to a population of federated devices, each of which holds a set of local data and a local model. These models are trained on the local data and the model weights are then retrieved by the central server to be combined using a predefined fusion algorithm, to create a new global model containing the new knowledge accumulated from the local models. This process is repeated for a number of iterations until the global model converges. Figure 5.3 shows a common process (strategy) followed to realize an FL training between a server and a corpus of devices. Figure 5.3 showcases a simple FL strategy for realizing a training session.

To get an idea about the modeling of the methodology process, we can depict a mathematical formula. Of course, since the process is directly connected to the fusion algorithm used, the FL process can be defined in a number of ways. For simplicity, we shall use the federated averaging algorithm to explain the process. Eqn (5.1) shows the process of fusing the local models from the remote devices in one global model [6].

$$w_G^k = \frac{1}{\sum_{i \in N} D_i} \sum_{i=1}^{N} D_i w_i^k. \tag{5.1}$$

Equation (5.1) Federated aggregation algorithm (FedAvg).

Here, the global model on the kth iteration is represented by w_G^k and the remote ith model at that iteration is represented by w_i^k. Each node holds a set of local data $D_{i \in \mathbb{N}}$ and local models w_i.

5.2.2 Key components

For the implementation of the described architecture, the system defines three main components [7] in order to realize the operation of the training, namely, a) the orchestrator, b) the aggregator, and c) the worker/client. Figure 5.2 shows how these components fit into the federated architecture.

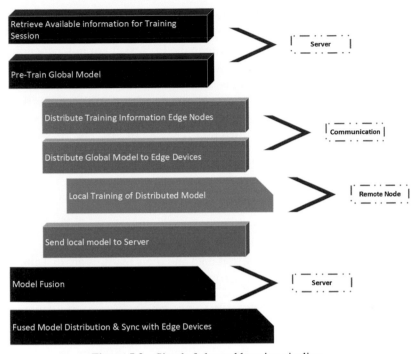

Figure 5.3 Simple federated learning pipeline.

5.2.2.1 Orchestrator

The orchestrator is responsible for managing the federated learning process, including initiating the FL session, selecting the population of devices, organizing the data, algorithm, and pipeline, setting the training context, managing communication and security, evaluating the performance, and, finally, synchronizing the FL procedure.

5.2.2.2 Aggregator

The aggregator is responsible for incorporating the updates from the local models into the global model. In some cases, the orchestrator also acts as the aggregator, particularly for smaller networks or certain security or operational requirements. The aggregator also implements security and privacy measures to protect the FL server and workers from any malicious actors.

5.2.2.3 Worker

The worker, also known as the party, is responsible for the local training that takes place during the FL training session. The worker is the owner of the data and updates its model based on the newly received version of the global model after the local training and global model generation by the aggregator. The worker has the option of participating in the FL session or not, depending on resource allocation or criticality.

The abovementioned components established the foundation of the methodology. Depending on the type and nature of the deployment, these components can have additional responsibilities and placement or some extra components might be added. The different types of FL are described in the next section.

5.2.3 Types of federated learning

There is a variety of different federated learning application types that depend on a multitude of characteristics. A main characteristic that defines the type of the methodology applied is the way that data and their features are distributed and used by the different nodes. In particular, based on the data, we have the following:

- **Horizontal federated learning:** This type of approach trains models on data that is horizontally partitioned across different devices or entities. For example, training a model on data from different hospitals or different companies (Figure 5.4).
- **Vertical federated learning:** This type of federated learning trains models on data that is vertically partitioned across different devices or

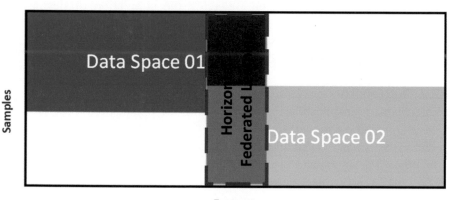

Horizontal Federated Learning

Figure 5.4   Horizontal federated learning.

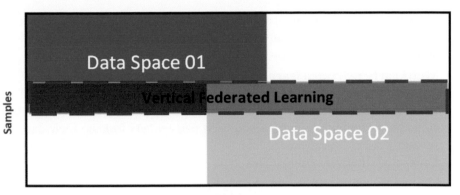

Vertical Federated Learning

Figure 5.5   Vertical federated learning.

entities. For example, training a model on data from different features of the same patient (Figure 5.5).

- **Federated transfer learning:** This type of federated learning is focused on adapting a model pre-trained on one dataset to another related dataset (Figure 5.6).

However, the type of the federated learning approach used is not limited to the distribution of the data for the specific use case but depends on other characteristics such as the deployment constraints, the criticality of the data

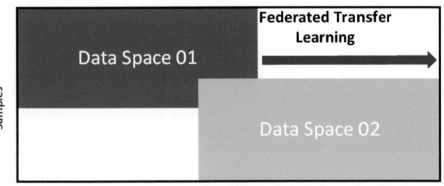

Federated Transfer Learning

Figure 5.6   Federated transfer learning.

and infrastructure, and the nature of the task tackled. These preconditions orient the methodology and technique to adapt to the problem at hand and include the following approaches:

- **Multi-party federated learning:** This type of FL is similar to horizontal FL, but the data is under multiple parties' control. This type of federated learning is useful for the scenarios where data is not centralized but spread across multiple parties and each party wants to keep their data private.
- **Federated meta-learning:** This type of FL is focused on training a model that can adapt to new tasks or domains quickly by leveraging knowledge from previous tasks or domains.
- **Federated domain adaptation:** This type of FL is focused on adapting a model trained on one domain to work on another domain.
- **Federated few-shot learning**: This type of FL is focused on training a model that can learn to classify new classes with only a few examples.
- **Federated reinforcement learning:** This type of FL is focused on training a model using the reinforcement learning approach on the edge devices.

5.2.4 Model fusion algorithms

As mentioned before, the underlying core of the training procedure is the aggregation algorithm that undertakes the fusion of the distributed models into one optimized global model. Thus, the aggregation algorithm is a crucial component of FL as it determines the final performance of the global model. The most commonly used aggregation algorithm is federated averaging, which takes the average of the local models' weights to form the global model. However, there are other aggregation algorithms that can be used depending on the specific use case. For example, some algorithms weigh the contributions of the local models based on the quality of their data or the computational resources available on the device. These algorithms can help to mitigate the impact of data availability and device heterogeneity. Additionally, some algorithms use techniques such as differential privacy to protect the privacy of the data on the edge devices during the aggregation process. Overall, the choice of aggregation algorithm can have a significant impact on the performance and privacy of the final global model and should be carefully considered when implementing FL. Table 5.1 presents some of the common and state-of-the-art fusion algorithms that are widely used in different settings.

Table 5.1 Common fusion algorithms used in FL.

Algorithm	Year	Description	Benefits
FedAvg [1]	2017	An iterative model averaging FL framework	Reduces communication cost by locally computed updated aggregation
Zoo [8]	2018	Composable services to deploy ML models locally on edge	Reduces latency in data processing, and minimizes the raw data revealed
FedPer [9]	2019	Federated learning with personalization layers	Improves results with data heterogeneity, and communication cost
FedAsync [10]	2019	Asynchronous federated optimization framework	Improves flexibility and scalability and tolerates staleness
FedCS [11]	2019	Client selection for FL with heterogeneous resources	Improves performance and reduces training time
BlockFL [12]	2019	Blockchained federated architecture	Optimizes communication, computation, and latency
FedMa [13]	2020	Federated matched averaging algorithm for FL	Improves accuracy and communication cost
FedAT [14]	2020	Synchronous intra-tier training and asynchronous cross-tier training	Improves accuracy and reduces communication cost

5.3 Federated Learning vs. Traditional Centralized Learning

Federated learning is different from traditional centralized learning [15] in several ways. The most significant difference is that in traditional centralized learning, the data is collected and stored in a central location, where it is used to train the model. In contrast, federated learning keeps the data on the edge devices and trains the model locally on each device. This allows for the training of models on large amounts of data without the need to transfer it and also the ability to handle non-independent and identically distributed (IID) data. Additionally, federated learning preserves data privacy and security as the data never leaves the edge devices. This makes federated learning particularly well-suited for scenarios where data is sensitive or distributed across multiple devices. However, it is important to keep in mind that federated learning has its own set of challenges such as communication overhead, data availability, and model divergence.

Table 5.2   Comparison between federated and centralized learning.

Federated learning	Traditional centralized learning
Data remains on edge devices	Data is collected and stored in a central location
Model trained locally on each device	Model trained on centralized data
Suitable for non-IID data	Assumes data is IID
Preserves data privacy and security	Data privacy and security may be at risk
Requires communication between devices	No communication required between devices
Scales horizontally and vertically	Scales vertically
Suitable for sensitive or distributed data	Not suitable for sensitive or distributed data
Can handle many edge devices	Limited by the amount of data that can be centralized
Can have challenges such as communication overhead and model divergence	Fewer challenges than federated learning

5.3.1 Advantages and disadvantages of federated learning

By itself and as it is probably apparent, the federated learning approach is vast and, in its range, it encapsulates major advantages but also some drawbacks. As in all fields, the optimal deployment of federated learning is the fine line between the tradeoff of these advantages and drawback and strictly depends on the application of the methodology. For example, there might be some applications that require better model generalization but in expense of the communication efficiency of the network. Table 5.3 enumerates some of these advantages and disadvantages of federated learning in order to provide a better view of its utility.

5.3.2 Real-world examples of federated learning

5.3.2.1 Smart farming

In smart farming, federated learning can provide several benefits [16] by allowing for the training of models on data that is decentralized and spread across multiple devices or entities. The use case integrates IoT data from crops and animal care infrastructures, AR smart glasses, and other heterogeneous IoT devices, which can be difficult to source and gather in a central place to train a single AI model. By utilizing federated learning, it allows to train models on data that is distributed across great distances, making it possible to:

Table 5.3 Advantages and disadvantages of federated learning.

Advantages	Disadvantages
Collaborative learning: Allows multiple devices or entities to collaboratively train a model while keeping their data on-device. This allows for the training of models on large amounts of data without the need to transmit or centralize it.	**Data availability**: Data availability can be an issue in federated learning, as not all devices or entities may have access to the same data or may have data of different quality.
Data privacy and security: Allows for the training of models without compromising the privacy and security of the data. This is particularly important in scenarios where data is sensitive or distributed across multiple devices.	**Communication overhead:** Requires communication between the devices or entities, which can be a bottleneck, especially if the devices are located in different geographical locations.
Edge computing: Allows devices to train models locally, which can reduce the need for transmitting large amounts of data over the network. Additionally, it enables the training of models that can be deployed on resource-constrained devices, such as IoT sensors or mobile phones.	**Model divergence:** Can suffer from model divergence, where the local models may not converge to a common global model due to the non-IID data distribution on the devices.
Handling non-IID data: It is particularly well-suited for training models on non-IID data that is commonly found in the real-world scenarios.	**Latency:** Can suffer from latency issues, as it requires communication between the devices or entities to exchange model updates.
Scalability: It is highly scalable and can handle a large number of devices or entities.	**Complexity:** Can be complex to implement and requires a lot of communication and coordination between the devices or entities.

- Formulate best practices for farming and livestock production in expanding the specific market by discovering weaknesses in the agricultural systems and providing insightful predictions to help end-users make informed decisions about their infrastructure's operations.
- Formulate rules and quantified metrics for optimum conditions in terms of (animal) behavior, psychiatry, food quality, nutrition, and agriculture environment by training models on the diverse data sources from different scenarios.
- Increase farm and livestock production by using AI-supported strategies that improve agricultural systems' sustainability, productivity, and risk.

- Provide feedback on how to ensure proper decision support by using the knowledge accumulated from the local models to improve the global model.

5.3.2.2 Smart, sustainable, and efficient buildings

In the use case of smart, sustainable, and efficient buildings, FL can provide several benefits [17]. By using IoT data in smart buildings to optimize the energy footprint and automate building management using AI-based solutions, FL can be used to train models on large amounts of data from multiple devices or entities, while keeping the data on-device. This allows for the training of models on large amounts of data without the need to transmit or centralize it, which can help to preserve the privacy and security of the data.

5.3.2.3 Industrial supply chains

In the context of the industrial supply chain use case, FL can provide significant benefits by improving the forecasting accuracy [18] for fulfilling the demand from retailers and agencies, who are attempting to satisfy the demand from their consumers. This is achieved by utilizing the abundance of product codes, complexity of certain manufacturing processes, and short lifetime of most products in the supply chain, which make production scheduling and market-oriented forecasting challenging. In this frame, FL allows for the collaborative training of models across different supply chains of the end-user, without the need to transfer or centralize the data. This can improve the forecasting accuracy by leveraging the knowledge and data from different product codes produced by the end-user. Additionally, the use of FL can protect the data privacy and resources of the end-user's infrastructure, by keeping the data on-device, and avoiding the need for centralizing and transferring it. Furthermore, by applying this technique to optimize the forecasting accuracy and using the heterogeneous data from different product codes, it can lead to the end-user's better decision making and better supplier—customer relationship.

5.3.2.4 Industrial infrastructures

In the use case of mixed reality and ML-supported maintenance and fault prediction of IoT-based critical infrastructure, the benefit of FL is its ability to predict the behavior of industrial devices, such as controllers, in order to identify potential defects and malfunctions. This enables the end-user to monitor and prevent problems in the operation of each industrial infrastructure. The technique is applied to a large number of industrial devices that are divided and installed in decentralized optical switches. The use case makes use of the ability of federated learning to handle many edge devices, both horizontally by scaling to more devices such as small form-factor pluggable (SFP) modules or switches and vertically by applying a hierarchical model optimization. This allows for more efficient and accurate predictions and maintenance operations for the critical infrastructure.

5.3.2.5 Medical sector

Federated learning can bring several benefits to the medical sector [19], [20], particularly in a use case of a collection of hospitals across a large distance. Some of the benefits include:

- **Data privacy and security:** Allows for the training of models without compromising the privacy and security of the patients' data. This is particularly important in the medical sector where data is sensitive and regulated.
- **Handling non-IID data:** It is particularly well-suited for training models on non-IID data, which is commonly found in the medical sector. By training models on the local data from different hospitals, the models can learn from diverse patient populations, resulting in more robust models.
- **Edge computing:** Allows hospitals to train models locally, which can reduce the need for transmitting large amounts of data over the network. Additionally, it enables the training of models that can be deployed on resource-constrained devices, such as mobile devices used by clinicians and nurses.
- **Collaborative learning:** Allows multiple hospitals to collaboratively train a model while keeping their data on-device. This allows for the training of models on large amounts of data without the need to transmit or centralize it.
- **Scalability:** It is highly scalable and can handle a large number of hospitals across a large distance. This makes it suitable for large-scale healthcare studies and research.
- By using, hospitals can train models on their local data without sharing any sensitive information across the network, while still being able to build models that generalize well to different patient populations. This can lead to better diagnosis, treatment, and ultimately patient outcomes.

5.4 Implementing Federated Learning

Implementing federated learning requires a few key components. First, a centralized server is needed to aggregate the models trained on the local devices and distribute the updated global model back to the devices. Second, there should be a mechanism for the local devices to communicate with the central server and securely exchange model updates. Third, a mechanism for data partitioning is needed to ensure that the devices are training models on non-overlapping data. Fourth, a method for combining the local models into a global model, such as federated averaging, is necessary. Lastly, it is important to have a way to evaluate the performance of the model and monitor the FL process. Additionally, it is important to have a good understanding of the underlying deep learning model and the data that are being used. It is also important to consider the security and privacy aspects of the FL process, as well as the network infrastructure to ensure that the devices can communicate effectively with the central server.

5.4.1 Tools and frameworks available

Since its introduction, federated learning has continuously been explored and integrated into a variety of commercial and industrial applications. To support the migration from conventional deep learning, a lot of diverse frameworks have been proposed and used to both deploy or experiment with the FL methodology. Table 5.4 enumerates some of the most used frameworks that exist today.

5.4.2 Challenges

Despite the many potential benefits of federated learning, there are still some challenges that need to be addressed before it can be widely adopted. These

Table 5.4   Available federated learning frameworks and tools.

Framework	Type
Tensorflow federated [21]	Research
FATE [22]	Production
Flower [23]	Production/research
PySyft [24]	Production/research
IBM federated [25]	Production/research
Leaf [26]	Research
OpenFL [27]	Production/research

include issues related to data privacy and security, as well as the need for robust methods for aggregating updates from multiple devices. Additionally, it requires the design of efficient algorithms to handle the high-dimensional and non-IID data across the devices, and more. Therefore, it is an active area of research and development, with many ongoing efforts aimed at addressing these challenges and making the approach more practical and widely applicable. Common challenges in the federated learning domain include problems that derive by its innate nature, such as:

- **Untrusted sources:** O ne of the challenges is the presence of untrusted sources, which can be devices or entities that may not have the same level of security or data privacy as the other participants. This can lead to potential breaches of security or privacy and can compromise the integrity of the model.
- **Adversarial attacks:** FL is also vulnerable to adversarial attacks, where an attacker may attempt to manipulate the local models or the global model, leading to a decrease in the accuracy of the model.
- **IID and non-IID data processing:** FL requires the data distributed across the devices or entities to be identically independently distributed (IID), which is not always the case. In scenarios where data is non-IID, the local models may not converge to a common global model, leading to a decrease in the accuracy of the model.
- **Synchronization problems:** FL requires coordination and communication between the devices or entities, and synchronization problems can occur if the devices or entities are not able to communicate or coordinate effectively.
- **Small number of participants:** FL requires a large number of devices or entities to participate in order to effectively train a model. If the number of participants is small, the model may not be able to effectively learn from the data.
- **System infiltration:** In FL, since the data is distributed across multiple devices or entities, it can be vulnerable to infiltration by malicious actors who can attempt to access the data or manipulate the models.

5.5 Conclusion

Federated learning is a novel methodology created on the basis of distributed training of AI models, heavily oriented at keeping the distributed data private while also optimizing the models and the resources used. It is particularly useful in the industrial and critical infrastructure domain, as it allows for the integration and optimization of AI in these systems without compromising their integrity. FL offers several advantages in terms of deployment, scalability, and security; however, it also poses some challenges in terms of implementation, communication, and model optimization, especially when considering the distribution of the distributed resources. It is a status quo in today's AI applications. The chapter focuses on introducing the basics of the federated learning methodology, the application of FL in decentralized critical infrastructures, outlining the advantages and disadvantages and different techniques used in the field. It provides practical examples of FL's deployment in various infrastructures such as power production facilities, agricultural sensor networks, and smart homes and more while also summarizing the currently available sources.

Acknowledgements

This work has received funding from the European Union's Horizon 2020 research and innovation program under Grant Agreement No. 957406 (TER-MINET).

References

[1] H. B. McMahan, E. Moore, D. Ramage, S. Hampson and B. A. y Arcas, "Communication-Efficient Learning of Deep Networks from Decentralized Data," Proceedings of the 20th International Conference on Artificial Intelligence and Statistics, AISTATS 2017, February 2016. W364W7352

[2] "Federated Learning: Collaborative Machine Learning without Centralized Training Data – Google AI Blog," [Online]. Available: https://ai.googleblog.com/2017/04/federated-learning-collaborative.html.W364W7352

[3] J. K. Konečnťy, H. B. Mcmahan and D. Ramage, "Federated Optimization:Distributed Optimization Beyond the Datacenter," November 2015. W364W7352

[4] I. Siniosoglou, V. Argyriou, S. Bibi, T. Lagkas and P. Sarigiannidis, "Unsupervised Ethical Equity Evaluation of Adversarial Federated Networks," ACM International Conference Proceeding Series, August 2021. W364W7352

[5] J. Konečný, H. B. McMahan, F. X. Yu, P. Richtárik, A. T. Suresh and D. Bacon, "Federated Learning: Strategies for Improving Communication Efficiency," October 2016. W364W7352

[6] W. Y. B. Lim, N. C. Luong, D. T. Hoang, Y. Jiao, Y. C. Liang, Q. Yang, D. Niyato and C. Miao, "Federated Learning in Mobile Edge Networks: A Comprehensive Survey," IEEE Communications Surveys and Tutorials, vol. 22, no. 3, pp. 2031-2063, July 2020. W364W7352

[7] I. Siniosoglou, P. Sarigiannidis, V. Argyriou, T. Lagkas, S. K. Goudos and M. Poveda, "Federated Intrusion Detection in NG-IoT Healthcare Systems: An Adversarial Approach," IEEE International Conference on Communications, June 2021. W364W7352

[8] J. Zhao, R. Mortier, J. Crowcroft and L. Wang, "Privacy-Preserving Machine Learning Based Data Analytics on Edge Devices," AIES 2018 - Proceedings of the 2018 AAAI/ACM Conference on AI, Ethics, and Society, pp. 341-346, December 2018. W364W7352

[9] M. G. Arivazhagan, V. Aggarwal, A. K. Singh and S. Choudhary, "Federated Learning with Personalization Layers," December 2019. W364W7352

[10] C. Xie, O. Koyejo and I. Gupta, "Asynchronous Federated Optimization," March 2019. W364W7352

[11] T. Nishio and R. Yonetani, "Client Selection for Federated Learning with Heterogeneous Resources in Mobile Edge," IEEE International Conference on Communications, Vols. 2019-May, April 2018. W364W7352

[12] H. Kim, J. Park, M. Bennis and S. L. Kim, "Blockchained on-device federated learning," IEEE Communications Letters, vol. 24, no. 6, pp. 1279-1283, June 2020. W364W7352

[13] H. Wang, M. Yurochkin, Y. Sun, D. Papailiopoulos and Y. Khazaeni, "Federated Learning with Matched Averaging," February 2020. W364W7352

[14] Z. Chai, Y. Chen, A. Anwar, L. Zhao, Y. Cheng and H. Rangwala, "FedAT: A High-Performance and Communication-Efficient Federated Learning System with Asynchronous Tiers," International Conference for High Performance Computing, Networking, Storage and Analysis, SC, October 2020. W364W7352

[15] M. Asad, A. Moustafa and T. Ito, "Federated Learning Versus Classical Machine Learning: A Convergence Comparison," July 2021. W364W7352

[16] T. Manoj, K. Makkithaya and V. G. Narendra, "A Federated Learning-Based Crop Yield Prediction for Agricultural Production Risk Management," 2022 IEEE Delhi Section Conference, DELCON 2022, 2022. W364W7352

[17] U. M. Aïvodji, S. Gambs and A. Martin, "IOTFLA : AA secured and privacy-preserving smart home architecture implementing federated learning," Proceedings - 2019 IEEE Symposium on Security and Privacy Workshops, SPW 2019, pp. 175-180, May 2019. W364W7352

[18] T. Li, A. K. Sahu, A. Talwalkar and V. Smith, "Federated Learning: Challenges, Methods, and Future Directions," IEEE Signal Processing Magazine, vol. 37, no. 3, pp. 50-60, August 2019. W364W7352

[19] M. Joshi, A. Pal and M. Sankarasubbu, "Federated Learning for Healthcare Domain - Pipeline, Applications and Challenges," ACM Transactions on Computing for Healthcare, vol. 3, no. 4, pp. 1-36, November 2022. W364W7352

[20] N. Rieke, J. Hancox, W. Li, F. Milletarì, H. R. Roth, S. Albarqouni, S. Bakas, M. N. Galtier, B. A. Landman, K. Maier-Hein, S. Ourselin, M. Sheller, R. M. Summers, A. Trask, D. Xu, M. Baust and M. J. Cardoso, "The future of digital health with federated learning," npj Digital Medicine 2020 3:1, vol. 3, no. 1, pp. 1-7, September 2020. W364W7352

[21] Federated Learning | TensorFlow Federated. W364W7352

[22] "Fate," [Online]. Available: https://fate.fedai.org/.W364W7352

[23] "Flower: A Friendly Federated Learning Framework," [Online]. Available: https://flower.dev/.W364W7352

[24] "PySyft - OpenMined Blog," [Online]. Available: https://blog.openmined.org/tag/pysyft/.W364W7352

[25] "IBM Federated Learning - IBM Documentation," [Online]. Available: https://www.ibm.com/docs/en/cloud-paks/cp-data/4.0?topic=models-federated-learning-tech-preview.W364W7352

[26] "LEAF - A Benchmark for Federated Settings," [Online]. Available: https://leaf.cmu.edu/.W364W7352

[27] "OpenFL - Creative expression for desktop, mobile, web and console platforms," [Online]. Available: https://www.openfl.org/.W364W7352

[28] L. Li, Y. Fan, M. Tse and K. Y. Lin, "A review of applications in federated learning," Computers & Industrial Engineering, vol. 149, p. 106854, November 2020. W364W7352

[29] I. Siniosoglou, P. Sarigiannidis, Y. Spyridis, A. Khadka, G. Efstathopoulos and T. Lagkas, "Synthetic Traffic Signs Dataset for Traffic Sign Detection & Recognition in Distributed Smart Systems," Proceedings - 17th Annual International Conference on Distributed Computing in Sensor Systems, DCOS 2021, pp. 302-308, 2021. W364W7352

6

Analysis of Privacy Preservation Enhancements in Federated Learning Frameworks

Z. Anastasakis[1], S. Bourou[1], T. H. Velivasaki[1], A. Voulkidis[1], and D. Skias[2]

[1]Synelixis Solutions S.A., Greece
[2]Netcompany-Intrasoft S.A., Greece
E-mail: anastasakis@synelixis.com; bourou@synelixis.com;
terpsi@synelixis.com; voulkidis@synelixis.com;
Dimitrios.Skias@netcompany-intrasoft.com

Abstract

Machine learning (ML) plays a growing role in the Internet of Things (IoT) applications and has efficiently contributed to many aspects, both for businesses and consumers, including proactive intervention, tailored experiences, and intelligent automation. Traditional cloud computing machine learning applications need the data, generated by IoT devices, to be uploaded and processed on a central server giving data access to third parties raising privacy and data ownership concerns. Federated learning (FL) is able to overcome these privacy concerns by enabling an on-device collaborative training of a machine learning model without sharing any data over the network. However, model sharing can also potentially reveal sensitive information. Therefore, federated learning needs additional privacy-preserving techniques to enable fully private machine learning model sharing and training. In this chapter, privacy-preserving techniques for federated learning are studied. In addition, a comparative analysis of state-of-the-art federated learning frameworks against privacy-preserving techniques is presented. The analysis comprises the identification of main advantages and disadvantages for eight

FL frameworks as well as the investigation of the frameworks under criteria related to their FL features and privacy preservation options.

Keywords: Federated learning, privacy preserving, Internet of Things, artificial intelligence, machine learning.

6.1 Introduction

Artificial intelligence (AI) produces insights by automatically identifying patterns and detecting anomalies on data collected or generated using IoT sensors and other devices. Machine learning (ML) is almost everywhere nowadays, from small wearable devices and smartphones to powerful super-computers ensuring fast and accurate data analysis. Moreover, IoT devices generate a great amount of data every day and, thus, raise significant concerns about privacy and ownership of the collected or generated data.

Traditional machine learning applications require their training and testing data to be located in a central cloud server. This raises privacy and data ownership concerns. Furthermore, IoT devices are already capable of processing a vast amount of data due to their powerful hardware specifications, making it possible for local data processing and analysis. Thus, edge computing is witnessing great interest especially after the emergence of 5G.

Nevertheless, data privacy is the most fundamental objective regarding data access and processing. This has led to the elaboration of strict data privacy legislations such as the Consumer Privacy Bill of Rights in the U.S. and the European Commission's General Data Protection Regulation (GDPR). For example, Articles 5 and 6 of the GDPR state that data collection and storage should be restricted to only what is user-consented and decidedly indispensable for processing.

To address privacy issues, Google [1] introduced federated learning (FL), a specific approach in edge computing. Federated learning is able to overcome the privacy concerns that emerge in a central cloud-based architecture by enabling an on-device collaborative training of a machine learning model without sharing any data over the network. This is achieved by initializing the training of a global machine learning model on a central server for a few iterations to obtain some initial weights. These model weights are then sent to the participants (data owners), which use their own resources to locally train the machine learning model. After training, each client sends its own updated weights to the server, which is responsible to aggregate the weights from all the different clients and produce a new global model. This process is repeated for several iterations until the global model reaches a certain desired accuracy level or reaches the limit set for the number of iterations. Federated learning aims to train an ML model privately by sharing model parameters (weights of the model) than sharing the data itself. This feature enables machine learning models to run on local and private data. However, model sharing can also potentially reveal sensitive information. Therefore, FL needs additional privacy-preserving techniques to enable fully private machine learning model sharing and training. Differential privacy (DP) and secure multiparty computation and homomorphic encryption (HE) constitute the most popular privacy-preserving techniques for FL systems.

6.2 Privacy-preserving Federated Learning

6.2.1 Federated learning frameworks

Several open-source federated learning frameworks have been developed to apply distributed learning on decentralized data but also to enhance privacy and security. Google proposed TensorFlow Federated [2], an open-source framework for federated learning and other computations on decentralized data. Another open-source federated learning framework is PySyft, which was introduced by OpenMined [3]. PySyft is suitable for research in FL and allows the users to perform private and secure deep learning. PySyft is also integrated into PyGrid [4], a peer-to-peer platform for federated learning and data privacy, which can be used for private statistical analysis on the private dataset as well as for performing FL across multiple organization's datasets. WeBank's AI department introduced FATE (federated AI technology enabler) [5], an open-source framework that supports FL architectures and secure computation of various machine learning algorithms. FATE is an industrial-grade framework mostly oriented toward enterprise solutions. The authors in [6] presented Flower, a friendly open-source federated learning framework that is ML framework agnostic and provides higher-level abstractions to enable researchers to experiment and implement on top of a reliable stack. Another promising open-source federated learning framework is Sherpa.ai, which is presented in [7] and incorporates federated learning with differential privacy. Sherpa.ai results as a combination of machine learning applications in a federated manner with differential privacy guidelines. FedML [8] is an open-source federated learning framework and benchmarking tool for federated machine learning. FedML supports three computing paradigms: on-device training for edge devices, distributed computing, and single-machine simulation. FedML promotes diverse algorithmic research due to the generic API design and the comprehensive reference baseline implementations. Another well-known open-source federated learning framework is the PaddleFL [9]. In PaddleFL, researchers can easily replicate and compare different federated learning algorithms while they can easily be deployed in large-scale scenarios. Leaf [10] is a modular benchmarking framework for federated learning with applications including federated learning, multi-task learning, meta-learning, and on-device learning. OpenFL [11] is another open-source federated learning framework for training ML algorithms using the data-private collaborative learning paradigm of FL. OpenFL works with machine learning pipelines built on top of TensorFlow and PyTorch and is easily customizable to support other machine learning and deep learning frameworks. NVIDIA FLARE [12] is a domain-agnostic, open-source, and extensible SDK for federated learning, which allows porting existing ML/DL workflow to federated settings and supports common privacy preservation techniques. In the following sub-sections, a more extended analysis is given for each framework. In Section 6.3.2, a thorough comparative analysis on these federated learning frameworks is presented toward the scope of IoT-NGIN.

6.2.2 Privacy preservation in federated learning

While FL is resilient and resolves, up to a point, data governance and ownership issues, it does not guarantee security and privacy by design. A lack of encryption can allow adversaries to abduct personally identifiable data directly from the processing nodes or interfere with the communication process, expose network vulnerabilities, and perform attacks. In addition, the decentralized nature of the data complicates data handling and curation. Moreover, in the case where algorithms running on the nodes are not encrypted, or the updates are not securely aggregated, the possibility of data leakage grows. Additionally, the algorithms can be tampered with, reconstructed, or get stolen (parameter inference), which can be strictly forbidden for most applications. Federated learning can be vulnerable to various backdoor threats (bug injection, inference, and model attacks) on different processing steps. Therefore, additional measures are essential to protect data from adversarial attack strategies such as data poisoning and model poisoning attacks. In Table 6.1, three major attacks against the dataset with their description and a basic example for each case are listed, while in Table 6.2, algorithmic-based attacks are presented.

Table 6.1   Various attacks against the data in a federated learning system.

Attacks against the dataset	*Description*	*Example*
Re-identification attack	Recover an individual's identity by exploiting similarities to other datasets and exposing the data characteristics.	Exploiting similarities between data distributions and actual values from other datasets in which the same individual is contained.
Dataset reconstruction attack	Determine an individual's characteristics from the training process without accessing the data itself.	Using multiple statistical information (probabilities, distributions, etc.) to get data points that correspond to a single individual.

Table 6.2   Major attacks against algorithms that run in a federated learning system.

Attacks against algorithm	*Description*	*Example*
Adversarial attack	Manipulation of the input to an algorithm with the goal of altering it, most often in a way that makes the manipulation of the input data impossible to detect by humans.	Compromising the computation result by introducing malicious training examples (model poisoning).
Model-inversion/reconstruction attack	Derivation of information about the dataset stored within the algorithm's weights by observing the algorithm's behavior.	Using generative algorithms to recreate parts of the training data based on algorithm parameters.

In general, the goal of an adversary during data poisoning is to alter the data according to their preferences. This can be done by ingesting a mixture of clean and false data into the training flow. For example, in [13], the result of an image classification learning task can be vulnerable to a data poisoning attempt by a mislabeling or a false-labeling operation. Wang refers to different defense mechanisms from simple data management to more sophisticated and robust approaches. Data sanitization is a rather basic defense, while pruning (removing neurons in a network) seems more reliable. Nonetheless, the pruning technique raises concerns regarding privacy-preserving in federated learning. In [14], [15], and [16], some legitimate defenses for these attacks are proposed, although backdoor attacks become stronger and more adjective.

Model poisoning attack refers to partial or full model replacement during training. The authors in [17] and [18] describe possible attacks and argue about various defenses (SMC, DP, etc.). Generative adversarial networks (GANs) [19] can be one of the most vicious threats in federated learning. The authors in [20] exploit defenses against GAN-based attacks and present the anti-GAN framework to prevent adversaries from learning the real distribution of the training data. On the other hand, GANs in [21] are utilized as a defense mechanism against adversarial attacks in federated learning systems. As a conclusion, FL is vulnerable to various attacks and great attention must be given to the defense mechanisms and tools; otherwise, it will not be possible for an FL system to fulfill its privacy-preserving objectives.

6.2.3 State-of-the-art approaches in privacy-preserving federated learning

Although FL enables on-device machine learning, it does not guarantee security and privacy. The fact that the private data are not shared with the central server is for sure an advantage; yet, there are ways to extract private information from the data. After the shared model is trained on the user's device based on its own private data, the trained parameters (model weights) are sent to the central server, and through an aggregation mechanism, the global model is composed. During the model transfer, it is possible for an adversary to extract information about the private data from those trained parameters. For example, in [22], the authors indicate that it is possible to extract sensitive text patterns, e.g., the credit card number, from a recurrent neural network that is trained on users' data. Therefore, additional mechanisms are required to protect data disclosure from attack strategies, which are subject to privacy-preserving methods in FL. The major approaches that can be employed in FL for data protection are differential privacy, homomorphic encryption, and secure multiparty computation.

Differential privacy (DP) is a method that randomizes part of the mechanism's behavior to provide privacy [23], [24]. The motivation behind adding randomness (either Laplacian or Gaussian) into a learning algorithm is to make it impossible to reveal data patterns or insights that correspond either to the model and the learned parameters or to the training data. Therefore, the DP provides privacy against a wide range of attacks (e.g., differencing attacks, linkage attacks, etc.) [25]. The method of introducing noise to the data can result in great privacy but may compromise accuracy. Therefore, there is a tradeoff between applying differential privacy and achieving a high level of model accuracy. However, the authors in [25] present a method, which applies privacy-preserving without sacrificing accuracy.

Another privacy-preserving technique is the secure multiparty computation (SMC), a well-defined cryptographic-based technique that allows a number of mutually suspicious parties to jointly compute a function before training a model while preserving the privacy of the input data [26], [27]. In the case of ML applications, the function can be the model's loss function at training, or it could be the model itself during inference. The challenge of applying SMC on a large-scale distributed system is the communication overhead, which increases significantly with the number of participating parties.

Homomorphic encryption [28] secures the learning process by applying computations (e.g., addition) on encrypted data. Specifically, an encryption scheme is characterized as homomorphic, when standard operations can be applied directly to the cypher data, in such a way that the decrypted result is equivalent to performing analogous operations to the original encrypted data [29], [30]. For machine learning methods, homomorphic encryption can be applied when training or inference is performed directly on encrypted data (cyphertexts). In scenarios, where large mathematical functions are implemented to cyphertext space, a major bottleneck of homomorphic encryption emerges. The properties of homomorphic encryption schemes confront several limitations, related to encryption performance.

Alternative hybrid approaches that combine SMC with DP and account dishonest participants exist. In [31], authors confront the inference risk of SMC and the low accuracy that DP presents due to the noise injection by combining them. Furthermore, they propose a tunable trust parameter attribute by additively HE, which considers many trust scenarios. HybridAlpha method [32] establishes a multi-input functional encryption (public-key cryptosystem) scheme to prevent inference attacks on SMC. HybridAlpha introduces a trusted third party to derive public keys to parties who intend to encrypt their data before training. Wang [33] presented HDP: a differential private framework for vertical federated learning (cross-silo). HDP-VFL does not rely on HE or on third-party collaborators to assure data privacy; therefore, it is easy to implement and is rather fast. Chain-PPFL [34] can achieve privacy-preserving without compromising the model accuracy using SMC and DP in a "trust-but-curious" way. The proposed communication mechanism constructs a serial chain frame that transfers masked information between participants. In addition, chain-PPFL does not require encryption or obfuscation before transmitting information because it uses the P2P encrypted secure transmitted channel, thus requiring less resources. The authors in [35] present a fully decentralized federated learning process (BlockFlow) as a more resilient approach against adversarial and inference attacks. BlockFlow adopts blockchains as computational platforms and, contrarily to other methods, does not require a central trusted part. Unlike other methods, there is no need for a centralized test dataset and different parties share DP models with each other.

6.2.4 Comparison of federated learning frameworks considering privacy preservation

Considering the extensive analysis presented above, for the FL methods/tools and the privacy-preserving approaches, comparative analysis for federated learning frameworks is conducted and presented in this section. The comparison refers to the FL frameworks analyzed in Section 6.2.1 and for which the main benefits and drawbacks are briefly presented in Table 6.3.

The comparison among the FL frameworks listed in Table 6.3 is based on the following criteria:

- **Criterion 1:** This criterion is based on basic federated learning features. The operating system support, the federated learning categorization, e.g., if it supports cross-silo or cross-device setups, which machine learning and deep learning libraries (TensorFlow, PyTorch, etc.) do the framework supports and if there is a Federated attack simulator.
- **Criterion 2:** This includes three computing paradigms; the standalone simulation that gives the possibility for a user to apply FL scenarios in simulation; the distributed computing capability that shows if an FL framework is capable of performing in a distributed environment where participants are different devices; the capability of on-device training for IoT and other mobile devices that normally have limited hardware resources.
- **Criterion 3:** If FL frameworks include common FL algorithms and configurations like federated average [36], decentralized FL, vertical FL, and split learning [37].
- **Criterion 4:** An essential characteristic for an FL framework is the existence of privacy-preserving mechanisms and also what types of privacy-preserving methods are supported by the frameworks. In cases where privacy-preserving techniques are not presented, the FL framework must give the capability to integrate such mechanisms.

Table 6.3 Main pros and cons of the federated learning frameworks.

FL framework	Main pros	Main cons
NVIDIA FLARE	1. It supports training in real-life scenarios 2. It supports a high number of clients 3. It is customizable, supporting the integration of ML models implemented via state-of-the-art ML frameworks, such as TensorFlow and PyTorch 4. It supports privacy reserving methods, such as percentile privacy, homomorphic encryption, and MPC, which can also be combined 5. It comes with good documentation and large community	1. It does not support on-device training 2. Its performance drops as the number of parties increases 3. It does not support heterogeneous clients
FATE	1. Production ready 2. High-level interface 3. Provides many FL algorithms 4. Containerized – Kubernetes support	1. It does not establish any differential privacy algorithms 2. Its high-level interface relies too much on a poorly documented domain-specific language 3. It does not have a core API; so developers must modify the source code of FATE to implement custom FL algorithms 4. It does not use GPUs for training
Flower	1. Provides a template API that allows users to easily transform ML pipelines to FL 2. Very easy to develop and ML framework-agnostic 3. Supports a great number of clients 4. It is really customizable	1. It does not have any differential privacy algorithms 2. It is relatively new and the support community is not that big 3. It does not provide secure aggregation
PySyft & PyGrid	1. Rather easy to use 2. It has the largest community of contributors among the FL frameworks	1. PySyft is only for one server and one client (duet) and can run only in simulation mode 2. PyGrid is needed in order to develop real FL scenarios
TFF	1. It integrates seamlessly with existing TensorFlow ML models	1. As of the time of writing, it can be used only in the simulation mode because it does not support

Table 6.3 (Continued.)

FL framework	Main pros	Main cons
	2. It is easy to use due to its familiarity	the federated operation mode 2. The data used for training cannot be loaded from the remote worker itself but must be partitioned and transferred through the central server
Sherpa.ai	1. Relatively easy to use because of the Jupiter notebooks, etc. 2. Implements FL algorithms and it is easy to customize them	1. Poor documentation 2. Small community with only seven contributors 3. The project's repository is not active (4+ months after the latest update) 4. Can run only in the simulation mode 5. Limited applicable scenarios
FedML	1. On-device training for edge devices including smartphones and Internet of Things (IoT) 2. Distributed computing 3. Growing community 4. Multi-GPU training support	1. No privacy-preserving techniques are applied. Only a secure aggregation technique is implemented 2. The multiple available modules for different situations might lead to drawbacks and create overheads
PaddleFL	1. It provides a high-level interface for some basic and well-known FL aggregators and implements a differentially private algorithm 2. It provides enough privacy-preserving methods such as DP, MPC, and secure aggregation	1. It is fairly difficult to use it because it uses a little-known DL platform 2. It has poor documentation and has a small community — only 12 contributors 3. It is not compatible with other frameworks and that is a major drawback
Leaf	1. It provides some basic federated learning mechanisms such as the federated averaging aggregator 2. It is modular and adaptive 3. It enables reproducible science	1. It does not provide any benchmark for preserving privacy in an FL setting 2. It does not offer as much official documentation or tutorials 3. Limited federated learning capabilities; it is mainly for production purposes

- **Criterion 5:** In order for an FL framework to be flexible and adaptive, documentation, tutorials, and community support are significant.

Table 6.4 Federated learning framework comparison ($\frac{1}{2}$).

FL framework	NVIDIA FLARE	FATE	Flower	PySyft + PyGrid	TFF
Standalone simulation	Yes	Yes	Yes	Yes	Yes
Distributed computing	Yes	Yes	Yes	Yes	Yes
On-device training (mobile, IoT)	No	No	Yes — depends on the network	Yes	No
FedAvg	Yes	Yes	Yes	Yes	Yes
Decentralized FL	Yes	No	Yes	No	No
FedNAS	No	No	Yes	No	No
Vertical federated learning		Yes	Yes	No	No
Split learning	Yes	No	Yes	Yes	No
Privacy-preserving methods	Yes (HE, percentile privacy, exclude Vars, DP)	No	(Yes) (PATE — implemented in IoT-NGIN, known as FedPATE [39])	Yes (SMC, HE)	Yes (DP)
DP noise type	No	No	Yes	No	No
Adaptive differential privacy	No	No	No	No	No
Subsampling methods to increase privacy	No	No	No	No	No
Documentation and community support	Large	Partial — mostly in Chinese	Yes Growing rapidly	Yes	Yes
Secure aggregation	Yes	Yes	Future implementation		No

- **Criterion 6:** Secure aggregation [38] algorithm implementation to further enhance privacy.

Table 6.5   Federated learning framework comparison (2/2).

FL framework	Sherpa.ai	FedML	PaddleFL	OpenFL
Standalone simulation	Yes	Yes	Yes	Yes
Distributed computing	No	Yes	Yes	Yes
On-device training (mobile, IoT)	No	Yes	No	No
FedAvg	Yes	Yes	Yes	Yes
Decentralized FL	No	Yes	Yes	Yes
FedNAS	No	Yes	No	No
Vertical federated learning	No	Yes	Yes	Yes
Split learning	No	Yes	Yes	Yes
Privacy-preserving methods	Yes (DP)	No	Yes (SMC, DP)	Yes (SMC, DP)
DP noise type	Yes	No	Yes	Yes
Adaptive differential privacy	Yes	No	Yes	Yes
Subsampling methods to increase privacy	Yes	No	Yes	Yes
Documentation and community support	Yes	Stable	Partial	Partial but growing
Secure aggregation	No	Future implementation	Yes	Yes

- **Criterion 7:** Nowadays, training on GPUs especially for deep learning tasks is essential. Especially for limited hardware resources on devices, GPUs have shown remarkable computation capabilities compared to CPUs.
- **Criterion 8:** All the FL frameworks in comparison are open-sourced but with different licenses and therefore of different usage limitations.
- **Criterion 9:** More general properties and characteristics of the FL frameworks. To be more specific, an FL framework must be easy to use, adaptive, preserve interoperability, flexibility, and privacy.

The characteristics of each FL framework against the nine identified criteria are tabulated in Tables 6.4 and 6.5.

Based on the tables above, privacy-preserving methods are available for NVIDIA FLARE, Flower, PySyft & PyGrid, TensorFlow Federated, Sherpa.ai, PaddleFL, and OpenFL; however, the exact privacy-preserving methods supported differ across the FL frameworks. On the other hand, Flower, PySyft & PyGrid, and FedML support on-device training.

6.3 Conclusion

This chapter has provided a critical review of federated learning theory, tools, and algorithms in relation to providing string privacy protection guarantees for individual nodes' data and models. We have explained why federated learning is necessary for privacy-preserving machine learning with many clients on decentralized data. We have proceeded with providing an extensive comparative analysis over open-source FL tools, mainly under the prism of privacy preservation, providing guidance for experimentation, according to underlying application requirements. Considering the outcomes of this analysis, three FL frameworks (NVIDIA FLARE, and Flower with PATE and TFF) have been selected for applying privacy-preserving federated learning in pilot use cases. Specifically, the project considers NVIDIA FLARE in "Traffic Flow & Parking Prediction" and "Crowd Management" use cases in the Smart City Living Lab, as well as in "Crop diseases prediction & irrigation precision" in the Smart Agriculture Living Lab. Moreover, Flower (integrated with PATE) has been considered in training ML models for classification tasks, relevant to the scope of the "Crop diseases prediction & irrigation precision" use case, as well. In addition, research on training ML models in large-scale settings for tabular data classification in the scope of network attack detection has been considered for the Smart Energy Living Lab. Future work aims at enhancing privacy in state-of-the-art open source FL frameworks, suitable for researching FL under real settings in the context of ensuring data privacy across the integrated IoT, edge, and cloud continuum.

Acknowledgement

The work presented in this document was funded through H2020 IoT-NGIN project. This project has received funding from the European Union's Horizon 2020 research and innovation program under Grant Agreement No. 957246.

References

[1] Google Research, "Federated Learning: Collaborative Machine Learning without Centralized Training Data," Google, 2017. [Online]. Available: https://ai.googleblog.com/2017/04/federated-learning-collaborative.html.W428W7321

[2] K. Bonawitz, H. Eichner, W. Grieskamp, D. Huba, A. Ingerman, V. Ivanov, C. Kiddon, J. Konečný, S. Mazzocchi, H. B. McMahan, T. Van Overveldt, D. Petrou, D. Ramage and J. Roselander, "Towards Federated Learning at Scale: System Design," in Proceedings of Machine Learning and Systems, Palo Alto, CA, USA, 2019. W428W7321

[3] T. Ryffel, A. Trask, M. Dahl, B. Wagner, J. Mancuso, D. Rueckert and J. Passerat-Palmbach, "A Generic Framework for Privacy Preserving Deep Learning," in NeurIPS 2018 Workshop on Privacy-Preserving Machine Learning, Montréal, 2018. W428W7321

[4] J. Konecný, H. B. McMahan, D. Ramage and P. Richtárik, "Federated Optimization: Distributed Machine Learning for On-Device Intelligence.," ArXiv, 2016. W428W7321

[5] Y. Liu, T. Fan, T. Chen, Q. Xu and Q. Yang, "FATE: An Industrial Grade Platform for Collaborative Learning With Data Protection," Journal of Machine Learning Research, 2021. W428W7321

[6] D. J. Beutel, T. Topal, A. Mathur, X. Qiu, J. Fernandez-Marques, Y. Gao, L. Sani, K. Hei Li, T. Parcollet, P. Porto Buarque de Gusmão and N. D. Lane, "Flower: A Friendly Federated Learning Research Framework," arXiv, 2020. W428W7321

[7] N. Rodríguez-Barroso, G. Stipcich, D. Jiménez-López, J. A. Ruiz-Millán, E. Martínez-Cámara, G. González-Seco, M. V. Luzón, M. A. Veganzones and F. Herrera, "Federated Learning and Differential Privacy: Software tools analysis, the Sherpa.ai FL framework and methodological guidelines for preserving data privacy," Information Fusion, vol. 64, pp. 270-292, 2020. W428W7321

[8] C. He, S. Li, J. So, X. Zeng, M. Zhang, H. Wang, X. Wang, P. Vepakomma, A. Singh, H. Qiu, X. Zhu, J. Wang, L. Shen, P. Zhao, Y. Kang, Y. Liu, R. Raskar, Q. Yang and Annavaram, "FedML: A Research Library and Benchmark for Federated Machine Learning," CoRR, 2020. W428W7321

[9] D. Dong, W. Zhang and Q. Jing, "PaddleFL," GitHub, [Online]. Available: https://github.com/PaddlePaddle.[Accessed2022].W428W7321

[10] S. Caldas, S. M. Karthik Duddu, P. Wu, T. Li, J. Konečný, H. B. McMahan, V. Smith and A. Talwalkar, "LEAF: A Benchmark for Federated Settings," Workshop on Federated Learning for Data Privacy and Confidentiality, 2019. W428W7321

[11] P. Foley, M. J. Sheller, B. Edwards, S. Pati, W. Riviera, M. Sharma, P. N. Moorthy, S.-h. Wang , J. Martin, P. Mirhaji, P. Shah and S. Bakas, "OpenFL: the open federated learning library," Physics in Medicine & Biology, 2022. W428W7321

[12] H. R. Roth, Y. Cheng, Y. Wen, I. Yang, Z. Xu, Y.-T. Hsieh, K. Kersten, A. Harouni, C. Zhao, K. Lu, Z. Zhang, W. Li, A. Myronenko, D. Yang, S. Yang, N. Rieke, A. Quraini and C. Chen, "NVIDIA FLARE: Federated Learning from Simulation to Real-World," in nternational Workshop on Federated Learning (NeurIPS 2022), New Orleans, USA, 2022. W428W7321

[13] H. Wang, K. Sreenivasan , S. Rajput, H. Vishwakarma, S. Agarwal, J.-y. Sohn, K. Leew and D. Papailiopoulos, "Attack of the Tails: Yes, You Really Can Backdoor Federated Learning," in 34th Conference on Neural Information Processing Systems (NeurIPS 2020), Vancouver, Canada, 2020. W428W7321

[14] K. Liu, B. Dolan-Gavitt and S. Garg, "Fine-Pruning: Defending Against Backdooring Attacks on Deep Neural Networks," in International Symposium on Research in Attacks, Intrusions, and Defenses, 2018. W428W7321

[15] J. Steinhardt, P. Wei Koh and P. Liang, "Certified Defenses for Data Poisoning Attacks," in 31st Conference on Neural Information Processing Systems (NIPS 2017), Long Beach, CA, USA, 2018. W428W7321

[16] S. Wang, X. Wang, S. Ye, P. Zhao and X. Lin, "Defending DNN Adversarial Attacks with Pruning and Logits Augmentation," in 2018 IEEE Global Conference on Signal and Information Processing (GlobalSIP), 2018. W428W7321

[17] Z. Sun, P. Kairouz, A. Theertha Suresh and . H. B. McMahan, "Can You Really Backdoor Federated Learning?," in 2nd International Workshop on Federated Learning for Data Privacy and Confidentiality at NeurIPS 2019, 2019. W428W7321

[18] E. Bagdasaryan, A. Veit, Y. Hua, D. Estrin and V. Shmatikov, "How To Backdoor Federated Learning," in Proceedings of the 23rdInternational Conference on Artificial Intelligence and Statistics (AISTATS) 2020, Palermo, Italy, 2020. W428W7321

[19] I. Goodfellow, J. Pouget-Abadie , M. Mirza , B. Xu , D. Warde-Farley , S. Ozair , A. Courville and Y. Bengio, "Generative Adversarial Networks," Commun. ACM, vol. 63, no. 11, p. 139–144, 2020. W428W7321

[20] X. Zhang and X. Luo, "Exploiting Defenses against GAN-Based Feature Inference Attacks in Federated Learning," arXiv, 2020. W428W7321

[21] S. Taheri, A. Khormali, M. Salem and J.-S. Yuan, "Developing a Robust Defensive System against Adversarial Examples Using Generative Adversarial Networks.," Big Data Cogn. Comput., vol. 4, no. 11, 2020. W428W7321

[22] N. Carlini, C. Liu, Ú. Erlingsson, J. Kos and D. Song, "The Secret Sharer: Evaluating and Testing Unintended Memorization in Neural Networks," in USENIX Security 2019, 2019. W428W7321

[23] M. Abadi , A. Chu, I. Goodfellow, H. B. McMahan, I. Mironov, K. Talwar and L. Zhang, "Deep Learning with Differential Privacy," in Proceedings of the 2016 ACM SIGSAC Conference on Computer and Communications Security (CCS '16), Vienna, Austria, 2016. W428W7321

[24] F. McSherry and K. Talwar, "Mechanism Design via Differential Privacy," in 48th Annual IEEE Symposium on Foundations of Computer Science (FOCS'07), 2007. W428W7321

[25] C. Dwork and A. Roth, The Algorithmic Foundations of Differential Privacy, vol. 9, Now Publishers Inc., 2014. W428W7321

[26] Q. Yang, Y. Liu, T. Chen and Y. Tong, "Federated Machine Learning: Concept and Applications," ACM Trans. Intell. Syst. Technol., vol. 10, no. 2, pp. 2157-6904, 2019. W428W7321

[27] C. Zhao, S. Zhao, M. Zhao, Z. Chen, C.-Z. Gao, H. Li and Y.-a. Tan, "Secure Multi-Party Computation: Theory, practice and applications," Information Sciences, vol. 479, pp. 357-372, 2019. W428W7321

[28] C. Lefebvre, "On data," Journal of Pidgin and Creole Languages, vol. 115, no. 2, 2000. W428W7321

[29] L. T. Phong, Y. Aono, T. Hayashi, L. Wang and S. Moriai, "Privacy-Preserving Deep Learning via Additively Homomorphic Encryption," IEEE Transactions on Information Forensics and Security, vol. 13, no. 5, pp. 1333-1345, 2018. W428W7321

[30] C. Gentry, "A Fully Homomorphic Encryption Scheme," Dissertation, 2009.W428W7321

[31] S. Truex, N. Baracaldo, A. Anwar, T. Steinke, H. Ludwig, R. Zhang and Y. Zhou, "A Hybrid Approach to Privacy-Preserving Federated

Learning," in Proceedings of the 12th ACM Workshop on Artificial Intelligence and Security (AISec'19), London, United Kingdom, 2019. W428W7321

[32] R. Xu, N. Baracaldo, Y. Zhou, A. Anwar and H. Ludwig, "HybridAlpha: An Efficient Approach for Privacy-Preserving Federated Learning," in Proceedings of the 12th ACM Workshop on Artificial Intelligence and Security (AISec'19), London, United Kingdom, 2019. W428W7321

[33] C. Wang, J. Liang, M. Huang, B. Bai, K. Bai and H. Li, "Hybrid Differentially Private Federated Learning on Vertically Partitioned Data," ArXiv, 2020. W428W7321

[34] Y. Li, Y. Zhou, A. Jolfaei, D. Yu, G. Xu and X. Zheng, "Privacy-Preserving Federated Learning Framework Based on Chained Secure Multiparty Computing," IEEE Internet of Things Journal, vol. 8, no. 8, pp. 6178-6186, 2021. W428W7321

[35] V. Mugunthan, R. Rahman and L. Kagal, "BlockFLow: An Accountable and Privacy-Preserving Solution for Federated Learning," ArXiv, 2020. W428W7321

[36] I. Mironov, "Rényi Differential Privacy," in 2017 IEEE 30th Computer Security Foundations Symposium (CSF), 2017. W428W7321

[37] N. Papernot and I. Goodfellow, "Privacy and machine learning: two unexpected allies?," cleverhans-blog , 2018. [Online]. Available: http://www.cleverhans.io/privacy/2018/04/29/privacy-and-machine-learning.html.W428W7321

[38] C. He, M. Annavaram and S. Avestimehr, "FedNAS: Federated Deep Learning via Neural Architecture," in CVPR 2020 Workshop on Neural Architecture Search and Beyond for Representation Learning, 2020. W428W7321

[39] IoT-NGIN, "D3.3 - Enhanced IoT federated deep learning/ reinforcement ML," H2020 - 957246 - IoT-NGIN Deliverable Report, 2022.W428W7321

7

Intelligent Management at the Edge

**Mohammadreza Mosahebfard[1], Claudia Torres-Pérez[1],
Estela Carmona-Cejudo[1], Andrés Cárdenas Córdova[1],
Adrián Pino Martínez[1], Juan Sebastian Camargo Barragan[1],
Estefanía Coronado[1,2], and Muhammad Shuaib Siddiqui[1]**

[1]i2CAT Foundation, Spain
[2]Universidad de Castilla-La Mancha, Spain
E-mail: reza.mosahebfard; claudia.torres; estela.carmona; andres.cardenas;
adrian.pino; juan.camargo; estefania.coronado; shuaib.siddiqui@i2cat.net;
estefania.coronado@uclm.es

Abstract

AI/ML techniques play a key role in 5G/6G networks providing connectivity
to IoT devices. In such scenarios, not only is it necessary to run time-sensitive
applications with strict latency requirements without human intervention, but
it is also key to apply automation techniques at both the application and the
network levels. The chapter is composed of three sections. In the first section,
we present different cloud native (CN) technologies enabling scalable, cost-
efficient, and reliable IoT solutions. The second section details different
distributed and hierarchical monitoring frameworks and metrics collection
schemes as inputs to AI engines. In the last section, application placement
problems focused on delay minimization in geographically distributed single-
cluster environments are first discussed. Afterwards, application placement
issues ensuring latency requirements for the applications and energy consumption in distributed multi-access edge computing (MEC) systems using
AI pipelines are presented.

Keywords: AI/ML, edge computing, edge intelligence, edge optimization,
edge automation, 5G/6G networks, IoT, monitoring frameworks, distributed
MEC, application placement.

135   DOI: 10.1201/9781032632407-9

7.1 Introduction to Intelligence at 5G/6G Networks Edge

Edge computing refers to bringing computing resources and capabilities closer to the devices that generate or consume data. This can help to reduce latency, improve performance, and increase security. It also facilitates both edge automation and intelligence. On the other hand, according to 5GPPP, high-performance next generation networks will be operated via a scalable management framework enabling service provisioning time from 90 hours to 90 minutes, by reducing the network management OPEX by at least 20% compared to current networks [1]. A promising solution to achieve 5G networks with a level of intelligence similar to that of humans as well as lower levels of latency is the combination of artificial intelligence (AI) and edge computing. AI at the edge refers to the use of AI algorithms and models at the edge of a network, closer to the end-user generating or consuming the data, which results in performance improvement and latency reduction.

7.1.1 Edge automation

7.1.1.1 State of the art

Two of the main international organizations and standardization bodies, namely 3GPP and ETSI, have defined requirements, features, and key technologies in the context of the 5G edge. The 5G 3GPP system architecture [2] is intended to support edge computing by enabling services such as the Internet of Things (IoT), industrial solutions, smart energy, connected health, autonomous driving and more. Another contribution from 3GPP involves studying the management aspects of edge computing, where several edge scenarios and use cases are explored and potential deployment solutions are discussed [3]. Following this line of work, enhancements regarding edge computing management and connectivity models have been proposed [4], which include a number of concepts such as self-organizing networks (SON) and network data analytics function (NWDAF). SON is an automation technology designed to streamline and simplify planning, configuration, management, optimization, and healing. SON architectures are conceived in three variants, centralized SON, distributed SON, and hybrid SON. Each variant is a key technology with the main aim of integrating legacy mobile radio access networks (RAN) [5]. Recent advancements in AI/ML techniques have led to an increased interest in SON with cognitive features combined with the software/hardware decoupling movement – via network function virtualization (NFV), and/or multi-access edge computing (MEC) – leading to greater network agility. NWDAF was introduced to provide a standard method to collect data supporting 5G core network functions and operation administrations and management systems [6].

ETSI has also published several reference architectures and specifications of the aforementioned NFV and MEC initiatives. By using zero-touch network and service management (ZSM), end-to-end network management can be achieved with minimal or no human intervention. ZSM facilitates collaborative management interactions between all layers of the network through the use of closed-loop automation, AI, adaptive ML, and cognitive technologies [7], abstracting the 5G network edge resource management. On the radio side, open RAN refers to the disaggregation movement of hardware and software in wireless telecommunications as well as to create open interfaces between them [8].

7.1.1.2 Key enablers

To meet edge automation expectations several vital technologies are required, including distributed data collection, real-time processing, and edge automation for 5G slicing. Both distributed data collection and real-time processing require streaming, in-memory storage management, and computing close to the edge in order to minimize latency and maximize bandwidth. In addition, stakeholders need to plan, design, and activate several customized network slices rapidly to provide customers with different 5G services. Slice elasticity, the ability to scale up or down in response to performance changes, also has become a must. To this end, by forecasting the upcoming traffic with AI/ML techniques, network slices can be optimized by minimizing resource usage while meeting quality of service (QoS) or customer requirements. A critical component of successful 5G service delivery is network slicing. A network slice is considered as a collection of networking and computational resources forming a dedicated network that provides an end-to-end connectivity to hosted applications and services [9]. Stakeholders are able to plan, design, and activate several customized network slices on demand. Moreover, slice elasticity, which is defined as the ability to scale up or down in response to variations in performance, is critical. In this regard, AI/ML techniques play an important role, since forecasting the upcoming traffic allows the slice to be adjusted (using a proactive rather than reactive model) to minimize resource consumption, meet QoS requirements, and perform lifecycle management tasks on existing slices.

7.1.2 Edge intelligence

5G/6G networks and AI/ML are closely related with edge devices of limited computing power are able to leverage 5G/6G network edge intelligence by distributing the computation, which is driven by the use of AI/ML techniques and distributed intelligence. A joint perception environment could be formed of real-time metrics collected from devices in the network. A perception environment of this type groups decisions in order to enhance the efficiency, productivity, and safety of several 5G edge applications. Such shared intelligence will be enhanced by the use of a hybrid and distributed architecture. By combining 5G edge networks with MEC architectures, distributed learning [10], and collaborative intelligence [11], real-time distributed intelligence and collaboration are becoming tangible. Intent-based networking [12], which has recently been applied to the RAN, is another promising idea that is undergoing development and adaptation for B5G networks.

7.1.2.1 State of the art

A flexible and hybrid architecture, both centralized and distributed, is critical for edge intelligence architectures. In terms of communication, a number of developments have been made, including direct device-to-device and multi-hop communication, which are mentioned in 3GPP standards [13]. They have been combined with 5G scenarios via the cellular vehicle-to-everything (V2X) paradigm to meet KPIs in verticals such as autonomous driving. In terms of radio management, intent-based RAN management is becoming increasingly important. It consists of altering the configuration of the RAN from the setting of technical parameters to the specification of connectivity services, allowing service providers to prioritize users and services based on their device capabilities and use cases.

Another integral part of edge intelligence is real-time access and analysis of data, along with concepts such as explainable AI (XAI), named data networks, joint optimization of communication and computing, distributed machine learning, and meta-learning, which are examples of technologies that will pave the way for B5G and 6G edge networks [14].

7.1.2.2 Key enablers

XAI is a set of methods and techniques for producing accurate and explainable models, along with explaining how and why the algorithm arrives at a specific solution, leading to an output that is comprehensible and transparent for humans. Another technology that is helping to meet the increasingly ambitious performance requirements is multi-access traffic management at the edge. By using the multi-access protocol and multiple access management [15], different technologies can be handled seamlessly. A multi-access protocol stack consists of two layers; a convergence sublayer that manages access path selection, multi-link aggregation, and more multi-access-specific tasks, and an adaptation sublayer that handles tunneling, security, and NAT.

In addition, joint optimization of computation and communication is quite a transcendental point to take into account in 5G/6G networks, as it helps to improve performance while managing both computation and radio resources intelligently. Lastly, distributed and federated learning are techniques that enable edge intelligence without transferring data to the cloud. Such learning techniques employ a collaborative learning model in which each element has a partial view of the system. As opposed to fully distributed learning where nodes must collaborate peer-to-peer, federated learning manages the collaboration through a central coordinator.

7.1.3 Edge computing and 5G/6G: a cloud native architecture

The current edge computing ecosystem is dynamic and evolutionary, which is the combination of the classic edge computing with several existing technologies and techniques including cellular networks, CN, and AI/ML. Thus, there is no de facto standard set of tools for implementing 5G/B5G edge computing architectures; however, the direction of such edges is becoming clearer. A number of factors have been identified as driving the adoption and evolution of edge architectures [16]. These include connectivity, applications exposed via APIs, the use of increasingly intelligent orchestrators, service exposure and optimization, and free open-source software [17].

From a technological point of view, CN technologies seem to be a perfect fit for edge architectures. In order to meet emerging 5G standards and provide flexibility for multi-vendor managed networks, edge solutions that are based on automation and intelligence need to be designed and developed as cloud-native architecture. The concept of CN is to decompose applications into a set of microservices that can be developed and deployed independently, in order to accelerate and optimize the DevOps lifecycle of software systems. A container orchestrator is responsible to schedule microservices to run on compute nodes by packaging them into lightweight containers. The CN approach is concerned with the way applications are developed and deployed, rather than only the place where they are executed [18]. Kubernetes, also known as k8s, has been adopted by the Cloud Native Computing Foundation

(CNCF) [19] as the open-source management tool for microservice-oriented applications. In CN architectures, streaming solutions such as Kafka [20] and Rabbit-MQ [21] are seamlessly integrated, along with publish–subscribe protocols such as MQTT [22] and data lake technologies such as Spark, which, by generating insights on edge nodes, reduces the need to transport data all the way to the cloud. In spite of the fact that these technologies were developed for different requirements, they complement each other perfectly in certain circumstances.

Container technology and Kubernetes orchestration framework provide scalability, cost-efficient, and reliable solutions. Hybrid k8s clusters with heterogeneous architectures provide the flexibility needed for the successful implementation of IoT applications. As the number of microservices in a scenario increases, it can be challenging to understand the interactions and identify and track errors. The service meshes can be used to resolve this problem [23], where linkerd [24] are currently being positioned as the *de facto* solution to the problem. Due to the operator's trend, Kubernetes has evolved from a declarative to an imperative model, where a set of controllers perform the required actions to match the intended state. OpenShift [25] is an example of a tool that adopts this concept, while several aspects, such as multi-cluster management, multi-cloud connectivity solutions, and workload migration, require further investigation.

Furthermore, 5G/6G edge architectures could benefit from the adoption of extended Berkeley filter packer (eBPF) technology [26]. It is emerging that different tools based on this technology, such as Cilium [27], allow a code to run within the kernel without the need to compile the entire kernel, providing unparalleled flexibility, as well as promising improvements in key areas such as security, networking, and monitoring, where AI will have a significant impact.

7.2 Distributed Telemetry

The field of intelligent networking has gained momentum in recent years due to the popularity of machine learning models and artificial intelligence systems in the telecommunications industry [28]. The concept of intelligent networking is mainly concerned with optimizing the management and performance of different network segments, such as radio, computing, and transport networks, each of which has heterogeneous objectives and approaches. As an example, some concepts, such as SON, address autonomic or cognitive self-managed networks [29]. Nevertheless, to cope with those characteristics, cognitive self-managed systems require strong telemetry systems to be aware of the behavior and performance of each of the elements composing the network infrastructure and the service communications. It is the consistent metrics that feed into the self-management systems enabling intelligent management models to achieve better results and, therefore, improve the performance of communication networks. However, due to the nature of current networks, thons of metrics gathered from segments that span several administrative domains significantly increase the complexity of the telemetry systems. This means that telemetry systems should be able to provide well-organized and differentiated metrics from each source so that they may be able to expose metrics per customer, per service, and per network element on demand.

As 5G networks are based on cloud-native and distributed services, multiple logical networks can be created and coexisted in a common infrastructure through technological enablers such as NFV [30], software defined networking (SDN) [31], and edge/cloud computing. Logical networks refer to the network slicing communication paradigm enabled by 5G networks by nature, which allows for the allocation of slices per service and per client. Since network slicing spans different network segments, edge computing must be capable of dealing with network slicing capabilities [32]. To meet the performance requirements and quality of service expected by users, several critical, time-sensitive, and less-consuming services are being moved to edge computing [33]. As a result, intelligent systems are also moving toward edge environments so that they can manage different services running at the edge that may belong to different vertical clients or network slices. Telemetry systems must adapt to paradigms such as network slicing, multi-tenancy, and multi-domain as well as to environments so that they can monitor aspects of these services in a flexible and dynamic manner. Monitoring systems may have to update their sources where metrics are collected frequently when services change.

Basically, the telemetry systems are a control framework that gives a detailed view of the state of a system. It allows assuring the desired operation of infrastructure resources as well as to analyze the performance of each virtualized service. The monitoring systems have existed since the emergence of IP networks with the aim to mitigate failures, attacks, and undesired behavior. As networks have evolved, monitoring systems have adapted and sophisticated their metrics acquisition models to better address unpredictable (proactive) and predictable (reactive) situations that violate operator-provided service level agreements (SLAs). Addressing proactively a monitoring situation means foreseeing events that can be mitigated in advance through the execution of specific actions. Proactive methods are based entirely on machine learning models that analyze patterns in historical data and anticipate future behavior. This is the core concept where intelligent networks are built. However, reactive methods refer to executing actions at the exact moment that an event occurs, which violates the SLAs. This principle has been widely used in most control systems. However, since the democratization of machine learning models, control systems are tending to use hybrid control methods depending on the requirements of SLAs and use cases. However, the performance methods are independent of the monitoring systems but depend on the type and quality of metrics they receive from the monitoring systems. Consequently, monitoring systems must meet the needs of each method to assure adequate control of services and resource infrastructure. In terms of monitoring system design, it is difficult to anticipate all the needs of the methods, but if they provide better visibility of each of the elements that comprise the communication service, the methods will be more likely to provide better performance.

In this context, previous research has focused on specific aspects of monitoring. For example, in [34], the authors make a study on traffic differentiation detection where they focus on presenting strategies and tools to monitor network traffic. On the other hand, in [35], the authors present a survey on network security monitoring. Here, the paper reviews the approaches and tools focused on network security aspects. In [36], the authors focus their attention on an exhaustive study of platforms for monitoring cloud environments. They detail both licensed and open-source tools. The important aspect of a monitoring system is to be able to perform all these types of monitoring with a single robust telemetry framework.

The following sections will provide a detailed description of the hierarchical and distributed monitoring architectural framework for 5G and 6G networks that provide flexibility and visibility of metrics obtained from both communication services and network infrastructure. Section 7.2.1 gives a detailed description of each component composing the architectural framework.

7.2.1 Hierarchical and distributed monitoring framework

The main objective of the distributed and hierarchical monitoring framework is to collect, organize, and expose the data flow, resource, and configuration metrics generated by each of the network segments. The system is hierarchical because its components are distributed across several layers of view or management levels where data is aggregated, filtered, and isolated. This allows metrics to be persisted and exposed at different levels, even with different levels of granularity. The different levels of monitoring are fed by separate and distributed monitoring agents deployed by the operator in each network segment.

Figure 7.1 illustrates the design of the architectural framework of the hierarchical and distributed monitoring system. In this case, two levels of metrics abstraction are defined. In addition, each level allows centralizing and persisting the metrics obtained from the network segments. This makes it easier for each network segment to have several monitoring agents and a common metrics centralizer. For example, for access networks such as Wi-Fi, small cells, and eNBs, monitoring agents could be deployed for each of them to interact directly and to extract the metrics generated in each network equipment. These monitoring agents are then aggregated to the first-level aggregators, where the metrics can be exposed and visualized by customers and operators. The same case would be for NFV infrastructure (NFVI) nodes, where there will be several types of monitoring agents deployed, both for the NFV node itself and for each of the virtualized network functions (VNFs) running on it. Similarly, these metrics may be aggregated, exposed, and visualized by one or more top-level aggregators, depending on the need of the use cases or customers. However, the communication service and network infrastructure of a network operator may be composed of multiple access networks, NFVI nodes, and transport networks; so there will be multiple first level aggregators. This is the motivation behind the use of a second level of aggregation, where the metrics collected by the first level aggregators are centralized. The second level of aggregation allows a network operator and customers in general to have a global view of the current state of the network infrastructure and the communication services running on it. It facilitates filtering by first-level aggregation nodes, without having to worry about which monitoring agent is being referred to when extracting a metric.

7.2.1.1 Monitoring agents

Monitoring agents are software tools that interact directly with network elements. They can be run directly on the network equipment or they can be run as services in edge/cloud computing. Monitoring agents are known as node exporters, which take all the metrics and push them to the top-level aggregator so that they can be understood and visualized. There are monitoring agents designed by default for different types of network elements, while others can be customized (pushgateways) and run as a set of scripts that interact directly with the operating system of the network element to extract the metric.

7.2.1.2 Aggregators – monitoring servers

Aggregators are instances of time series databases (TSDB) in charge of collecting and centralizing the metrics exposed by the monitoring agents. The aggregators persist the metrics for a given time to allow operators, users, or other components to access the historical information provided by the monitoring agents. In addition, they allow metrics to be visualized and operationalized to contextualize them in human-understandable units of measurement. Currently, many of the network services are deployed in conjunction with a metrics aggregator dynamically, which generates the need to implement a static second-level aggregator. There are several alternatives

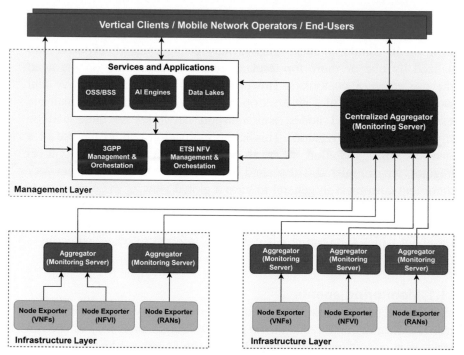

Figure 7.1   Architectural framework of the distributed and hierarchical monitoring system.

in the TSDB market; however, the most popular ones are Prometheus[1], InfluxDB[2], TimeStream[3], and TimescaleDB[4]

7.2.1.3 Centralized aggregator − monitoring server

The centralized aggregator is in charge of collecting the metrics exposed by the first-level aggregators. In other words, it adds the first-level aggregators as direct targets and is not aware of the number of monitoring agents that exist in the system. This level of abstraction allows operators to dynamically scale and manage first-level aggregators that are dynamically deployed alongside network services. On the other hand, the centralized aggregator also allows visualizing the metrics exposed by all monitoring agents by filtering them by each first-level aggregator. One tool that acts as a centralized aggregator is Thanos[5]. It has the same working principle as Prometheus.

7.3 AI Pipelines for the Edge-to-cloud Continuum

While the development and deployment of 5G mobile networks is ongoing, extensive research efforts are currently being directed toward the requirements of future 6G mobile networks, covering aspects such as architecture, enabling technologies, key features, and requirements. Among these, network cloudification is one clear 6G architectural trend. Moreover, 5G network developments are already paving the way to support a massive number of end devices across the cloud continuum [37].

Research challenges related to the massification of end devices in 5G networks are often related to the placement of applications and network functions that might be distributed across multiple devices spanning the cloud continuum [38], and to the optimization of strict latency, reliability, and bandwidth requirements.

As the 6G paradigm introduces a shift to the full digitalization of the real world, some additional critical aspects need to be considered, such as efficient interworking with IoT devices, the support of advanced, novel edge computing solutions, and adequate cloud support for network operation. In this regard, the native support of AI and ML in 6G can provide innovative

---

[1] https://prometheus.io/
[2] https://www.influxdata.com/
[3] https://aws.amazon.com/es/timestream/
[4] https://www.timescale.com/
[5] https://thanos.io/

solutions, for example, related to the optimization of network functions and distributed applications [39]. AI and ML techniques will become critical to automate decision-making processes in 6G and enable the implementation of predictive orchestration mechanisms.

However, the intertwining of communication and computation algorithms in 6G requires suitable in-network governance mechanisms. In particular, every infrastructure and service component in the network must be controllable by the tenant, which requires very versatile, pervasive, and automatic resource control capabilities [40]. This calls for the design of a 6G-native AI fabric that caters for the diversity of resources and end devices across the cloud continuum, which should be able to provide not only novel, natively embedded governance capabilities but also the ability to optimize the use of resources in the network in an energy-efficient manner.

7.3.1 Native AI for distributed edge-to-cloud environments

6G is promising to become a networking technology whose management and behavior are meant to be closer to human's brain reasoning. The vision must also include the native incorporation of AI processes capable of handling network functions more efficiently (e.g., intelligent network management and wireless resource configuration) as well as training and executing AI-based models [41], [42].

Networking ecosystems have also evolved from the point of view of the distribution of the radio and computational resources. In this regard, future mobile networks are expected to be fully geographically distributed and managed by different entities and operators, and even based on several administrative domains (see Figure 7.2). Related to this, the highly distributed telemetry systems at different network segments make available huge data volumes which, although provide a full vision of the system's status, also multiply the difficulty in knowledge extraction. Therefore, despite the improvement expected in availability level and network performance, together with the high-dimensional data, it will greatly increase the complexity of management and error handling, making it impractical for human operators [43]. For that reason, an AI-enabled architecture able to build knowledge natively and act autonomously is the goal of 6G networks.

Adopting the aforementioned AI processes as well as regular user applications at the edge of the network brings, however, new challenges to next-generation networks. Undoubtedly, the increase in heterogeneity of both edge nodes and application requirements, the computational limitation of

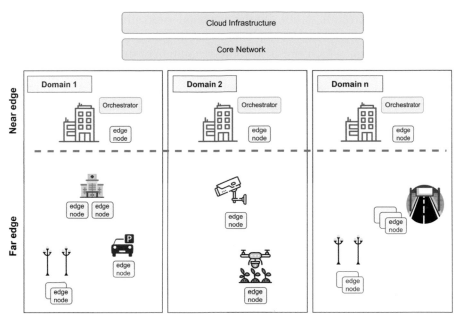

Figure 7.2 Example of a highly distributed and independently managed edge infrastructure.

the edge nodes, and the dynamic change of user demands make intelligent resource management approaches able to ensure the data privacy become essential [44]. More specifically, application and function placement can be considered one of the key resource allocation problems, especially as we deal with highly heterogeneous and distributed infrastructure involving computational and communication resources [45], [46]. Therefore, there is a need for intelligent and distributed placement solutions that provide decisions without sharing the data belonging to each administrative domain or independent system.

In this regard, distributed and federated learning have been demonstrated to provide excellent performance due to the ability to collaboratively build a model without data transferring, therefore avoiding data privacy issues and extra overheads in the data transmission process [47], [48]. Similarly, reinforcement learning has shown promising results in tackling this challenge in centralized scenarios, such as in the works proposed in [49] and [50].

Most of the recent research related to application placement is related to either (i) computational offloading at the edge from end-user devices, (ii) latency-aware processes at the radio side, and (iii) edge infrastructures where telemetry data is not distributed, or in which the various nodes are managed by the same orchestration entity. On the one hand, offloading approaches for energy saving in the mobile devices tend to neglect the energy consumption of the edge servers, which are also more resource-constrained than cloud infrastructures. This issue could be made worse by uneven distributions of users in the geography, which could also make edge placement algorithms waste energy having nodes with very low resource utilization instead of being powered off. On the other hand, the maximum latency supported by applications must also consider the link delay depending on the placing node and the processing time. In essence, it should ensure that besides meeting the application requirements, also the QoS constraints are ensured in a unified manner, especially for the time-sensitive applications. In the next subsections, these problems are greatly discussed, especially when they are addressed by AI processes in highly distributed (and administratively independent) systems.

7.3.1.1 Energy saving in distributed edge computing

Extensive research has been performed in MEC to optimize the energy consumption of computationally intensive tasks, given the limited resources of the servers used. Application placement algorithms are increasingly important at the edge since, among other consequences, computational tasks offloaded to the cloud can result in lower utilization of MEC resources and higher power consumption. The performance of applications could be affected due to the demanding application requirements that can limit the storage and capacity of end devices. In addition, in future 6G networks, expected to be extremely geo-distributed in terms of computational resources, centralized orchestration approaches could lead to constant interaction between central entities and result in energy consumption.

The state of the art highlights the need to focus on the placement of applications and workloads that produce lower energy consumption. Moreover, it is to be considered not only the energy consumed by the application itself when it is running but also some transactions when moving applications across several nodes. This can be the case of the follow-me scenario. In this case, energy consumption on edge servers, migrations from edge servers to cloud servers and between edge servers must be taken into account. In addition, other approaches suggest maintaining the edge servers in an idle state or low consumption and activating the server when a new application arrives. However, not all works consider all possible sources of energy consumption, because depending on the use case, it might be more necessary to prioritize the minimization of expenditure in some sources of consumption than in others.

Numerous research contributions that attempt to solve this problem aim to strike a balance between performance metrics and energy efficiency. Machine learning techniques have been widely used in this topic, due to their ability to make predictions from data and to obtain assumptions about the environment without prior knowledge. For application placement, forecasting methods predict periodic changes from time series considering the edge node data as input and the geographic location information [51]. The authors of [52] aim to reduce the total energy of each user, including local computation and wireless transmission energy under a federated learning approach. However, the energy consumption on only the terminal side is addressed in [53]. Reinforcement learning and its variants are oriented to minimize the long-term energy consumption and have been demonstrated to be a good alternative for these kinds of scenarios [54]. For instance, some authors consider application placement with multiple metrics in dynamic environments as a problem to solve with distributed learning approach [53].

7.3.1.2 Latency-aware AI processes in edge computing

As stated previously, one of the key enablers of the incoming generation of network services is the ability to bring the processing power near to the final user, using edge computing as a tool to decrease the potential delays in end-to-end communications. The management of this delay is particularly important in ultra-reliable low-latency communications (URLLC) as an inappropriate delay would generate misbehavior in time-sensitive applications, affecting use cases as diverse as smart living, Industry 4.0, or autonomous vehicles [55]. Essentially, selecting the proper host to implement the service application placement is critical if the stringy delay requirements of the applications are to be fulfilled. Contrary to what might be expected, the host's selection is not a trivial labor, as different elements contribute to the final decision. However, it is not sufficient to consider the current delay of the proposed hosts. Additionally, it is essential to account for the processing delay after the application has been instantiated in the server, the computational characteristics of the host, the distance between the host and the users, and an increasing number of secondary parameters.

Considering the previously mentioned constraints, human decision-making would be time-consuming and error-prone, making it necessary to implement an automated decision-making system instead. Traditional optimization models include the use of algorithms that perform numerical analysis and mathematical optimization methods [56], [57]. However, considering the dynamicity of the network, a system that is able to adapt to this type of changes is necessary, excluding the possibility of using traditional optimization models. Incidentally, machine learning models excel in this type of conditions and are natively suited to handle data in time-series format and with an abundance of data categories. Machine learning models can solve optimization problems successfully and accurately and at the same time being flexible enough to adapt to the unique changes of the network, showing more generalization capabilities than its traditional counterpart.

As such, ML processes have been proven to be suitable for solving the best placement location for delay-constrained applications. When deployed on a centralized point of the network architecture, ML models use as input the parameters that are monitored through the network orchestrator or the network management service. These parameters are affected directly or indirectly by the end-to-end delay; so it is especially important to measure KPIs that are linked with the propagation delay, the processing delay, and the radio communication delays, among others. Under this statement, the authors of [58] look to maximize the quality of experience (QoE) by analyzing packet loss rate, packet error rate, and latency under a two-level deep reinforcement learning model that suggests the best application position. Similarly, in [59], a deep reinforcement learning model is introduced, which uses transmission delay, propagation delay, and execution delay to reach a compromise between the application requirements and the server capacity. Finally, the work in [60] uses parameters directly obtained from the end-users, in a deep reinforcement learning configuration, to generate a tradeoff between the current performance delay-oriented and the cost of running the application. To do so, it searches for a balance between the delay experienced by the user and the cost taken from the network provider while distributing the application. Consequently, according to the state of the art, deep reinforcement learning is a good fit for scenarios whose initial inputs are unknown and adapts well to the latency-related metrics in application placement problems, providing flexibility and adaptability to an ever-changing network environment.

Acknowledgements

This work has been mainly supported by the EU H2020 research and innovation program IoT-NGIN with Grant Agreement No. 957246. It has also been supported by the EU "NextGenerationEU/PRTR," MCIN, and

AEI (Spain) under project IJC2020-043058-I, and by the Grant ONOFRE-3 PID2020-112675RB-C43 funded by MCIN/AEI/10.13039/501100011033.

References

[1] 5GPPP, A Pre-Structuring Proposal Based on the H2020 Work Programme. [Online]. Available: https://5g-ppp.eu/coverage-plans/

[2] 3GPP, System Architecture for the 5G System (5GS), V.17.1.1, 3GPP TS 23.501, 2021.

[3] 3GPP, Study on management aspects of edge computing, V16.0.1, 3GPP TR 28.803, 2019.

[4] 3GPP, 5G System Enhancements for Edge Computing, V1.0.0,, 3GPP TS 23.54, 2021.

[5] 5G; Self-Organizing Networks (SON) for 5G networks (3GPP TS 28.313 version 16.0.0 Release 16), 2020.

[6] 3GPP, 5G; 5G System; Network Data Analytics Services; Stage 3 (3GPP TS 29.520 version 15.3.0 Release 15), 2019.

[7] ETSI, "Zero-touch network and Service Management (ZSM); Reference Architecture, ETSI GS ZSM 002 V1.1.1," 2019.

[8] O-RAN, "O-RAN Architecture Description", v05.00, O-RAN, WG1, 2021.

[9] A. Papageorgiouet al., "On 5G network slice modelling: Service-, resource-, or deployment-driven?" *Computer Communications*, vol. 149, pp. 232–240, 2020, doi: 10.1016/j.comcom.2019.10.024.

[10] P. S. Dutta, N. R. Jennings and L. Moreau, "Cooperative Information Sharing to Improve Distributed Learning in Multi-Agent Systems," *Journal of Artificial Intelligence Research*, vol. 24, p. 407–463, 2005, doi: 10.1613/jair.1735.

[11] I. V. Bajić, W. Lin and Y. Tian, "Collaborative Intelligence: Challenges and Opportunities,"*2021 IEEE International Conference on Acoustics, Speech and Signal Processing (ICASSP)*, pp. 8493-8497, 2021, doi: 10.1109/ICASSP39728.2021.9413943.

[12] Cisco, "Intent based networking". [Online]. Available: https://www.cisco.com/c/en/us/solutions/intent-based-networking.html

[13] 3GPP, "Overall Description of Radio Access Network (RAN) Aspects for Vehicle-to-Everything (V2X) based on LTE and NR", 3GPP TR 37.985, V.16.0.0," 2020.

[14] 3GPP, "Integrated Access and Backhaul Radio Transmission and Reception", 3GPP TS 38.174, V.16.3.0," 2021.

[15] 5G Americas, "5G Edge Automation and Intelligence" White Paper, 2021.

[16] RFC 8743, "Multi-Access Management Service," [Online]. Available: https://www.rfc-editor.org/rfc/rfc8743.txt

[17] Ericsson, "Edge computing and deployment strategies for communication service providers," [Online]. Available: https://www.ericsson.com/en/reports-and-papers/white-papers/edge-computing-and-deploymen t-strategies-for-communication-service-providers.

[18] 5G Americas, "Distributed Compute and Communications in 5G" White Paper, 2022.

[19] Cloud Native Computing Foundation (CNCF). CNCF Cloud Native Definition v1.0, [Online]. Available: https://github.com/cncf/toc/bl ob/master/definition.md

[20] Kafka. [online]. Available: https://kafka.apache.org/

[21] RabbitMQ. [online]. Available: https://www.rabbitmq.com/

[22] MQTT. [online]. Available: https://mqtt.org/

[23] Linkerd Documentation. What is a service mesh? [online]. Available: https://linkerd.io/what-is-a-service-mesh/

[24] Linkerd. [Online]. Available: https://linkerd.io/

[25] OpenShift. [Online]. Available: https://www.redhat.com/en/technologi es/cloud-computing/openshift

[26] eBPF Documentation. What is eBPF? [online]. Available: https://ebpf.i o/what-is-ebpf

[27] Cilium. [Online]. Available: https://cilium.io/

[28] P. V. Klaine et al., "A Survey of Machine Learning Techniques Applied to Self-Organizing Cellular Networks," in *IEEE Communications Surveys & Tutorials*, vol. 19, no. 4, pp. 2392-2431, 2017, doi: 10.1109/COMST.2017.2727878.

[29] T. Meriem et al., "ETSI white paper no. 16 gana - generic autonomic networking architecture reference model for autonomic networking, cognitive networking and self-management of networks and services," 2017.

[30] M. Mosahebfard, J. S. Vardakas and C. Verikoukis, "Modelling the Admission Ratio in NFV-Based Converged Optical-Wireless 5G Networks," *in IEEE Transactions on Vehicular Technology*, vol. 70, no. 11, pp. 12024-12038, 2021, doi: 10.1109/TVT.2021.3113838.

[31] M. Dalgitsis et al., "SDN-Based Resource Management for Optical-Wireless Fronthaul," in: *(eds) Enabling 6G Mobile Networks*, Springer, Cham. 2022, doi: 10.1007/978-3-030-74648-3_14.

[32] A. Cárdenas et al., "Enhancing a 5G Network Slicing Management Model to Improve the Support of Mobile Virtual Network Operators," in *IEEE Access*, vol. 9, pp. 131382-131399, 2021, doi: 10.1109/ACCESS.2021.3114645.

[33] J.-M. Fernandez, I. Vidal, and F. Valera, "Enabling the orchestration of IoT slices through edge and cloud microservice platforms," *Sensors*, vol. 19, no. 13, p. 2980, 2019, doi: 10.3390/s19132980.

[34] H.-C. Hsieh, J.-L. Chen, and A. Benslimane, "5G virtualized multi-access edge computing platform for IoT applications," *Journal of Network and Computer Applications*, vol. 115, pp. 94–102, 2018, doi: 10.1016/j.jnca.2018.05.001.

[35] T. Garrett et al., "Monitoring Network Neutrality: A Survey on Traffic Differentiation Detection," in *IEEE Communications Surveys & Tutorials*, vol. 20, no. 3, pp. 2486-2517, 2018, doi: 10.1109/COMST.2018.2812641.

[36] I. Ghafir et al., "A Survey on Network Security Monitoring Systems," *IEEE 4th International Conference on Future Internet of Things and Cloud Workshops (FiCloudW)*, pp. 77-82, 2016, doi: 10.1109/W-FiCloud.2016.30.

[37] G. Aceto et al., "Cloud monitoring: A survey," *Computer Networks*, vol. 57, no. 9, pp. 2093-2115, 2013, doi: 10.1016/j.comnet.2013.04.001.

[38] The 5G Infrastructure Association (5GIA), "European Vision for the 6G Network Ecosystem", white paper, 2021, doi: 10.5281/zenodo.5007671.

[39] E. Carmona Cejudo, and M. S. Siddiqui, "An Optimization Framework for Edge-to-Cloud Offloading of Kubernetes Pods in V2X Scenarios," *IEEE Globecom Workshops (GC Wkshps)*, 2021, doi: 10.1109/GCWkshps52748.2021.9682148.

[40] M. Ericson et al., "6G Architectural Trends and Enablers," *IEEE 4th 5G World Forum (5GWF)*, pp. 406-411, 2021, doi: 10.1109/5GWF52925.2021.00078.

[41] K. B. Letaief et al., "Edge Artificial Intelligence for 6G: Vision, Enabling Technologies, and Applications," in *IEEE Journal on Selected Areas in Communications*, vol. 40, no. 1, pp. 5-36, 2022, doi: 10.1109/JSAC.2021.3126076.

[42] A. Bandi, "A Review Towards AI Empowered 6G Communication Requirements, Applications, and Technologies in Mobile

Edge Computing," *6th International Conference on Computing Methodologies and Communication (ICCMC)*, pp. 12-17, 2022 doi: 10.1109/ICCMC53470.2022.9754049.

[43] E. Coronado et al., "Zero Touch Management: A Survey of Network Automation Solutions for 5G and 6G Networks," in *IEEE Communications Surveys & Tutorials*, 2022, doi: 10.1109/COMST.2022.3212586.

[44] M. Giordani et al., "Toward 6G networks: Use cases and technologies", *IEEE Communications Magazine*, vol. 58, no. 3, pp. 55-61, 2020, doi: 10.1109/MCOM.001.1900411.

[45] C. R. de Mendoza et al., "Near Optimal VNF Placement in Edge-Enabled 6G Networks," *25th Conference on Innovation in Clouds, Internet and Networks (ICIN)*, pp. 136-140, 2022, doi: 10.1109/ICIN53892.2022.9758116.

[46] Y. Li et al., "Joint Placement of UPF and Edge Server for 6G Network," *IEEE Internet of Things Journal*, vol. 8, no. 22, pp. 16370-16378, 2021, doi: 10.1109/JIOT.2021.3095236.

[47] J. Song and M. Kountouris, "Wireless Distributed Edge Learning: How Many Edge Devices Do We Need?," *IEEE Journal on Selected Areas in Communications*, vol. 39, no. 7, pp. 2120-2134, 2021, doi: 10.1109/JSAC.2020.3041379.

[48] S. Yu et al., "When Deep Reinforcement Learning Meets Federated Learning: Intelligent Multi-timescale Resource Management for Multi-access Edge Computing in 5G Ultradense Network," *IEEE Internet of Things Journal*, vol. 8, no. 4, pp. 2238-2251, 2021, doi: 10.1109/JIOT.2020.3026589.

[49] A. Dalgkitsis, P. -V. Mekikis, A. Antonopoulos, G. Kormentzas and C. Verikoukis, "Dynamic Resource Aware VNF Placement with Deep Reinforcement Learning for 5G Networks," *IEEE Global Communications Conference*, 2020, doi: 10.1109/GLOBECOM42002.2020.9322512.

[50] A. Talpur and M. Gurusamy, "DRLD-SP: A Deep-Reinforcement-Learning-Based Dynamic Service Placement in Edge-Enabled Internet of Vehicles," *IEEE Internet of Things Journal*, vol. 9, no. 8, pp. 6239-6251, 2022, doi: 10.1109/JIOT.2021.3110913.

[51] D. Li, M. Lan, and Y. Hu, "Energy-saving service management technology of internet of things using edge computing and deep learning", *Complex & Intelligent Systems*, vol. 8, no. 5, pp 3867–3879, 2022, doi: 10.1007/s40747-022-00666-0.

[52] Z. Yang et al., "Energy Efficient Federated Learning Over Wireless Communication Networks", *IEEE Transactions on Wireless Communications*, vol. 20, no. 3, pp. 1935-1949, 2021, doi: 10.1109/TWC.2020.3037554.

[53] M. Goudarzi, M. Palaniswami, and R. Buyya, "A Distributed Deep Reinforcement Learning Technique for Application Placement in Edge and Fog Computing Environments", *IEEE Transactions on Mobile Computing*, 2020, doi: 10.1109/TMC.2021.3123165.

[54] H. Zhou et al., "Energy Efficient Joint Computation Offloading and Service Caching for Mobile Edge Computing: A Deep Reinforcement Learning Approach", *IEEE Transactions on Green Communications and Networking,*, 2022, doi: 10.1109/TGCN.2022.3186403.

[55] Č. Stefanović, "Industry 4.0 from 5G perspective: Use-cases, requirements, challenges and approaches," *11th CMI International Conference: Prospects and Challenges Towards Developing a Digital Economy within the EU*, pp. 44-48, 2018, doi: 10.1109/PCTDDE.2018.8624728.

[56] H. Badri et al. "A Sample Average Approximation-Based Parallel Algorithm for Application Placement in Edge Computing Systems", *2018 IEEE International Conference on Cloud Engineering (IC2E)*, pp. 198-203, 2018, doi: 10.1109/IC2E.2018.00044.

[57] R. Yu, G. Xue and X. Zhang, "Application Provisioning in FOG Computing-enabled Internet-of-Things: A Network Perspective," *IEEE INFOCOM 2018 - IEEE Conference on Computer Communications*, pp. 783-791, 2018, doi: 10.1109/INFOCOM.2018.8486269.

[58] I. Alqerm and Jianli Pan. "DeepEdge: A New QoE-Based Resource Allocation Framework Using Deep Reinforcement Learning for Future Heterogeneous Edge-IoT Applications". *IEEE Transactions on Network and Service Management*, vol. 18, no. 4, pp. 3942–3954, 2021. doi: 10.1109/TNSM.2021.3123959.

[59] P. Gazori, D. Rahbari, and Mohsen Nickray. "Saving time and cost on the scheduling of fog-based IoT applications using deep reinforcement learning approach". *Future Generation Computer Systems*, vol. 110 pp. 1098–1115, 2020. doi: 10.1016/j.future.2019.09.060.

[60] Y. Chen et al., "Data-Intensive Application Deployment at Edge: A Deep Reinforcement Learning Approach," *IEEE International Conference on Web Services (ICWS)*, pp. 355-359, 2019, doi: 10.1109/ICWS.2019.00064.

8

IoT Things to Service Matchmaking at the Edge

Nisrine Bnouhanna[1] and Rute C. Sofia[2]

[1]Technical University of Munich, Germany
[2]fortiss Research Institute of the Free State of Bavaria for Software Intensive Systems and Services – affiliated with the Technical University of Munich, Germany
E-mail: bnouhanna.nisrine@gmail.com; sofia@fortiss.org

Abstract

This chapter debates on the use of Machine Learning (ML) to support edge-based semantic matchmaking to handle a large-scale integration of IoT data sources with IoT platforms. The chapter starts by addressing the interoperability challenges currently faced by integrators, the role of ontologies in this context. It continues with a perspective on semantic matchmaking approaches, and ML solutions that can best support a cognitive matchmaking. The chapter then covers a use case and pilots that are being developed with a new open-source middleware, TSMatch, in the context of the Horizon 2020 EFPF project, for the purpose of environmental monitoring in smart manufacturing.

Keywords: Machine learning, semantic technologies, matchmaking.

8.1 Introduction

Manufacturing environments are becoming increasingly digitized to improve the overall process and business efficiency. Sensors and actuators (Internet of Things devices) are heavily integrated into manufacturing environments,

157   DOI: 10.1201/9781032632407-10

and interconnected to edge and cloud via heterogeneous communication protocols, such as the Message Queuing Telemetry Transport (MQTT) [1] or the Open Platform Communications Unified Architecture (OPC UA) [2], [3]. The integration and discovery of sensors and their interconnection to the edge or cloud implies heavy human intervention, being error prone. Moreover, as devices within an devices within an industrial environment are often acquired from different vendors, interoperability at different levels (device, protocol, domain, etc.) [4] is a significant issue in IoT.

Semantic sensor technologies [4], such as the Web of Things (WoT), provide a way to define IoT devices via expressive, uniform descriptions of metadata and data meaning, thus assisting in lowering the barrier of interoperability between IoT devices and IoT platforms.

Similarly, IoT services can be seen as a subset of web-based services, and, therefore they can be described via semantic technologies.

Therefore, describing semantically IoT devices and services is a methodology that provides a way to lower the interoperability barrier. However, semantic data annotation is still being tied to specific protocols. For instance, OPC UA specifies robotics specifications, which are not necessarily compatible with the specifications provided by other protocols.

Semantic matchmaking can assist in bringing this level of automation to IIoT. In this context, semantic matchmaking relates with using the meaning and information content provided by IIoT device descriptions (Things Descriptions (TD)) to match it with the meaning of offered IIoT services, e.g., environmental monitoring, abnormal pattern detection, etc.

Currently, semantic matchmaking requires the use of ontologies to discover semantic similarity between the two semantic descriptions − in the case of this work, Thing and Service − to detect the "semantic distance" between the two elements.

Ontologies are therefore a key component of semantic interoperability, as they provide the foundation and capability for devices to interpret and infer knowledge from datasets. However, the application of ontologies is complicated due to three major problems: i) fragmentation and vendor-lock; ii) cross-domain interoperability; iii) lack of open tools and application examples [5]. Fragmentation may be reduced via the development of information models that are universal, based on open standards, such as the ETSI Smart Applications Reference Ontology (SAREF) [6], and not based on specific protocols or vendors. Cross-domain interoperability requires a new approach to ontologies, in particular, the application of a universal language and a universal universal approach that can assist the mapping between domain-based ontologies, such as that happening with the methodology of the Industrial Ontology Foundry-core (IOF-core)[1] for industry, and the core ontology for biology and biomedicine (COB)[2] for the biomedical domains. SAREF is a key reference in this context.

While ontologies provide an easier way to interpret data across IIoT infrastructures, the need for a higher degree of automation still persists.

The focus of this chapter, therefore, relates with a debate on the definition and use of semantic matchmaking in IIoT environments, to improve the overall interoperability. The main contributions of this chapter are as follows:

- To provide an understanding of semantic matchmaking and the under-lying semantic technologies that are applied in the context of IIoT environments.
- To explain the current challenges and propose guidelines to circumvent them.
- To explain how semantic matchmaking can be applied in the context of edge−cloud environments.

The chapter is organized as follows. After this introductory section, Section 8.2 provides background on semantic matchmaking. Section 8.3 presents a specific applicability case derived from the application of an open-source semantic matchmaking middleware, TSMatch. Section 8.4 explains the current challenges faced when applying semantic matchmaking between IoT Things and services. Section 8.5 debates on proposals to further support an intelligent, adaptive, and semantic matchmaking for IIoT. Section 8.6 concludes the document.

8.2 Semantic Matchmaking and Current Approaches

In general, semantic matchmaking refers to the mapping between two con-cepts, entities, or descriptions focusing on how similar the semantic meaning of the matched concepts is, while identifying the relationship between them [6].

Semantic matchmaking is used in various fields such as web services [7], [8], information retrieval [9], [10], and in various vertical domains such as vertical domains such as smart cities [11] or health [12]. A typ-ical application of semantic matchmaking in the context of web services

---

[1] https://industrialontologies.org
[2] https://obofoundry.org/ontology/cob.html

is service composition, where several existing web services are combined using semantic matchmaking between the services' descriptions, to provide enriched descriptions of services. There are also several scenarios where semantic matchmaking is applied to retrieve information. The most common is web search engines and recommendation systems. Semantic matchmaking has also been used in vertical domains as an interoperability solution to enable communication between various entities.

Semantic matchmaking is especially useful for large-scale IoT environments, since the large number of connected devices/Things need to effectively communicate between each other and with other services, to reach its full potential. However, applying semantic matchmaking to IoT needs to be adjusted to the specific conditions and needs of IoT environments, e.g., the diversity of attributes for sensors, the different units applied, etc. An additional challenge to address in the context of IoT environments is the matching of devices/Things across different vertical domains, as fine-grained matching is required. For example, semantic matchmaking should be able to differentiate between a temperature sensor of an environment and a temperature sensor of a machine and accordingly match the adequate sensor to the service request.

There are several methods and technologies used to achieve semantic matchmaking depending on the scenario, requirements, and the type of entities to be matched. Overall, semantic matchmaking can be categorized in three main approaches: knowledge-based, statistical, and hybrid [19].

Knowledge-based approach refers to using a predefined knowledge containing statements such as rules, facts, and constraints to provide a semantic match between entities. A common example of such an approach is ontology-based matching, where reasoning is used to find similarities and relations between the semantic description entities.

Knowledge-based semantic matchmaking approaches tend to be accurate and provide fine-grained matching since they are based on pre-built and expert knowledge and models combined with logical reasoning. However, they may lead to false negatives caused by the limitations of the knowledge used. For example, if two concepts are semantically synonymous but defined differently in their terminological definitions, the similarity between the two is not captured and a reasoner would fail to find the match between the two concepts. Moreover, knowledge-based semantic matchmaking approaches are complex, require long design time, demand high maintenance to keep the knowledge-base up to date, and are associated with long processing time [16], [17].

A **statistical approach** is based on analyzing the frequency of occurrence of certain terms used in the semantic descriptions of the entities to be matched and use statistical tools such as lexical resources (e.g., WordNet[3]/distance measures (e.g., cosine similarity) or ML (e.g., clustering techniques [13]) to define their semantic similarity. Statistical-based semantic matchmaking is considered to be less complex compared to the knowledge-based approach; it also tends to require less processing time due to less complex computation. However, for applications that require fine-grained matching, statistical-based approaches are usually not suitable since the processing and transformation of the data causes loss of semantic information, thus leading to more generic matching.

Hybrid approach refers to semantic matchmaking solutions that combine both knowledge-based and statistical approaches to mitigate the advantages and disadvantages of both approaches [14], [15]. Hybrid approaches may assist in overcoming the disadvantages of both the knowledge-based and statistical categories. However, identifying the effective way to combine and take advantage of both techniques remains a challenge.

8.3 TSMatch, an Example of Semantic Matchmaking for IIoT

TSMatch [22] is an open-source middleware[4] that supports semantic matchmaking between IoT data sources (Things) and IoT services. TSMatch contributes to solve the challenge of semantic interoperability, by providing an automated matchmaking solution between IoT devices and IoT services, which relies on semantic technologies. The proposed solution is based on the following two assumptions: i) each IoT device has a semantic description; ii) each IoT service can be described semantically based on an ontology.

The TSMatch middleware has been developed and applied in industrial environmental pilots (TRL6) in the context of the **Horizon 2020 European Connected Factory Platform for Agile Manufacturing (EFPF)** project[5], and a demonstrator is available and interconnected to the EFPF data spine via the fortiss IIoT Lab.

---

[3] https://wordnet.princeton.edu/
[4] https://git.fortiss.org/iiot_external/tsmatch
[5] https://www.efpf.org/

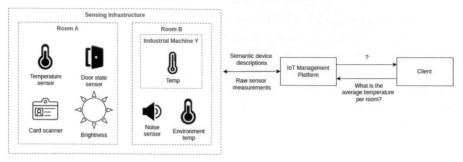

Figure 8.1   Example of a smart facility interconnected to an IoT platform.

As an example that may assist in understanding the operation of semantic matchmaking, let us consider Figure 8.1 standing for a smart factory shopfloor, integrating multiple sensors.

In the shopfloor, machines from different vendors, with coupled sensors attached on them, are expected. Moreover, sensors are also used to monitor the environment, e.g., CO_2, temperature, humidity, etc. Employees of this facility are using wearable devices, tablets, and smart phones, which also have sensing capabilities. In this scenario, different IoT platforms have been acquired to different vendors. Therefore, each platform considers different semantic standards to support an interoperable data exchange. Data exchange is supported by a data bus across the factory, and the different platforms rely on specific communication protocols to exchange data, e.g., OPC UA, MQTT Sparkplug, etc. Different services, e.g., data analytics tooling, environmental monitoring services, and certification services, are interconnected to the data spine via software-based connectors that have been specifically devised for this purpose, by the different vendors, or by an integrator.

Some of these services run on the so-called edge (close to the field-level devices, e.g., on the shopfloor) and others run on the cloud. On this scenario, the semantic matchmaking process can occur on the cloud or on the edge. Placing the matchmaking on the edge is expected to lower latency and also reduce energy consumption, as most of the data processing (including aggregation) is performed closer to the end-user.

TSMatch (rf. to Figure 8.2) aims at providing this type of support, being developed to run as an edge-based service. Following a client-server approach and consisting of multiple containerized microservices, TSMatch comprises a server-side, **the TSMatch engine**, and a **TSMatch client**. The TSMatch engine is composed of two main functional blocks and several interfaces:

- **Semantic matchmaking**. Performs semantic matchmaking between IoT Things descriptions (stored on a database) and ontologies. The result is a set of enriched data nodes, which are also stored in a database.
- **Data aggregation**. Sensor data aggregator.
- **Ontology interface**. Provides support for ontologies to be imported into TSMatch.
- **Connectors**. Different connectors, e.g., Mosquitto to RabbitMQ; HTTP/REST, etc.

The input and output of the matchmaking and data aggregation processes are stored on a local Neo4J database, storing Things descriptions, service descriptions, ontologies, and new data nodes (aggregated Things based on a category, e.g., temperature measurement).

The end-user interacts with the TSMatch engine via an Android app (TSMatch client). Moreover, TSMatch relies on the following external components:

- **An MQTT broker.** TSMatch currently relies on an MQTT broker based on Mosquitto as message bus. The TSMatch client and engine interconnect to the Thing discovery: IoT Thing discovery is supported via Coaty.io[6].
- **Service registry**. Holds a set of service descriptions. Currently holds environment monitoring service specification examples based on OWL and WSDL, which the user can select via the TSMatch client.

8.3.1 Setup

The TSMatch operation considers two phases. During setup, TSMatch performs discovery of existing IoT devices via the coaty.io open-source middleware, and ontologies can also be imported.

For discovery, it is assumed that IoT devices have an integrated coaty agent or are interconnected to a hub that holds such agent. Therefore, when an IoT device boots up or becomes active after a period of inactivity, it publishes its TD via coaty. These TDs are stored on the local database co-located to the TSMatch engine. The semantic matchmaking module subscribes to Thing discovery events. When a new TD is received, or when there is a change in the TD, then the semantic matchmaking process computes the new data elements

---

[6] https://coaty.io/

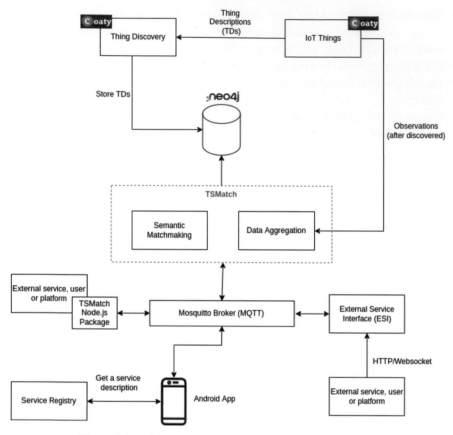

Figure 8.2   High-level perspective of the TSMatch architecture.

as described in the next subsection and stores the new data nodes on the local database (graphDB).

8.3.2 Runtime

Before running the semantic matchmaking algorithm, the TD files as well as the names of the ontology elements are pre-processed to clean up the data, i.e., to perform tokenization, remove punctuation, etc. After the pre-processing step, the TDs are passed to one of the selected semantic matchmaking algorithms. The algorithm matches the given TDs to the ontology elements. Then a relation is created in the graph database between each TD and the ontology nodes that it is being compared with.

```
. . .
"sensor": {
    "name": "LightIntensity",
    "description": "Light intensity in Lux",
    "type": "object",
    "readOnly: "true",
    "properties": {
        "LightIntensity": {
            type": "number",
            "readOnly": true
        }
    }
    . . .
}
. . .
```

Figure 8.3 Description of a service enriched with information from the FIESTA-IoT ontology.

An example of a TD description is provided in Figure 8.3, where the "name" and "description" attributes (first level attributes) will be used by the algorithm to perform a check against ontologies' categories. The algorithm performs multiple interactions based on a depth search on the respective provided ontology/ies.

The matchmaking relies on a Natural Language Processing (NLP) neural network-based approach that has been compared with i) a statistical approach, based on sentence similarity; iii) a clustering-based approach. The NLP neural network model-based approach (W2VEC) has been tested and shown to achieve better results in comparison to a clustering approach derived from K-means, and to a cosine similarity approach [23][7,8].

After matches are found, the relations between the nodes representing sensor descriptions and specific categories of ontologies are created.

The third step on the algorithm concerns data aggregation. Upon receiving a service request, the data aggregation module checks for the aggregated TD nodes on the database, subscribes (via MQTT) to data from the respective

---

[7] https://github.com/fiesta-iot/ontology.
[8] https://git.fortiss.org/iiot_external/tsmatch/-/tree/master/dataset/ontology

sensors, and performs data aggregation based on a simple average function. Based on the service example described in Figure 8.3, the algorithm discovers TDs stored in the database with a stored relation to "Illuminance," "Lux," "LightSensor," and "Environment."

Ontology nodes also on the database. It sends a response back to the requesting service (on the TSMatch client), providing information about the sensors, based on the TDs as shown in Figure 8.4. Moreover, the algorithm gets data from the respective IoT devices (via MQTT, as a subscriber) and then performs data aggregation (simple average) and periodically sends the results to the requesting service, as shown in Figure 8.5.

Figure 8.4   TSMatch client, interface that obtains the available descriptions of existing sensors in an infrastructure in real time.

Monitor

Get observations from available IoT Things

Temperature - room: 1 floor: 15 building: HT2

Temperature - room: 1 floor: 16 building: HT

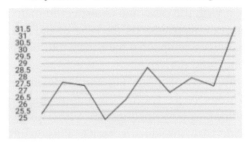

Figure 8.5 TSMatch, temperature monitoring, aggregated results derived from the TSMatch ML-based matchmaking process.

8.4 Semantic Matchmaking Challenges for IoT

As mentioned earlier, semantic matchmaking can be applied to various fields including IoT; however, with each field of application, new requirements and challenges are to be considered. Based on the scenario described earlier, the objective is to semantically match the semantic description of IoT Things with Services, to achieve a finer data matching, and to be able to provide enriched data-based services. Besides providing semantic matchmaking between the IoT Things attributes (e.g., temperature attribute) and the service input signature, other aspects need to be considered, as follows:

- **Integration of functional and non-functional requirements**. To ensure a match that supports interoperability between the IoT Things and the services, non-functional requirements beyond security may be relevant to be integrated. An example of a non-functional requirement could be data compliance aspects, for instance.
- **Integration of user requirements**. Users in this scenario can be the manager of the facilities where the IoT Things are located. Such user requirements can be provided in the form of user preferences (e.g., preference in terms of non-functional service requirement, for instance, cost), but also in the form of quality of experience (QoE) feedback (e.g., level of satisfaction with the outcome of a specific match process). This way, the user can put constraints on the type of IoT data to be utilized and shared with services or specify the bandwidth constraints that may impact the frequency and data rate.
- **Integration of context-awareness**. The aim is to consider the surrounding context of Things (e.g., room temperature for a specific sensor installed on a machine in a room) together with Things attributes (e.g., temperature provided by the sensor itself). This would provide fine-grained and more accurate matching since it allows the differentiation between sub-types and application of IoT Things.
- **Integrate in the semantic approach design energy awareness and processing time reduction**. To meet far edge constraints, use semantic approaches that reduce the processing time (e.g., real-time requirements) and power consumption, among other aspects.
- **Interoperability across domains**. IoT is applied to various vertical domains. In many IoT scenarios, communication and integration across domains is required; hence, it is necessary to reduce the limitation associated with using a knowledge-based approach mainly due to the risk of having incomplete and complex models that require high maintenance.
- **Integration of a feedback loop to the user, to improve QoE**. Provide useful feedback to both the user and the service about the matching process (e.g., ranking of matches, information about the criteria selected for the match).

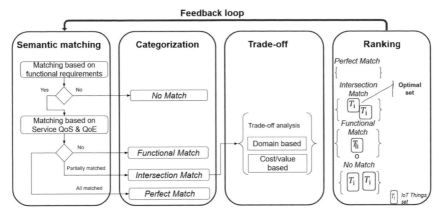

Figure 8.6   IoT Things to service semantic matchmaking approach.

- **Integration of a learning approach**. IoT solutions are constantly evolving; hence, building a matching solution that is able to learn from the previous matches to improve future matches is key.

8.5 Evolving Semantic Matchmaking at the Edge

To fulfill the requirements of semantic matchmaking between existing IoT Things and services at the edge, we propose the following five-step approach as illustrated in Figure 8.6, which are further described in the next subsections.

1. **Hybrid semantic matchmaking**: After discovering the available IoT Things descriptions and receiving the service semantic request, use a hybrid semantic approach to match both the functional and non-functional requirements of the service with the IoT Things while considering user requirements (e.g., QoE) as constraints.
2. **Categorization**: Group IoT Things based on the semantic matchmaking results, to reflect the degree of matched requirements.
3. **Tradeoff**: In case of a partial match of functional and non-functional requirements of the service, use tradeoff analysis to optimize for a specific goal to support the identification of an optimal set of IoT Things.
4. **Ranking**: Considering the results of the categorization and the tradeoff analysis, rank IoT Things sets and highlight the match criteria and optimization goal to the user and the IoT service to support further decisions.

5. **Feedback loop**: Use previous matched results to learn and optimize the hybrid semantic matchmaking and tradeoff analysis.

8.5.1 Hybrid semantic matchmaking

Hybrid semantic matchmaking brings together the advantage of both knowledge-based and statistical categories. A novel approach also needs to fulfill the requirements described in Section 8.3. Such a hybrid approach is based on an algorithm that takes into consideration the novel aspects of integrating IoT service requirements, IoT user requirements, and IoT Things attributes.

Such an automated semantic matchmaking algorithm needs to be able to find similarities between criteria required by the service, the user, and the features of the existing IoT Things.

First, the main parameters to be matched for the service are the service functional requirements meaning the service requested IoT input data and the service QoS, for example, sampling rate, resolution, or delay of the IoT data. Second, the user requirements or QoE refer to the user criteria to accept/be satisfied with the provided functionality and integration between the IoT Things and the service. Such a user could be the manager of the environment hosting the IoT Things. For instance, a user can specify requirements regarding the network usage, IoT Things energy consumption in case of battery-operated IoT Things, or the type of data shared, e.g., public (i.e., services requesting such data can have access without permission), private (i.e., requires permission from the user), or restricted data (i.e., cannot be shared with external services). Finally, some of the key aspects of the IoT Things descriptions to be considered in the semantic matchmaking are as follows:

- The IoT Things observed property, for example, temperature, occupancy, and presence.
- The IoT Things observation type, which refers to the value type created based on environmental stimuli, for example, 27°C.
- The IoT Things feature refers to the specific feature we are observing or measuring its property, for example, environment, machine, human, etc.
- The IoT Things spatial property is the area of observation or location, for instance, a factory in a specific city.
- The IoT Things capabilities group the set of specifications that describe aspects of the provided observations such as range and accuracy.

Now that we identified the various concepts to be matched, the next step is to use hybrid semantic matchmaking to identify which IoT Things fulfill the needed requirements. Thus, the main phases of the hybrid semantic matchmaking approach are illustrated in Figure 8.7.

As a first step, IoT Things are discovered using an IoT crawler or a web of things search engine (WoTSE). These tools can assist in automatically identifying existing IoT devices in an infrastructure, and in storing their TDs [18]. Then, relevant concepts for matching are retrieved from the descriptions, e.g., IoT Thing name, observed property, feature of interest, spatial property, capabilities, pre-processed, stored, accuracy, sampling rate, etc. This is an ongoing process to update, remove, or add IoT Things information to reflect the current state of the IoT environment.

The second step aims at organizing and grouping the IoT Things information. The goal is to match the incoming service requests with a subset of IoT Things relevant for the service instead of the full set to reduce processing time and computations. Different machine learning methods can be used for that purpose, for instance, clustering and categorization methods. Clustering algorithms are unsupervised learning techniques used to group similar data points without prior knowledge of the groups, while categorization algorithms are a supervised learning technique where a model is trained to predict the category/class based on labeled data. In IoT scenarios, the categories are not predefined and depend on the set of IoT Things available in an environment. Creating a fine list of IoT Things categories would be challenging and would need to be updated constantly to reflect the constant development of new

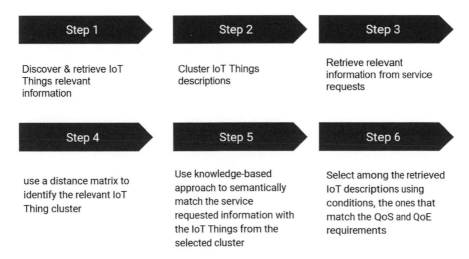

Figure 8.7 Steps of the proposed hybrid semantic matchmaking approach.

solutions. Thus, unsupervised learning techniques such as clustering methods seem to be more suitable for grouping a set of IoT Things without prior knowledge of the groups and classes available in the environment. Different clustering methods can be selected, such as centroid-based clustering (e.g., k-means), ensity-based clustering (e.g., Density-based Spatial Clustering of Applications with Noise (DBSCAN)), hierarchical clustering (e.g., agglomerative hierarchical clustering), or distribution-based clustering (e.g., Gaussian mixture model), to name a few.

Selecting the adequate unsupervised learning technique would need to consider the following requirements:

- IoT Things information is non-numerical data that may have different dimensions and incomplete information.
- Small number of IoT Things in the environment.
- Limited computation power on the edge.
- Varying number of clusters depending on the IoT Things available in the environment.

A potential unsupervised learning technique to investigate is hierarchical clustering since it is known to handle non-numerical data with different dimensions and incomplete data. It does not require a predefined number of clusters, can determine the number of clusters based on the data, and is able to work with a small amount of data. However, the main disadvantages of hierarchical clustering are its high computational complexity and lack of scalability, especially for large amounts of data. Hence, different clustering methods might be used depending on the scale of the IoT environment in consideration.

The third step relates to retrieving and pre-processing relevant information from the service, e.g., service description text, location, domain, service input, and required QoS. As the fourth step, the algorithm can use a distance (similarity) matrix to match the service-requested information (functional requirements) to the centroid of each cluster to identify the most relevant cluster of IoT Things. In step 5, the algorithm would apply a knowledge-based approach to semantically match the service-requested information with the selected cluster. Depending on the specific identified cluster domain, a specific ontology could be considered, or a standard (such as SAREF) may assist in interoperability across different domains/different ontologies.

Finally, a rule- and condition-based approach is used to identify if the selected IoT Things meet the required QoS requirements of the service and the user QoE. Thus, the input from the user and the requirements from the service should be extracted based on which the set of rules are developed. Then, performance data from the IoT Things are analyzed against these rules to determine if they meet the service requirements. It is important that the IoT Things performance data are updated over time along with an ongoing evaluation to assure that these requirements are met over time.

The proposed hybrid semantic approach has the advantage of using clustering techniques and similarity matrix to reduce the problem space of the ontology matching, leading to less processing time while maintaining fine-grained matching. Moreover, existing standard ontologies can be automatically selected and used depending on the scenario, hence removing the need to develop and maintain a cross-domain ontology. Different concepts from different stakeholders are included in the matching process to ensure a comprehensive IoT Thing to service matching solution. However, the matching accuracy is influenced by the clustering algorithm, which may cause false positives and the selected ontology form the knowledge-based matching ; therefore, it is important to use the feedback loop to help automatically adjust the clustering parameters and select the adequate ontology to improve the precision.

8.5.2 Categorization

Based on the semantic matchmaking, the next stage is to categorize and group the IoT TDs based on the level of identified matches. Therefore, we propose the following categories, which can be derived from the results of the hybrid semantic matchmaking process.

- **Exact match**: When all three selection criteria are met, which include the IoT service required IoT data input, QoS, and the user QoE.
- **Functional match**: When only the functional requirements are matched. For example, a set of IoT Things that can provide the environmental temperature at location A is found; however, they do not meet both the user QoE and the IoT service QoS.
- **Intersection match**: Refers to having a functional match plus partially matched QoS and QoE requirements. This is a challenging category since IoT Things falling in this category would need to be ranked. For example, if one set of IoT Things fulfills all functional requirements plus two service QoS and one user QoE while another set meets all functional requirements plus one (different) IoT QoS and one (different) user QoE, how can both sets be compared?

- **No match**: When the service functional requirements cannot be matched.

8.5.3 Tradeoff

For the intersection match category, a further analysis is required to rank the set of IoT Things that fall into this group. The analysis should enable the comparison between different QoS and QoE requirements to permit ranking. One option is to use tradeoff analysis to serve a specific optimization goal. The optimization goal can be either defined by the user or derived from the operation domain and adjusted using the feedback loop. A domain-based tradeoff analysis, for instance, would optimize to fulfill the domain-specific requirements; therefore, the requirements relevant to the domain in question have higher value and hence higher ranking.

Using the categorization of IoT Things combined with the tradeoff analysis matching, the goal is to identify the optimal set of IoT Things among available ones by ranking them and providing useful information to the service and the user regarding the selection criteria such as the list of matched concepts and the optimization goal used. We proposed the following ranking classes:

- **Perfect match**: Provide a list of IoT Things that match perfectly functional, QoE, and QoS requirements.
- **Intersection match**: If no-perfect match is not available, select a set of IoT Things that match the functional requirements as well as partial QoS and QoE requirements. This ranking is affected by the tradeoff process since it creates various IoT Things selections, taking into consideration the optimization goal of the tradeoff analysis.
- **Functional match**: A set of IoT Things that only fulfill the functional requirements.

8.5.4 Feedback Loop

Based on the IoT service selected/used set of IoT Things compared to the identified optimal set of IoT Things, a feedback loop can be established to enable learning. Various information can be adjusted such as automatically associating a tradeoff goal to a specific domain, identifying relevant QoS and QoE for a specific IoT domain, adjusting the clustering algorithm's parameters, re-evaluating the similarity measures used, or reducing the processing time by focusing on specific aspects most relevant for the service category.

8.6 Conclusion

Semantic matchmaking provides a way to tackle some interoperability challenges in IoT environments, via the use of semantic definitions of sensors, actuators, machines, and IoT services. Based on standardized approaches, and on the use of supervising-based approaches, it is feasible to reduce the operational cost of setting up and maintaining large-scale IoT infrastructures. While there are solutions, such as TSMatch, which perform such matchmaking already with some degree of freedom, the increasing variety of vendor-based approaches across different vertical domains require an approach that considers unsupervised learning.

Hence, in this chapter and to further provide an answer to the challenges of semantic matchmaking between IoT Things and services on the edge, a five-step approach is proposed. The approach includes using a hybrid semantic matchmaking to match between the IoT Things extracted information and the service requests, categorize the matching results based on the completeness of the match, use tradeoff analysis to decide on the ranking of partial matches, rank the IoT Things subset from no-match to perfect-match, select the optimal IoT Things subset that meets the service request and finally use a feedback loop to improve the process. Overall, the approach aims to optimize on the edge identification of an optimal set of IoT Things to fulfill the requirements of the service including its quality of service while considering the user requirements and the specifications of IoT scenarios and use cases as constraints.

Acknowledgements

The work described in this chapter has been partially supported by the H2020 projects EU-IoT project funded by the European Union's Horizon 2020 Research and Innovation Programme under Grant Agreement no. 956671 and H2020 DT-ICT-07-2018-2019 project "European Connected Factory Platform for Agile Manufacturing" (EFPF) under Grant Agreement no. 825075.

References

[1] Sebastian Raff. The MQTT Community. Available online: https://gith ub.com/mqtt/mqtt.github.io/wik.

[2] OPC Foundation. OPC Unified Architecture: Interoperability for Industrie 4.0 and the Internet of Things. pp. 1-44. Available online: https://opcfoundation.org/wp-content/uploads/2017/11/OPC-UA-Interoperability-For-Industrie4-and-IoT-EN.pdf

[3] Leitner, S.-H.; Mahnke, W. OPC-UA/Service-Oriented Architecture for Industrial Applications; Technical Report; ABB Corporate Research Center: 2006.

[4] Gergely Marcell Honti, Janos Abonyi, "A Review of Semantic Sensor Technologies in Internet of Things Architectures", *Complexity*, vol. 2019, Article ID 6473160, 21 pages, 2019. https://doi.org/10.1155/2019/6473160

[5] EU-IoT OntoCommons Ontological Interoperability report.

[6] Giunchiglia, F., & Shvaiko, P. (2003). Semantic matching. The Knowledge Engineering Review, 18(3), 265-280.

[7] Ferrara, A., Montanelli, S., Noessner, J., & Stuckenschmidt, H. (2011, May). Benchmarking matching applications on the semantic web. In Extended Semantic Web Conference (pp. 108-122). Springer, Berlin, Heidelberg.

[8] Gmati, F. E., Ayadi, N. Y., Bahri, A., Chakhar, S., & Ishizaka, A. (2016, April). Customizable Web services matching and ranking tool: Implementation and evaluation. In International Conference on Web Information Systems and Technologies (pp. 15-36). Springer, Cham.

[9] Wan, S., Lan, Y., Guo, J., Xu, J., Pang, L., & Cheng, X. (2016, March). A deep architecture for semantic matching with multiple positional sentence representations. In Proceedings of the AAAI Conference on Artificial Intelligence (Vol. 30, No. 1).

[10] Wang, J., Pan, M., He, T., Huang, X., Wang, X., & Tu, X. (2020). A pseudo-relevance feedback framework combining relevance matching and semantic matching for information retrieval. Information Processing & Management, 57(6), 102342.

[11] Ru, L., Zhang, B., Duan, J., Ru, G., Sharma, A., Dhiman, G., ... & Masud, M. (2021). A detailed research on human health monitoring system based on internet of things. Wireless Communications and Mobile Computing, 2021.

[12] Hasan, S., & Curry, E. (2014). Approximate semantic matching of events for the internet of things. ACM Transactions on Internet Technology (TOIT), 14(1), 1-23.

[13] Akritidis, L., Fevgas, A., Bozanis, P., & Makris, C. (2020). A self-verifying clustering approach to unsupervised matching of product titles. Artificial Intelligence Review, 53(7), 4777-4820.

[14] Cassar, G., Barnaghi, P., Wang, W., & Moessner, K. (2012, November). A hybrid semantic matchmaker for IoT services. In 2012 IEEE International Conference on Green Computing and Communications (pp. 210-216). IEEE.

[15] Klusch, M., Fries, B., & Sycara, K. (2006, May). Automated semantic web service discovery with OWLS-MX. In Proceedings of the fifth international joint conference on Autonomous agents and multiagent systems (pp. 915-922).

[16] Otero-Cerdeira, L., Rodríguez-Martínez, F. J., & Gómez-Rodríguez, A. (2015). Ontology matching: A literature review. Expert Systems with Applications, 42(2), 949-971.

[17] Shvaiko, P., & Euzenat, J. (2011). Ontology matching: state of the art and future challenges. IEEE Transactions on knowledge and data engineering, 25(1), 158-176.

[18] F. Skarmeta, J. Santa, J. A. Martínez, J. X. Parreira, P. Barnaghi, S. Enshaeifar, M. J. Beliatis, M. A. Presser, T. Iggena, M. Fischer et al., "Iotcrawler: Browsing the internet of things," in 2018 Global Internet of Things Summit (GIoTS). IEEE, 2018, pp. 1-6.

[19] Fenza, Giuseppe, Vincenzo Loia, and Sabrina Senatore. "A hybrid approach to semantic web services matchmaking." International Journal of Approximate Reasoning 48.3 (2008): 808-828.

[20] N. Bnouhanna, E. Karabulut, R. C. Sofia, E. E. Seder, G. Scivoletto and G. Insolvibile, "An Evaluation of a Semantic Thing To Service Matching Approach in Industrial IoT Environments," 2022 IEEE International Conference on Pervasive Computing and Communications Workshops and other Affiliated Events (PerCom Workshops), 2022, pp. 433-438, doi: 10.1109/PerComWorkshops53856.2022.9767519. Pisa, Italy.

[21] E. Karabulut, N. Bnouhanna, R. C. Sofia, ML-based data classification and data aggregation on the edge. inProc. ACM CoNext2021, December 2021, Munich, Germany. Student poster. https://doi.org/10.1145/3488 658.3493786.

[22] N. Bnouhanna, R. C. Sofia and A. Pretschner, "IoT Thing to Service Matching" 2021 IEEE International Conference on Pervasive Computing and Communications Workshops and other Affiliated Events

(PerCom Workshops), 2021, pp. 418-419, vol 1, pp 418-419, DOI; 10.1109/PerComWorkshops51409.2021.9431128

[23] E. Karabulut, R. C. Sofia, J. Ott, https://www.overleaf.com/project/61d ff801dd153d87a37f1460.Masterdissertation,2022.Shortversionundersu bmission(2023).

9

A Scalable, Heterogeneous Hardware Platform for Accelerated AIoT based on Microservers

R. Griessl[1], F. Porrmann[1], N. Kucza[1], K. Mika[1], J. Hagemeyer[1],
M. Kaiser[1], M. Porrmann[2], M. Tassemeier[2], M. Flottmann[2],
F. Qararyah[3], M. Waqar[3], P. Trancoso[3], D. Ödman[4], K. Gugala[5],
and G. Latosinski[5]

[1]Bielefeld University, Germany
[2]Osnabrück University, Germany
[3]Chalmers University of Technology, Sweden
[4]EMBEDL AB, Sweden
[5]Antmicro, Poland
E-mail: rgriessl@techfak.uni-bielefeld.de;
fporrmann@techfak.uni-bielefeld.de;
nkucza@techfak.uni-bielefeld.de; kmika@techfak.uni-bielefeld.de;
jhagemey@techfak.uni-bielefeld.de; mkaiser@techfak.uni-bielefeld.de;
mporrmann@uni-osnabrueck.de; marco.tassemeier@uni-osnabrueck.de;
mflottmann@uni-osnabrueck.de; qararyah@chalmers.se;
waqarm@chalmers.se; ppedro@chalmers.se; zouzoula@chalmers.se;
daniel@embedl.ai; kgugala@antmicro.com; glatosinski@antmicro.com

Abstract

Performance and energy efficiency are key aspects of next-generation AIoT
hardware. This chapter presents a scalable, heterogeneous hardware platform
for accelerated AIoT based on microserver technology. It integrates several
accelerator platforms based on technologies like CPUs, embedded GPUs,
FPGAs, or specialized ASICs, supporting the full range of the cloud−edge-
IoT continuum. The modular microserver approach enables the integration

179   DOI: 10.1201/9781032632407-11

of different, heterogeneous accelerators into one platform. Benchmarking the various accelerators takes performance, energy efficiency, and accuracy into account. The results provide a solid overview of available accelerator solutions and guide hardware selection for AIoT applications from the far edge to the cloud.

Keywords: IoT, machine learning, AIoT, microserver, deep learning, (far) edge-computing, FPGA, accelerator, energy-efficiency, performance classification.

9.1 Introduction

Looking into novel architectures optimized to accelerate the computation of neural networks, adaptable and scalable hardware solutions tailored to the applications' requirements are a key component. A fully featured, heterogeneous hardware platform integrating several accelerators is described and evaluated in the following. Over the last years, a large number of diverse DL accelerators in the form of special ASICs or IP cores, as well as GPU- or FPGA-based solutions, have been introduced in the market. This chapter focuses on benchmarking, and a comparative evaluation of selected accelerators regarding performance, energy efficiency, and accuracy is performed. Together with the seamless integration of DL into the IoT hardware platforms, the benchmarking methodology is used for further optimizing applications toward performance and energy efficiency. The presented work has been part of the VEDLIoT project [1]. In this chapter, we present a summary of the results obtained. More details are available in the respective project deliverables [2], [3].

9.2 Heterogeneous Hardware Platform for the Cloud-edge-IoT Continuum

This section deals with the hardware architecture and presents the different accelerators evaluated. It also acts as an introduction and classification for the different accelerators used in the benchmarking section.

The hardware platform can be used as a joint infrastructure for different developments. It supports a wide range of AIoT applications that can be addressed using a flexible communication infrastructure and exchangeable microservers. Figure 9.1 shows the RECS platforms covering application

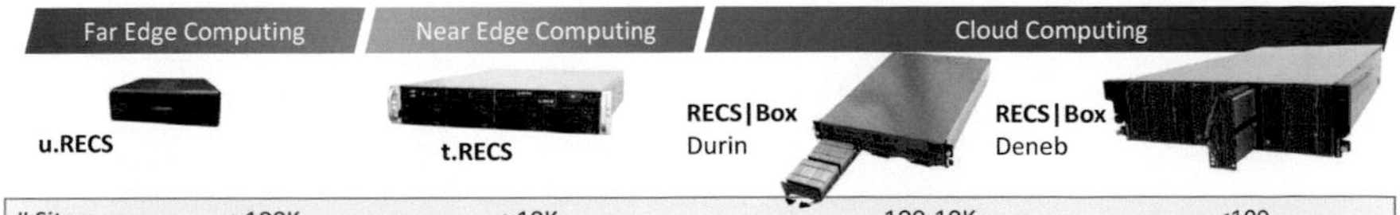

# Sites	>100K	>10K	100-10K	<100
Footprint	Custom	Compact (1RU)	Medium (2RU)	Large (3RU)
Power Budget	<30 W	< 500 W	500 W – 2 KW	> 2 KW
# Microserver	max 2	up to 3	up to 48	up to 144

Figure 9.1 Overview of modular and scalable RECS platforms.

domains from embedded/far-edge computing toward cloud computing. All platforms commonly target heterogeneous computing with tightly coupled microservers. The cloud computing platform RECS|Box consists of either two or three rack units and aims for high-density applications using hundreds of microservers with high-bandwidth communication requirements. t.RECS houses up to three microservers in one rack unit and focuses on edge computing scenarios with low-latency demands like image and video processing use cases or 5G base stations. u.RECS rounds off the range of the RECS family toward low-power and compact embedded computing.

Microservers are based on industry-standard computer-on-module (COM) form factors, allowing for flexible and heterogeneous processing. On the one hand, RECS|Box and t.RECS support microservers that are based on COM express and COM-HPC server and client standards. The u.RECS, on the other hand, supports multiple compact form factors for far-edge computing, including SMARC, Jetson NX, Xilinx Kria, and Raspberry Pi compute modules.

9.2.1 Cloud computing platform RECS|Box

The RECS|Box platform is available in two different chassis sizes. The small chassis with 2U (Durin) is meant as a starter chassis, mainly for evaluation and non-datacenter use cases, while the 3U (Deneb) chassis is to be used in larger installations. The RECS|Box server architecture supports microservers based on x86 (e.g., Intel Xeon), 64-bit ARM mobile/embedded SoCs, 64-bit ARM server processors, FPGAs, GPUs, as well as other PCIe-based acceleration units. The smaller Durin can be equipped with up to 9 high-performance (HP) microservers or with 48 low-power (LP) microservers, and the larger Deneb can host 27 HP microservers or 144 LP microservers. The large amount of microservers inside the systems requires a sophisticated

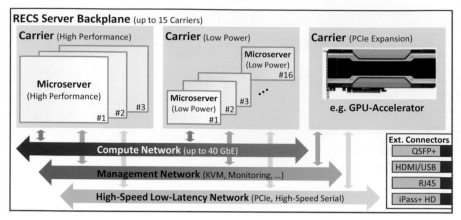

Figure 9.2　Communication architecture of RECS|Box platform.

communication infrastructure. Therefore, the RECS|Box comes up with multiple communication standards depicted in Figure 9.2.

The basis is the Ethernet network. It provides multiple 1 and 10 Gbit/s links to every microserver. Furthermore, it is internally switched and supports upstream bandwidth toward the top of the rack (ToR) switch up to 120 Gbit/s, combining three 40 Gbit/s links. In addition to the Ethernet communication infrastructure, a dedicated high-speed low-latency (HSLL) communication network is integrated into the RECS|Box architecture. It consists of two levels. On the physical level, the HSLL can directly connect high-speed serial links between microservers, as commonly available in FPGA modules. For processor-driven microservers (e.g., x86 based), the second level is PCIe-based direct host-2-host communication. Similar to the Ethernet network, it is internally switched and provides bandwidth of up to 56 Gbit/s to every microserver. The bandwidth toward a PCIe ToR switch is up to 336 Gbit/s, combining three 112 Gbit/s links.

9.2.2 Near-edge computing platform t.RECS

While the RECS|Box cloud hardware, described in the section above, focuses on data center applications, the edge server architecture supports local applications with high demands for low-latency, safety, and security. Especially applications with user interaction require local (pre-) processing and reduction of large amounts of data, which are difficult to achieve using a cloud-based approach. Three microserver modules of the COM-HPC standard

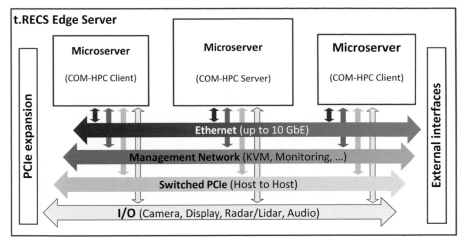

Figure 9.3 Communication architecture of t.RECS platform.

can be placed on the carrier board, supporting microservers based on x86 (e.g., Intel Xeon), 64-bit ARM server processors, FPGAs, GPU SoCs (e.g., NVIDIA Jetson AGX), as well as PCIe-based acceleration units via the PCIe expansion slot.

The t.RECS has a powerful and scalable communication infrastructure as shown in Figure 9.3. It is derived from the RECS|Box cloud platform and provides the basis for closely coupled heterogeneous compute nodes. The internal bandwidth for Ethernet, as well as HSLL, is the same as that in the RECS|Box, but the external bandwidth is reduced to single external links of 40 Gbit/s for Ethernet and 112 Gbit/s for HSLL.

9.2.3 Far-edge computing platform u.RECS

The architecture of the u.RECS is presented in Figure 9.4. The two integrated module slots support the SMARC 2.1 standard and the NVIDIA Jetson NX standard. In addition to the two module slots, a PCIe M.2 slot and an mPCIe slot are integrated, which can be used to add further accelerators or communication methods, such as 5G, to the u.RECS. Furthermore, communication options, e.g. Ethernet or PCIe and energy measurement methods, are integrated on the board to make the u.RECS a perfect fit for a wide range of AIoT use cases.

The NVIDIA Jetson NX module slot is capable of supporting Xavier NX and Orin NX SoC modules. These modules have ARM CPUs combined

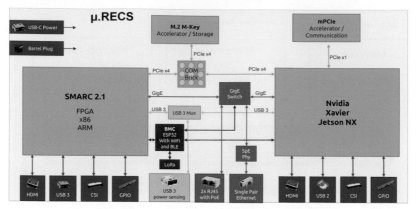

Figure 9.4 Architecture of u.RECS platform.

with latest NVIDIA GPU technology. Support for the SMARC 2.1 standard gives the u.RECS access to a wide range of COMs and ML accelerators, as SMARC modules are available in the market through different module manufacturers, such as Congatec, ADLINK Technology, or others. The SMARC slot can be equipped with, among others, the following types of microservers:

- ARM CPU (e.g., i.MX 8)
- x86 CPU (e.g., Atom CPU)
- FPGA (e.g., Xilinx Zynq UltraScale+)

There are a number of additional ML accelerators that can be equipped in or connected to an M.2 or mPCIe slot. Additionally, it is possible to connect accelerators via USB 3.0 and access them from one of the compute modules. Furthermore, with the u.RECS, it is possible to measure the energy of an accelerator connected via USB. Accelerators supported this way include:

- Intel Myriad X
- Hailo-8
- Google Coral

9.3 Accelerator Overview

There are many accelerators available for a wide range of applications, from small embedded systems with power budgets in the order of milliwatt to cloud platforms with a power consumption exceeding 400 W. Figure 9.5 provides an overview of the different accelerators using a double logarithmic plot, grouping them into three groups, depending on their peak performance values

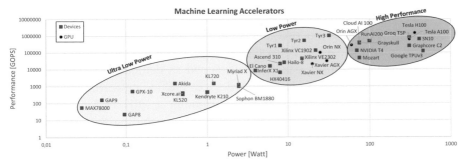

Figure 9.5 Theoretical performance of AI accelerators and classification into performance groups.

(in giga-operations per second). It should be noted that values provided by the vendors are used; so no normalization regarding technology, precision, or architecture is performed. On average, an energy efficiency of about 1 Tera Operation per W (1 TOPS/W) is achieved. In the following paragraphs, the main characteristics of the three performance groups are discussed.

Ultra-low power (<3 W): The ultra-low power group of accelerators is mainly devices integrating energy-efficient, microcontroller-style cores combined with compact accelerators for DL-specific functions. They are focusing on generic IoT applications like the Maxim MAX78000, the Ambient Scientific GPX-10, or the BrainChip Akida, providing only simple analog or digital interfaces. Other devices such as the Greenwave GAP 8 and GAP 9, the Canaan Kendryte K210, or the Kneron KL530 and KL720 also aim at vision processing, providing an additional camera interface. Typically, those devices are directly designed into the application itself without using a modular or microserver-based approach, simply because all interfaces and peripherals are integrated. Only the Bitmain Sophon BM1880 and Intel Myriad X are providing a generic USB interface and are designed to act as accelerator devices attached to a regular host processor. None of these devices integrates external memory controller interfaces. Based on its wide availability, the Intel Myriad X device is included in the benchmarking activity.

Low power (3−35 W): While the previous group of accelerators is focusing on applications with a very low-power envelope (often in a battery-powered environment with no special requirements regarding cooling), the low-power group of accelerators includes accelerators for a wide range of applications in automation and automotive. All devices include high-speed interfaces for external memories, and peripherals, as well as high-speed communication toward other processing devices or host systems, such as PCIe, proving excellent capabilities for a modular, microserver-based approach as supported by the RECS platform. Apart from the Hailo-8, the FlexLogix InferX X1, and the VSORA Tyr family, which are designed as dedicated accelerators attached to an external host processor, all devices include powerful, general-purpose application processors, capable of running a fully fledged Linux operating system. In addition to specialized ASICs including the Coherent Logix HX40416, the Blaize El Cano, or the Huawei Ascend 310, this group also includes embedded GPUs from NVIDIA, in particular, the Jetson family, starting from the Nano and TX2, via the Xavier NX and Orin NX devices all the way up to the AGX Xavier. The Xilinx Versal Core AI VC1902 and Versal Edge AI VE2302 are explained in detail in the following section.

High performance (>35 W): The high-performance group of accelerators includes devices with up to 450 W of TDP, suitable for both inference and training use cases, typically deployed in the form of a PCIe extension cards for edge or cloud servers. Besides the classical NVIDIA Tesla GPGPUs including Tesla V100, A100, and H100, also dedicated ASICs like the Groq TSP, the SambaNova SN10, the Graphcore C2, or the Google TPUv3 are part of this cluster. In addition, also powerful inference ASICs like the SimpleMachines Mozart, the Tenstorrent Grayskull, the Qualcomm Cloud AI 100 Chip, or the Untether AI RunAI200 are included. As a reference, also a consumer-class NVIDIA Geforce GTX 1660 GPU has been included in the benchmarking. The NVIDIA Jetson AGX Orin is also part of this group due to its high power envelope, although it is part of the embedded NVIDIA Jetson family.

9.3.1 Reconfigurable accelerators

Field programmable gate arrays (FPGAs) are a promising alternative to GPUs and TPUs. Due to their reconfigurable architecture, these devices can be adapted to the specific requirements of an application, making them promising candidates for the resource-efficient processing of machine learning algorithms. For acceleration of deep learning models on their FPGAs, Xilinx provides a dedicated IP core, the deep-learning processor unit (DPU). Various FPGA devices are already available in the RECS system, and new devices like Xilinx Versal are expected to be added in the near future. For the easy yet efficient integration of new reconfigurable accelerators into the RECS system, an FPGA base design has been developed, supporting the flexible communication facilities of the RECS platform.

A key advantage of FPGAs over ASICs is their reconfigurability, enabling highly optimized designs for specific application scenarios. However, this reconfigurability comes at a significant overhead in terms of power and performance. This overhead is reduced by the integration of embedded processors and fixed-function units (like DSP blocks and embedded memories) in modern FPGAs. An additional method to increase the resource efficiency of reconfigurable architectures is partial dynamic reconfiguration, enabling, e.g., to switch between different accelerators at runtime. Dynamic reconfiguration can be used to enable the system to automatically adapt to changing environmental conditions, like weather changes, when running a neural network on camera data. In general, accelerators with different power, performance, and accuracy footprints can be selected at runtime.

Figure 9.6 provides an overview of the architecture and supported interfaces of the base design for the u.RECS. For heterogeneous systems, the PCIe interface connects the reconfigurable accelerator to other compute modules and accelerators on the u.RECS. The base design was created with the Xilinx Vitis Core Development Kit (2021.2) in the Vivado block design environment. When targeting different FPGAs or FPGA platforms, the base design needs to be adapted, e.g., because of changed internal or external interfaces. Additionally, other pre- or post-processing steps may be required, as well as a change of the complete application runtime. Hence, a wide variety of different FPGA implementations can be expected, which are difficult to

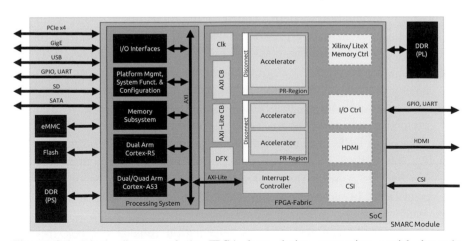

Figure 9.6 Block diagram of the FPGA base design supporting partial dynamic reconfiguration.

manage by hand. Therefore, we have set up a scripting environment that automates the configuration and build process. All necessary calls to the Vitis build system are automated, enabling an easy transition to new platforms. The entire hardware platform as well as the software infrastructure are built automatically, including the configuration of the processing system and the Linux environment. Changes to the FPGA base design, like additional interfaces, located in the FPGA fabric, can be done directly in the script. This is especially important for easy migration between the different FPGAs supported by the RECS platform.

For the evaluation of performance and energy efficiency, various combinations of Xilinx FPGAs and DPU configurations have been generated with the scripting approach described above. UltraScale+ FPGAs have been used, ranging from small (ZU3EG) to large (ZU15EG) devices. The DPUs can be parameterized to match the application requirements, e.g., by varying the inherent parallelism in terms of the peak number of operations per clock cycle. In the next section, FPGA implementations are named by the device and the integrated DPU variant. To give an example, ZU15 2xB4096 refers to a ZU15EG device that integrates the base architecture together with two B4096 DPUs, each capable of processing 4096 INT8 operations per clock cycle. The DPUs are running at a reduced clock frequency of 200 MHz, limited by power constraints of the used boards.

In addition to Xilinx UltraScale+ FPGAs, we have also evaluated the energy efficiency of the new Xilinx Versal architecture, utilizing a VC1902 on the VCK190 evaluation system. The reconfigurable SoCs combine an ARM processing system with a programmable logic fabric and a variety of I/O interfaces. In addition to the classical FPGA-based SoCs, the VC1902 integrates new DSP engines, AI engines, and a network-on-chip infrastructure for communication between the heterogeneous computing resources. For deep learning applications, especially the 400 AI engines are of high interest, promising a significant increase in performance and energy efficiency compared to DPU implementations on the reconfigurable fabric. For the development, Xilinx Vitis AI version 2.5 has been used together with Xilinx Vitis 2022.1. A wide range of configurations can also be selected for the Versal DPU. In our implementation, C32B6 refers to an architecture with six batch handlers, utilizing 32 AI engine cores per batch handler, for a total of 192 AI engines. The implementation runs at a clock frequency of 333 MHz for the programmable logic and 1.25 GHz for the AI engines.

9.4 Benchmarking and Evaluation

9.4.1 Methodology

The evaluation of different accelerators and their corresponding hardware manufacturer's optimization toolchains was conducted using a standard set of convolution neural network (CNN) models. The evaluation utilized three state-of-the-art CNNs – ResNet50 [4], MobileNetV3 [5], and YoloV4 [6] – all of which are from the domains of image recognition and classification. The models were represented using the open neural network exchange (ONNX) [7], which is an open standard for ML algorithms.

For evaluation purposes, two widely used benchmarking datasets were employed: common objects in context (COCO) [8], a comprehensive database for object detection, segmentation, and captioning, and ImageNet [9], the most frequently used dataset for image classification in the large-scale visual recognition challenge (ILSVRC). ImageNet contains 1000 object categories and has 1,281,167 training images, 50,000 validation images, and 100,000 test images. Three versions of each model (ResNet50, MobileNetV3, and YoloV4), each with a different precision, were evaluated. The first version was the original trained model with 32-bit floating-point precision (FP32), followed by two quantized versions of the original model: 16-bit floating-point precision (FP16) and 8-bit integer precision (INT8). The toolchains used for evaluation are summarized in Table 9.1.

In order to evaluate the merit of the hardware platforms for various deployment scenarios with different goals and constraints, we used the following metrics divided into four categories:

- System metrics: **peak performance** in giga-operations per second (GOPS) and **idle power**[1] in Watts (W).

---

[1] The idle power is measured as to determine a more accurate power consumption for the execution.

Table 9.1 Toolchains used for evaluation.

Hardware	Toolchain	Version
NVIDIA GPUs	TensorRT SDK	7.1.3 and 8.0.1 [10]
Intel CPUs, Myriad	OpenVINO	2021.4.1 [11]
Xilinx FPGAs	Vitis AIVitis	1.3 and 2.5 (Versal)2021.2 and 2022.1 (Versal)
Google Coral TPU	TensorFlow [12]TensorFlow Lite	2.4 and 2.52.4 and 2.5
Hailo-8	Hailo Software Suite	4.8.1

- Performance metrics: **inference time** in seconds (s), **achieved performance** in GOPS, and **power consumption** in Watt (W).
- Quality metrics: **accuracy** in percentage (%) and **mean average precision** (mAP or mAP@X) in percentage (%).
- Efficiency metrics: **power efficiency** in GOPS per Watt (GOPS/W).

In this evaluation, two quality metrics were evaluated, each suited for the targeted CNN domain. For image classification, the most crucial quality metric is accuracy, which represents the number of correct classifications divided by the number of images. Accuracy was measured in two ways: top-1 that accuracy measures the frequency of the model prediction with the highest probability matching the ground truth; and top-5 accuracy that measures if the top 5 highest-probability predictions include the ground truth. For object detection, the relevant quality metric is mean average precision (mAP or mAP@X). mAP@X is the area under the precision–recall curve with an intersection over union (IoU) threshold X. For instance, mAP(.50) means that a positive detection must have a minimum IoU of 50%, with everything below being marked as a false detection with a precision of 0%. Another form of mAP is mAP@X:Y, calculated as the average AP over a range of minimum IoUs. We reported the mAP@X:Y from $X = 0.5$ to $Y = 0.95$, with a step size of 0.05.

To determine the power consumption, we utilized tools provided by the hardware vendors, and when these were not available, we used laboratory instruments. For the NVIDIA accelerators, we employed the utilities **Tegrastats** and **nvidia-smi**. The NVIDIA Jetson-Nano was an exception, where, due to the absence of integrated tools, we used an external power meter. The Intel Myriad and its host module were measured using a Tektronix MDO4054B oscilloscope. The Google Coral TPU and its host module were also measured with the same oscilloscope. The power consumption of Hailo-8 was measured inside an NVIDIA Xavier NX evaluation system by plugging it into the M.2 PCIe port and excluding the power consumed by the CPU module. For FPGA-based systems, the complete system power, including external memory and I/O interfaces, was measured. Notice that the power consumption values are also necessary to determine the efficiency metric (typically measured in GOPS/W).

It is important to mention that, due to the limited space, only the evaluation results for the YoloV4 model are presented in this chapter. However, the conclusions in this chapter are still relevant to the results of all other tested models.

9.4.2 Evaluation results

As mentioned before, the optimization toolchains for the evaluated accelerators are vendor-specific and vary between architectures. Despite using the same source for the DL models, we needed to ensure that all devices were performing the same computations and produce comparable results. To validate this, we measured the mAP(.50) and mAP(.50:.95) for each device. Our findings show that the mAP is significantly influenced by the software toolchain used to compile and quantize the models. Therefore, the mAP was grouped into categories based on vendor and quantization (FP32, INT8), as depicted in Figure 9.7.

The NVIDIA FP32 category encompasses all results obtained from NVIDIA devices that used 32-bit floating point (FP32) quantization. The OpenVINO FP32 category combines the results from x86-based processors and the Myriad DL accelerator that employed FP32 quantization.

Furthermore, tests were also conducted using FP16 quantization, but since they only show minor deviations from FP32 ($<0.1\%$), only FP32 and INT8 results are presented here. For the NVIDIA INT8 category, which encompasses all NVIDIA devices using 8-bit integer quantization, the quantization was done using training data from the COCO dataset with the toolchain. The Xilinx INT8 and Hailo-8 INT8 categories were based on pre-quantized models from each vendor's model zoo. Our attempts to quantize the YoloV4 model for these categories resulted in poor precision outcomes. This highlights the significant impact that specific toolchains and hardware expertise can have on quantization and precision.

Figure 9.7 compares the mAP of all tested architectures with the YoloV4 model. Most of the architectures show slight deviations of less than 5%, with the exception of the Xilinx INT8 result, which is nearly 8% lower. Further analysis was conducted by examining the recall–precision gradients for each of the 80 classes the YoloV4 model is trained on. Figure 9.8 presents an example of this analysis, showing the mAP(.50) recall–precision gradients, where objects with an IoU larger than 50% are considered positive detections and are displayed with their corresponding precision. Objects with an IoU less than 50% are considered negative detections and are set to a precision of 0%, which is why the orange and yellow precisions are not present in the figure. Class I (toothbrush) showed the highest deviation for INT8 quantization among the tested devices, with the NVIDIA and Xilinx accelerators performing relatively poorly compared to the Hailo-8 accelerator. This is by far the class with the highest deviation, unlike class II (vase), where all

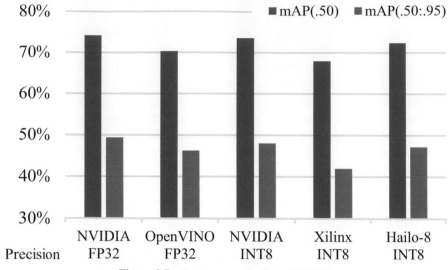

Figure 9.7　Accuracy evaluation of YoloV4.

Figure 9.8　mAP(.50) recall−precision gradients using INT8 for classes I: toothbrush II: vase and accelerators. (a) NVIDIA; (b) Hailo-8 c: Xilinx.

accelerators performed similarly. A detailed analysis of the results, including all 80 COCO classes for each accelerator with floating point and integer quantization, showed that most classes behave like class II. This provides confidence that the accelerators in the evaluation are performing the same tasks and that the results are comparable.

The evaluation in Figure 9.9 shows the achieved performance in GOPS and the power consumption in Watt (W) for the execution of YoloV4 on the different hardware systems. Similar results are obtained for both ResNet50 and MobileNetV3. The notations next to the accelerators (B1, B4, and B8) indicate batch sizes of 1, 4, and 8. For those cases, the metrics are for the complete execution of the batch. It is important to note that the power consumption of all PCIe-based accelerators (Myriad, GTX1660, V100, and

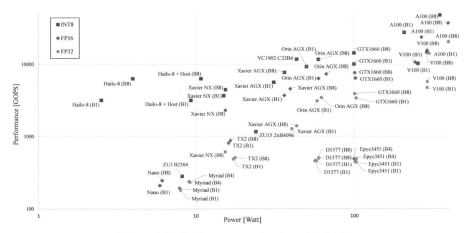

Figure 9.9 Performance evaluation of YoloV4.

A100) has been measured without the host system. For Hailo-8, both cases (with and without the host system) are considered.

Figure 9.9 serves as a reference for making hardware choices based on performance and power requirements. The results can be applied to a variety of use cases by taking into consideration the power domains depicted in Figure 9.5.

Two x86 systems (D1577 and Epyc3451) are provided as a reference to demonstrate the superiority of DL accelerators over traditional processing systems. In terms of energy efficiency, noteworthy platforms include Hailo-8, Xavier NX, Xavier AGX, VC1902, Orin AGX, and A100, catering to different domains, as shown in Figure 9.5.

In this evaluation, three reconfigurable devices (ZU3, ZU15, and VC1902) have also been studied. On the one hand, the Xilinx Zynq devices (ZU3 and ZU15) exhibit relatively low performance compared to the specialized accelerators, as they are basic FPGAs that utilize the Xilinx DPU accelerator. On the other hand, the Xilinx Versal (VC1902) boasts significantly higher performance and energy efficiency due to its built-in DL accelerators. Among all reconfigurable devices, the VC1902 shows the best energy efficiency with INT8 quantization.

The energy efficiency comparison in Figure 9.10 reveals a clear gap between classical processing systems (D1577 and Epyc3541) and DL accelerators. Even older DL accelerators (TX2, Nano, and Myriad) offer better efficiency. Newer GPU-based accelerators (Xavier NX, Xavier AGX, and Orin AGX) provide good efficiency but are obviously surpassed by dedicated

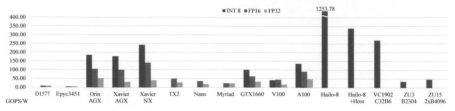

Figure 9.10   Efficiency evaluation of YoloV4. The missing bars for certain platforms represent cases where the precision is not supported.

ASIC-based accelerators (Hailo-8 and VC1902). It is important to note that the power measurement of all PCIe-based accelerators was reported without the power for the host system. The Hailo-8 presents a significant lead when compared to Xavier NX and VC1902.

Overall, this evaluation shows that, when considering the different points in the compute continuum, as presented in Figure 9.9, the Hailo-8 and Xavier NX are well-suited for far-edge computing platforms, while Xavier AGX, VC1902, and Orin AGX fit into near-edge computing platforms, and the A100 can be deployed in cloud computing platforms.

9.5 Conclusion

The main topic of this chapter is the evaluation of heterogeneous AIoT hardware, in particular, accelerators, for deep learning applications. In addition, the RECS hardware platforms are introduced, supporting the complete continuum of heterogeneous cloud, edge, and IoT applications. Especially for scenarios with low power budgets, energy efficiency is crucial, which is only achieved by using specialized hardware accelerators. A set of relevant accelerators was presented and classified into three different performance groups according to their processing capabilities. Besides ASIC- and GPU-based accelerators, emphasis has been put on reconfigurable architectures, presenting a DPU-based FPGA architecture for easy integration of dedicated DL algorithms.

The evaluation methodology was described in detail, discussing the used DL models, corresponding datasets, and used specific toolchains. The performance and efficiency metrics GOPS and GOPS/W were introduced and the quality metrics mAP(0.50) and mAP(0.50:0.95) were used for YoloV4. The power measurement used for this evaluation was described.

Since toolchains are vendor-specific, an evaluation of the accuracy, of the model running on different architectures, was performed. An in-depth analysis of recall−precision gradients per class shows that the results of different architectures using different toolchains are still comparable. The YoloV4 evaluation shows an extensive overview of modern DL accelerators and their performance as well as their energy efficiency. The outcome of this chapter provides a guideline for hardware selection in the area of DL accelerator, ranging from far-edge computing up to cloud computing.

Acknowledgements

This publication incorporates results from the VEDLIoT project, which received funding from the European Union's Horizon 2020 research and innovation program under Grant Agreement No. 957197.

References

[1] Martin Kaiser, Rene Griessl, Nils Kucza, et al. VEDLIoT: Very Efficient Deep Learning in IoT. In *2022 Design, Automation & Test in Europe Conference & Exhibition (DATE)*, pages 963-968, 2022.

[2] Rene Griessl, Karol Gugala, Elaheh Malekzadeh, et al. D 3.1 – Evaluation of existing architectures and compilers for DL, October 2021. VEDLIoT project deliverable.

[3] Rene Griessl, Marco Tassemeier, Pedro Trancoso, Karol Gugala, et al. D 3.3 – Evaluation of the DL accelerator designs, October 2022. VEDLIoT project deliverable.

[4] Kaiming He, Xiangyu Zhang, Shaoqing Ren, and Jian Sun. Deep Residual Learning for Image Recognition. In *Proceedings of the IEEE conference on computer vision and pattern recognition*, pages 770-778, 2016.

[5] Andrew Howard, Mark Sandler, Grace Chu, Liang-Chieh Chen, Bo Chen, Mingxing Tan, Weijun Wang, Yukun Zhu, Ruoming Pang, Vijay Vasudevan, et al. Searching for MobileNetV3. In *Proceedings of the IEEE/CVF international conference on computer vision*, pages 1314-1324, 2019.

[6] Alexey Bochkovskiy, Chien-Yao Wang, and Hong-Yuan Mark Liao. YoloV4: Optimal speed and accuracy of object detection. *arXiv preprint arXiv:2004.10934*, 2020.

[7] Junjie Bai, Fang Lu, Ke Zhang, et al. ONNX: Open Neural Network Exchange. https://github.com/onnx/onnx,2019.

[8] Tsung-Yi Lin, Michael Maire, Serge J. Belongie, Lubomir D. Bourdev, Ross B. Girshick, James Hays, Pietro Perona, Deva Ramanan, Piotr Doll'a r, and C. Lawrence Zitnick. Microsoft COCO: Common Objects in Context. *CoRR*, abs/1405.0312, 2014.

[9] Jia Deng, Wei Dong, Richard Socher, Li-Jia Li, Kai Li, and Li Fei-Fei. ImageNet: A large-scale hierarchical image database. In *2009 IEEE conference on computer vision and pattern recognition*, pages 248-255. Ieee, 2009.

[10] Huang Rao, Chen et al. TensorRT. https://github.com/NVIDIA/Tensor RT,2013.

[11] Paramuzov Lavrenov, Churaev et al. OpenVINO. https://github.com/o penvinotoolkit/openvino,2013.

[12] Martín Abadi, Paul Barham, Jianmin Chen, Zhifeng Chen, Andy Davis, Jeffrey Dean, Matthieu Devin, Sanjay Ghemawat, Geoffrey Irving, Michael Isard, et al. TensorFlow: A System for Large-Scale Machine Learning. In *12th USENIX symposium on operating systems design and implementation (OSDI 16)*, pages 265-283, 2016.

10

Methods for Requirements Engineering, Verification, Security, Safety, and Robustness in AIoT Systems

Marcelo Pasin[1], Jämes Ménétrey[1], Pascal Felber[1], Valerio Schiavoni[1], Hans-Martin Heyn[2], Eric Knauss[2], Anum Khurshid[3], and Shahid Raza[3]

[1]University of Neuchâtel, Switzerland
[2]Gothenburg University, Sweden
[3]Research Institutes of Sweden AB, Sweden
E-mail: marcelo.pasin@unine.ch; james.menetrey@unine.ch; pascal.felber@unine.ch; valerio.schiavoni@unine.ch; hans-martin.heyn@gu.se; eric.knauss@cse.gu.se; anum.khurshid@ri.se; shahid.raza@ri.se

Abstract

This chapter presents methods for requirements engineering, verification, security, safety, and robustness with a special focus on AIoT systems. It covers an architectural framework dealing with requirements engineering aspects of distributed AIoT systems, covering several clusters of concern dealing with the context description of the system, learning environment of the deep-learning components, communication concerns, and a set of quality concerns, such as ethical aspects, safety, power, security, and privacy aspects. Each cluster contains a set of architectural views sorted into different levels of abstraction. In addition, it introduces WebAssembly as an interoperable environment that would run seamlessly across hardware devices and software stacks while achieving good performance and a high level of security as a critical requirement when processing data off-premises. To address security aspects in AIoT systems, remote attestation and certification mechanisms are

197   DOI: 10.1201/9781032632407-12

introduced to provide a TOCTOU (time-of-check to time-of-use) secure way of ensuring the system's integrity.

Keywords: IoT, machine learning, AIoT, requirements engineering, TOC-TOU, WebAssembly, verification, security, safety, robustness.

10.1 Introduction

More and more traditional algorithms are replaced by models based on deep learning. Deep learning has proven to be successful in solving problems of large complexity, such as natural language processing or facial recognition tasks. In addition, systems tend to be broken down into different components, to be placed where they are most needed and can be most efficient. By establishing high-bandwidth connections between all kinds of different devices and allowing many different system configurations, the components of the distributed system become part of what is known as the Internet of Things (IoT). When combining deep learning with the properties of IoT, new concerns might arise that are not yet foreseen by standards and literature. The new concerns include aspects such as data quality, heuristic deep-learning modeling, learning of the models, or even new ethical considerations.

Applying disruptive systems and methods in real-world applications relies on advances in development methodology. New methods for effectively describing requirements for AI-based algorithms that are distributed over IoT devices from edge to the cloud and how they relate to end-user concerns and needs are a crucial part of the solution. These methods build the foundation for specifying components of such systems in a way that enables to reason about robustness and safety as well as to enable security, privacy, and trust by design. AIoT systems contain both traditional software and hardware components and AI components running on specialized AI acceleration hardware. The challenge is not only to specify and design the AI components but also to integrate them together with the traditional components into an overall AI-enabled system.

10.2 Architecture Framework for AIoT Systems

Architecture frameworks (AF) provide a reusable knowledge structure for designing an AIoT system. An AF organizes architectural descriptions into different architectural views [6]. Different architectural views allow for decomposing the design task into smaller and specialized subtasks, each task specifically suitable to serve a certain design aspect of the system.

10.2.1 State-of-the-art for AI systems architecture

In a research agenda for engineering AI systems, the authors provide a list of challenges when developing architectures for systems with AI components [7]: Providing the right (quality of) data used for training, establishing the right learning infrastructure, building a sufficient storage and computing infrastructure and creating a suitable deployment infrastructure. The latter includes monitoring the behavior of the AI systems under operation because it might only be possible to detect and correct flaws in an AI system after deployment. Furthermore, AI systems do not only consist of AI components but also rely also on conventional software and hardware components. The development of AI components and traditional system components must therefore be aligned to avoid unwanted technical debt [11]. However, as Woods emphasizes, traditional architecture frameworks, such as the 4+1 architectural view model by Kruchten [9], do not account for data and algorithm concerns connected to AI component development [10]. Generally, new stakeholders (e.g., data engineers, or governmental agencies overseeing the use of AI in society), and new concerns connected to AI like data quality aspects, ethical considerations such as fairness or explainability, and eventually many more, need to be represented through new architectural viewpoints. An example of such an additional viewpoint is a learning viewpoint governing the view on the machine learning flow [12]. Developing AI components is a hierarchical, yet also iterative task: Prepare training data and environment, create a suitable model, train and evaluate the model, tune, and repeat training, and eventually deploy and monitor the runtime behavior of the trained model [7, 13]. To fulfill a stakeholder's goal with a system, its design needs to be decomposed into different levels of system design, and consistency needs to be ensured to satisfy high-level requirements [14]. In addition, the system design must also allow for **middle-out development**, where existing components need to be integrated into the overall system design (e.g., transfer-learning from existing AI models or integration of off-the-shelf components). Murugesan et al. propose a hierarchical reference model which supports the appropriate decomposition of requirements to the composition of the system's components [15]. In their model, they define how components can be decomposed into subcomponents. To ensure consistency between the system architecture and the requirements, they define the terms consistency, satisfaction, and acceptability. One major advantage of their model is that, if the decomposition of system components is done correctly, these components can be independently specified and developed.

In summary, a major challenge in AI system design is the lack of design patterns, standards, and reference architectures that support the co-design of traditional software components and AI components [16]. When designing a system, a range of quality aspects, such as safety, security, and privacy needs to be considered. For AI systems, ethical aspects such as explainability of decisions, fairness, and participation play an important role during the system design process. Therefore, the architectural framework for AIoT shall not only support the seamless design and integration of traditional software components and AI components but also allow for all necessary quality concerns to be considered as early as possible in the design process.

10.2.2 A compositional architecture framework for AIoT

The main goal is to introduce an architecture framework based on compositional thinking suitable for developing distributed AI-based systems. The idea of an architectural framework is to provide a knowledge structure that allows the division of an architectural description into different architectural views [6]. An architectural view expresses "the architecture of a system from the perspective of specific system concern" [17]. The conventions of how an architectural view is constructed and interpreted are given through a corresponding architectural viewpoint. Several views on the architecture of the system-of-interest allow for factoring the design task into smaller and specialized tasks.

For a given concern, there exist several views at different levels of abstraction. A hierarchical design process allows for the co-evolution of requirements and architecture, known as the "twin peaks of requirements and architecture" [19, 20]. Based on ideas from compositional thinking, an evolution of system architectures seems possible by establishing suitable descriptions of the abstraction levels for the architectural views, their classification into clusters of concern, and the relation between the views. We call the framework "compositional" because it is built up from different "modules," called clusters of concern, at different levels of abstraction [18].

10.2.3 Clusters of concern

Clusters of concerns are determined through the identified use cases based on the operational context and high-level goals for the desired AI system. For example, privacy might not be of concern for an AI-based diagnostic system detecting faults of a welding robot, but safety could be of paramount concern. Four major groups of concerns emerged for the architecture framework:

Behavior and context contains aspects that concern the static and dynamic behavior of the system, as well as the context and constraints for the desired behavior. To describe an architecture reflecting the desired behavior of the system, two clusters of concern are introduced: **Logical Behavior** covers views that are concerned with the static behavior of the system, and **Process Behavior** covers views concerned with the dynamic behavior of the system. The **Context and Constraints** cluster of concern covers views on the system that define the context and limits the design domain for AI systems. For AI systems, it is beneficial, sometimes even required, to explicitly state the desired context and to define views on the constraints and the design domain of the system. An example is the Operational Design Domain of automated vehicles.

Means and resources contains aspects of the system that enable the desired behavior. The concerns in this group include views that allow to the description of the resources and means available for the system to execute the desired behavior in a given context.

Typical views include the hardware architecture and component design of the system under the cluster of concerned **hardware**. Additionally, three AI-related clusters of concern have been identified that are fundamental "means to execute a desired behavior."

First, the concerned **AI models** contain views that describe the setup and configuration of the required AI model, including the choice of the right deep-learning model. For example, the classification of objects in an optical video stream requires a different deep neural network configuration and then recognizing commands in a voice recording or predicting trajectories of other vehicles in the vicinity. Choosing the right AI model setup is a system design decision which requires suitable views on the AI model in relation to the overall system.

Furthermore, the learning strategy of the AI model has a paramount impact on the final behavior of the AI system. The **learning** cluster of concern covers views on the system that allows for defining and setting up the learning environment of the AI model. This can include the definition of training objectives and views that outline the chosen optimizer for training. Planning and preparing the learning of the AI model therefore becomes a "mean to execute a desired behavior" within an AI system. Learning can be conducted through preparing training datasets, or, in the case of reinforcement learning, could be done in a simulated environment.

Data strategy contains views that support collection and selection for training, validation, and runtime data of the AI model. Views can describe methods for data creation, data selection, data preparations, and runtime monitors of data used by the AI. Trained with the flawed datasets (e.g., bias present in the data), the behavior of the AI system will exhibit the flaws learned during the learning process (e.g., it will show a bias in the decisions). The concerns of an **AI model**, **Learning**, and **Data Strategy** have many dependencies on each other, which will be expressed through correspondence.

Communication deals with aspects of data, connectivity, and communication between nodes or components of the desired system, which is one major concern when developing distributed systems, such as automotive systems, or systems in the IoT. Communication is what drives the IoT. Two clusters of concerns have been identified: First, **Information** accumulates views on the system that model the information and data exchanged in and through the system-of-interest. Second, the cluster of concern **Connectivity** contains views on the means of communication available to the system and its resources.

Quality concerns basically encompasses all quality aspects described through quality attributes, which can affect the architecture of the system. Examples are safety, security, privacy, robustness, and ethical concerns. The latter can include aspects such as fairness and explainability. Recent legislation shows that ethical aspects become a central concern when developing AI systems [21]. This group contains concerns that influence the desired quality of the system. The cluster of concern **safety** provides an example here: Assume one is to follow the workflow of ISO 26262 [21]. The starting point to designing a safe system is to identify safety goals that the architecture, as part of the functionality-providing item, needs to fulfill. This is often done through a Hazard Identification and Risk Assessment (HARA), which provides abstract information applicable to the entire system. On the next lower level of abstraction, the functional safety concept provides a view of a more detailed system architecture that introduces functional safety requirements and redundancies (through safety decomposition in hardware and software components) with the aim to assure the fulfillment of the earlier specified safety goals. On the next more detailed level, the technical safety concept provides information on the technical realization of the functional safety concept. In addition, and not explicitly mentioned in ISO 26262, we propose that the runtime behavior and monitoring is part of the system design process.

For safety concerns, this could mean the introduction of safety degradation concepts and safety monitoring. Further identified relevant clusters of concerns for quality aspects of an AI system in the IoT are **Security**, **Privacy**, and **ethical aspects** such as Fairness and Transparency. For embedded systems, **Energy Efficiency** can be taken up as an explicit quality aspect covered by a separate cluster of concerns. Unlike previous architectural frameworks for the IoT, the compositional thinking in the architectural framework allows for co-designing the system to fulfill the explicitly identified quality concerns. It means that already early in the system development, correspondences between the views regarding the quality concerns and other views in the architecture description are established. The final system can then be said to be "Safe by design," "Secure by design," "Efficient by design," or "Fair by design."

Table 10.1 provides a list of viewpoints, which govern architectural views in the architecture framework, that we assume to be novel and relevant specifically toward the AI components of the system.

10.2.4 Levels of abstraction

The architectural views are not only sorted by clusters of concerns as discussed previously but also by their represented level of abstraction. We found it most beneficial to follow four levels of abstraction, specifically **knowledge and analytical level**, **conceptual level**, **design level**, and **runtime level**:

Knowledge and analytical level: The first level of abstraction includes architectural views that provide an abstract and high-level view of the system-of-interest. On that level, all views provide a way to describe the system and context on a knowledge level, which provides information for further, more concrete system development. For example, the high-level AI model view could elaborate on which functions should be fulfilled through an AI.

Conceptual level: On the next level of abstraction, the views provide a more concrete description of the overall system-of-interest. Components are not detailed yet, but the overall system composition becomes clear and the context of operation is clearly defined. For example, the AI model could be concretely shaped as a deep-learning network with a required amount of layers. All views on this level combined provide a system specification that sets the system-of-interest in context and elaborates on how the desired functionality is fulfilled.

Table 10.1   Description of clusters of concern in the framework.

Concern	Description
Behavior and Context	*Aspects that concern the static and dynamic behavior of the system, as well as the context and constraints for the desired behavior.*
Logical Behavior	Views that are concerned with the static behavior of the system.
Process Behavior	Views concerned with the dynamic behavior of the system.
Context and Constraints	Contains views on the system that define the context and limit the design domain.
Means and Resource	*Contains views on aspects of the system that enable the desired behavior.*
Hardware	Includes views on the hardware architecture and component design of the system.
AI models	Contains views that describe the setup and configuration of the required AI model. Views can include model design, for example, neural network setup or views detailing the configuration of the AI model.
Data strategy	Views that support collection and selection for training, validation, and runtime data of the AI model. Views can describe methods for data creation, data selection, data preparations, and runtime monitors of data used by the AI.
Learning	Covers views on the system that allows for defining and setting up the learning environment of the AI model. This can include the definition of training objectives and views that outline the chosen optimizer for training.
Communication	*Contains views of data, connectivity, and communication between nodes or components of the desired system.*
Information	Accumulates views on the system that model the information and data exchanged in and through the system-of-interest.
Connectivity	Contains views on the means of communication available to the system and its resources.
Quality Concerns	*Encompass quality aspects which can be described through non-functional requirements which affect the architecture of the system.*
Ethics	Views that regulate ethical aspects, such as fairness or transparency of the system.
Security	Views that ensure the security aspects of the system.
Safety	Contains views governing the safety aspects of the system. The views can stem from standards such as ISO 26262.
Energy Efficiency	This cluster of concerns contains views ensuring energy efficiency, especially for mobile devices.
Privacy	Here, views can be contained that ensure privacy requirements, such as for example requested by regulatory authorities.

Design level: The most concrete level at the design time of the system is the design level, which includes views that concretely shape the final system-of-interest. Resources are allocated to components, the AI model is configured to work most efficiently in the given environment, and the concrete component hardware architecture is defined. The solution specification describes the final embodiment of the system-of-interest.

Runtime level: Complex systems, both AI-driven and conventional, often require forms of monitoring and operations control. The purpose of runtime monitoring can be manifold: On one hand, monitoring a deployed system at a run time provides valuable feedback about its performance and reliability to developers and product owners. DevOps is an essential component of an agile development framework, and early detection of issues in a deployed system allows for a swift response from the developers. Furthermore, some requirements of the system might not be exhaustively testable before the deployment of the final system. This is especially the case for AI systems because we have to anticipate undesired behaviors of deployed AI algorithms. By constantly monitoring the decisions of the AI algorithm, such deviations from the intended behavior can be detected and mitigated, for example, through retraining or by "pulling the plug." Most AI systems are not "adaptive." They are trained and tested with a dataset representing the desired context in which the AI system is intended to operate in under the assumption of stationarity in the probability distribution of the data. In reality, the assumption of stationarity of the probability distributions does not hold in most cases, for example when the context, in which the AI operates, can change over time. Concepts like continual learning allow the AI to handle drifts in data distributions. However, continual learning requires runtime monitoring concepts to detect deviations from the currently learned context, and automatic data collection (and labeling) for autonomous retraining of the AI model. These aspects of changes in runtime behavior are described on the runtime level of abstraction in the compositional architectural framework.

The final conceptual model of a compositional architecture framework based on the stated propositions is illustrated in Figure 10.1.

10.2.5 Compositional architecture framework

Figure 10.2 presents a compositional architectural framework that includes all earlier identified concerns for distributed AI systems and all levels of abstractions for AIoT systems [18].

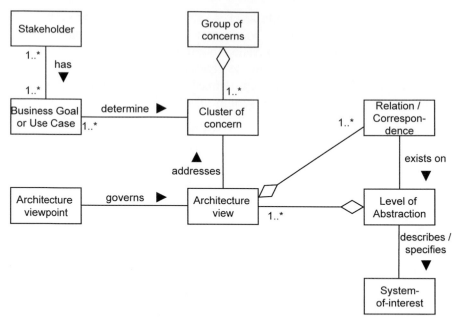

Figure 10.1   Conceptual model of a compositional architecture framework [18].

Business Goals and Use Cases												
Behaviour and Context			*Means and Resources*				*Communication*		*Quality Concerns*			
Logical Behaviour	Process Behaviour	Context & Constraints	Data Strategy	Learning	AI Model	Hardware	Information	Connectivity	Ethics	Privacy	Security	Safety
Analytical Level — Function components	Interaction	Context assumptions	Data ingestion	Training objectives	High level AI model	High level hardware architecture	Compilation	Interfaces	Ethic principles	Privacy impact analysis	Threat analysis (TARA)	Hazard analysis (HARA)
Conceptual Level — Logical components	Logical sequences	Context definition	Data selection	Training concept	AI model concept	System hardware architecture	Information model	Node connectivity	Ethic concept	Privacy concept	Cyber-security concept	Functional safety concept
Design Level — Computing ressource allocation	Resource sequences	Constraints / Design Domain	Data preparation / manipulation	Optimiser settings	AI model configuration	Component hardware architecture	Communication model	Resource connectivity	Ethic technical realisation	Technical solutions for privacy	Technical cyber security concept	Technical safety concept
Run Time Level — Behaviour monitoring	Adaptive behaviour	Context monitoring	Runtime data monitoring and collection	Manage continous improvements	AI model performance monitoring	Hardware performance monitoring	Data monitoring	Connectivity monitoring	Assessment / auditing of AI decisions	Assessment of privacy compliance	Security monitoring / threat response	Safety monitoring / safety degradition

Figure 10.2   Compositional architecture framework for AIoT systems, categorizing views in different clusters of concerns on different levels of abstraction [18].

10.2.6 Applying a compositional architecture framework in practice

Based on the experience of applying a compositional architectural framework, the following guideline can be provided:

Step 1: Identify clusters of concern. Clusters of concerns are identified. Initially, larger groups of concerns (such as functionality, hardware, communication, and quality) can be defined, which are then refined into atomic clusters of concerns.

Step 2: Identify levels of abstraction. Levels of abstractions are identified. The number of required levels depends on the size and complexity of system-of-interest and the development settings of the company. Three to four different levels of abstraction seem a good default.

Step 3: Add existing architectural decisions. Known architectural decisions are entered into the matrix. Most development projects do not start from scratch but instead must reuse or integrate into existing architectures. Prior knowledge, such as an existing component architecture, can be entered into the appropriate clusters of concerns and level of abstraction in the architecture matrix.

Step 4: Add missing architectural views. Architectural views are added. Relations (morphisms) are created between the architectural views at each level of abstraction such that no inconsistencies occur when looking at the system-of-interest from different architectural views.

Step 5: Add missing relations. All relations between architectural views must be mapped onto corresponding views of the next lower level of abstraction. If a relation between two architectural views on a higher level of abstraction does not have a correspondence on the next lower level of abstraction, the relation might be unnecessary and can be removed, or a corresponding relation needs to be created.

Step 6: Iterate if needed. During the system development, additional clusters of concern might be discovered that iteratively are added.

Steps 1–5 are illustrated in Figure 10.3. At each step, implied requirements on aspects related to the corresponding architecture view are identified and derived.

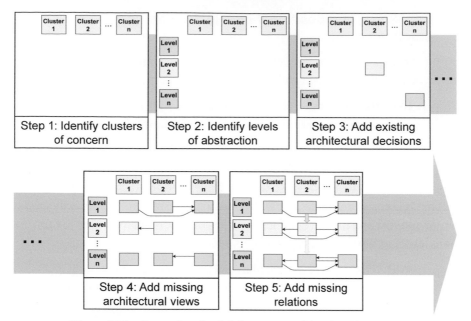

Figure 10.3 Steps taken for defining a compositional architectural.

10.3 WebAssembly as a Common Layer for the Cloud-edge Continuum

The cloud is an immense ecosystem of countless providers offering different virtualized services to supply an enormous demand for computer applications. Some of these applications ended up in the cloud to be more convenient or cheaper to maintain, others were initially built for the cloud for scalability and availability while relying on its naturally distributed and replicated nature. Clouds can also offer lower latency, more resiliency, or regulatory compliance. Regardless of the reason, **cloud computing** has probably become the most prominent infrastructure supporting applications today. With a growing number of multi-cloud software, dealing with heterogeneous cloud providers and technologies has become a common issue.

Telecommunication companies began deploying their own distributed infrastructure, installing small, cloud-like clusters closer to consumers of their services to improve performance, latency, or reliability. Local governments and other infrastructure providers such as energy and transportation followed suit, deploying their own small clusters of fairly powerful computing devices close to the human activities they support. The use of these highly distributed devices is collectively known as **edge computing**.

Today's scenario is completed by billions of sensing and actuating devices deployed around the globe, referred to as the **Internet of Things** or IoT. Such devices often have limited processing capabilities and perform simple tasks like measuring a temperature or turning a lightbulb on and off. They are connected to the Internet, more than often coordinating their function through edge devices, and connecting users through cloud services.

The combined existing infrastructure of IoT, edge, and cloud form an abstraction that is currently being called the cloud-edge-IoT continuum, or simply the **cloud-edge continuum**. This collective infrastructure is anything but continuous, as each part exists in a separate silo, built of proprietary solutions, as shown in Figure 10.4. Developers of applications spanning over the continuum must implement specific solutions for each silo, often built with incompatible software components. The lack of a seamless environment makes it much more difficult to profit from the collective advantages of the continuum.

Finally, applications shared by multiple users always counted on some sort of **security**, usually dealing with encryption, authentication, and access control, and there are many established tools. With the advent of the cloud, which is accessed over the Internet, security has become a fundamental part of all applications. Edge-cloud continuum application vendors, developers, and users need to rely on the entire continuum – cloud, edge, and IoT – to ensure their data is secure and their calculations are accurate.

An ideal seamless cloud-edge continuum should provide a lightweight execution environment with a similar (or even identical) software and hardware interface that allows unmodified code to run on any machine in the

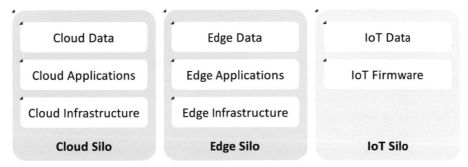

Figure 10.4   Independent cloud, edge, and IoT silos.

system. A typical cloud-only environment is already fairly complex, composed of several different hardware components, leveraged using extensive software components, managed by large engineering teams, and shared among many tenants. Adding edge and IoT to the picture shifts scale and heterogeneity to another dimension.

In this chapter, we propose using WebAssembly as the core component of a seamless environment spanning over the entire continuum. We advocate that the technology provided by WebAssembly is suitable for the implementation of applications on most hardware devices and software environments of the cloud-edge continuum, with the appropriate level of security. Modern hardware can execute WebAssembly with near-native code performance. Combined with special hardware features that guarantee the confidentiality and integrity of applications, WebAssembly abstracts the complexity of software development while providing a trusted environment. Naturally, as with any nascent technology, many parts needed to implement a seamless continuum are still missing.

In the sections that follow, we debate the drawbacks of existing software architectures in more detail. We then present WebAssembly and its benefits for implementing the continuum, in particular when supporting AIoT applications. We conclude with a few ideas for future work on the topic.

10.3.1 Building blocks of a seamless continuum for AIoT

There are already some initiatives for a common environment for cloud, edge, and IoT silos. In this section, we present a few popular ones and compare them to a solution using WebAssembly as proposed.

The java virtual machine (JVM) is one of the first practical implementations of common environments that address the problem of applications running on heterogeneous underlying systems. By and large, the JVM is one of the most comprehensive choices today, with implementations ranging from commodity servers to embedded devices. Still, the JVM supports very few programming languages and adds significant performance penalties compared to running C programs natively. Java programs depend on large numbers of class libraries, which imposes a large memory footprint for the execution of even the simplest programs.

Containers have recently emerged as an alternative to running applications in heterogeneous environments. They are, however, defined for specific architectures and a specific operating system interface, and recompilation is necessary to get containers that can run, for example, on Intel and Arm devices (popular as cloud and edge devices, respectively). WebAssembly has the generality of JVM and the ease of use of containers, making it possible to build cross-platform software that runs with negligible performance losses and a small memory footprint.

Deploying applications automatically in a distributed system involves addressing aspects such as access control and resource management, as well as monitoring and optimizing computing and communication. We are not aware of any practical, specific tool that covers the entire cloud-edge continuum. We do not deal with this problem here, but we suspect it would be possible to adapt many of the existing tools designed for the cloud, assuming the underlying systems become more homogeneous. Also, some authors have already started working on models for integrating cloud and edge devices into one seamless deployment system [23, 24].

Security has already proven essential in standard cloud systems, where application users must have guarantees that the confidentiality and integrity of their data will be respected. These guarantees are difficult to provide in a multi-tenant system, where co-tenants can abuse the system's vulnerabilities to discover (or infer) someone else's application data. Also, one common deterrent for cloud adoption is the provider's curiosity, because they have all the administrative power needed to inspect all content across all physical machines. From an opposite point of view, providers want to be protected from malicious tenants who may want to exploit infrastructure vulnerabilities for their own benefit.

Compared to the cloud, edge infrastructure is much more distributed. Edge devices are installed in end-user buildings and other shared infrastructures, even in public spaces, making it impossible to maintain physical control over all the resources. Same as with the cloud, edge administrators have physical access and control of the edge devices they manage. But contrary to the cloud, edge users are close to the devices and can even abuse them physically. We believe that edge infrastructures offer far fewer security guarantees than the cloud.

Most current popular computer architectures include some form of trusted execution environments (TEEs). They allow code execution in an isolated part of the CPU, where access by other software is architecturally impossible. A TEE can run a program and protect its data so that a machine administrator cannot access it. Current implementations usually have an additional execution mode in the processor and may even offer memory encryption for TEE data. The currently most popular implementation of TEE is Intel's Secure Guard Extensions (Intel SGX), for which commercial cloud services such as

Azure Confidential Computing already exist. For edge and IoT deployments, the most popular architecture (Arm) offers TrustZone as a TEE. Again, proprietary and incompatible solutions in the underlying hardware make it difficult to reuse trusted software components from cloud to edge and vice versa.

Confidential containers could be a viable alternative for deploying applications on the continuum, as suggested by Scontain [25]. They are similar to traditional containers, except they run entirely in a trusted environment. However, like other containers, they are platform dependent. They are also expensive in terms of the resources required in many cases since they can contain significant amounts of operating system functions. Microsoft's Azure Sphere follows the same idea, offering a unified programming model and support for trusted execution technologies. But it only supports a few programming languages and relies heavily on other Microsoft services.

By proposing WebAssembly as an execution model combined with trusted execution environments, we can provide a seamless portability base for running trusted applications. The same base can be used to deploy applications on edge or cloud devices, with similar security guarantees. Also, previous work [26] has shown that a double-sided sandbox enabled by a WebAssembly TEE provides better security for the provider and for the tenants. In the context of AIoT, securing proprietary machine learning models is of utmost importance. Leveraging TEEs as a security mechanism to offload inference removes the burden of having pervasive communication to the cloud and lowers the number of end-user information to transfer offshore. As a result, AIoT systems are more autonomous, while better preserving the owners' privacy, which is an essential concern in the years to come.

Many different IoT infrastructures have been deployed and are already continuously generating data that feed cloud applications worldwide. Components in the application chains (IoT to edge to cloud) can be updated independently to add new functionalities and eliminate vulnerabilities. There is increasing usage of federated machine learning, where edge devices work together to build a model without revealing all the details of each user's data, helping to protect privacy. **Remote software attestation** [27], which is usually paired with TEEs, also plays a fundamental role in such a dynamic, distributed scenario. It makes it possible to build trust in certain software components and to check their authenticity and integrity. It also allows ensuring that one is remotely communicating with a specific, verified program. We believe that attestation plays an essential role in building a fully trusted environment for running cloud-edge continuum applications. Hence, cloud applications can infer security guarantees from AIoT software using attestation, despite being in untrusted physical environments, and can delegate part of computations.

10.3.2 WebAssembly as a unifying solution

WebAssembly is a rather new and universal virtual instruction set architecture. Unlike previous cross-platform efforts such as Oracle's Java and Microsoft .NET, WebAssembly is being developed from the ground up by a consortium of open technology companies, including Microsoft, Google, and Mozilla. While originally designed to increase performance for active web pages, WebAssembly does not depend on web-related functionality and is increasingly used to build standalone applications. WebAssembly has many advantages to being used as a unified execution unit for the cloud-edge continuum. First, WebAssembly can be generated by compiling a variety of programming languages. Second, unlike Java and .NET, WebAssembly is lightweight, has minimal dependencies, and offers additional security benefits like sandboxing.

WebAssembly interacts with the operating system thanks to the WebAssembly System Interface (WASI), a standardized specification of a POSIX-like interface. It is designed with conciseness and portability in mind, allowing platforms to easily implement it, being ideal for constrained environments such as IoT and Edge devices and TEEs. Common compilers for languages like C and Rust seamlessly translate POSIX calls into WASI calls. In addition, WASI follows the concept of capability-based security, where access to each system resource must be granted by the runtime, such as file system or socket interactions, materializing a strong boundary between the applications and the operating system.

There are currently a few execution models for WebAssembly code: interpretation, just-in-time (JIT), and ahead-of-time (AOT) compilation. Runtimes like WAMR [28] can be adapted to offer one or more execution models, with different memory footprints (209 KiB for AOT, 230 KiB for interpretation, and 41 MiB for JIT). A growing list of toolchains (LLVM, Emscripten) already supports WebAssembly as a compile target for various source languages, including C, C++, and Rust, with other languages such as C#, Go, Kotlin, and Swift being under active development. For all these reasons, we believe WebAssembly is an attractive practical binary architecture choice to be used in the entire continuum.

10.3.3 The case for a TEE-backed WebAssembly continuum

Trusted execution environments aim to provide safe and trustworthy code execution on (remote) untrusted hardware. Hardware manufacturers have provided TEE implementations more than a decade ago, each one of them offering different features and security guarantees. The most influential TEEs that are currently marketed are Intel SGX [29], Arm TrustZone [30], and AMD Secure Encrypted Virtualization (AMD SEV) [31]. These technologies enable processing data in isolated memory areas that can neither be accessed nor tampered with by more privileged software, such as the operating system or the hypervisor. Hence, cloud providers and edge device owners with management rights or even physical control cannot access the data and computation of a tenant, protecting the confidentiality and integrity of their applications.

Cloud providers, such as Microsoft Azure and Google Cloud, already market confidential computing, and we expect widespread adoption of these services due to the demand driven by the cloud-edge continuum. We observe that the rich ecosystem of trusted environments largely varies in terms of security, threat models, and implementation. However, defining a common basis for trusted execution and making it widely available in both cloud and edge environments is essential for the continuum and the industry in general. For that reason, Arm, Intel, Microsoft, and others created the confidential computing consortium (CCC), supporting open-source projects for trusted execution technology under the umbrella of the Linux Foundation. A unified abstraction for TEEs in the cloud-edge continuum must take support and shape from such ongoing efforts. For that reason, the CCC is involved in many projects, such as Enarx [32] and Veracruz [33], which aim to provide WebAssembly support in TEEs independently from hardware.

In our previous work, we proposed a few solutions to execute general-purpose WebAssembly applications within TEEs. We developed Twine [34] to bring a WebAssembly runtime into Intel SGX enclaves, leveraging WASI to interact with the TEE facilities and the untrusted operating system. More recently, we proposed WaTZ [35], a trusted runtime for Arm TrustZone with added remote attestation. The latter, an essential feature for providing trust for remote applications, is surprisingly missing in Arm's architecture. We believe that industrial versions of our prototypes will help pave the way to build distributed applications on the cloud-edge continuum that providers, developers, and users can safely trust.

10.3.4 WebAssembly performance

We refer to our previous work for many experiments regarding WebAssembly performance. We first proposed a solution to run general-purpose WebAssembly applications inside Intel SGX TEEs, leveraging WASI to interact with the untrusted OS, while shielding the file system primitives to prevent eavesdropping. Later, we proposed a trusted runtime environment for Arm TrustZone with remote attestation of WebAssembly code. A more recent publication contains an extended version of this chapter, with some detailed performance figures [36]. We refer the reader to these publications for the full detail of our measurements.

In the performance measurements we made, we used WebAssembly inside TEEs to implement many frequent tasks done by useful programs. To measure the low-level cost of using WebAssembly, we used Polybench/C [37], a tool that implements several sorts of different programming language constructs frequently used, allowing us to compare the quality of different compilers. We observed similar performance losses when using WebAssembly on x86 and Arm architectures, with the execution time being increased by 30% on average.

To produce a comparison using more resources such as memory and disk, we compared the execution performance of SQLite, a widespread and embeddable database management system, as most real-world applications generate, store, and retrieve information to operate. As such, we used the built-in benchmarks of SQLite named Speedtest1 [38]. Each Speedtest1 experiment targets a single aspect of a database, such as selection using joins or the update of indexed records. In our evaluation, WebAssembly was almost three times slower than native code on an Intel x86 processor, and roughly two times slower in an Arm processor. Interestingly, since we made these performance comparisons at different moments in time, we could observe clear progress in the environment. WebAssembly was four times slower in the experiments we did two years earlier, using the same hardware and software, but with newer versions of the compiler and the runtime environment. These enhancements over the years strengthen the perspective of using WebAssembly as a universal, lightweight, yet versatile bytecode to enable platform independence across the continuum.

10.3.5 WebAssembly limitations

Although current compilers such as LLVM are mature enough to generate proper WebAssembly bytecode, the system call support currently offered by

WASI is rather limited. Extending WASI to be more POSIX-compliant would probably reduce the ability to use it in several, more protected, environments, such as web browsers. A different alternative is proposed by Emscripten, which directly translates the source code into POSIX functions and system calls. This helps to run older WebAssembly programs on POSIX systems with only a few modifications, but it reduces the portability. We note that the WebAssembly subgroup that focuses on standardizing WASI thoughtfully extends the specifications to be features-complete.

Running WebAssembly code incurs a performance overhead. Some programs can run up to three times slower than their native version, depending on the type of workload. This can be explained by many factors, such as increased register pressure, additional branch instructions, increased code size, stack overflow checks, and indirect call checks. While some of these issues can be compensated for by having compilers spend more time generating better code, other factors are a consequence of WebAssembly's design limitations, which would require changes in its specifications, at the cost of making it more difficult to implement.

WebAssembly uses linear memory to store the heap of a running program, with a limited number of 64KiB pages, for a total of 4GiB. While most software will not require more than this amount of linear memory, this may limit some server-side applications, such as training large deep-learning models or keeping large databases in memory. Recent proposals aim to extend this limit by increasing the number of allocable pages, raising the theoretical memory ceiling to 16 EiB (64-bits wide).

As with any young technology, WebAssembly still needs more efficient implementations for many useful features. Future contributors may suggest WebAssembly and WASI extensions to relax the constraints or extend the capabilities of the specification. For example, WASI-nn proposes adding a WASI machine learning module to facilitate model inference. We also anticipate that many current limitations for the cloud-edge continuum will disappear thanks to compiler advances, specification extensions, and better WebAssembly support for popular requirements.

10.3.6 Closing remarks concerning the common layer

It is impossible to precisely predict which will be the winning technology used to build the cloud-edge continuum. Yet, we envision it as an interoperable, scalable, and distributed system in which any piece of software can reside on any device, regardless of the underlying platform. Such capabilities will change the development lifecycle of future applications, allowing developers to focus on business value rather than spending time with the complexity of each individual piece of infrastructure. WebAssembly is perfectly suited to this task thanks to its abstraction of the operating system, device type, programming language, and the additional security guarantees it can offer with TEEs.

We briefly presented some performance results showing that WebAssembly is a viable alternative to running native applications, with acceptable overhead. We have covered many aspects of successfully adopting WebAssembly to implement the cloud-edge continuum. Many challenges remain to be overcome, such as improving interoperability with existing programming languages and extending WASI to better support more complex applications. Also, much progress is still necessary for terms of middleware, which connects the components of the continuum and simplifies the deployment and migration of applications. Thanks to the experience we acquired with WebAssembly and Trusted Computing ecosystems, we are confident that they are a well-suited software development foundation for building large-scale systems such as the cloud-edge continuum.

10.4 TOCTOU-secure Remote Attestation and Certification for IoT

A key component in securing connected IoT systems is ensuring the integrity of the IoT software-state and detecting any change. This is typically achieved with remote attestation (RA), which aims at verifying the state of the software/memory of an untrusted attester (i.e., an IoT device) by allowing a trusted verifier to engage in a challenge-response-based exchange of proof. RA mechanisms rely on hardware/software/hybrid Root-of-Trust. As a result of said attestation, the attester is certified with a certain level of assurance guaranteeing software-state integrity that impacts trust decisions within networked systems. The attestation often results in software updates or issuing certificates indicating device assurance levels. The certificates include information like the assurance evidence, device IDs, assurance level indicating the trustworthiness of the device, etc. This assurance certificate only guarantees that an IoT device has a verified software stack. IoT devices also need conventional X.509 certificates when strong authentication is required, which is enabled by public key infrastructure (PKI). There are efforts to bring conventional PKI to IoT [39–41], which meet IoT limitations such as resource constraints of the device, the dynamic operational environment, diversity in the supply chain, etc.

It is important that we do not define yet another certification infrastructure for assurance certification, and integrate assurance certificates with existing state-of-the-art PKI. This chapter addresses both of these problems: (i) providing digital certification for device assurance (ii) as well as integrating the new assurance certificates into the existing PKI certification, without compromising the standard compliance and without security properties.

More specifically, in this chapter, we introduce and detail AutoCert (**Auto**mated digital **Cert**ification) to provide TOCTOU security by combining Remote Attestation results about assurance of device health with standard public key infrastructure (PKI) authentication processes.

In the context of RA and certificates that reflect the attested state of the device, the time-of-check to time-of-use (TOCTOU) race condition may take effect. The time-of-check to time-of-use invalidity is a highly contextual problem, existing in remote attestation, operating systems, certifications, etc., and remains possible in this case as well. Due to the dynamic nature of IoT systems, the software state of the device may have changed in the delta time between the RA and the certificate issuance due to a software update, vulnerability exploitation, or software version update. Although potential solutions exist to prevent and resist TOCTOU attacks in trusted platform module (TPM)-based remote attestation, a solution that provides a mechanism to validate the current software-state against the attested state and use an assurance certificate without invoking RA again, is missing, and is critical in the IoT domain. However, a solution that provides a mechanism to validate the current software-state against the attested state in certificates without invoking RA again is also critical in the IoT domain.

10.4.1 AutoCert – proposed mechanism

The AutoCert mechanism is an automated procedure comprising interactions among an **IoT owner**, **IoT devices** as a part of a networked system, a trusted third-party responsible for attesting the device's software-state, for example, a Conformity Assessment Body (**CAB**), and a standard Certification Authority (**CA**) to enroll device certificates.

10.4.1.1 Pre-deployment

The manufacturer commissioned the IoT device with software, platform/device certificate, a dedicated TPM 2.0 chip, and a secure unique device identifier during device initialization. The platform certificate binds the TPM to the IoT device. The secure unique device identifier, that is, UDevID, is a hardcoded identity like a device URI, EUI, or DevID playing a role in IoT device identification in local and global networks.

The TPM's Root-of-Trust originates with a unique 2048-bit RSA key pair, known as the endorsement key (EK). The TPM restricts the use of the EK to a limited set of decryption operations as per the TCG rules, and it cannot be used directly for device authentication or digital signatures. Therefore, we generate a 2048-bit RSA key pair, the attestation key (AK), using the EK as a seed for attestation. The attestation certificate (CertAK) corresponding to the AK is also generated at this state by the IoT manufacturer. The IoT manufacturers and solution providers classify IoT devices into usage profiles based on their deployment scenario, for example, smart home, automotive, industrial, critical infrastructure, smart grid, etc. In AutoCert, the IoT owner assigns a device_profile to the IoT device to enable security policies for devices within a network. This categorization assists CAs and CABs in conducting reasonable risk assessment and vulnerability management throughout the device lifecycle. The IoT device is configured to boot with trusted software that measures (i.e., calculates the hash) the next software to be run and stores this hash in a platform configuration register using the TPM2_PCR_Extend function. This process continues through the OS kernel code resulting in a chain of measurement. In AutoCert, we propose configuring security-critical software, libraries, files, and executables as a part of this chain of measurements.

10.4.1.2 Remote attestation

AutoCert's remote attestation is built on the challenge/response interaction model from the RATS architecture. Before a device is attested (Figure 10.5), the IoT owner is responsible for generating the reference values corresponding to the device software/s and securely transferring them to the verifier. We assume a confidential exchange of these values. Before the remote attestation begins, the IoT owner sends a signed request to the CAB with the **UDevID** and device_profile of the IoT device. The CAB sends a signed attestation request containing a random nonce N and a **PCRSelection** is sent to the IoT device. The TPM2_Quote function is used to generate the evidence. The cryptographically strong random nonce N uniquely distinguishes the evidence, determines its freshness, and prevents replay attacks. We propose the generation of an integrity key pair, IK, by the IoT device and sending it along with the evidence for the creation of an integrity_proof. The IK is an

RSA key-pair, IK_{priv}, and IK_{pub} generated with the TPM2_Create function using the **PCRSelection**. Since any change in the security-critical software on the device is recorded with an update to the PCR using TPM2_PCR_Extend, the use of this **PCRSelection** in creating the IK ensures that this key will not be valid if the software-state of the device changes.

A valid TPM-generated attestation key, the *AK*, is used to sign TPM-generated evidence. It serves as a way for third parties to validate keys and data generated by a specific TPM on an IoT device. On receiving the evidence, the CAB validates the accompanying signature and compares the evidence against reference values. Following the attestation result and using a suitable risk assessment mechanism (not discussed in this work), the attester's assurance level is calculated against the device_profile. The results of attestation and the assurance level are used by the CAB to ensure the software-state integrity

10.4.1.3 TOCTOU and integrity_proof

The integrity key pair, IK, is proposed to address the TOCTOU race condition. The **PCRSelection** contains the measurements computed and stored during the measured boot, representing the IoT device's software-state.

Using these PCRs in RA and generating the IK_{priv} and IK_{pub} key pair creates a dependence of the IK on the software-state of the device. As soon as the software-state changes due to a new vulnerability or malicious update, the IK is invalidated.

This forms the core of AutoCert procedures and is a part of the proof of the IoT device's software-state integrity, as it strictly locks the IK to a valid state of the device. We compute an integrity_proof by aggregating the value of **PCRSelection** used in evidence generation, that is, **PCRIntegrity** and the IK_{pub}. The integrity_proof , assurance level, and **UDevID** are then shared with a trusted CA. The CA now possesses records of attested IoT devices against their **UDevID** and assurance attributes. These attributes are integrated with the IoT profile of the standard X.509 certificate using custom extensions. This certificate $Cert_{AC}$ reflects a CA-verified device identity (authentication) as well as the CAB-attested software-state of the IoT device (assurance).

10.4.1.4 Verification for TOCTOU security

The verification of this integrity_proof for TOCTOU security applies to all IoT devices using X.509 certificates for authentication and establishing secure DTLS communication sessions with clients.

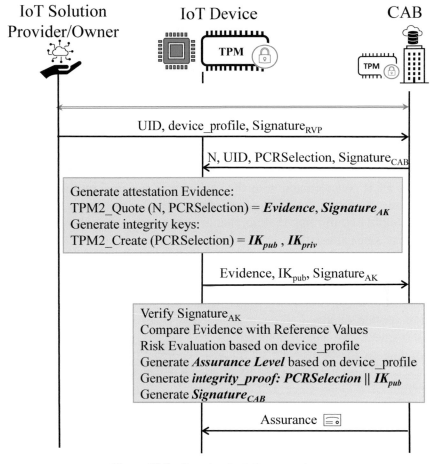

Figure 10.5 Remote attestation procedure.

To achieve assurance of the IoT device's software-state, the client performs two levels of integrity checks, as presented in Figure 10.6.

The first level of integrity check includes verifying the assurance level stated in the $Cert_{AC}$. This assurance level would form the basis of network access policies or authorization to access system resources.

However, as stated earlier, it is possible that the IoT device's software-state changes after the remote attestation process, or $Cert_{AC}$ enrollment. This can happen due to malware or vulnerabilities in existing software. This scenario presents itself as an instance of a TOCTOU attack, and checking the assurance level is insufficient in security-critical cases.

To eliminate this TOCTOU condition, AutoCert facilitates another level of integrity verification. To perform this Level2 integrity check, AutoCert introduces a lightweight service to ensure that the integrity_proof is valid. The verification process includes sending a random challenge by the client to the IoT device after signing it using the IK_{pub} from integrity_proof in the $Cert_{AC}$. Since the integrity_proof is locked to the state of the IoT device attested by CAB, it can only be decrypted by the IoT device if it possesses IK_{priv}, hence guaranteeing proof of possession. The IoT device decrypts the challenge, includes the current value of the **PCRIntegrity**, and signs it. The challenge ensures the freshness of this message exchange. The current value of the PCR concatenated with the challenge is received by the client, which verifies it against the PCR values from the integrity_proof, that is, the **PCRIntegrity** confirming that no changes have occurred concerning the software-state since attestation.

10.4.2 Implementation and experimental evaluation

As a proof-of-concept (PoC), we implemented the AutoCert setup with an attestation service on the IoT device, which is invoked when it receives an attest request. We also implemented an integrity verification service corresponding to the two levels of integrity checks. The experiments are performed using the OPTIGA TPM Evaluation Kit. The evaluation hardware is comprised of a Quad Core 1.2GHz, 64-bit Raspberry Pi 3 with 1 GB RAM and an Iridium board with OPTIGA SLM 9670 TPM 2.0. We choose TPM SLM 9670 for this evaluation since it is specially designed for use in automotive/industrial applications. The following set of experiments aims to measure the system-wide execution time of the proposed mechanism during different phases. We measured the round trip time (RTT) as the time elapsed from the start of each AutoCert phase until the completion of the phase. We measured the phases using a system clock in nanoseconds and iterated the experiments five to ten times to ensure statistical accuracy.

Phase 1 of AutoCert begins with a request to the CAB to initiate AutoCert remote attestation with the IoT device. The RTT of this phase is 28,800 ms. This phase is expected to execute during device assembly after the unique device keys are integrated into the hardware, and device software is installed. This does not interrupt runtime services like mutual authentication, where excessive delays disrupt services, timeout, or cancellation of operations.

Phase 2 of AutoCert is the certificate enrollment. On receiving a certificate enrollment request from the IoT device, the CA checks for assurance

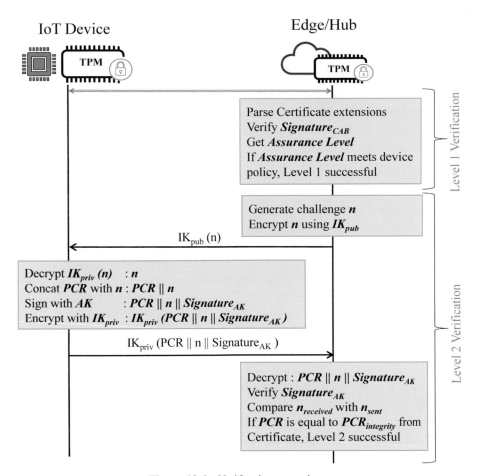

Figure 10.6 Verification procedure.

attributes received from the CAB, associated with the **UDevID** of the IoT device, and enrolls the certificate, including the assurance attributes. The enrollment of Cert$_{AC}$ with assurance attributes takes 7104 ms. This measurement merely gives an estimate of the generation of a certificate with additional extensions. In actual events, certificate issuance and enrollment time also vary depending on the computational capabilities of the CA and network capacity.

Phase 3 of AutoCert provides 2 levels of assurance to the communicating devices. The proposed level 1 integrity check attains a basic level of assurance. This begins by verifying the signature and the assurance level from the Cert$_{AC}$. An extended TOCTOU security of assurance is provided in level 2. The level 1 verification steps are executed in 0.7 ms, and the RTT for level 2 verification, including minor network delays between the two involved entities, is 4746 ms. The majority of the execution time during level 2 verification can be traced to the creation and loading of the encryption key. As these operations depend on the implementation of TPM specifications and adjacent function libraries, it is reasonable to state here that the RTT for level 2 verification is justified considering the hardware security guarantees provided by the TPM.

10.4.3 AutoCert – conclusion

This chapter presented AutoCert, addressing TOCTOU security in integrity certificates corresponding to software-state assurance in IoT devices and providing a standardized mechanism to distribute integrity certificates. Auto-Cert's remote attestation is based on IETF RATS relying on TPM2.0 for evidence generation. We have proposed the integration of the AutoCert mechanisms into existing standards to facilitate its adoption in the emerging PKI for IoT.

10.5 Conclusion

In this chapter, a compositional architectural framework was derived during focus groups within the project consortium. Compositional thinking allows for an effective co-design of all relevant concerns of the system-of-interest. Especially for AI components, the architectural framework allows for effective data selection, AI model development, and hardware design. Qualitative aspects, such as safety, security, and privacy, but also ethical aspects are explicitly considered throughout the design process. Furthermore, to ensure functionality and quality aspects of the system, the architectural framework considers monitoring concepts for runtime operations of the system.

In addition, a common layer for the cloud-edge continuum based on the WebAssembly virtual instruction set architecture is introduced. We discussed the historical context and the shortcomings of existing software development environments and shed light on what improvements can be implemented to arrive at seamless, secure applications across the continuum. We then presented WebAssembly's advantages for such applications, along with its preliminary performance comparison for executing benchmark payloads, thus supporting the concept's viability for building the unified technology.

Furthermore, we presented the time-of-check to time-of-use challenges that remote attestation and certification face in the context of AIoT systems. An overview of the seriousness and specificity of TOCTOU problems for IoT devices, resulting from resource constraints of such devices, was given, describing their operational environment, supply chain, vulnerability management, and others. Then, we highlighted the importance of developing a solution capable of software validation appropriate for IoT devices and described AutoCert as a proposed mechanism.

Acknowledgement

This publication incorporates results from the VEDLIoT project, which received funding from the European Union's Horizon 2020 research and innovation program under Grant Agreement No. 957197.

References

[1] Joel Höglund, Samuel Lindemer, Martin Furuhed, Shahid Raza. PKI4IoT: Towards Public Key Infrastructure for the Internet of Things. Computers & Security journal (Elsevier), Volume 89, Pages 101658, February 2020

[2] Joel Höglund, Martin Furuhed, Shahid Raza. Lightweight Certificate Revocation for Low-power IoT with End-to-end Security. Journal of Information Security and Applications (Elsevier), Volume 73, 103424, March 2023

[3] Joel Höglund, Martin Furuhed, Shahid Raza. Towards Automated PKI Trust Transfer for IoT. The 3rd International Conference on Public Key Infrastructure and Its Applications (PKIA 2022), September 9-10, 2022.

[4] Anitha Murugesan, Sanjai Rayadurgam, and Mats Heimdahl. Requirements reference models revisited: Accommodating hierarchy in system design. Proceedings of the IEEE International Conference on Requirements Engineering, 2019-September:177–186, 2019.

[5] Nalchigar, S., Yu, E., Keshavjee, K., 2021. Modeling machine learning requirements from three perspectives: a case report from the healthcare domain. Requirements Engineering 26, 237–254.

[6] Patrizio Pelliccione, Eric Knauss, Rogardt Heldal, S. Magnus Ågren, Piergiuseppe Mallozzi, Anders Alminger, and Daniel Borgentun. Automotive Architecture Framework: The experience of Volvo Cars. Journal of Systems Architecture, 77:83–100, 2017.

[7] Bosch, Jan, Helena Holmström Olsson, and Ivica Crnkovic. "Engineering ai systems: A research agenda." *Artificial Intelligence Paradigms for Smart Cyber-Physical Systems* (2021): 1-19.

[8] Lucas Bernardi, Themis Mavridis, and Pablo Estevez. 150 successful machine learning models: 6 lessons learned at Booking.com. Proceedings of the ACM SIGKDD International Conference on Knowledge Discovery and Data Mining, pages 1743–1751, 2019.

[9] Phillippe Kruchten. Architecture blueprints—the "4+1" view model of software architecture, volume 12. ACM Press, New York, New York, USA, 1995.

[10] Eoin Woods. Software Architecture in a Changing World. IEEE Software, 33(6):94–97, 2016.

[11] Sculley, D., Holt, G., Golovin, D., Davydov, E., Phillips, T., Ebner, D., Chaudhary, V., Young, M., Crespo, J.F., Dennison, D., 2015. Hidden technical debt in machine learning systems. Advances in Neural Information Processing Systems 2015-January, 2503–2511.

[12] Henry Muccini and Karthik Vaidhyanathan. Software Architecture for ML-based Systems: What Exists and What Lies Ahead. Proceedings of the 43rd International Conference on Software Engineering,, mar 2021.

[13] Zhiyuan Wan, Xin Xia, David Lo, and Gail C. Murphy. How does Machine Learning Change Software Development Practices? IEEE Transactions on Software Engineering, 2020.

[14] Greg Giaimo, Rebekah Anderson, Laurie Wargelin, and Peter Stopher. Will it Work? Transportation Research Record: Journal of the Transportation Research Board, 2176(1):26–34, jan 2010.

[15] Anitha Murugesan, Sanjai Rayadurgam, and Mats Heimdahl. Requirements reference models revisited: Accommodating hierarchy in system design. Proceedings of the IEEE International Conference on Requirements Engineering, 2019-September:177–186, 2019.

[16] Silverio Martínez-Fernández, Justus Bogner, Xavier Franch, Marc Oriol, Julien Siebert, Adam Trendowicz, Anna Maria Vollmer, and Stefan Wagner. Software Engineering for AI-Based Systems: A Survey. Preprint, 1(1), 2021.

[17] International Organization for Standardization. ISO / IEC / IEEE 42010:2012: Systems and software engineering — Architecture description. Swedish Standards Institute, Stockholm, swedish standard edition, 2012.

[18] Heyn, Hans-Martin, Eric Knauss, and Patrizio Pelliccione. "A compositional approach to creating architecture frameworks with an application

to distributed AI systems." *Journal of Systems and Software* (2023): In print.

[19] Bashar Nuseibeh. Weaving Together Requirements and Architectures. Computer, 34(3):115–119, 2001.

[20] Jane Cleland-Huang, Robert S. Hanmer, Sam Supakkul, and Mehdi Mirakhorli. The twin peaks of requirements and architecture. IEEE Software, 30(2):24–29, 2013.

[21] European Commission. Regulation of the European Parliament and of the Council laying down harmonised rules on Artificial Intelligence (Artificial Intelligence Act) and amending certain Union Legislative Acts, 2020.

[22] International Organization for Standardization. ISO 26262:2018: Road vehicles— Functional safety. International Organization for Standardization, Geneva, 2018.

[23] Luiz Bittencourt, Roger Immich, Rizos Sakellariou, et al., 'The Internet of things, fog and cloud continuum: integration and challenges', Internet of Things, vol. 3, pp. 134–155, 2018.

[24] Daniel Balouek-Thomert, Eduard Gibert Renart, Ali Reza Zamani, et al., 'Towards a computing continuum: Enabling edge-to-cloud integration for data-driven workflows', International Journal of High Performance Computing Applications, vol. 33, num. 6, pp. 1159–1174, 2019.

[25] Sergei Arnautov, Bohdan Trach, Franz Gregor, et al., 'SCONE: secure Linux Containers with Intel SGX', 12th Symposium on Operating Systems Design and Implementation, USENIX, 2016.

[26] David Goltzsche, Manuel Nieke, Thomas Knauth, et al. 'AccTEE: A WebAssembly-based Two-way Sandbox for Trusted Resource Accounting', 20th International Middleware Conference, ACM, 2019.

[27] Jämes Ménétrey, Christian Göttel, Anum Khurshid, et al., 'Attestation mechanisms for trusted execution environments demystified', 22nd IFIP International Conference on Distributed Applications and Interoperable Systems, Springer, 2022.

[28] WebAssembly micro runtime (WAMR), https://github.com/bytecodealliance/wasm-micro-runtime.

[29] Victor Costan and Srinivas Devadas, 'Intel SGX explained', IACR Cryptology ePrint Archive, 2016.

[30] Arm, 'Introducing Arm TrustZone', https://developer.arm.com/ip-products/security-ip/trustzone, 2019.

[31] Advanced Micro Devices. 'Secure Encrypted Virtualization API: Technical Preview', tech. rep. 55766, 2019.

[32] Enarx, https://enarx.io.

[33] Veracruz, https://veracruz-project.com.

[34] Jämes Ménétrey, Marcelo Pasin, Pascal Felber, et al., 'Twine: an embedded trusted runtime for WebAssembly', 37th International Conference on Data Engineering, IEEE, 2021.

[35] Jämes Ménétrey, Marcelo Pasin, Pascal Felber, et al., 'WaTZ: a Trusted WebAssembly runtime environment with remote attestation for Trust-Zone', 38th International Conference on Distributed Computing Systems, IEEE, 2022.

[36] Jämes Ménétrey, Marcelo Pasin, Pascal Felber, et al., 'WebAssembly as a common layer for the cloud-edge continuum', 2nd Workshop on Flexible Resource and Application Management on the Edge, 2022.

[37] Louis-Noël Pouchet et al., 'PolyBench/C the polyhedral benchmark suite', 2018.

[38] Lv Junyan, Xu Shiguo, and Li Yijie, 'Application research of embedded database SQLite', International Forum on Information Technology and Applications, IEEE, 2009.

[39] Joel Höglund, Samuel Lindemer, Martin Furuhed, Shahid Raza. PKI4IoT: Towards Public Key Infrastructure for the Internet of Things. Computers & Security journal (Elsevier), Volume 89, Pages 101658, February 2020

[40] Joel Höglund, Martin Furuhed, Shahid Raza. Lightweight Certificate Revocation for Low-power IoT with End-to-end Security. Journal of Information Security and Applications (Elsevier), Volume 73, 103424, March 2023

[41] Joel Höglund, Martin Furuhed, Shahid Raza. Towards Automated PKI Trust Transfer for IoT. The 3rd International Conference on Public Key Infrastructure and Its Applications (PKIA 2022), September 9-10, 2022.

Part III

Blockchain Solutions for Trusted Edge Intelligence in IoT Systems

11

Decentralized Strategy for Artificial Intelligence in Distributed IoT Ecosystems: Federation in ASSIST-IoT

Eduardo Garro[1], Ignacio Lacalle[2], Karolina Bogacka[3,4], Anastasiya Danilenka[3,4], Katarzyna Wasielewska-Michniewska[3], Charalambos Tassakos[5], Anastasia Theodouli[6], Anastasia Kassiani Blitsi[6], Konstantinos Votis[6], Dimitrios Tzovaras[6], Marcin Paprzycki[3], and Carlos E. Palau[2]

[1]Prodevelop S. L., Spain
[2]Communications Department of Universitat PolitÃÍcnica de València, Spain
[3]Systems Research Institute, Polish Academy of Sciences, Poland
[4]Warsaw University of Technology, Poland
[5]TwoTronics GmbH, Germany
[6]The Centre for Research & Technology, Greece

Abstract

Decentralization of the IoT ecosystems poses several challenges whenever AI is applied in a shared fashion. Diverse locations, alongside privacy concerns, require the use of holistic strategies, where various environments effectively collaborate while avoiding data disclosure. In this context, this chapter proposes a use case to demonstrate the appropriateness of the solution brought by the ASSIST-IoT project. Specifically, multiple geographic and computing locations, which are close to the automotive surface defects detection scanners, work together to improve AI outcomes, scaling those to a large fleet of vehicles.

Keywords: Federated learning, Internet of Things, decentralization, edge-cloud continuum, surface defects detection.

231   DOI: 10.1201/9781032632407-14

11.1 Introduction

The current transition from cloud-like centralized datacenters to more decentralized systems, where geographically dispersed edge devices live, fosters an unprecedented paradigm shift with disruptive effects in the convergence between the physical and digital world. Here, orchestrating intelligence (AI) promises to be a key driver for enabling low-latency applications with high reliability in multitude of use cases (e.g., automotive, industrial automation, personalized health, etc.). In addition, moving intelligence closer to the edge, relaxing the dependence from a central location could contribute to bandwidth savings, and energy-efficiency and help to preserve data security/privacy [14].

The previous is aligned with reference to European entities in the field. First, the European Strategy for Data includes at its heart the need for decentralization to ensure flexibility and agility in matching demand/supply, and responsiveness while reducing resource consumption through flexible federation and a "fair business offer" [3]. Besides, according to the Alliance for the Internet of Things Innovation (AIOTI) roadmap [7], the next release (v6) of its high-level architecture will focus on artificial intelligence and machine learning (AI) for the next-generation IoT systems (NG-IoT). The success of using AI/ML to solve NG-IoT problems will highly depend on the quality and quantity of available training data. However, while traditional ML approaches typically rely on the central management of training data, such an approach does not seem to be feasible or practical in the next era of IoT. The reasons for this are, on the one hand, data privacy and regulatory compliance and, on the other hand, technical burdens associated with the growing amount of data to be collected and transferred to "a central location." In this context, decentralized AI solutions are needed.

11.1.1 Decentralized AI

The term distributed intelligence has at least two meanings: (a) **collective intelligence** and (b) **decentralized AI**.

The main mechanisms of the collective intelligence are: (a) *cognition* in terms of sensing, (b) *cooperation* as multiple (semi-) autonomous entities exchanging data to jointly establish what needs to be done, and (c) *coordination*, conceptualized as a mechanism crucial for the realization of workflows, where specific actions depend on the results of other actions. If those mechanisms are understood in the most convenient way, it is not very difficult to envision scenarios, in which collective intelligence can be claimed to materialize within NG-IoT ecosystems.

On the other hand, decentralized AI (sometimes also called distributed AI) is a subfield of AI research, dedicated to the development of distributed solutions for problems. It is often seen as a predecessor to the research devoted to software agents and (multi-)agent systems. Still, within the scope of this book, we referred this action to *distributed problem solving*. The main idea is that, for example, completing the training of neural networks with (very) large datasets would require on a single node a substantial amount of time (hours, days, or even weeks) and resources, whereas if multiple computing nodes are tightly coupled, the "training work" can be divided among them, leading to more efficient use of resources in lower operational time. In this way, distributed AI is somehow related to parallel computing. Here, it is important to realize that the most common parallel computing methods and approaches have been designed for a single stakeholder (i.e., a single user, or a company), being the sole owner of all of the data used for model training. However, it has to be realized that, for the past few years, the situation has been rapidly evolving. Among others, the following trends brought about the changes:

- Proliferation of powerful handheld devices with multiple sensors, which generate streams of data that users may want to control.
- Fast drop of price and size of sensors (and actuators), which can be placed "everywhere" and can belong to "anybody."
- Availability of small and inexpensive processors designed for machine learning (e.g., NVIDIA Jetson Nano series devices), which can be placed in almost any location within the IoT ecosystem.
- Increase in the number of wireless networks with high bandwidth and range, which are used to establish communication channels between sensors, actuators, edge devices, computing nodes, gateways, cloud(s), etc.
- Progress in research, development, and deployment of the IoT ecosystems, in almost all areas of day-to-day activities.
- Advances in methods, and their implementations, that can be used in various ML scenarios.

As a result, the vision of a single owner of data, which is stored in a centralized location and used to train model(s) to realize its own (individual) goals, starts to be supplanted by approaches that can facilitate coopetition. Here, coopetition is understood as a scenario where multiple entities (e.g., data owners) compete in one context (e.g., as producers of medicines) and cooperate in another, e.g., as providers of knowledge for the development of shared machine learning models. Notably, this implies certain orchestration and harmonization workload that must be performed among topologically– and likely geographically– disperse devices, therefore becoming larger than single-node parallelization.

11.1.2 Federated learning

Federated learning (FL) [10], [12] is one of the most recent developments in the area of decentralized AI. FL is an approach to train AI/ML models involving multiple datasets stored in "local nodes." In other words, in FL, a shared (global) model is trained collaboratively by multiple parties, which protect their (private) training datasets. After each "round" of local training, the model parameters are "combined into the central model." After the update is completed, the updated central model is redistributed and used either in the training or in the inference processes. Typically, the updated version of the global model is sent back to the nodes that participated in the training. However, there exist FL scenarios, in which "new nodes" participate in each training round (see, for instance, [11]). The training process is completed, when the common model meets specific stopping criteria. Here, it should be noted that while the typical training of a neural network is reported, FL is model-independent; i.e., any model that can be trained on local data and updated centrally can be used.

It should be noticed that the notion of parties participating in FL training might refer to a wide spectrum of possibilities; starting from small edge devices, cameras, or mobile phones, up to enterprise-scale data centers located in different countries or even different companies and organizations. With that scope in mind, ASSIST-IoT project [1] moves forward in this decentralized AI direction, by providing an FL infrastructure to be used to instantiate FL in future NG-IoT systems. This infrastructure is under con-struction and is being deployed in a real-life industrial scenario. This chapter presents the ASSIST-IoT FL system in detail, in the context of a specific use case of the project focused on automotive sector. Here, the deployment will realize an FL-based surface defect detection, applied without compromising the data privacy of a large fleet of vehicles that pass through the scanners in their individual locations.

The remainder of the chapter is organized as follows. Section 11.2 intro-duces the different concepts of federated learning, while section 11.3 presents the adopted ASSIST-IoT FL architecture, detailing the different enablers designed and implemented within the scope of the project. Next, Section 11.4 presents the specific case study and the current deployment situation. Finally, conclusions are drawn in Section 11.5.

11.2 Federated Learning Principles

In order to successfully design the appropriate ASSIST-IoT FL system, the project has followed the FL taxonomy identified in [9] that relies on five main aspects:

- **Communication architecture:** While in a centralized design the parameter updates on the global model are always done in a central manager, also called aggregator or collector, in a decentralized design, there is not a single point of truth (there is no manager element). The most commonly known example of a centralized FL architecture is the Google Keyboard - Gboard for mobile keyboard predictions [8].
- **Scale of federation:** The FL systems can be categorized into two typical types by the scale of federation: *cross-silo* and *cross-device*. The differences between them lie in the number of parties and the amount of data stored in each party. In *cross-silo*, the parties can be either independent organizations or independent data centers of a single organization. In *cross-device*, on the contrary, the number of parties is relatively large and each party has a relatively small amount of data as well as computational power, the parties usually being IoT devices.
- **Data partitioning:** FL systems are also categorized in horizontal or vertical data partitioning based on how data are distributed over the sample and feature spaces. In *horizontal data partitioning*, the datasets of different parties have the same feature space but little intersection on the sample space, so that the parties can train the local models using their local data with the same model architecture. In *vertical FL*, the datasets of different parties have the same sample space but differ in the feature space.
- **ML model:** Since FL is used to solve ML problems, the parties usually want to train state-of-the-art ML models. The most popular ML models are *neural networks (NN)*, which achieve state-of-the-art results in many AI tasks, like image classification and word prediction; *decision trees*, which are highly efficient to train and easy to interpret compared with NNs; and *linear models* (e.g., linear regression, logistic regression, and

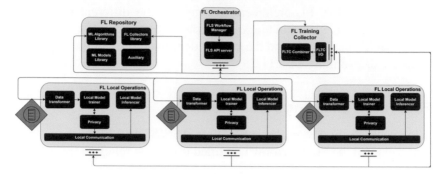

Figure 11.1 ASSIST-IoT FL system formed by four enablers.

support vector machines), which are well-known and easy-to-use ML models.

- **Privacy mechanism:** Although, ideally, local data is not expected to be exposed in FL, the exchanged model parameters may still leak sensitive information about the data. The most well-known privacy mechanisms include *cryptographic methods* or *differential privacy*.

11.3 Federated Learning System of ASSIST-IoT Project

According to the previously described categorization, and feature implementation options, the proposed ASSIST-IoT FL system for the automotive pilot uses the following configuration:

- Communication architecture: Centralized
- Scale of federation: Cross-device
- Data partitioning: Horizontal
- ML model: Neural Network
- Privacy mechanism: Differential privacy

The proposed ASSIST-IoT FL system block diagram and flow chart are shown in Figure 11.1. As it can be seen, four main functional blocks can be distinguished. These functional blocks are named **enablers** and are used as an abstraction term in the project acting as the cornerstone elements of the ASSIST-IoT architecture. In essence, an enabler is a collection of software *components* – running on nodes – that work together to deliver a specific functionality of a system, that is, ASSIST-IoT enablers are not atomic but presented as a set of interconnected components. It should be noticed that multiple enablers may be used in a system to deliver a more complex *service*, leveraging features of the involved enablers. Additionally, one of the most important design principles that distinguish *components* from *enablers* is that the components from different enablers cannot directly communicate unless a RESTful API endpoint has been explicitly developed for that purpose.

Regarding the regular call flow in this particular deployment, it starts with the model training. To do so, a proper training job configuration is submitted to FL orchestrator that propagates it to FL training collector and candidate FL local operations to execute the job. Then, FL training collector collaborates with FL local operations to finally obtain new global model aggregated from successive local updates. To support the process, FL repository is used to store all required intermediate and final information and metadata. After successfully finalizing the training job, the new global model can be used for local inference by FL local operations.

The following sections describe the four ASSIST-IoT FL enablers in detail [13].

11.3.1 FL enablers

11.3.1.1 FL Orchestrator

FL orchestrator is the enabler responsible for specifying and managing FL workflow(s)/pipeline(s), including:

- FL job scheduling;
- Management of the FL lifecycle;
- Selection and delivery of initial version(s) of the shared model;
- Delivery of the version(s) of models used in various stages of the process, such as training stopping criteria;
- Handling the different "error conditions" that may occur during the FL process.

It is formed by two components:

- **FLS API server:** Offers a REST API to allow for the communication and interaction with the other enablers of the FL system. Although the communication of model updates and configuration between the FL training collector is carried out via gRPC, all traffic between the FL orchestrator or the FL repository and the rest of the enablers is exchanged using a RESTful API. Hence, it allows to retrieve information or perform FL management actions, to FL local operations, FL training collector, and FL repository.

• **FLS workflow manager:** This component is in charge of defining the workflow for a specific instance of the FL lifecycle. Workflow description specifies, among others, the source of initial configuration (e.g., minimum number of FL local operations needed for federated training, number of training rounds for carrying out the federated learning process, the initial shared ML model to be used, evaluation criteria method and required accuracy value, method used for parameter aggregation, and required encryption mechanisms), and lifecycle management (e.g., evaluating the number of FL local operations connected, or the number of training rounds finished provided by the FL training collector).

11.3.1.2 FL Repository

The FL repository is used to store all information necessary to conduct the FL process (configuration, models, algorithms, etc.). It consists of two components, one holding the FastAPI, server which is in constant contact with the second component that encapsulates the MongoDB database.

This database is used to store initial ML models, already trained ML parameters suitable for specific datasets and formats, multiple averaging approaches, as well as additional functionalities that may later be needed, including data transformations and IP addresses of potential client instances present in the FL system of ASSIST-IoT. ML model weights are kept in the form of GridFS chunks in order to allow them to exceed the size of 16 MB (which they sometimes do).

The FastAPI server serves just as a gatekeeper to the MongoDB instance, allowing for the easy performance of specific queries (and only performing those queries).

11.3.1.3 FL Training Collector

The FL training process involves several independent parties that commonly collaborate in order to provide an enhanced ML model. In this process, the different local update suggestions shall be aggregated accordingly. This duty within ASSIST-IoT is tackled by the FL training collector, which resides in a centralized location and is also in charge of delivering back the updated model. Therefore, its functionalities are:

• Aggregation of local updates of the ML model prepared by independent parties as a part of a model enhancement process by means of the specialized FL averaging mechanisms and FL training collector I/O components.

- Supplying specific FL local operations with any additional configuration they might need by communicating via gRPC.
- Configuration of the employment of privacy mechanisms on edge (in the case of differential privacy) or just aggregating the weights in a manner compliant with those mechanisms (in the case of homomorphic encryption).
- Delivering back to the parties the updated model using the established gRPC connection, synchronizing the training, and later obtaining the results of local training.
- In some cases, the FL training collector may also conduct performance evaluation on the global model throughout training. For this purpose, it will also use the data transformation module (in order to pre-process the test data before the evaluation). More information about the data transformation module will be presented in a later section.

11.3.1.4 FL Local Operations

The FL local operations is the enabler embedded in each involved party performing local training. Its components and their respective functionalities are:

- **Data transformer** is used for the verification of local data format compatibility with the data formats required by the models being trained, as well as for application of the required data transformations using predefined transformers if needed. For more details about the data transformation module, please refer to the next section.
- **Local model trainer** is in charge of getting the local results that are later on passed to the FL training collector to carry out the proper aggregation method over the common shared model.
- **Local model inferencer**, as its name suggests, carries out the inference process of the final shared ML model over new incoming data.
- **Privacy**. There are two privacy mechanisms available out of the box provided by ASSIST-IoT enablers: differential privacy with adaptive clipping and homomorphic encryption. The differential privacy mechanism was based on [5] and [6]. Here, the influence of the model update supplied by a given client is not clipped according to a fixed clipping threshold but adaptively modified throughout training. Although the Gaussian noise and clipping is applied on the side of FL local operations, FL training collector is responsible for most of the metric computation needed to adjust the clipping. Homomorphic encryption, on the other

hand, requires a significant additional computation on the side of FL local operations, with only small adjustments needed on the side of the FL training collector. Therefore, the computational and communications overhead introduced by the homomorphic encryption currently prohibits its use beyond the training of very simple models using a specially adapted version of the federated averaging strategy.

- **Local communication** is the RESTful API that acts as the entrance and exit gate of the FL local operations with the rest of the enablers of the FL system. The FL local operations can also additionally establish a gRPC connection with the FL training collector.

11.3.2 Secure reputation mechanism for the FL system via blockchain and distributed ledger

In addition to the baseline FL features, an external distributed ledger enabler will be included in the next iteration of the pilot. It would provide a secure reputation mechanism for all the local operators. The reputation mechanism therefore will constitute a safe guard mechanism that prevents free-riders from freely accessing the global model without contributing to it and also malicious adversaries from poisoning the global model [17]. To do so, blockchain technology has been proposed. This technology allows the secure maintenance of a distributed ledger among several parties without the need of a trusted centralized authority using a consensus algorithm. Blockchain technologies depending on whether we refer to permissionless or permissioned blockchain networks can ensure different security aspects. For permissionless blockchain networks, transparency, decentralization, immutability, and traceability of shared data can be ensured, while permissioned networks can ensure private transactions by granting access to the data of the distributed ledger only to authorized users who have the right permissions [2], [15], [16].

The integration of the DLT enabler with the FL baseline system is illustrated in Figure 11.2. The DLT enabler will calculate reputation scores for each FL local operator instance, which will be stored on a permissioned blockchain network that allows only authorized users to have access to the scores and also to participate in the consensus algorithm that updates them. This consequently will increase the privacy of the reputation score data. Next, FL training collector will send the weights from the FL local operations and the weights from the global model to the distributed ledger (DLT).

The final reputation score for each FL local operations will be calculated using the cosine similarity between the weights of FL local operations and the aggregated weight [17]. The final reputation score for each local operator

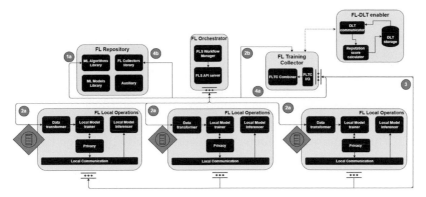

Figure 11.2 ASSIST-IoT FL-DLT enabler.

will be stored in the DLT along with the reputation set that contains the FL local operations who would be considered reputable in this round (if their calculated score is not below a given threshold). The FL training collector will query on an on–off strategy to the reputation scores and reputation set, so that further decisions on the penalties or incentives for the FL local operations may be taken.

In detail, the FL-DLT enabler depicted in Figure 11.2 is composed of three components:

- **Distributed ledger (DLT) communicator:** This component is a RESTful API that receives weights from the training collector, and it also fetches from the DLT storage and sends back to the training collector the reputation scores and reputation set.
- **Reputation score calculator:** This component applies the reputation mechanism and calculates the scores for each local operator in each training round. It also maintains a reputation set containing all the reputable local operators.
- **Distributed ledger (DLT) storage:** This component stores the reputation scores and the reputation set to the distributed ledger.

11.4 ASSIST-IoT FL Application in an Automotive Defect Detection Use Case

11.4.1 Business overview and context of the scenario

During the last years, the digitalization pressure and optimization needs are deeply studied in the automotive field. AI-based surface inspection of the vehicle exterior is seen as a well-promised common case of the previous one, where precisely FL can hold a primary role. For instance, in the proposed validation scenario, where images are taken by cameras in arch scanners that are installed in various locations and potentially in garages owned by different entities. First, it relaxes the need of sharing data (privacy and aversion concerns). Second, it reduces the dependency on network connection vís-a-vis a centralized, cloud approach of data gathering and AI application. Third, it moves the focus to the work close to the action (where scanners are), in terms of end-user interaction. This is relevant as this interaction actually inserts labeled training and validation data; thus, efficiency is improved.

In the proposed case, the goal is for a FL-powered deep learning system to relax the bandwidth usage and the overall network dependency and to provide faster and more accurate detection of defects (currently up to 15 minutes). The FL solution will need to deal with cameras that capture data and metadata of 50–300 colored, high-resolution images per vehicle analyzed (Figure 11.3). Then the system mounted forward data via fiber optics, 4G, and 5G to a cloud location. Edge locations (where scanners reside) are equipped with an intelligent storage system with local buffering (but have limited storage capacity) and provide a direct connection to end users that annotate human-visualized defects. There, the associated front-end software must handle a hundred thousand images, offering advanced, application-centered visualization, and display with an optional focus on existing damages and AI proposal. It must be considered that the data can be very heterogeneous due to different models, locations, scanner owner, and indoor/outdoor position, among others. Therefore, the AI-based inspection can strongly support both manual users reviewing or automated inspection and evaluation procedures to monitor and determine the vehicle's exterior conditions. Due to the nature of the task, the consideration of the images of many scanners for the AI-model training has large impact on the overall quality of the global AI models in the current cloud approach

From the federated learning point of view, the task setup may look as follows (Figure 11.3). Either scanners or individual cameras can operate as federated clients, performing both model training and inference tasks, with the central server being responsible for coordinating the processes, like training, testing, aggregating, and distributing the latest version of the global model.

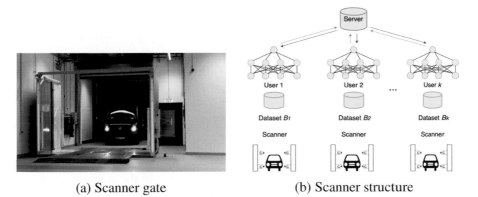

(a) Scanner gate   (b) Scanner structure

Figure 11.3   Car damage recognition - scanner gate.

11.4.2 Proposed solution and benefits of decentralized learning strategy

The application of AI and specifically FL to the automotive use case enables to optimize the process of damage recognition with respect to current situation. First, application of AI and inference close to the sources of the data will enable faster processing of the data and recognition of situations that need special handling. Second, the benefits coming with using FL-based approach can be identified compared to the centralized approach. The centralized approach is an alternative in which all data collected on local devices (e.g., scanner cameras) is sent to the server (cloud) and processed there to train the model or inference on using the trained model. Therefore, FL allows the described use case to benefit from the following:

- Significantly reduced or practically non-existing necessity to transfer privacy-sensitive data. As a result, the whole dataset is never stored in a centralized manner, but local datasets are available on client nodes and used there to train the local versions of the model. This increases overall data privacy which is important when considering multi-stakeholder environment with coopetition. This is relevant for the selected application case due to the aforementioned aversion and privacy concern existing while scanners are owned by multiple entities (and even in single scenarios). Cameras are subject to confidentiality rules, as they may contain private information of both the vehicle owner and the company that performs the damage inspection.
- Decreased need for data storage capacities on the server side and reduced data transfer between local devices and server (cloud). This is

specifically important in big data environments. This would help entities using the scanner-based installation to be more efficient and accurate on their predictions, as the need of communication toward cloud would be relaxed and the annotation by company stuff would leverage (limited) edge storage capacities instead of submitting upwards.

- Improved inference speed, as the location of the global model on the local nodes implies that no communication between the source of the data and the server (cloud) for generating predictions is intended and all the inference happens close to the device that generated the data. As indicated in the business case description, this is the main goal of the application of FL system, aiming to reduce the (up to) 15 minutes current timeframe for predictions.
- Personalization availability. Due to the previously described reasons for local data heterogeneity, federated clients may require additional uptraining on their local data for better model performance, and FL provides an easy way to produce a more personalized tool for vehicle damage detection that takes into consideration features of the local dataset, while still benefiting from the generalized knowledge from the multiple entities that participated in the joint training.
- Global model aggregation techniques can be used to mitigate the effect of the heterogeneity of damage and vehicle types present on the client nodes. Here, allowing local training of models, which can grasp more nuances related to usual vehicles in a specific location (e.g., vans), would enhance the depth of knowledge that can be applied to other sites with less volume of such. Therefore, FL system is capable of adapting to task-specific challenges and site-specific data.

Figure 11.4 shows how enablers proposed in the ASSIST-IoT FL architecture can be combined in the system deployed for automotive defect detection use case. Here, the *FL local operations* run on clients (cameras), whereas *FL orchestrator*, *FL training collector*, and *FL repository* are located in the cloud. The main goal is to distribute the processing, instead of sending all the images to the cloud and processing it centrally. Here, although the centralized topology seems to be a good choice for initial implementation, it can be foreseen that a more complex topology (e.g., hierarchical) may be ultimately needed [4]. One of the reasons is that in an extended deployment, groups of scanners may belong to different stakeholders that all want to benefit from the good detection model but without disclosing their data.

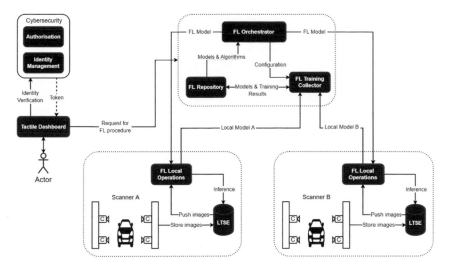

Figure 11.4 FL architecture for the automotive defect detection use case.

Note that, on the diagram, besides aforementioned FL enablers, additional enablers designed and implemented within ASSIST-IoT are included addressing: *cybersecurity* (specifically authentication and authorization), *long-term storage* (the *long-term storage enabler* can provide local storage of images for FL clients), and *tactile dashboard* (for visualizations needed in the system). Upon reflection, it is easy to see that these elements can provide all additional functions needed in the considered ecosystem.

11.4.3 Proposed validation

Federated learning experiments for the car damage detection use case were performed based on the mask-RCNN model for object detection and segmentation. During the federated training, separate cameras were treated as federated clients. Initial experiments were performed with a total of eight cameras, although in the future scenarios, more populated experiments are expected.

The evaluation of the FL model is based on the holdout evaluation dataset, which consists of images, representing a comprehensive set of possible inference scenarios. This dataset also includes images with no detected damages at all, in order to properly test the model's capability to accurately detect both damages and their absence. An example of the damage detected by the model is shown in Figure 11.5.

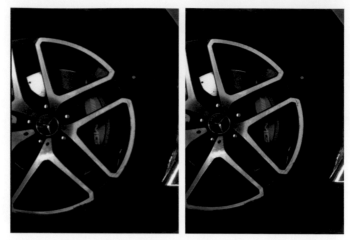

Figure 11.5   Rim damage detection example (target – left; result – right).

The metrics taken into account are appropriate for the task of object detection and segmentation. The main performance indicators, therefore, are precision, recall, and the resulting F1 score per damage category with the IoU (intersection over union) threshold set at a reasonable value. For the deployed model, the appropriate IoU is expected to be around 0.5.

Apart from the calculated performance indicator, an expert-based evaluation is also implied. As the system is expected to assist human professionals during their damage evaluation activities, their feedback will provide the necessary information for further model improvements.

Finally, for the evaluation of the use case, the following KPIs have been identified and will be controlled and verified: (i) increase of detected defects on the car exterior, (ii) faster vehicle inspection compared to the current process (planned at least 30% increase), and (iii) minimization of data transfer (planned at least 50% increase).

11.5 Conclusions

Decentralized AI promises to be a relevant innovation to be incorporated to Next-Generation IoT deployments. From the viewpoint of decentralized intelligence, ASSIST-IoT has focused on Federated Learning. This technique relies on training machine learning models in coopetition manner –a joint cooperation and competition approach– over heterogeneous nodes located at different locations and with different computing capabilities. For doing so, strategies to locally train the models, centrally orchestrate the averaged updates, and a way to bring back the trained model for either further training or infererence to those edge devices is needed. Rooting on relevant references and based on the novel architecture provided by the project, an FL system has been designed and it is being developed.

One of the many applications that such a system could have is materialized in a real-life use case brought by ASSIST-IoT, consisting of leveraging edge computing in various locations to train ML algorithms that detect defects on vehicles' surfaces. The usage of ASSIST-IoT's FL system allows to improve inference speed as well as reduce the network bandwidth needs to the cloud, while keeping the data in the local environments, thus increasing security and privacy. The use case is currently being trialed and some early evaluation activities are providing optimistic outlooks. Final results of the experiment will be presented in future works.

Acknowledgements

This work is part of the ASSIST-IoT project that has received funding from the EU's Horizon 2020 research and innovation program, under Grant Agreement No. 957258.

References

[1] ASSIST-IoT project. https://www.assist-iot.eu. Accessed: 2023-01-06.
[2] Permissioned blockchain vs. permissionless blockchain: Key differences.
https://cointelegraph.com/blockchain-for-beginners/permissioned-blockchain-vs-permissionless-blockchain-key-differences. Accessed: 2023-01-13.
[3] The European Data Strategy, 202.
https://ec.europa.eu/commission/presscorner/detail/en/fs_20_283. Accessed: 2023-01-06.
[4] *Introducing Federated Learning into Internet of Things ecosystems – preliminary considerations*, 07 2022.
[5] Galen Andrew, Om Thakkar, Brendan McMahan, and Swaroop Ramaswamy. Differentially private learning with adaptive clipping. *Advances in Neural Information Processing Systems*, 34:17455–17466, 2021.

[6] Daniel J Beutel, Taner Topal, Akhil Mathur, Xinchi Qiu, Titouan Parcollet, and Nicholas D Lane. Flower: A friendly federated learning research framework. *arXiv preprint arXiv:2007.14390*, 2020.

[7] O. Elloumi, M. Carugi, J. P. Desbenoit, G. Karagiannis, and P. Murdock. AIOTI-WG3-High Level Architecture (HLA) Release 5.0. 2020.

[8] Andrew Hard, Kanishka Rao, Rajiv Mathews, Françoise Beaufays, Sean Augenstein, Hubert Eichner, Chloé Kiddon, and Daniel Ramage. Federated learning for mobile keyboard prediction. *CoRR*, abs/1811.03604, 2018.

[9] Ahmed Imteaj, Urmish Thakker, Shiqiang Wang, Jian Li, and M. Hadi Amini. A survey on federated learning for resource-constrained iot devices. *IEEE Internet of Things Journal*, 9(1):1–24, 2022.

[10] Latif U. Khan, Walid Saad, Zhu Han, Ekram Hossain, and Choong Seon Hong. Federated learning for internet of things: Recent advances, taxonomy, and open challenges. *CoRR*, abs/2009.13012, 2020.

[11] Brendan McMahan, Eider Moore, Daniel Ramage, Seth Hampson, and Blaise Aguera y Arcas. Communication-efficient learning of deep networks from decentralized data. In *Artificial intelligence and statistics*, pages 1273–1282. PMLR, 2017.

[12] H. Brendan McMahan, Eider Moore, Daniel Ramage, and Blaise Agüera y Arcas. Federated learning of deep networks using model averaging. *CoRR*, abs/1602.05629, 2016.

[13] Marcin Paprzycki, Maria Ganzha, Katarzyna Wasielewska, and Piotr Lewandowski. Devsecops methodology for ng-iot ecosystem development lifecycle - assist-iot perspective. *Journal of Computer Science and Cybernetics*, 37(3):321-337, Sep. 2021.

[14] Yuji Roh, Geon Heo, and Steven Euijong Whang. A survey on data collection for machine learning: A big data - ai integration perspective. *IEEE Transactions on Knowledge and Data Engineering*, 33(4):1328–1347, 2021.

[15] Siamak Solat, P. Calvez, and Farid Naït-Abdesselam. Permissioned vs. permissionless blockchain: How and why there is only one right choice. *Journal of Software*, 16:95 – 106, 12 2020.

[16] Muhammad Habib ur Rehman, Khaled Salah, Ernesto Damiani, and Davor Svetinovic. Towards blockchain-based reputation-aware federated learning. In *IEEE INFOCOM 2020 - IEEE Conference on*

Computer Communications Workshops (INFOCOM WKSHPS), pages 183–188, 2020.

[17] Xinyi Xu and Lingjuan Lyu. A reputation mechanism is all you need: Collaborative fairness and adversarial robustness in federated learning. *arXiv preprint arXiv:2011.10464*, 2020.

12

Achieving Security and Privacy in NG-IoT using Blockchain Techniques

Vasiliki Kelli[1], Anna Triantafyllou[1], Panagiotis Radoglou-Grammatikis[1], Thomas Lagkas[2], Vasileios Vitsas[2], Panagiotis Fouliras[3], Igor Kotsiuba[4], and Panagiotis Sarigiannidis[1]

[1]University of Western Macedonia, Greece
[2]International Hellenic University, Greece
[3]University of Macedonia, Greece
[4]iSolutions Labs, Ukraine
E-mail: vkelly@uowm.gr; atriantafyllou@uowm.gr; pradoglou@uowm.gr; tlagkas@cs.ihu.gr; vitsas@it.teithe.gr; pfoul@uom.gr; igor.kotsiuba@isolutions.com.ua; psarigiannidis@uowm.gr

Abstract

The centralization of data is a current practice in information systems that do not fit into the novel next-generation computing concept. Such a paradigm aims to support the distribution of information, processing, and computing power. Blockchain is a technology supporting the recording of information for distributed and decentralized, peer-to-peer applications, which has emerged in the last decade, with the initial focus being on the finance sector. A highly valuable feature of blockchain is its capability of enhancing the security of data due to the immutability of the information stored on the ledger. In this chapter, the definition, details, applications, and benefits of this technology will be explored. In addition, the ways in which blockchain increases security and privacy will be described. Finally, the pairing of blockchain with other next-generation, cutting-edge technologies will be investigated.

Keywords: Blockchain, security, privacy, peer-to-peer.

251 DOI: 10.1201/9781032632407-15

12.1 Introduction – What Is Blockchain?

Technology has become an aspect of daily life for most of the world's population. Intelligent devices able to capture, gather, process, and distribute information have become a necessity for an ever-increasing number of domains, ranging from the simplistic use of smart home gadgets to the highly critical medical sector. Intelligent devices have become such an integral part of contemporary society, which each human is estimated to own 9.3 devices, by the year of 2025 [1]. Such a massive number of data-driven devices is expected to significantly increase the volume of data to be processed and stored. After all, Internet of Things (IoT) contributed to the creation of the concept of Big Data, which is defined as highly variable data, produced at high velocity, and is arriving in big volumes. Next-generation IoT (NG-IoT) is a novel concept in computing, aiming to extend IoT in a human-centric, distributed manner. As such, objects, services, and technologies offered to the end-users are combined to achieve optimal end-user satisfaction, while the processing of data occurs in the edge, closer to the user, yielding faster response times.

Contemporary information systems mostly focus on processing and storing data in a central manner. This means that data travels from each data source to a central entity for further management. However, this task is becoming increasingly difficult due to the high volume and variety of the produced information; as such, the effective storage and rapid analysis of data becomes the main concern. In addition, centralization is often associated with security and privacy issues, due to data traveling through unsecure channels to the central entity, or due to the single-point-of-failure problem, which dictates that the entire process will fail, if the central entity's operation is disrupted.

The issues described in the paragraphs above have contributed to a current effort to shift from the use of the concept of centralization in IoT to the concept of decentralization. Consequently, information, processing, and other aspects are distributed across devices, recanting the single-point-of-failure problem. The significance of the shift toward decentralization has become prominent due to the rise of the NG-IoT concept in computing, where instead of relying on cloud solutions for data processing, all management occurs in various distributed edge nodes, closer to the end-user.

Blockchain is the technology mostly associated with decentralization and thus plays a key role in the NG-IoT concept. Although this technology became well-known through the launch of the first digital cryptocurrency, Bitcoin, in 2009, the idea was initially described by a person under the

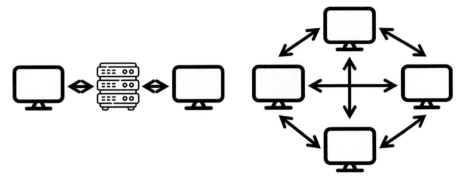

Figure 12.1 Centralized systems (left) and decentralized systems (right).

pseudonym "Satoshi Nakamoto" in 2008 [12], [13]. The concept behind blockchain states that it serves as a system to record information, in an immutable manner. This information is duplicated, and every participant in the blockchain network owns a copy of it. In particular, a blockchain is a digital ledger of transactions cryptographically signed and grouped into blocks. Each new block is cryptographically linked to the previous one, while it undergoes validation through a consensus decision by the network's members, in order to be added to the blockchain [2]. Due to blockchain's function of distributing copies of the data on the chain across the network, conflicts regarding data differences due to malicious actions are easily resolved, while its cryptographic nature boosts security [11]. Since blockchains follow an append-only policy and every member owns a copy, it is impossible for old blocks to be deleted or modified, making data on the chain tamper-resistant [14].

In order to cryptographically sign and link blocks to each other, hash functions are used by blockchain technology. Hashing refers to the application of a function to an input of any kind, leading to an output, or digest, of a specific size. Well-known hash functions include secure hash algorithm 256 (SHA-256), which produces an output of 256 bits, message-digest 5 (MD-5), which digests the input into 128 bits, and SHA-1, which produces a 160-bit output. Hash functions are one-way, meaning that they cannot be reversed, while the slightest change to the input will lead to a digest vastly different [15]. This makes hash functions optimal for verifying the veracity of data stored in the blocks. In addition, it is impossible to find inputs that lead to the same digest. As such, the utilization of hashing is able to highly elevate the security in blockchain technology.

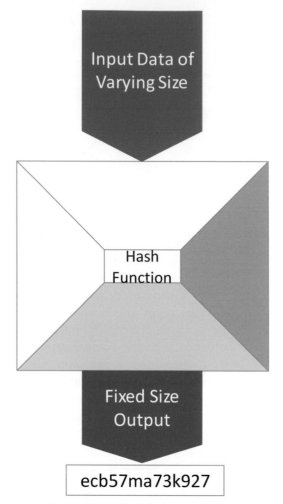

Figure 12.2 Hash function operation.

Figure 12.3 depicts a basic diagram of a blockchain network. As discussed, each block contains transactions, the calculated hash of its header, and the hash of the previous, or parent block. In blockchains, the first block created is called the genesis block and it is the only one that does not contain the hash of the previous block [3]. The header hash is generated by taking as an input information such as the timestamp, the block's data, and the parent block's hash. Hashing allows traceability of potentially malicious changes, contributing to blockchain's secure nature.

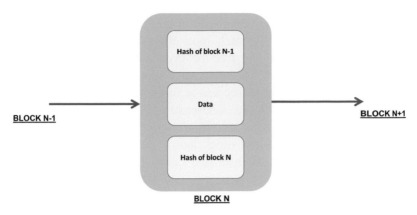

Figure 12.3 Blockchain architecture.

Blockchain is a versatile, easily integrable technology promising to elevate the security levels of the respective application areas. The versatility of this technology comes from the fact that it can be used in varying ways – from verifying transactions to securely storing any kind of data. Thus, blockchain has become an integral part of NG-IoT, as it can be effectively combined with other NG-IoT technologies and concepts such as artificial intelligence (AI), federated learning, cybersecurity, and edge and cloud computing [22]. Blockchain can support secure sharing of model updates in a centralized federated learning setting, as the model updates can be wrapped as transactions and stored in the blocks; thus, their integrity can be ensured by the federated clients [23]. In addition, blockchain can support a fully peer-to-peer AI training systems, where model updates are stored directly on the chain by the participants in the peer-to-peer network [24]. Finally, blockchains can be used for logging of actions, authentication, and authorization in a critical NG-IoT setting, as a cybersecurity solution [25], [26].

12.2 Permission-less and Permissioned Blockchain

Blockchains are categorized based on who can publish new blocks. If there is no restriction on who can append new blocks on the chain, then the blockchain is considered to be permission-less. On the other hand, if only certain entities are allowed to publish new blocks on the chain, then the blockchain is considered to be permissioned.

Permission-less or public blockchains allow anyone with access to the network to read and publish new blocks and make transactions [16]. Usually, such blockchain networks are used primarily in the finance sector and, more specifically, in cryptocurrencies. As such, blockchains that are categorized as permission-less are open-source and free for anyone to download them and take participation in the network. However, such blockchains face probable security threats as entities can have free access to the network and thus some may try to maliciously publish blocks. Consensus mechanisms, explained in Section 12.3, aim to resolve such issues.

In contrast with permission-less blockchains, permissioned blockchain networks rely on a central or decentralized entity to allow access to the chain. In case a centralized entity is responsible for granting access, then this entity should be trustworthy. Private and consortium blockchains are both permissioned, with the former being administered by a single entity, while the latter is being administered by a group of organizations. If users are not registered by the entity to the network, then they are not able to publish new blocks, while they may not be able to read blocks, as reading can be restricted by the entity of authority. In case users have permission to join the network, they should prove through methods such as certificates that they are allowed to access to blockchain. Such blockchain networks are predominantly utilized by organizations that prefer to keep their transactions and data private and more secure. Organizations may employ permissioned blockchain to manage inventory and their supply chain, amongst other options. Permissioned blockchains may be especially useful in NG-IoT use cases where sensitive data is stored on the ledger, such as hospitals and smart grids; thus, authentication should be required to obtain the stored information.

Finally, hybrid blockchains combine the characteristics of both a permissioned and a permission-less blockchain network. Specifically, the members of the network are able to regulate and allow the accessibility of the network to other users, while the hybrid blockchain users decide whether transactions are made public [4]. This makes hybrid blockchains a customizable approach to blockchain networks.

12.3 Consensus Mechanisms

As blockchain networks are composed of distributed and trustless systems, a mechanism to allow all the nodes to reach an agreement on the validity of the blocks to be published and the status of the ledger is required. This issue is especially highlighted due to the lack of a trustworthy central authority able to regulate and manage all actions in the network. In addition, malicious actions may be an issue for permission-less ledgers, due to the unregulated

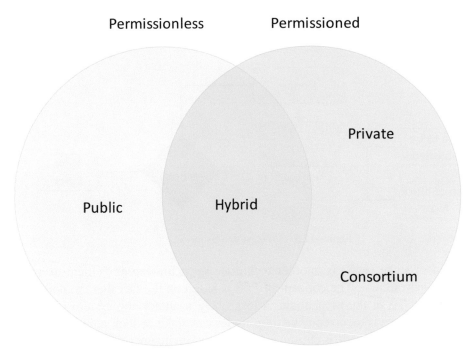

Figure 12.4 Permissioned and permission-less blockchains.

nature of such blockchains, and thus actors may attempt to alter the state of the blockchain. To address this concern, consensus mechanisms are used by the blockchain to allow the nodes to achieve trust and security between them and reach an agreement regarding the state of the decentralized ledger.

Proof of work (PoW), otherwise known as mining, is a procedure in which the participants of the mining process are required to calculate the hash value of the header of the block to be appended to the ledger [17]. Specifically, the hash value should remain below a given target value. To achieve this, miners have to find a nonce number, which is able to yield a lower or equal hash value, when added to the block's header. When a miner is able to solve the puzzle and find a nonce that yields a lower hash value, they send the block with the nonce found to the rest of the network for verification. The rest of the nodes hash the block header with the nonce, verify the work conducted by the miner, and proceed by appending the new block to their copy of the blockchain [5]. PoW consensus model was first seen in Bitcoin. As the calculation of the nonce is quite a challenging task with high computational difficulty, the miner able to find the nonce is usually rewarded.

For the Bitcoin blockchain, the publishing miner receives cryptocurrency as a reward mechanism.

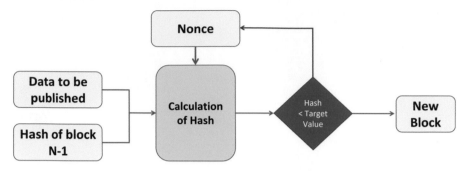

Figure 12.5 PoW consensus model.

Proof of stake (PoS) is another technique for achieving agreement in a trustless environment. The concept of PoS is based on the fact that the node with more stake in the blockchain is less likely to attack the system [18]. In essence, in a cryptocurrency setting, nodes can stake or lock coins in the system. A validating node is chosen in a semi-random manner, as the decision is also based on how many coins the node has staked for the procedure. Once the block is validated and published in the blockchain, the validator receives a reward in the blockchain's cryptocurrency. Such a consensus model does not require the computational and processing effort the PoW model requires and is not as energy-demanding as the latter [19].

12.4 Smart Contracts

Smart contracts, initially introduced in 1994 by a computer scientist and cryptographer named Nick Szabo, aim at the utilization of blockchain technology for automating the execution of a contract [20]. Specifically, smart contracts are computer programs that are able to self-execute when the conditions

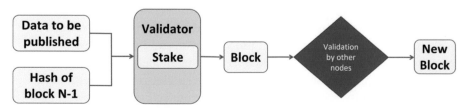

Figure 12.6 PoS consensus model.

described in the terms are fulfilled, similarly to regular contracts. Those terms are enclosed in the smart contract's code, and if an event described in the terms occurs, the smart contract is triggered and executed.

Since smart contracts leverage blockchain technology, they benefit from blockchain's secure, immutable, and tamper-resistant nature. Reliability is also ensured as all activities are trackable and verifiable through the distributed ledger. To define a smart contract, the participating parties agree on its conditions, which are then translated into code following "if/then" statements, to describe the possible scenarios [21]. Next, the smart contract is stored in the blockchain network, as displayed in Figure 12.7. This means that all participants in the network have a replica of the contract. In case a condition that is included into the description of the contract is met, then the transaction described gets executed.

Although smart contracts have a wide area of possible applications, as they arc applicable to the legal industry, real estate, healthcare, insurance, and logistics, they are most predominantly seen in the finance sector. Specifically, smart contracts can contribute to adding transparency in financial transactions. A simple example would be the purchase of goods by a buyer; if money is deposited, then the order is confirmed by the seller.

A relatively new type of smart contracts is the Ricardian Smart Contract. In contrast with regular smart contracts, the Ricardian contracts are legally

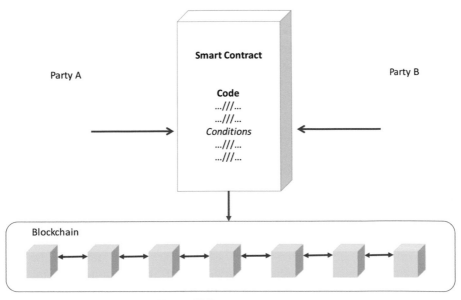

Figure 12.7 Smart contracts.

binding between the participating entities. Similar to smart contracts, they use blockchain to function and they are also verified by the blockchain network. The emerging concept of NG-IoT heavily supports the transition to a ubiquitous computing era, through human-centric advancements. Therefore, Ricardian Smart Contracts contribute to NG-IoT's aim as a human-centric blockchain application, as such contracts are presented both in a human-readable format, as well as a computer-readable format. Such a shift from static agreements to dynamic, legally binding computer code facilitates the transition to a pervasive computing era through NG-IoT, where agreements become automatically enforced, transparent, and verifiable through a peer-to-peer manner. Overall, smart contracts are a secure and reliable way to facilitate and automate the agreement procedures between the participating entities.

12.5 Blockchain Applications for Security and Privacy

Blockchain technology is considered to be the foundation of cryptocurrencies, as the concept of it was initially introduced in a cryptocurrency context [27]. Although blockchain was first designed for such applications, its utility has since been expanded and blockchain technology has become applicable in a wide area of industries [11]. This occurs not only due to blockchain's secure nature but also due to its distributed, peer-to-peer aspect. Contemporary businesses are striving to disengage from traditional centralized solutions and are currently leaning toward the utilization of decentralized systems.

Decentralization allows industries to eliminate the necessity of trusting a single central entity. This is why blockchain technology is an attractive solution for multiple areas where the establishment of trust in an untrustworthy environment is needed. Blockchain especially benefits modern supply chain systems. Supply chains are defined as the activities that contribute to the journey of materials from the initial suppliers to the final customers [6]. Some supply chain activities are product development, production, and logistics. In such a context, blockchains can be used for locating the origins of a product, providing open access to supply chain data and automating the process of transactions through the utilization of smart contracts.

Another application of blockchain would be the very timely concept of smart property. Smart property is a combination of NG-IoT and blockchain, which provides and controls ownership of a smart object through the blockchain infrastructure through the utilization of smart contracts. This is especially useful due to the emergence of smart objects and their vast integration in contemporary lifestyle. As such, the distributed objects in a human-centric NG-IoT ecosystem are assigned to an appropriate owner through smart contracts. Nick Szabo explains the concept of smart property through an example where in case a person misses a payment for a car loan, then a smart contract would revoke the digital keys to operate the car [7].

Blockchain's reliability and immutability has made this technology an asset of high value to critical industries as well. Such application areas require data to remain unaltered and require tamper-proof history of transactions. This is the reason why blockchains are especially useful in the healthcare industry. Due to their decentralized nature, blockchains are excellent for storing and managing access to electronic medical records (EMRs), which is an electronic representation of a patient's health-related data [28], [30]. As such, EMRs can be presented to the participants of the network in a uniform format, achieving interoperability between different institutions, which is one of the main goals of NG-IoT. This is especially useful in case a patient needs to receive treatment in a foreign country; their records can be made immediately accessible to the medical personnel in the distributed NG-IoT ecosystem, taking appropriate actions. Furthermore, in accordance with the General Data Protection Regulation (GDPR) introduced in the European Union, patients can have control over their data, choosing to make their EMRs available to the respective data consumer [8], [29]. Finally, blockchains can be utilized for the challenging task of remote patient monitoring through smart contracts, where patient sensor data is checked by a smart contract and if an emergency occurs, the authorized medical personnel gets timely notified [9].

Finally, this peer-to-peer technology shows great potential for integration in the cybersecurity industry, due to the multitude of benefits it offers. Specifically, another important application of the blockchain technology would be the attestation of devices and services. In an NG-IoT network that consists of multiple heterogeneous intelligent objects where security is highly critical, it is of essence to verify the integrity of the software running on the devices. Blockchain can be used to establish trust through distributed attestation in an unreliable IoT and NG-IoT ecosystem [10]. Due to the immutability that characterizes blockchain, data regarding the identification of devices in the network can be stored in the ledger; this way, unregistered devices with possibly malicious code will not be able to impact the critical network. Finally, blockchains may be utilized for logging events in a critical infrastructure. As such, the output of systems responsible for security, such as intrusion

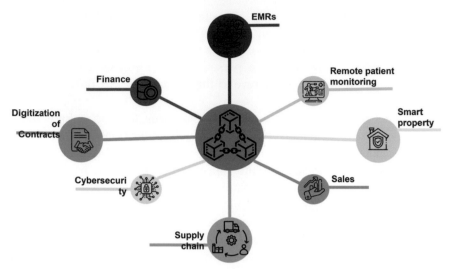

Figure 12.8   Examples of blockchain application.

detection systems (IDS), can be registered in the chain providing traceability and transparency of events.

12.6 Conclusion

The rise of the utilization of heterogeneous intelligent devices in an NG-IoT ecosystem has led to the necessity for decentralization of tasks and processes. Furthermore, the novel concept of NG-IoT calls for the interplay of emerging technologies through a human-centric, decentralized manner. In addition, a growing number of industries and businesses are striving to disengage from centralized solutions for the management of processes, data storage, and securing their systems. This way, the single-point-of-failure issue that centralized solutions may encounter is eliminated. Blockchain technology allows the secure decentralization of those processes. Due to its cryptographic nature, blockchain is immutable, transparent, and is able to establish trust in an unreliable environment. As described in this chapter, blockchain is the key component for multiple industries, including the financial industry, supply chains, healthcare, and cybersecurity. To this end, this trustworthy peer-to-peer technology promises to transform and secure the respective application areas, through its highly valuable benefits.

Acknowledgements

This project has received funding from the European Union's Horizon 2020 research and innovation program under Grant Agreement No. 957406 (TERMINET).

References

[1] B. Safaei, A. M. Hosseini Monazzah, M. Barzegar Bafroei and A. Ejlali, "Reliability Side-Effects in Internet of Things Application Layer Protocols," 2017.

[2] D. Yaga, P. Mell, N. Roby and K. Scarfone, "Blockchain technology overview," 2018.

[3] A. Bosu, A. Iqbal, R. Shahriyar and P. Chakraborty, "Understanding the motivations, challenges and needs of Blockchain software developers: a survey," *Empirical Software Engineering,* August 2019.

[4] A. Alkhateeb , C. Catal , G. Kar and A. Mishra, "Hybrid Blockchain Platforms for the Internet of Things (IoT): A Systematic Literature Review,"*Sensors,* February 2022.

[5] C. Natoli, J. Yu, V. Gramoli and P. Veríssimo, "Deconstructing Blockchains: A Comprehensive Survey on Consensus, Membership and Structure," 2019.

[6] D. Dujak and D. Sajter, "Blockchain Applications in Supply Chain," in *SMART Supply Network*, 2019.

[7] G. Foroglou and A. Lali Tsilidou, "Further applications of the blockchain," 2015.

[8] C. C. Agbo, Q. H. Mahmoud and . J. M. Eklund, "Blockchain Technology in Healthcare: A Systematic Review," *Healthcare,* April 2019.

[9] F. B. Ashraf and R. Reaz, "IoT-Blockchain in Remote Patient Monitoring," 2021.

[10] U. Javaid, M. N. Aman and B. Sikdar, "Defining trust in IoT environments via distributed remote attestation using blockchain," 2020.

[11] D. M. H. Miraz and M. Ali, "Blockchain Enabled Enhanced IoT Ecosystem Security," 2018.

[12] S. Nakamoto, "Bitcoin: A Peer-to-Peer Electronic Cash System," 2008.

[13] J. Ducrée, "Satoshi Nakamoto and the Origins of Bitcoin – The Profile of a 1-in-a-Billion Genius," 2022.

[14] P. Xi, X. Zhang, L. Wang, W. Liu and S. Peng, "A Review of Blockchain-Based Secure Sharing of Healthcare Data," *Applied Sciences,* August 2022.

[15] D. Li, P. Ding, Y. Zhou and Y. Yang, "Controlled Alternate Quantum Walk based Block Hash Function," 2022.

[16] M. Ayenew, H. Lei, X. Li, Q. Weizhong, E. Abeje, W. Xiang and A. Tegene, "Enhancing the performance of permissionless blockchain networks through randomized message-based consensus algorithm," *Peer-to-Peer Networking and Applications,* November 2022.

[17] Y. PoTsang, C. H. Wu and C. K. Man Lee, "BlockTrainHK: An online learning game for experiencing blockchain concepts," *SoftwareX,* July 2022.

[18] E. Deirmentzoglou, G. Papakyriakopoulos and C. Patsakis, "A Survey on Long-Range Attacks for Proof of Stake Protocols," *IEEE Access,* February 2019.

[19] C. T. Nguyen, D. T. Hoang, D. N. Nguyen, D. Niyato, H. T. Nguyen and E. Dutkiewicz, "Proof-of-Stake Consensus Mechanisms for Future Blockchain Networks: Fundamentals, Applications and Opportunities," *IEEE Access,* June 2019.

[20] N. Szabo, "Formalizing and Securing Relationships on Public Networks," *First Monday,* September 1997.

[21] S. Wang, L. Ouyang, Y. Yuan, X. Ni, X. Han and F.-Y. Wang, "Blockchain-Enabled Smart Contracts: Architecture, Applications, and Future Trends," *IEEE Transactions on Systems, Man, and Cybernetics: Systems,* November 2019.

[22] Y. Lu, X. Huang, Y. Dai, S. Maharjan and Y. Zhang, "Blockchain and Federated Learning for Privacy-Preserved Data Sharing in Industrial IoT," *IEEE Transactions on Industrial Informatics*, June 2020.

[23] S. Awan, F. Li, B. Luo and M. Liu, "Poster: A Reliable and Accountable Privacy-Preserving Federated Learning Framework using the Blockchain," November 2019.

[24] U. Majeed and C. S. Hong, "FLchain: Federated Learning via MEC-enabled Blockchain Network," September 2019.

[25] W. Pourmajidi and A. Miranskyy, "Logchain: Blockchain-Assisted Log Storage," July 2018.

[26] D. Li, W. Peng, W. Deng and F. Gai, "A Blockchain-Based Authentication and Security Mechanism for IoT," July 2018.

[27] S. Singh and N. Singh, "Blockchain: Future of financial and cyber security," December 2016.

[28] X. Zhang and S. Poslad, "Blockchain Support for Flexible Queries with Granular Access Control to Electronic Medical Records (EMR)," May 2018.

[29] "General Data Protection Regulation Info" [Online]. Available:https: //gdpr-info.eu/

[30] V. Kelli, P. Sarigiannidis, V. Argyriou, T. Lagkas and V. Vitsas, "A Cyber Resilience Framework for NG-IoT Healthcare Using Machine Learning and Blockchain," June 2021.

Part IV

Novel IoT Applications at the Cloud, Edge, and "Far-edge"

Part V

New Tools, Applications in the
digital Editions Workflow

13

Enabling Remote-controlled Factory Robots via Smart IoT Application Programming Interface

Ivo Bizon Franco de Almeida[1], Rania Rojbi[1], Nuria Molner[2], and Carsten Weinhold[3]

[1]Vodafone Chair Mobile Communication Systems, Technische Universität Dresden, Germany
[2]iTEAM Research Institute of Universitat Politècnica de València, Spain
[3]Barkhausen Institut gGmbH, Germany
E-mail: ivo.bizon; rania.rojbi@ifn.et.tu-dresden.de; numolsiu@iteam.upv.es; carsten.weinhold@barkhauseninstitut.org

Abstract

This chapter explores the potential of the Internet of Things (IoT), a network capable of delivering real-time control, touch, and sensing/actuation information, to reshape industrial communication and transform operations in various industries. It covers the technological trends, from legacy industrial networks to emerging industrial wireless networks. It also examines the 5G networks' role in the key Tactile Internet applications developed for the iNGENIOUS project.

Keywords: Internet of Things (IoT), Tactile Internet, Industry 4.0, 5G.

13.1 Introduction

In the early days of mobile wireless communications, such as the second generation (2G) of mobile communications, and the first releases of

WI-FI, they were mainly employed for message exchange and data collection applications. More recently, it became an emerging technology in industrial applications and an indispensable component in today's life. It has not only connected a very large number of the world's population to the Internet, but also, in the last few years, provided connectivity between intelligent devices and machines creating the Internet of Things (IoT). IoT has gained a lot of interest and it has been introduced in different sectors including health, entertainment, and, in particular, in the industrial environment, where it determines the conditions for factories to evolve to the era of the fourth industrial revolution.

IoT applied in the industrial sector can be described as a network of sensors, machines, and monitoring devices connected to the internet and connected to each other. These different components collect data, analyze it, and interact together to continuously carry industrial processes and maintain a constant and efficient workflow. In the case of deviation, the IoT system issues an alert.

As wireless communication continues to be developed, unprecedented applications could be realized. Recently, the network became capable of communicating in real-time haptic information, e.g., touch, motion, and vibration, besides control and actuation commands in addition to the conventional audio−visual data traffic. This communication is ensured through highly reliable internet connectivity. Thus, the concept of the Tactile Internet appeared [1].

Tactile Internet is defined as a reliable network that allows real-time remote access, data exchange, and control of objects (real and virtual objects). It added an extra dimension to wireless communication by allowing real-time machine-to-machine and human-to-machine interactive systems while being highly available, reliable, and secure. In particular, Tactile Internet provides a promising opportunity to reshape industrial wireless communication and transform the operation of many existing industrial systems. It is also a promising technology to realize new use cases (UCs) such as in healthcare and industrial transportation.

Moreover, as 5G technology advances, it opens up new opportunities for smart manufacturing applications. One potential area of implementation is in UCs where wired solutions are impractical, such as mobile robots or automated guided vehicles (AGVs), which require high-performance and scalable wireless technology. Additionally, 5G can be used to improve flexibility and eliminate wear and tear on cables in situations where additional sensors are added to machinery.

This chapter explores the capabilities of IoT in the context of Industry 4.0 characterized by the integration of advanced technologies to improve efficiency and productivity. The iNGENIOUS project, a European Union-funded research project, serves as a prime example of how IoT can be utilized in such an industry. The Factory UC of the iNGENIOUS project specifically focuses on the implementation and demonstration of IoT in a real-world industrial setting. This chapter studies Tactile IoT in industrial environments. It focuses on the role of 5G wireless networks, which have the potential to revolutionize the way Tactile IoT is used in factories and warehouses. It explores how 5G networks can improve the speed, reliability, and scalability of Tactile IoT applications, enabling new and innovative use cases. This part focuses also on one of the key areas where IoT is being applied in the Factory UC of the iNGENIOUS project, which is in the use of automated guided vehicles (AGVs), within a warehouse or factory.

To conclude, this chapter delves into the capabilities of IoT in smart factories and warehouses, with a specific focus on the iNGENIOUS project's Factory UC. The utilization of AGVs and Tactile Internet in the Factory UC serves as an example of how IoT is capable of improving efficiency and productivity in industrial environments.

13.2 IoT Application for Supply chain

Supply chains are one of the most complex parts of business operations since they require synchronization and collaboration between different business segments and actors. In this context, IoT and data analytics applications can play a key role, since they are able to contribute to the optimization of operations, resolve issues, and identify potential bottlenecks across different segments like factories, warehouses, transportation, logistics, or maritime ports. The following presents several examples of IoT applications in supply chains.

13.2.1 IoT applications in smart factories and warehouses

Nowadays, many companies in the industrial manufacturing sector are carrying out smart factory initiatives where systems and devices are expected to become fully interconnected, and where the data among devices can provide valuable insights for improving production efficiency. In this context, next-generation IoT (NG-IoT) technologies will not only enable optimization of the industrial operations but also will affect product, development, storage, and delivery processes, thanks to the efficient use of the data.

The use of NG-IoT applications to connect sensors and establish machine-to-machine (M2M) communication protocols will help factories and warehouses to get real-time data at every stage of the supply chain with communication services offering high levels of reliability and availability (up to 99.999% for control and up to 99.9% for sensing), low latencies (below 10ms), and accurate positioning (≤ 0.5 m) [2]. Additionally, the combination of IoT applications with cloud-based management systems and artificial intelligence modules can improve machinery operation and asset management procedures [3], thus allowing companies to know the location and status of machinery and goods while predicting risky events like machinery failures or low-stock events.

Other innovations like automated guided vehicles (AGVs) will be able to calculate the shortest route for product delivery, reducing the amount of time needed to complete the operation together with fuel costs. At the same time, by connecting IoT platforms and enabling the exchange of data between supply chain players through distributed ledger technology (DLT) solutions, factories and warehouses will be able to track the different events that take place when products are manufactured and when orders are delivered out of the facilities.

Some examples of IoT applications in smart factory and warehouse scenarios are:

- MindSphere industrial IoT solution [4] developed by Siemens is an industrial IoT as a service solution that uses advanced analytics and AI to power IoT solutions from the edge to the cloud. Thanks to MindSphere, factories and warehouses can ingest and visualize immediate real-time data and analytic results in one centralized location with no development required. For that purpose, it includes different components such as an asset manager, fleet manager, usage transparency, or operator cockpit.
- Amazon Web IoT services for industrial [5] developed by Amazon is an industrial IoT solution that combines machines, cloud computing, and analytics to improve industrial processes' performance and productivity. Thanks to this AWS module, factories and warehouses can cover different use cases such as predictive quality and predictive maintenance or asset condition monitoring. A detailed set of the different components together with their role within the AWS industrial IoT (IIoT) architecture is shown in Figure 13.1.

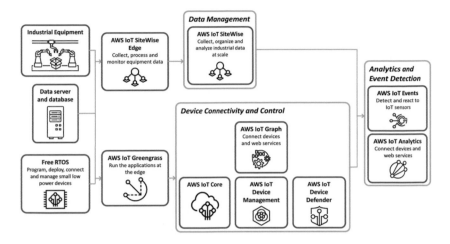

Figure 13.1 AWS IoT architecture. Figure adapted from AWS website: https://aws.amazon .com/de/iot/solutions/industrial-iot/

13.3 Tactile IoT Applications

Tactile Internet is an evolution of IoT characterized by extremely low latency in combination with high availability, reliability, and security. Tactile IoT applications are designed to perform certain tasks by monitoring input data and altering output data accordingly.

These applications involve remote interactions between objects, such as humans, physical machines, or virtual ones, while preserving similar perceptions as when the objects are directly connected. These interactions include remote accessing, perceiving, manipulating, or controlling real or virtual objects or processes and are distinguished by the requirements of ultra-reliable and low-latency communication (URLLC) within 5G networks to achieve perceived real-time response.

The main task is realized by means of one or more processes that define the relations between a set of inputs and a set of outputs. The outputs of some processes might be used as input to others. An exemplary procedure could be: if a bell rings, check the identity of the person and open the door if the person is found in a whitelist. In this case, the input data is the bell signal, and the process is to check the identity of the person, which can be accomplished by sending a command to a camera to take a picture. This leads to a second procedure where the input is now the image, the process is face detection, and the action is to open the door or decline entry.

IoT is commonly associated with the massive deployment of light devices such as sensors and switches with relaxed timing requirements. Tactile internet IoT includes a wide range of applications that are technically distinguished by stringent end-to-end latency requirements.

13.3.1 Tactile Internet applications encountered in supply chain stages

IoT has the potential to revolutionize the way supply chains operate. There are a variety of IoT applications that are currently available for use in supply chain management such as real-time response, predictive maintenance, and smart inventory management. The integration of IoT technology into supply chain operations can bring significant cost savings, improved delivery times, and early identification of issues.

The exact definition of real-time response depends on the application. Accordingly, two main scenarios are encountered:

- Human-in-loop: Here, humans should be able to remotely interact with real or virtual objects and perceive different auditory, visual, and haptic feedback with the same experience when directly dealing with the physical objects. This requires a hyperspectral imaging (HSI) device such as haptic gloves, virtual reality (VR) headset, to translate the human actions to machine-type commands, and the machine feedback to human perceived signals. This category of applications is specifically driven by the challenges of remotely conveying the sensing of haptic touch and kinesthetic muscular movement for humans, in addition to the timing requirements of closed-loop control systems.
- Machine-in-loop: This corresponds to the connection of machines, such as sensors, actuators, robots, and control processes to a computer-based simulation model. In this case, the different interactions should lead to a realistic environment and performance as when the different identities are directly or closely connected.

Tactile applications have practical use in supply chain operations. For example, teleoperation and automation can improve working conditions and increase productivity in logistics. In addition, it enables autonomous applications, e.g., in transportation and warehouse management. These applications are outlined in more detail below.

13.3.1.1 Teleoperation

This application allows a human user to operate a device or machine located in a remote area. Teleoperation enables performing a task in hazardous or inaccessible environments to ensure workers' safety, and it can also be employed to provide comfortable working conditions. Additionally, it allows one operator to control multiple objects (e.g., one driver for more than one AGV). In contrast to conventional remote control, the tactile version of it, depicted in Figure 13.2, offers a realistic experience as the user feels like they are operating a physical device. It is important to note that the application involves one or more robots and one acts as the master and the rest as slaves. The master robot is responsible for receiving commands from the operator and relaying them to the slave robots. A key aspect of this architecture is that not all robots need to be connected to the central server executing the orders, reducing the load in the network, especially if they connect to the master using any type of connectivity for short distances, such as device-to-device (D2D) communications. However, one bottleneck of this architecture is that all communication goes through the master robot, and if it fails, the whole system has problems. For that, the master operator and the slave teleoperator device exchange haptic signals, such as forces, position, velocity, vibration, and torques, in addition to video and audio signals by means of an HSI. The HSI encodes the human actions to commands understood by the teleoperator and translates the feedback from the teleoperator to signals perceived by the human.

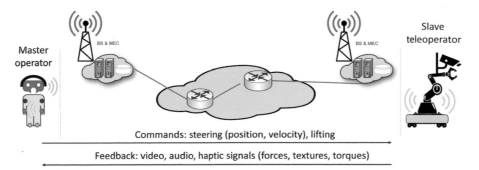

Figure 13.2 Tactile remote operation.

13.3.1.2 Autonomous driving

Mobility is essential for supply chains both for transporting goods and for handling raw materials and products in production lines. Autonomous driving enables smarter, more ecological, and safer movement of people and goods. Self-driving requires processing multiple types of information such as optical images, radar, etc., generated by sensors installed as part of the surrounding infrastructure or on vehicles. The sensed data are conveyed to a controller, which needs to compute and forward driving commands such as steering, braking, and acceleration within a latency constraint. Autonomous driving may also involve platooning, where it is required to control the speed of a line of vehicles traveling in the same direction.

As an example, AGVs are an attractive option for efficient material transportation within factory plants and warehouses. However, current technology hinders flexibility, as sensor and command data processing are carried out at the device, rather than a central command unit. To solve this issue, a common application programming interface (API) that allows communication among AGVs, controlling units, and sensors appears as an attractive way to implement such technology.

13.3.1.3 Industrial automation

Industrial closed-control loop has URLLC requirements similar to those of tactile internet. Thus, the first application is to replace the wired industrial network with a wireless one, as illustrated in Figure 13.3, which leads to greater flexibility and reduced cost of installation and maintenance, especially for connecting moving devices. This flexibility has inspired new industrial applications that connect people, objects, and systems. The conventional human−machine interface (HMI), which typically consists of a display, input terminal, and software for gathering data and altering control parameters, can be replaced by alternative augmented reality (AR) or virtual reality (VR)

Figure 13.3 From fixed conventional automation to flexible tactile automation.

interfaces. Mobile platforms such as AGVs and mobile robots can be programmed to perform various scenario-dependent tasks instead of fixed robot arms dedicated to certain tasks. This allows more efficient use of resources and forms the core of next-generation industrial applications.

13.4 Industrial and Tactile Application Programming Interface (API)

In the context of the emerging Industry 4.0 framework [6], the next-generation factories are expected to be efficient, flexible, dynamic, self-organized, and able to produce customized products rather than a massive number of products as in conventional factories. This requires flexible deployment and reconfiguration of production tools, in addition to a dynamic network to fulfill different requirements for connecting people and physical and virtual machines in real and virtual environments. Accordingly, the factory infrastructure, which includes different types of sensors, actuators, processing units, and network resources, will be considered as a ubiquitous computing platform that is ready to execute customized end-user applications. These applications are composed of multiple tactile and non-tactile processes. The tactile processes comprise available tactile applications as discussed in Section 13.3, such as remote operations, autonomous driving, and automation. The other processes involve non-time critical missions such as data collection for monitoring, surveillance, predictive maintenance, and reporting. Aligned with the concept of tactile internet, which focuses on providing a seamless experience when interacting with remote objects as dealing with a direct object, the tactile applications will provide similarity in programming remote distributed terminals as they are on a single computer (see Figure 13.4).

- The processing and storage capabilities act like multi-core processors and memories, which are used in the execution of specific tasks.
- The I/O domain consists of devices, which can be simple inputs (sensors), outputs (actuators), or a stand-alone device with local inputs and outputs, such as tactile HSI.
- The network provides the connection bus system to interconnect the I/O with the processors and memories.
- The network management and orchestration play the role of operating system and expose different APIs that abstract the hardware and provide the programming tools that are used by software developers like system calls as they program a single device, such as a smartphone.

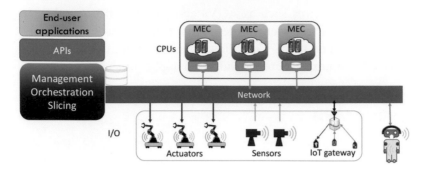

Figure 13.4 Network computer architecture.

• The end-user application runs on top of the network operating system.

As in any computer architecture, a compiler is required to translate the programming code to the hardware language and to ensure at least that some constraints are respected at the compile time. In the network scenario, the compiler is responsible for provisioning the required network and processing resources to fulfill different process requirements in terms of latency, reliability, and data rate, and to consider dynamic conditions such as mobility and changing environment. In addition, run-time error handling should be thoroughly considered to avoid any malfunctioning of the operating system. For instance, to check if a device is already in use by other applications, the communications key performance indicators (KPIs) are fulfilled, and proper release of unused resources is.

Connecting wireless terminals for computer systems is already implemented in everyday life, such as monitors, keyboards, mice, headsets, cameras, and remote controls. However, when considering stringent timing requirements in terms of latency and synchronization between many devices, existing operating systems and connectivity approaches are not sufficient.

5G wireless communication infrastructure is a key enabler for future industrial ecosystems and has become widely available in industrial sites. The sensors and actuators within factory plants can be regarded as available manufacturing resources that can be programmed to produce specific products according to particular specifications. After the production of a determined number of pieces or after the identification of possible product improvements, the resources should be easily rearranged to continue the production with the new specific requirements. In contrast, the current production lines are built to perform repetitive tasks without flexibility. For realizing such a flexible production technique, a software abstraction from the actual physical devices has to be designed. This conceptual abstraction is defined as an industrial and tactile application programming interface (API). In short words, the industrial and tactile API consists of a set of functions that enable the application developer to get data in and out of the system in a unified framework. Within this context, first, a set of common functionalities have been identified as an essential part of the API that enables user-defined applications to exchange data easily and securely.

The industrial and tactile API has to provide different levels of abstraction to effectively serve its purpose. Specifically, three levels can be identified:

1. End-user application development API: This level is crucial as it provides the end user with a simple and easily comprehensible graphical interface for instantiating new applications and presents data in a format that is understandable by the end user.
2. Mid-level function library: This level is important as it contains functions that do not need to be directly used by the end user, such as an object detection algorithm.
3. Low-level API: This level is crucial as it contains functions for data packet formatting and specification of parameters for the physical communication link based on the requirements given by the end user. These functions are fundamental in ensuring proper communication and data transfer between the devices.

For instance, AGVs are attractive options for automated material transportation within factories, as they can improve efficiency and reduce downtime. However, current technology limits the flexibility and dynamic control of multiple AGVs from a central command unit. To solve this, a common data exchange structure via an API is necessary, allowing AGVs, controlling units, and sensors to communicate and perform tasks. A smart IoT API also facilitates the recognition and initial configuration of devices for communication.

13.4.1 Proof-of-concept within the iNGENIOUS project

To demonstrate this concept within iNGENIOUS [7], the integration between a non-3GPP compliant radio access technology, and a management and orchestration (MANO) entity is carried out using JavaScript object notation

(JSON) format, which consists of an open standard file format for data exchange. A JSON file stores various data types in key-value pairs in a human-readable format, with the keys serving as names and the values containing the related data. An example is illustrated in Figure 13.5. It is commonly used for APIs because of its lightweight to exchange information due to its small file size and it is easy to read/write compared to other data formats, as it is written in an organized and clean way.

In our case, the MANO sends a JSON file containing the resource allocation for each application, and the radio controller unit extracts this information and distributes the resources accordingly.

In AGVs UC for the iNGENIOUS project, an end-to-end (E2E) platform is developed for remotely controlling AGVs in the port area. The primary motivation for enabling remote operation is to improve the driver's safety by avoiding possible hazardous situations related to operating in industrial areas. This is achieved by designing a complete IoT system that enables the vehicle

```
{
"Robot": {
        "ID":"AGV",
        "NavigationRange":{
                "max":"50m",
                "min":"20m",
                },
        "MaxSpeed": "1.2m/s",
        "MaxLoad":"35kg",
        "BatteryLife":"12h",
        "Weight":"100kg",
        "Camera":"Yes"
        "RequiredDataRate":"5Mbps"
```

Figure 13.5 Example of a JSON file containing information about an AGV device: this information is shared with the IoT application developer.

operator to have continuous situational awareness of the vehicle status and surrounding environment and enables real-time communication of necessary control signals to operate the AGV safely.

In the following, an exemplary set of functionalities is described for an industrial application of AGVs. Within the Factory UC, factory inspection is defined as an application where an AGV travels along a predefined track with a camera and sensors integrated. The video and environmental information collected by the AGV are sent to a remote user that monitors the factory site. The quality of the video can be specified at the beginning of the application by the user. The graphical user interface of such an application is illustrated in Figure 13.6. This example will be illustrated within the iNGENIOUS Factory UC.

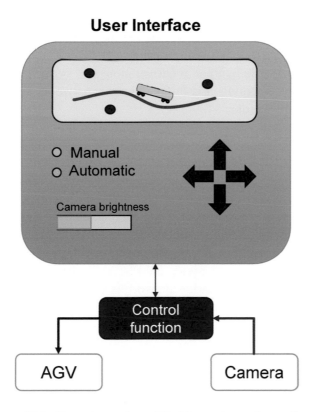

Figure 13.6   Exemplary end-user UI of factory inspection application.

The identified functionalities that have to be available from the industrial and tactile API are:

- Start, stop, and adjust the AGV's speed.
- Transfer the measurements from the AGV to the end user.
- Capture the current image frame and store it in the user's database.
- Transfer AGV's position to the end user.
- Translation of MANO resource allocation to PHY parameters.

The identified connection types of the devices are:

- AGV: UDP frames.
- Camera: UDP frames.

13.5 Conclusion

This chapter explores the potential of Tactile Internet in industrial communication, which aims to provide wireless real-time control and manipulation. It examines the role of Tactile Internet in current industrial systems, evaluating its potential in legacy, emerging, and future industrial networks, in particular within the iNGENIOUS project.

Within iNGENIOUS, it was shown that the operation of the Tactile Internet requires defining interfaces for communication between devices and access to the network. Therefore, the network techniques should be flexible to provide a similar experience for the application developer as programming on a computer by abstracting the hardware and network functionalities.

Moreover, this chapter suggests that the Tactile Internet, through high-performance wireless connectivity, would enable the transition toward wireless for industrial control, simplifying the design of legacy systems and enabling remote operation in various industries. It also notes that the emerging 5G wireless communication network is likely to be the winning technology for the Tactile Internet.

Acknowledgements

This work has been partially supported by the European Union's Horizon 2020 research and innovation program through the project iNGENIOUS under Grant Agreement No. 957216.

References

[1] A. Aijaz und M. Sooriyabandara, "The tactile internet for industries: A review," Proceedings of the IEEE, Bd. 107, pp. 414-435, 2018.

[2] A. Varghese und D. Tandur, "Wireless requirements and challenges in Industry 4.0," in 2014 International Conference on Contemporary Computing and Informatics (IC3I), Mysore, India, 2014.

[3] C. She, C. Sun, Z. Gu, Y. Li, C. Yang, V. H. Poor und B. Vucetic, "A Tutorial on Ultrareliable and Low-Latency Communications in 6G: Integrating Domain Knowledge Into Deep Learning," Proceedings of the IEEE, Bd. 109, pp. 204-246, 2021.

[4] K. E. Kulawiak, "Manufacturing the platform economy: An exploratory case study of MindSphere, the industrial digital platform from Siemens," University of Oslo, Oslo, 2021.

[5] Amazon Web Services, Inc, "Overview of Amazon Web Services: AWS Whitepaper," Amazon, https://d1.awsstatic.com/whitepapers/aws-overv iew.pdf,2021.

[6] A. Germán Frank, L. Santos Dalenogare und N. Fabián Ayala, "Industry 4.0 technologies: Implementation patterns in manufacturing companies," International Journal of Production Economics, Bd. 210, pp. 15-26, 2019.

[7] iNGENIOUS Consortium, "INGENIOUS - Next-Generation IoT Solutions for the Universal Supply Chain," 2022. [Online]. Available: https://ingenious-iot.eu/web/.[Accessed2023].

14

A Practical Deployment of Tactile IoT: 3D Models and Mixed Reality to Increase Safety at Construction Sites

Piotr Sowiński[1,2], Tina Katika[3], Fotios K. Konstantinidis[3], Anna Dabrowska[4], Ignacio Lacalle[5], Angelos Amditis[3], Carlos E. Palau[5], and Marcin Paprzycki[1]

[1]Systems Research Institute, Polish Academy of Sciences, Poland
[2]Warsaw University of Technology, Poland
[3]Institute of Communication and Computer Systems, Greece
[4]Central Institute for Labour Protection – National Research Institute, Poland
[5]Communications Department of Universitat Politècnica de València, Spain

Abstract

This chapter elaborates on the usage of mixed reality equipment (Microsoft HoloLens 2) and software (enablers based on the ASSIST-IoT project) for improving the safety and health of blue-collar workers at a construction site. Building upon a proven methodology and architecture, the chapter summarizes the introduction of network technologies and techniques as well as other mechanisms (such as ultra-wideband communication) that allow Tactile Internet principles to be realized in the proposed scenario.

The user interface of the mixed reality device and an engagement study are described, along with future validation and demonstration activities assessing the appropriateness of the proposed system, both at the laboratory and a construction site located in Poland.

Keywords: Mixed reality, Internet of Things, Tactile Internet, edge–cloud continuum, construction safety, ultra-wideband, semantic integration.

285   DOI: 10.1201/9781032632407-18

14.1 Introduction

In the year 2020, a record number of fatal accidents at work accompanying construction activities was reported [6]. According to the EUROSTAT, the majority of these activities took place at construction sites, making it one of the most dangerous work environments. Unpredictable weather conditions, changing environment, demanding work activities, as well as increasing involvement of subcontractors observed recently in the construction sector are undoubtedly the factors influencing workers' safety. These factors are particularly hard to manage in a traditional–collective way, on an occasional basis. The emergence of Tactile Internet technologies makes it possible to create better support systems for the management of occupational risks, particularly in workplaces where environmental conditions are subject to dynamic changes that can have serious consequences for human health and life [24].

The deployment of Tactile Internet technologies for occupational safety and health (OSH) management significantly contributes to a paradigm shift from traditional methods of carrying out collective risk assessment for specific groups of workers to assessment methods, which allow to determine the level of risk individually for each worker. Moreover, the existing periodical risk assessment approaches can be replaced by continuous monitoring of hazards in the working environment in real time [23]. Finally, the introduction of properly adjusted prevention measures has become possible, thanks to early warning OSH systems based on immersive and Tactile Internet technologies.

Immersive technologies, such as mixed reality (MR), allow their users to efficiently interpret physical and digital information while understanding their spatial relations. MR keeps the end-users engaged in an environment enriched with related digital content without disconnecting and isolating them from their surroundings. At the same time, MR offers a unique opportunity to enhance safety communication in construction as it enables a human-centric approach through better interaction of the end-users with the IoT environment [13].

Head mounted devices (HMDs) and particularly the recent development of lightweight, commercially available Microsoft HoloLens 2 bring three-dimensional (3D) models out of the screen and provide users with the ability to engage and interact with data and media more intuitively while experiencing and understanding designs and structures [22]. HoloLens 2 is a powerful HMD that can substitute a computer, a screen, and a keyboard while boasting more processing power than an average laptop and can be used anytime, anywhere. In various setups, it demonstrated its ability to protect its end-users from external factors that may impact their health and safety [19]. MR has the capacity to bring 3D data to life by putting information in front of users' eyes without changing or adjusting the data format. This way, project management and delivery methods become more efficient, less costly, and less time-consuming, and the communication and collaboration among parties are also improved [2].

In the face of networking needs, there are challenges in transmitting real-time information from edge devices to MR devices [14]. In terms of Tactile Internet, which is the main pillar in the development of the proposed architecture, a set of tools are used to reduce the latency, guaranteeing extremely low round-trip delays with excellent availability, reliability, and security for human–machine and interaction-centric real-time applications. Those tools are mainly deployed in the data management layer, which manages all operations associated with data collecting, delivery, and processing to perform essential data-related services.

The stringent requirements of Tactile Internet systems drive the need for deploying the services in a distributed manner, and on the edge (as close to the data and the user as possible). The complexity of hand-crafting and managing such deployments quickly becomes overwhelming, and thus dedicated tools for service management and orchestration are needed [7], [8].

The multi-modal information about the construction site must be collected from a variety of sensors in real time. One key challenge here is personnel and asset tracking inside and outside buildings. To this end, ultra-wideband (UWB) tags and anchors can be used to provide live location data, with low power consumption. The collected highly heterogeneous data must be integrated by the IoT system. This problem of data integration has long been recognized as a key challenge in implementing IoT platforms [9]. The different parts of a system can be maintained by different, independent stakeholders, which rules out an "authoritative" approach to integration – in which a single, central body decides upon all schemas and protocols. Thus, solutions are needed to manage the inherently decentralized landscape of data formats and schemas.

Therefore, the aim of this chapter is the introduction of network technologies and techniques as well as other mechanisms (such as semantic data integration, ultra-wideband communication) that allow Tactile Internet principles to be realized in the construction environment, following the objectives:

- using mixed reality equipment and edge-based software for improving the health and safety of workers;
- employing state-of-the-art network technologies at a construction site based on Tactile Internet needs;
- solving the data integration problem with modern approaches to streaming semantic annotation and translation;
- tracking workers and assets in real-time using ultra-wideband communication;
- deploying the solution in an edge-cloud context with the use of the ASSIST-IoT reference architecture.

14.2 Solution Architecture

To address the challenges outlined above, a solution was devised, based on the ASSIST-IoT reference architecture for next-generation IoT. Figure 14.1 presents the overall solution architecture. ASSIST-IoT deployments consist of encapsulated enablers (sets of microservices, jointly providing functionalities to the system) and other custom components. The enablers and custom components are deployed in a virtualized (Kubernetes) environment [7] and orchestrated via a novel MANO-based custom software delivered by the project [8].

The proposed system aims to provide the OSH manager with digital tools that facilitate performing inspections and alert the manager of unusual or dangerous situations. Through the MR enabler (using a head mounted device – HMD), the OSH inspector obtains contextual visual data about activities that occur at their location or dangerous events from the construction area. The MR enabler is integrated with the Tactile Dashboard, the Semantic Repository, the Long Term Storage, and the Edge Data Broker enablers.

The Tactile Dashboard enabler displays data in real time using user-friendly and interactive visuals, providing the capability to configure the MR enabler in each scenario. The Semantic Repository serves as a nexus for data models used on the construction site. This includes storing 3D and BIM models of the site. The function of the Long Term Storage enabler (LTSE) is to provide safe and robust storage for other enablers and store important data such as workers' medical and training records. Lastly, the Edge Data Broker provides a common point for IoT devices and services to broadcast their data in a streaming manner. The integration between the MR enabler and the Edge Data Broker enables other components to easily transfer messages to the MR enabler by publishing data to a particular topic to which the MR is subscribed.

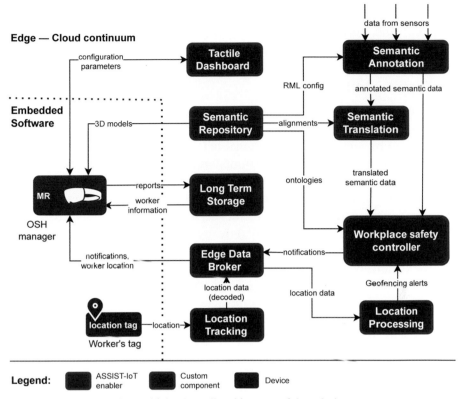

Figure 14.1 Overall architecture of the solution.

The MR enabler depends heavily on the Edge Data Broker to gather essential data for its operation.

The "central" component responsible for processing most of the logic is the workplace safety controller. It aggregates incoming streams of data and performs live operations on them. For example, it is tasked with detecting UV over-exposure of workers. To determine the total exposure of a worker, the information about the worker's location must be aggregated with live weather data and the BIM model of the construction site to determine the amount of shade in a given area. When the workplace safety controller detects abnormally high UV exposure, it emits a notification to the MR enabler so as to inform the OSH manager of the situation. Geofencing boundaries and other types of safety hazards are monitored in a similar manner as well.

The proposed solution faces a number of architectural challenges. The most significant are: the Tactile Internet aspect (low-latency interfaces with immediate feedback); data integration (integrating heterogenous data sources and services); and, finally, the mixed reality interface. These three key aspects are discussed in detail in the following subsections.

14.2.1 Tactile internet aspect

Tactile Internet (TI) is one of the latest advent technologies that play a major role in next-generation IoT (NG-IoT) environments. An NG-IoT deployment is characterized by including all traditional IoT capabilities (devices discovery, data connection, visualization of monitored information, etc.) besides adding new traits such as 5G, AI-based functions, edge/fog computing, and software-defined networking/network function virtualization (among other technologies), considering Tactile Internet as one of the key objectives. All of the previous can be achieved only by modular architectures that use reliable, fast underlying networks to support very low latencies. An application is considered to be *tactile* when it allows a seamless sensation of touch (resolution of 1000 Hz). In general terms, according to European Commission-promoted initiatives, it is crucial to include TI's strict limitations in the architectural decisions of any forthcoming IoT/distributed systems reference architectures [5].

Formally, according to the International Telecommunication Union Standardization Sector (ITU-T), Tactile Internet is defined as *extremely low latency, in combination with high availability, reliability, and security*. In practical terms, it means enabling haptic human–machine interaction, opening up the establishment of use cases like heavy machinery handling, remote surgery, or, as in this case, ultra-real-time awareness of construction workers' status. The authors of this work consider, drawing from the experience gained in the ASSIST-IoT project, that TI must be understood as a system that (i) successfully carries haptic data (in this work, from sensors, BIM models, and MR glasses) by (ii) relying on communication (leveraging, among others, UWB) meeting the requirements of (a) low latency, (b) high reliability, and (c) high data throughput.

In this regard, for what concerns the proposed deployment, communication latency poses a critical obstacle. This is a usual barrier whenever adopting IoT systems in many applications [26], [27]. High latency can even make the technology entirely unfeasible for a given application. In the past decade, a variety of communication protocols and standards were established and implemented by the community to tackle this issue. These protocols emphasize the need for giving special attention to the quality of service (QoS) and quality of experience (QoE) for various applications [17]. In order to ensure low latency (that will facilitate designing Tactile Internet scenarios), it is realized to place computation closer to the user (where tactile data is generated). In technical topological terms, this means shifting the processing workload to the edge of the network.

Several architectures and works [16] have proposed to follow a primary–secondary approach relying on edge computing. This is achieved via reducing connectivity to a few links and by setting up a primary gateway node (at the edge) to connect secondary devices to the network. Using this architecture (inspired by IEEE 1918.1), information is encoded, optimizing data transmission, and the security and privacy are clearly enhanced.

To support such needs as well as to comply with the latter requirement exposed above, the Edge Data Broker enabler (EDBE) was developed, whose filtering and ruling capabilities reduce the number of transmitted messages, while the quality of service (QoS) is adapted based on the use case requirements. These scriptable capabilities allow data to be routed and processed in real time, with the specific pipelines being triggered by predetermined criteria. Their seamless integration allows for edge-based filtering and decentralized data-consuming strategies, which cuts network traffic and latency dramatically, fulfilling the requirements of Tactile Internet. Following those design principles, human–machine collaboration is enabled in applications such as Construction 4.0 [20], Industry 4.0, virtual reality, and augmented reality [15].

Several enablers and components in the proposed deployment connect to EDBE via the MQTT protocol. For the needs of semantic integration (described in detail in the following subsection), the Semantic Annotation and Semantic Translation enablers communicate in a streaming manner. Here, EDBE ensures that the data is routed locally to the nearest available consumer, minimizing latencies. To address the needs of processing geospatial data, the Location Tracking enabler produces streams of location data from each tracked asset. The Location Processing enabler is then able to run complex geospatial queries on the gathered data. Finally, the workplace safety controller component aggregates streaming MQTT data from various sources and emits the necessary notifications and alerts.

An experimental feature, currently being investigated in the hopes of further lowering the latencies, is the novel Jelly RDF streaming protocol [27]. It is meant to provide high-performance, low-latency streaming of semantic data between the semantic enablers and the workplace safety controller.

14.2.2 Data integration

The challenge of integrating data from heterogenous sources is well-addressed by ASSIST-IoT enablers in the data management plane: the Semantic Annotation enabler, Semantic Translation enabler, and the Semantic Repository enabler. This technological stack provides a robust set of tools for addressing data integration using ontologies and Semantic Web technologies [1]. Here, the Semantic Annotation enabler annotates non-semantic streaming data using RML mappings [4], giving it explicit meaning. The Semantic Translation enabler in turn translates the semantic data to allow the consumers to understand the meaning of data represented using different ontologies [10]. The semantic translation and annotation processes are applied to data gathered from sensors present on the construction site.

The final piece of the data integration solution is the Semantic Repository enabler, which serves as a "nexus" for all schemas, ontologies, and other data models used in the deployment. The repository offers robust versioning and metadata support, allowing all other components to stay synchronized with each other, with regard to the used data models. In this use case, the repository stores (among others) ontologies used by the workplace safety controller, RML configuration files for semantic annotation, alignment definitions for semantic translation, the BIM model of the constructed building, and the 3D models of the building displayed to the users.

14.2.3 Mixed reality interface

The MR enabler is a standalone native application that is deployed on a head mounted device (Microsoft HoloLens 2) to monitor the worksite and notify the OSH manager about incidents or undesirable behavior. It visualizes information from the BIM model, including construction components and dangerous zones. The MR enabler collects, curates, and then displays the required information related to the construction site and the workers.

Upon establishing a connection to the Edge Data Broker, the MR enabler starts receiving data to visualize. The data, from long-term storage or real-time data streams, is requested according to its relevance to the user at a specific time and location. When displaying the data and other content, the authorization and access rights of the end-user are taken into account. More specifically:

- Blue-collar worker's ID, medical and training data, are retrieved from the Long Term Storage enabler for the OSH manager to verify their compliance with the expiration dates. Alerts and notifications from localization services ensure that construction workers move around areas that are safe and where they are authorized and trained.

- Manipulation of the BIM models, where the OSH manager can manipulate the BIM models to be informed about dangerous zones and evacuations routes.
- Environmental conditions such as ambient temperature and UV radiation are also reaching the MR enabler through the EDBE to ensure that workers function at suitable conditions.

Many functionalities of the MR enabler ensure that the required information is collected, such as location and proximity data, exceeding of the physiological parameters thresholds, weather conditions, personal identification information, training and medical records, building information, alerts, and notifications. At the same time, the MR enabler supports activities that improve the overall health and safety management. More specifically, we have the following:

Connection to the EDBE to consume data. In the case of the MR enabler, it connects wirelessly to an edge gateway device, where the Edge Data Broker is deployed and subscribes to multiple topics in order to be able to consume/produce data that other enablers produce and consume.

Importing of the BIM models through the Semantic Repository. The BIM visualization functionality relies on the loading of the BIM model from Semantic Repository in a way that can be visualized through the MR

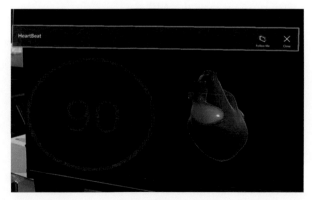

Figure 14.2 In this figure, real-time data is visualized to the MR device, which are produced by a worker's wristband.[2]

Figure 14.3 The BIM model visualized through the MR glasses upon conversion to the required format through the laboratory facilities.

device. The dangerous zones are included in the model, as presented in Figure 14.3 and updated by the construction site's owner.

Manipulation of BIM. The MR enabler is designed in a way that allows the user to manipulate the 3D model rendered in order to provide a better understanding of the information linked to it, while the manipulation handles are presented in Figure 14.4.

Generation of reports. Using the reporting feature, as it is presented in Figure 14.5, the OSH manager can report unusual or dangerous situations, while the reports are transmitted to the LTSE.

Displaying alerts and notifications. This activity includes the alerts and notifications that the inspector receives in case of a dangerous event within the construction site via the MR device.

Figure 14.4 The model has handles at the model's corners that enable the user to scale the model. The handles in the center of the BIM edges enable the user to rotate the model in each direction. The user may then move the 3D model freely inside their range.

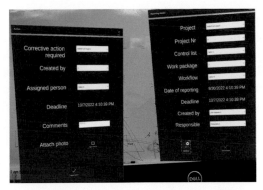

Figure 14.5 The reporting function is visualized, where the OSH inspector can produce a human-centric report when they identify misalignments during the inspection procedure.

Figure 14.6 The user interface of the various alerts coming from other systems (such as weather station, fatigue monitoring, and location management system about danger zones unauthorized access) is presented.

14.3 Evaluation

To ensure that the developed MR application is user friendly, the visuals and user interface (UI) elements were designed after UI/UX research [12]. As a result, a custom UI was built focusing on an immersive, usable, and familiar user interface environment with a low cognitive load process to improve user engagement and avoid common usability errors. At the same time, the user path was defined upon interviews with construction stakeholders to analyze their needs and the goals of this application. This allowed to define the trail from the very first contact of the health and safety manager with the MR application to their final action. Along with information gathering, prototypes were built to determine the capabilities and complexities of a successful enabler. Both qualitative and quantitative research were performed to gain insights and other analytics that favor the UX design.

Considering the human-centric approach adopted in ASSIST-IoT, the designed mixed reality interface will be also subjected to the evaluation process with end-user participation. Mlekus et al. [21] proved that user experience characteristics significantly affect technology acceptance. Low user acceptance means less frequent use, lower job satisfaction, and performance losses [3], [18], [29]. In order to determine the level of acceptance of MR technology, Rasimah et al. [25] used the metrics of personal innovativeness, perceived enjoyment, perceived ease of use, perceived usefulness, and intention to use. According to their findings, perceived usefulness was the most important factor determining further intention to use MR technology. Therefore, the feedback coming from end-users, being a result of the evaluation process, is recognized to be crucial for the successful deployment of Tactile IoT.

The questionnaire-based methodology for evaluating whether the MR technology can enhance safety-related communication on construction sites was also adopted by Dai et al. [2]. The authors demonstrated a great degree of willingness to adopt MR technology for enhancing safety on construction sites. Advantages of MR over currently used communication methods such as phone calls, walking to people to talk, and video conferencing were highlighted. In particular, instant access to information, context-based perception, and visual interaction were indicated as factors highly contributing to effective communication at the construction site. According to Dai et al. [2], communication with the use of HoloLens was reported as more accurate and efficient than with the use of traditional methods. However, still some issues have been identified as responders indicated, e.g., that it was hard to wear HoloLens and walk at the same time or that the field of view was limited.

Using the technology acceptance model (TAM) and its variations for MR technology evaluation is a known and appreciated method based on collection of responses to questionnaires [11], [28]. However, in the literature also some limitations of this method are indicated, which are particularly related to subjective means of evaluation, including interpersonal influence. Therefore, evaluation methodology assumed both laboratory and field trials including subjective and objective assessment of user experience and technology acceptance. In terms of objective assessment, special focus will be paid to the analysis of the influence of provided MR interfaces on psychophysical load with the use of biofeedback methods. Conclusions from both the subjective and objective assessment will be a basis for further MR interface improvement.

14.4 Conclusions and Future Work

The proposed approach for ensuring the health and safety of construction workers presents a significant paradigm shift in how this problem is addressed in practice. In modern, demanding, and dynamic work environments, it is no longer sufficient to perform periodical risk assessment studies – instead, the safety of the site must be monitored in real time. This would be unattainable without the use of novel technologies, such as the Tactile Internet, mixed reality, and semantic data integration; all combined in a next-generation IoT environment. The proposed solution architecture exemplifies how these abstract approaches can be put to work in a specific use case, using the ASSIST-IoT reference architecture. Moreover, the preliminary evaluation methodology of the solution is presented. In the future, a detailed evaluation of the system will be performed, in the demanding environment of an active construction site.

Acknowledgements

This work is part of the ASSIST-IoT project that has received funding from the EU's Horizon 2020 research and innovation program under Grant Agreement No. 957258.

References

[1] Tim Berners-Lee, James Hendler, and Ora Lassila. The Semantic Web. *Scientific american*, 284(5):34–43, 2001.

[2] Fei Dai, Abiodun Olorunfemi, Weibing Peng, Dongping Cao, and Xiaochun Luo. Can mixed reality enhance safety communication on construction sites? an industry perspective. *Safety Science*, 133:105009, 2021.

[3] Sarv Devaraj and Rajiv Kohli. Performance impacts of information technology: Is actual usage the missing link? *Management Science*, 49(1):273–289, 2003.

[4] Anastasia Dimou, Miel Vander Sande, Pieter Colpaert, Ruben Verborgh, Erik Mannens, and Rik Van de Walle. RML: a generic language for integrated RDF mappings of heterogeneous data. In *Ldow*, 2014.

[5] EU-IoT. Research & innovation - Next Generation IoT. https://www.ng iot.eu/research-innovation/.

[6] EUROSTAT. Accidents at work - statistics on causes and circumstances. https://ec.europa.eu/eurostat/statistics-explained/index.php?title=Accid ents_at_work_-_statistics_on_causes_and_circumstances#Workstation _accidents, 2022. Accessed: 2022-12-06.

[7] Alejandro Fornés-Leal, Ignacio Lacalle, Carlos E Palau, Paweł Szmeja, Maria Ganzha, Marcin Paprzycki, Eduardo Garro, and Francisco Blanquer. ASSIST-IoT: A reference architecture for next generation Internet of Things. In *New Trends in Intelligent Software Methodologies, Tools and Techniques*, pages 109–128. IOS Press, 2022.

[8] Alejandro Fornés-Leal, Ignacio Lacalle, Rafael Vaño, Carlos E Palau, Fernando Boronat, Maria Ganzha, and Marcin Paprzycki. Evolution of MANO towards the cloud-native paradigm for the edge computing. In *Advanced Computing and Intelligent Technologies*, pages 1–16. Springer, 2022.

[9] Maria Ganzha, Marcin Paprzycki, Wiesław PawĂĆowski, Paweł Szmeja, and Katarzyna Wasielewska. Semantic interoperability in the Internet of Things: An overview from the INTER-IoT perspective. *Journal of Network and Computer Applications*, 81:111–124, 2017.

[10] Maria Ganzha, Marcin Paprzycki, WiesĂĆaw Pawłowski, Paweł Szmeja, and Katarzyna Wasielewska. Streaming semantic translations. In *2017 21st International Conference on System Theory, Control and Computing (ICSTCC)*, pages 1–8, 2017.

[11] Wilma Lorena Gavilanes López, Blanca Rocio Cuji, Maria Jose Abásolo, and Gladys Lorena Aguirre Sailema. Technological acceptance model (tam) using augmented reality in university learning scenarios. In *2019 14th Iberian Conference on Information Systems and Technologies (CISTI)*, pages 1–9. IEEE, 2019.

[12] Marc Hassenzahl and Noam Tractinsky. User experience-a research agenda. *Behaviour & information technology*, 25(2):91–97, 2006.

[13] Tina Katika, Fotios K Konstantinidis, Thomas Papaioannou, Aris Dadoukis, Spyridon Nektarios Bolierakis, Georgios Tsimiklis, and Angelos Amditis. Exploiting mixed reality in a next-generation IoT ecosystem of a construction site. In *2022 IEEE International Conference on Imaging Systems and Techniques (IST)*, pages 1–6. IEEE, 2022.

[14] Fotios K Konstantinidis, Ioannis Kansizoglou, Nicholas Santavas, Spyridon G Mouroutsos, and Antonios Gasteratos. Marma: A mobile

augmented reality maintenance assistant for fast-track repair procedures in the context of Industry 4.0. *Machines*, 8(4):88, 2020.

[15] Fotios K Konstantinidis, Nikolaos Myrillas, Spyridon G Mouroutsos, Dimitrios Koulouriotis, and Antonios Gasteratos. Assessment of industry 4.0 for modern manufacturing ecosystem: A systematic survey of surveys. *Machines*, 10(9):746, 2022.

[16] Ignacio Lacalle, César López, Rafael Vaño, Carlos E Palau, Manuel Esteve, Maria Ganzha, Marcin Paprzycki, and Paweł Szmeja. Tactile Internet in Internet of Things ecosystems. In *International Conference on Electrical and Electronics Engineering*, pages 794–807. Springer, 2022.

[17] R Deiny Mardian, Muhammad Suryanegara, and Kalamullah Ramli. Measuring quality of service (QoS) and quality of experience (QoE) on 5G technology: A review. In *2019 IEEE International Conference on Innovative Research and Development (ICIRD)*, pages 1–6. IEEE, 2019.

[18] Marco Giovanni Mariani, Matteo Curcuruto, and Ivan Gaetani. Training opportunities, technology acceptance and job satisfaction: A study of italian organizations. *Journal of Workplace Learning*, 25(1):455–475, 2013.

[19] Guy Martin, Louis Koizia, Angad Kooner, John Cafferkey, Clare Ross, Sanjay Purkayastha, Arun Sivananthan, Anisha Tanna, Philip Pratt, James Kinross, et al. Use of the HoloLens2 mixed reality headset for protecting health care workers during the COVID-19 pandemic: prospective, observational evaluation. *Journal of medical Internet research*, 22(8):e21486, 2020.

[20] Panagiotis Michalis, Fotios Konstantinidis, and Manousos Valyrakis. The road towards civil infrastructure 4.0 for proactive asset management of critical infrastructure systems. In *Proceedings of the 2nd International Conference on Natural Hazards & Infrastructure (ICONHIC), Chania, Greece*, pages 23–26, 2019.

[21] Lisa Mlekus, Dominik Bentler, Agnieszka Paruzel, Anna-Lena Kato-Beiderwieden, and Gunter W. Maier. How to raise technology acceptance: user experience characteristics as technology-inherent determinants. *Gruppe. Interaktion. Organisation. Zeitschrift fÃijr Angewandte Organisationspsychologie (GIO)*, 51(1):273–283, 2020.

[22] Andrzej Paszkiewicz, Mateusz Salach, Maria Ganzha, Marcin Paprzycki, Marek Bolanowski, Grzegorz Budzik, Hubert Wójcik, Fotios Konstantinidis, and Carlos E Palau. Implementation of UI methods and UX in VR in case of 3D printer tutorial. In *New Trends in Intelligent*

Software Methodologies, Tools and Techniques, pages 460–471. IOS Press, 2022.

[23] Daniel Podgórski. *New Opportunities and Challenges in Occupational Safety and Health Management*. CRC Press, 2020.

[24] Daniel Podgorski, Katarzyna Majchrzycka, Anna Dabrowska, Grzegorz Gralewicz, and Małgorzata Okrasa. Towards a conceptual framework of OSH risk management in smart working environments based on smart PPE, ambient intelligence and the Internet of Things technologies. *International Journal of Occupational Safety and Ergonomics*, 23(1):1–20, 2017.

[25] Che Mohd Yusoff Rasimah, Azlina Ahmad, and Halimah Badioze Zaman. Evaluation of user acceptance of mixed reality technology. *Australasian Journal of Educational Technology*, 27(8):1369–1387, 2011.

[26] Philipp Schulz, Maximilian Matthe, Henrik Klessig, Meryem Simsek, Gerhard Fettweis, Junaid Ansari, Shehzad Ali Ashraf, Bjoern Almeroth, Jens Voigt, Ines Riedel, et al. Latency critical IoT applications in 5G: Perspective on the design of radio interface and network architecture. *IEEE Communications Magazine*, 55(2):70–78, 2017.

[27] Piotr Sowinski, Katarzyna Wasielewska-Michniewska, Maria Ganzha, Wieslaw Pawlowski, Pawel Szmeja, and Marcin Paprzycki. Efficient RDF streaming for the edge-cloud continuum. In *Proceedings of the IEEE 8th World Forum on Internet of Things (in print)*, 2022.

[28] Maman Suryaman, Risma Fitriani, and Dian Budhi Santoso. The application of technology acceptance model in evaluating mixed reality as a learning strategy on classroom management. *Italienisch*, 12(2):494–505, 2022.

[29] Mark Turner, Barbara Kitchenham, Pearl Brereton, Stuart Charters, and David Budgen. Does the technology acceptance model predict actual use? a systematic literature review. *Information and Software Technology*, 52(1):463–479, 2013.

15

Haptic and Mixed Reality Enabled Immersive Cockpits for Tele-operated Driving

Raul Lozano[1], Miguel Cantero[2], Manuel Fuentes[2], Jaime Ruiz[3], Ignacio Benito[3], and David Gomez-Barquero[1]

[1]iTEAM Research Institute of Universitat Politècnica de València, Spain
[2]5G Communications for Future Industry Verticals S.L. (Fivecomm), Spain
[3]Nokia Spain S.A., Spain
E-mail: raulote@iteam.upv.es; miguel.cantcro@fivecomm.eu; manuel.fuentes@fivecomm.eu; jaime_jesus.ruiz_alonso@nokia.com; ignacio.benito_frontelo@nokia.com; dagobar@iteam.upv.es

Abstract

In the last few years, the use of automated guided vehicles (AGVs) and autonomous mobile robots (AMRs) has experienced a sustainable increase in different verticals such as factories and logistics. However, they still have some technical limitations that hamper their autonomous operation in unpredictable or dynamic environments, requiring them to be supervised and/or controlled by human operators. In such situations, current tele-operated driving (ToD) systems lack the required stimulation and spatial perception to precisely manipulate the AGVs/AMRs, besides suffering from real-time challenges that limit the accuracy of movement. This chapter describes a proposal to solve these problems, by combining low-latency 5G-IoT networks and immersive cockpits equipped with haptic and mixed-reality devices. It also explains how such devices provide intuitive feedback for ToD and facilitate context-aware decision-making. The results are validated in the context of two innovative demonstrations deployed in the environment of a seaport, where ToD of multiple AGVs/AMRs is supported by a 5G mm Wave network infrastructure.

Keywords: 5G, IoT, haptics, metaverse, mixed-reality, robotics.

15.1 Introduction

Automated robots, which can be mobile (i.e., autonomous mobile robot – AMR) or guided (i.e., automated guided vehicle – AGV), are becoming increasingly sophisticated machines capable of navigating without human input, thanks to the multiple sensors attached (e.g., LiDAR/RADAR, cameras, IMUs, ultrasounds, etc.). The data gathered by the different sensors is processed by powerful AI-assisted tools to detect people, obstacles, and patterns, and even to perform the robot's simultaneous location and mapping (SLAM). In a collaborative industrial environment with multiple robots working at the time, next-generation IoT networks will make possible not only the real-time communication among the robots and other assets to optimize the collaborative task but also the offloading of the complex AI algorithms to the edge/cloud computing infrastructure in order to mitigate the cost of hardware and allow the robot to complete more complex missions.

Self-driving vehicles have been proposed for plenty of applications in the literature, the majority of them motivated by security or economic reasons. For instance, AGVs/AMRs can be very useful in scenarios where the physical presence of human beings can pose a risk to their safety, such as fires, toxic gas leaks, chemical or nuclear contamination, manipulation of explosives, logistics, etc. Similarly, they are key for the inspection of critical infrastructures such as factories, power stations, refineries, railways, ports, etc., especially in remote locations or in the case of extensive infrastructures where inspection by a local operator would be very expensive or inefficient [1].

Nevertheless, when deploying the mentioned use cases to a real scenario, occasional failures occur, especially if the inputs are contradictory or unseen for the AI modules. In the unpredictable real world, there is a myriad of situations that expert human operators are more capable of solving than state-of-the-art robotics. Some identified situations where human's pattern recognition and judgment still outperform machines are [2]: (i) low visibility due to extraordinary weather or light conditions; (ii) confusing or malfunctioning traffic signals; (iii) unclear or handwritten text indications; and (iv) sensors providing conflicting data.

To overcome such issues, the use of tele-operated driving (ToD) systems as a safety backup is the best option, especially in critical tasks and tasks that involve transporting or manipulating dangerous cargo. The idea is that the AGV/AMR asks a remote operator to take control of the robot when it cannot handle the situation [3], delivering to him all the necessary sensor data (e.g., video stream, detected obstacles, telemetry information, etc.). In that regard, we consider the state-of-the-art solutions to provide insufficient time responsiveness and stimulus to perform ToD precisely and intuitively in any environment.

For a correct implementation of ToD, we identify that an appropriate IoT communication infrastructure along with dedicated protocols and an intuitive cockpit setup is needed. From the communication perspective, 5G seems to be the best candidate to satisfy the QoE requirements (e.g., strict throughput, latency, and loss rate), although they depend on multiple factors such as the level of control of the vehicle. From the application perspective, we propose to integrate the cockpit with a combination of head mounted displays (HMDs) and haptic devices to engage the user in multisensory and realistic 3D environments that facilitate the ToD. We think that such combination will be the standard for any kind of remote control in the next decade, transforming the ways humans interact over long distances and revolutionizing verticals such as healthcare, education, entertainment, and industry.

The rest of the chapter is structured as follows. Section 15.2 details the challenges of the state-of-the-art ToD systems, especially regarding real-time working. Section 15.3 proposes a generic architecture and components to overcome these challenges, identifying haptic communications, mixed reality, and 5G as the main enablers for ToD. Section 15.4 describes the implementation of the architecture and components into a proof of concept deployed in the environment of a seaport, including a KPI collection to study the viability of the use case. Finally, the chapter's conclusions and next steps are included in Section 15.5.

15.2 Tele-operated Driving challenges

15.2.1 Real-time issues

All the use cases described above intend to control the vehicle in real time, which is with an imperceptible latency for the user. This means that the system will only be felt as intuitive and natural if the end-to-end (E2E) latency of the system is below a certain threshold, the so-called human factor.

However, the studies found on the literature do not provide firm conclusions about the value of such threshold, with results that range from 10 to 400 ms. For example, the 5G Automotive Association (5GAA) defines a maximum admissible latency from 400 ms when the robot is only supervised to 120 ms when the operator fully controls the vehicle [4]. Moreover, the human reaction time depends on factors such as the age and qualification of the subject, the expectancy to the event, or the participating senses [5].

Regarding ToD specifically, the human factor for both sight and touch is also dependent on the characteristics of the application (e.g., velocity of the robot, size of the scenario, and other moving objects). In fact, some studies identify that the strictest human factors come from the combination of visual and tactile feedback controlling an immersive, highly dynamic visual scene, when an E2E latency of few milliseconds is needed in both senses for unnoticeable delay [6].

Unfortunately, such extremely low values cannot be satisfied with current technology, considering that sensors and actuators are usually the bottleneck of the application-level delay. For example, if the maximum E2E latency for a certain ToD application is 200 ms and the immanent latency of a modern operating robot is (in the best case) around 180 ms, only 20 ms are left for visual feedback, application processing, and network-level latencies. For a typically lower human factor for sight, this threshold is impossible to reach, although some studies propose to anticipate the user's intention via complex AI/ML algorithms [7]. On the other hand, the human factor for touch (i.e., around 10−50 ms) may be easier to satisfy, given that haptic actuators are quicker than mechanical ones, as is the case of Meta's haptic glove prototype, which was able to achieve haptic feedback delays of just 20 ms [8]. For that reason, we envision that by applying haptic feedback to ToD, the user can be warned about a certain danger faster than only using visual feedback.

Hence, the reduction of network-level latencies for ToD will not make the difference by itself but can contribute to enable some specific use cases. Under specific configurations, 5G networks target latencies down to 1 ms, which is a reduction between 30 and 50 ms compared with current networks. Nevertheless, the main challenge is not to achieve ultra-low latencies but to achieve them while maintaining high reliability and throughput. Even with dedicated networks and proper dimensioning, such combination requires combining two 3GPP families: (i) enhanced mobile broadband (eMBB) and (ii) ultra-reliable low-latency communications (URLLC), which entails challenging tradeoffs. On the one hand, increasing the reliability requires more resources for signaling, re-transmission, redundancy, and parity, resulting in an increase of the latency. On the other hand, low latency modes are only valid in a multi-user network for a fraction of the load in the system, and at the expenses of higher latencies for the rest of the users.

15.2.2 Immersive devices

The scope of ToD is closely linked to racing simulation games. Those games are intended to emulate the behavior of real-world cars, making the user feel to be physically in the vehicle through the use of racing cockpits equipped with haptic-feedback steering wheel, gearbox, and pedals. Nevertheless, the visual feedback is usually provided by one or several 2D screens, which do not provide a sufficiently immersive experience.

Although many consumer-grade VR HMDs are available in the market today (e.g., HTC Vive, Meta Quest, Sony Playstation VR, and Valve Index), their lack of quality content has made them commercially unsuccessful, discouraging developers to create more VR content for their games. Moreover, sophisticated peripherals capable of immersing the user into the in-game action, such as pass-through mixed reality (MR) HMDs (e.g., Varjo XR3, Meta Quest Pro, etc.), haptic vests (e.g., bHaptics TactSuite, OWO, etc.), or force-feedback haptic gloves (e.g., HaptX DK2, SenseGlove Nova, etc.), are at the moment industrial-grade devices due to their expensive prices.

We consider it a matter of time that the technology evolves enough to make immersive devices commercially attractive, allowing people to get immersed into artificial scenarios and witness new ways of interacting with tools and machines. Indeed, immersive devices have the potential for providing complex user interfaces and extended spatial perception that boosts human problem-solving and manipulative skills [9].

15.3 Immersive Cockpit Architecture and Components

15.3.1 Overall architecture

As the core part of any ToD scenario, the use of the immersive cockpit influences the design of the whole architecture and the rest of the actors involved, including network, AGVs/AMRs, or UEs. In the end, data flows are the essence of IoT; so the whole architecture must be oriented to exploit this data.

In order to supervise and/or control the AGVs/AMRs in industrial environments, where every task is critical, accuracy is the main requirement. Hence, it is critical to communicate the immersive cockpit and the AGVs/AMRs with low latency, while maintaining high reliability and throughput. Using Wi-Fi, LTE, or other IoT networks different from 5G might lead to in undesired accidents costing money and even potential injuries to people. 5G is the only network capable of offering advanced slicing or QoS-prioritization schemes.

The architecture we propose can be appreciated in Figure 15.1. It has three key parts [10]: (i) 5G mmWave antenna compliant with 3GPP Rel-15 (eMBB); (ii) indoor cockpit composed of MR HMD, haptic gloves, steering wheel, and pedals, connected to an MEC via fixed fiber and/or 5G hotspot; and (iii) AGV/AMR equipped with 360ž cameras, proximity sensors, and a 5G modem. Its flexible and versatile design allows for several AGVs/AMRs with different traffic priorities to be working simultaneously in the area.

There are four different data flows from or to the immersive cockpit. In the uplink, one unique flow is used to transmit driving commands to the AGV/AMR, either using the haptic gloves or the steering wheel. In the downlink, the ACK message to these commands contains the telemetry data, used to monitor the status of the robot. The E2E latency for the haptic data flow is expected to be between 20 and 30 ms. On the other hand, the video streaming is received in a different downlink data flow, which provides a 360ž first-person view of the area (displayed in VR or MR) with an expected latency of 100 ms. Finally, a security signal that contains the information about the LiDAR and depth cameras is used to create haptic feedback that warns about the obstacles and other events on the automated route.

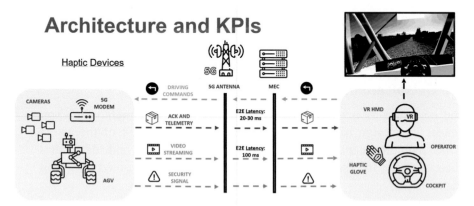

Figure 15.1   Data flows in the proposed architecture of the immersive cockpit [11].

15.3.2 Components

15.3.2.1 Head mounted displays

HMDs are devices that allow users to experience VR or MR. HMDs typically consist of a headset that includes a display and lenses, as well as sensors and other hardware for tracking the user's movements and providing a realistic experience. MR-backed tele-operation permits the 3D visualization of the scenario while displaying useful data acquired from the ambient using the robot's sensors, enriching the information for the drivers. This allows users to interact with virtual objects as if they were real, making the experience more engaging and realistic. One of the key advantages of MR headsets is their ability to track the user's movements in the real world, allowing to move around freely and interact with virtual objects in a natural way. In contrast, VR headsets often require users to stay in a fixed position, limiting their ability to interact with the virtual world. Additionally, the pass-through cameras of MR headsets can provide a more comfortable and natural experience for users, preventing motion sickness and other discomforts that can be caused by fully immersive VR experiences.

Hence, the immersive cockpit has been tested with two different HMDs (one MR and other VR). The first one is the Varjo XR-3, a high-end MR device with advanced features (e.g., hand tracking, eye tracking, and autonomous SLAM) and a top resolution of 70 pixels per degree. It also includes pass-through cameras and LiDAR sensors to enable the overlaying of virtual objects on the real world, perceived as photorealistic by the user. The second device tested is the famous Meta Quest 2, a pure VR device with lower resolution and simpler features but capable of working standalone (i.e., via Wi-Fi and not tethered to a PC). However, it was found out that the wired mode provides better latency and performance.

15.3.2.2 Haptic gloves

People trust on digital technologies to interact over long distances when they cannot be physically present in a certain place, either due to agenda overlaps or mobility restrictions. However, current approaches are limited to the communication of sight and hearing, which, although are becoming increasingly capable of simulating physical presence thanks to the development of metaverse technologies such as mixed reality and holograms, lack the ability to simulate physical interaction as touch does. In fact, it has been demonstrated that haptic interaction improves human performance over any kind of task [12], showing that the sense of touch is crucial for perceiving the environment. It seems logical to try to replicate these benefits in human—machine interaction, by implementing haptic communication into ToD. Haptic feedback can be used not only for ToD when the robot reaches its functional limits [13] but also for receiving information about the robot's state in the supervision mode [14].

Haptic communications are still an unexplored technology, meaning that the development of haptic applications, protocols, devices, and actuators is very poor. The few commercially available haptic devices are quite expensive and limited, which impedes the growth of the industry and the unlocking of the potential of haptic communications. In fact, the haptic glove used in our proof of concept is a prototype that only provides vibrotactile feedback, created by NeuroDigital Technologies.

The Sensorial XR haptic gloves feature 10 haptic actuators with LRA technology, one at each fingertip and five near the palm. Each LRA has 1024 vibration intensities with an amplitude up to 1.8 G and a resonant frequency of 205 Hz, ensuring a high level of realism and immersion. The gloves also have a low latency of under 30 ms, ensuring a seamless and responsive user experience [11]. In addition to the haptic actuators, the gloves also feature seven nine-axis IMUs working at 200 Hz. The IMUs allow for motion capture, enabling the gloves to track and replicate a user's hand movements in the MR environment. This is executed by the capture of abduction, adduction, and rotation degrees of freedom, providing a more detailed and accurate representation of hand movements compared to flex/blending sensors [15]. Finally, the gloves have four conductive fabric zones located in the thumb, middle, index, and palm. These allow for gesture capture, enabling the gloves to recognize and respond to specific hand gestures made by the user. A picture of the different sensors and actuators of the gloves can be seen in Figure 15.2.

The Sensorial XR haptic gloves can be used with either a wired or wireless connection to the supporting PC. The wired connection offers negligible latency and a sample rate of over 200 Hz, ensuring a high level of responsiveness and accuracy. The wireless connection uses Bluetooth 5.0 and has an added latency of 7.5 ms, with a lower sample rate of 120 Hz. The gloves come with a dedicated API programmed in C# language, which enables communication with the Unity3D application that defines their behavior after an event. The application can simulate complex sensations such as inter-finger collisions, surfaces rugosity, or customized vibrations, providing a rich and immersive VR experience. Figure 15.3 shows an example of how the haptic sensations can be applied to ToD, creating haptic feedback to warn about the obstacle closeness.

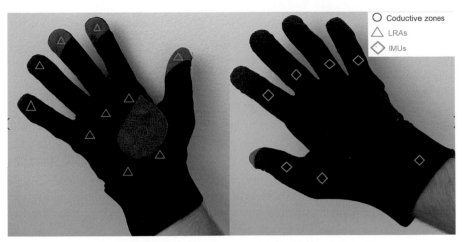

Figure 15.2 Sensors and actuators of Sensorial XR [16].

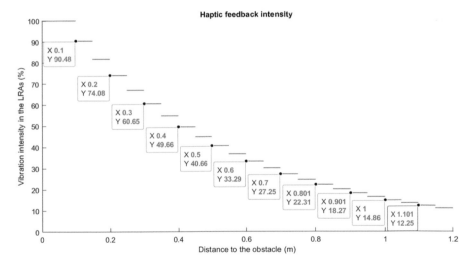

Figure 15.3 Haptic feedback intensity as a response to the obstacle closeness [16].

15.3.2.3 Wheels and pedals

The Logitech G29 is a high-performance racing wheel, pedals, and gearbox designed for use with gaming consoles and computers. The wheel features a durable, high-quality construction with a leather-wrapped steering wheel and stainless steel paddle shifters. The pedals are made of metal and feature a non-slip surface, while the gearbox offers six-speed manual shifting with a clutch pedal.

One of the standout features of the Logitech G29 is its force feedback system, which provides realistic and immersive racing experiences. Indeed, it has a dual-motor design, providing separate feedback for the wheel and pedals. The wheel also has a number of customizable buttons and dials, allowing users to customize their racing experience.

15.3.2.4 5G mmWave modems

The scarcity of mmWave modems and devices in the market has made it also challenging to implement such frequencies in our E2E solution. Only two of these devices were available for testing and integration, one on the AGV/AMR side and the other on the cockpit side. On the AGV/AMR side, we used an Askey mmWave 5G modem, which was directly connected to the AGV/AMR controller board. This modem also has a web user interface that allows for easy configuration. On the cockpit side, we used an Asus smartphone with mmWave capabilities, which was configured to create a VPN with the AGV/AMR. Both of these modems are capable of operating in the n258 5G band and provide an Ethernet link to the rest of the connected systems.

15.4 Proof of Concept

The huge traffic volume handled yearly by the port terminals, together with the variety of infrastructures and equipment managed by different stakeholders (e.g., terminal operators, maritime agencies, or logistic suppliers), make them one of the most complex parts of the supply chain.

We propose to digitalize and automate the port logistics by taking advantage of the data richness of IoT, implementing innovative use cases such as the "improvement of the driver's safety with mixed-reality and haptic solutions." It envisions a future when AGVs/AMRs will be used as mobile cranes to transport the ship containers around the port terminal, optimizing the loading and unloading of assets [15]. The ToD of the AGVs/AMRs will be available as a safety backup (i.e., for both supervision and total control), performed from a remote indoor cockpit to avoid accidents and hazardous situations for human operators. In an attempt to provide more intuitive and immersive ways of operating the AGVs/AMRs, the use of 2D screens and input devices (e.g., mice or keyboards) will be avoided. Instead, the immersive cockpit will be equipped by HMDs and haptic gloves, capable of providing multisensory information of the port area.

15.4.1 End-to-end use case description

To understand the role of the immersive cockpit within the use case, it is necessary to provide a whole picture about the scenario and actors involved. As a proof of concept before the deployment in the port terminal, several AGVs/AMRs are programmed to follow automated routes around a specific area, simulating the logistics operations. Simultaneously, a remote operator utilizes the immersive cockpit to supervise the task, with the possibility of controlling (i.e., changing or stopping) the route at any moment. In the extraordinary case that the robot's autonomous mode is not available (e.g., SLAM fail, or non-avoidable obstacle in the path), the control of the AGV/AMR totally shifts to the cockpit for a full ToD. During this manoeuver, the visual and haptic feedback provided by the immersive cockpits allows the user to precisely overcome the obstacle and put the AGV/AMR back in its route; so it can work autonomously again.

While the ToD cockpit is integrated with all the peripherals mentioned before (i.e., steering wheel, pedals, haptic gloves, and HMD), the supervision mode can alternatively be performed through an "on-site cockpit" composed by the haptic gloves only (see Figure 15.4). This intends to prove the potential of such devices as both IoT sensors and actuators, as well as to explore new ways of controlling the AGVs/AMRs.

15.4.2 Remote cockpit

The remote cockpit implements all the described components into a unified solution. However, although the hardware is important in order to enable the features desired, the software is the true important part. The XR application we implemented is an MR simulation of a car interior and exterior, as depicted in Figure 15.5. The Unity scene was created by modifying a car model using Blender software and then importing it into Unity. The GStreamer unity plugin is used to receive H264 video streams from multiple cameras, which are projected into four rectangles within the car scene. In addition, UDP C# scripts are used to receive telemetry and security information from the nodeJS cockpit application. This information is displayed in the car's user interface components and the steering wheel is also moved according to the movement of the physical steering wheel being used to remotely drive the AGV/AMR. The telemetry information retrieved from the AGV/AMR every 100 ms includes longitude and latitude GPS position, RTT in milliseconds for the UDP commands, steering angle of wheels, vehicle speed (m/s), traffic lights status if sent, engine RPM, driving mode, battery energy, and encountered objects if any. On the other hand, the security signal serves for haptically warning the user about the events on the route, including the case that autonomous mode is no longer available and ToD is required.

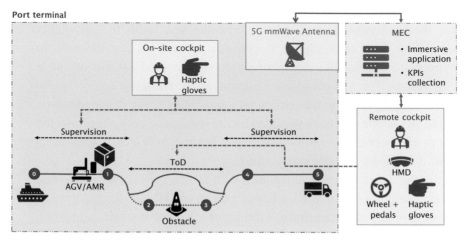

Figure 15.4   Immersive cockpit use case scenarios: route control (supervision) demo and ToD demo.

Figure 15.5   Remote cockpit implementation from first-person view (left) and third-person view (right).

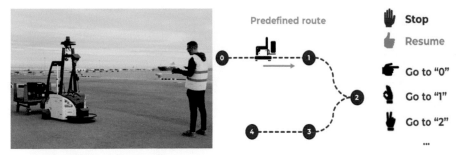

Figure 15.6 On-site cockpit implementation (left) and route control schema (right).

15.4.3 On-site cockpit

This cockpit is only used for supervision and command of the AGVs/AMRs, with the Sensorial XR haptic glove playing a pivotal role. The application is focused on using the Sensorial XR SDK interface to handle the data received from the haptic glove, including vibration levels, hand position and rotation, and gesture performed. This allows the user to easily control and manage the AGV/AMR's actions. The gestures that can be performed include: (i) going to a specific point in the route; (ii) stopping the movement; and (iii) resuming the movement (see Figure 15.6). This allows the user to avoid potential dangers for the robot, such as approaching an obstacle on the route, by receiving haptic feedback with an intensity that depends on the proximity of the obstacle, as depicted in Figure 15.3.

15.4.4 KPIs collection

In a first attempt to test the viability of the immersive cockpit implementation, the following KPIs were analyzed during the proof of concept deployed in the port:

- Round trip time (RTT)
- Video latency
- Video throughput
- E2E latency

First of all, the RTT is measured from the application layer, and, therefore, it considers the time that it takes for a UDP control command to be sent from the application (either from the gloves or the wheel/pedals) to an AGV/AMR, and for the AGV/AMR to send back the telemetry information to the application. The RTT is automatically calculated for each UDP message

Figure 15.7   Round trip time of remote driving command in Grafana.

and stored in a Grafana database, as Figure 15.7 shows. In order to effectively manage and store all the data, we have implemented a Grafana-based system in the MEC. This system receives asynchronous UDP messages from the nodeJS application on the HMD side through the use of a Telegraf plugin, which then injects the messages into the Influx DB database for storage. It can be appreciated that the RTT is very low, of around 7.5 ms, thanks to the use of a 5G network.

The video latency and throughput are jointly measured via slow-motion analysis, using the GStreamer tool to configure different video resolutions. In this case, the communication is only downlink (i.e., from the AGV/AMR to the cockpit), and both KPIs are measured from the cockpit perspective. Hence, the throughput captured is 2.5 Mbps for 360 p resolution, 8 Mbps for 720 p resolution, and 16 Mbps for 1080 p resolution. The same resolutions offer average latencies of 138.4, 156.4, and 173.6 ms, respectively; quite high values considering that no video codec is used.

Finally, the E2E latency is measured via slow-motion analysis too. We are aware that such method includes several biases such as the behavior of the peripherals, the slow-motion camera or the AGV/AMR; but we chose this method as a first approach, due to its simplicity. The E2E latency is measured on the on-site cockpit and includes the RTT plus delays of sensors/actuators of the cockpit and the AGV/AMR. However, we identified that the bottleneck may be the specific AGV/AMR being used. Hence, the data shown in Figure 15.8 demonstrates that, on average, there is a noticeable difference in perceived latency when an AGV/AMR is resumed on a route or sent to a specific point (735 ms) compared to when it is stopped (362 ms). This is due to the fact that it takes less time to mechanically stop the wheels using the brake than it does to start movement.

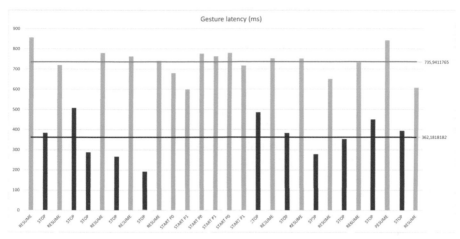

Figure 15.8   Perceived E2E gesture latency.

15.5 Conclusion

This chapter has explored the benefits of using immersive cockpits for ToD and supervision of AGVs/AMRs in real time, identifying key enabling factors such as haptic communication, mixed reality, and 5G. In order to demonstrate the viability of this technology, a proof of concept was deployed in a port environment with the goal of improving operator safety through indoor ToD. It was found that, while the literature defines an end-to-end (E2E) latency threshold of under 50 milliseconds for immersive ToD, this is currently not feasible due to mechanical limitations.

The performance metrics collected during these demonstrations resulted in average E2E gesture latencies of 362 ms for braking and 736 ms for acceleration, despite a network RTT latency of only 7.5 ms. Regarding the E2E video latency, the average values are between 138.4 and 173.6 ms, depending on the resolution demanded. These despair results, with a great gap between the E2E gesture latency and the RTT or video latencies evidence that the robot's mechanical actuators, are the primary bottleneck for ToD, and therefore the E2E gesture latency can be widely reduced using more mechanically advanced AGVs/AMRs.

Nevertheless, it must be considered that such mechanical latency is also present when manually driving the vehicle, not only when tele-operating it. Hence, more relevant KPIs (such as the communication and application latencies) should be prioritized when studying the real-time viability of immersive ToD. The low RTT provided by the 5G network, together with the low E2E video latency obtained show that the application latency is acceptable for this use case. Moreover, rudimentary subjective tests performed on different users that participated in the proof of concept agreed that the ToD was intuitive and smooth, whereas the latency was almost un-noticeable. In addition, throughput measurements showed that this ToD application has minimal bandwidth requirements that can be easily satisfied by 5G Release 15 (eMBB) networks.

Despite these challenges, the proof of concept showed the potential of haptic and mixed reality assisted ToD to revolutionize industries and logistics in the coming decades. We consider this use case to be completely open to future improvements and technological advances. Haptic communication will continue to be explored through the creation of an immersive laboratory at the Universitat Politècnica de València in late 2023, where QoE-based optimizations will be conducted for various sectors including education, industry, and logistics.

Acknowledgements

This work has been partially supported by the European Union's Horizon 2020 research and innovation program through the project iNGENIOUS under Grant Agreement No. 957216.

References

[1] D. Mourtzis, J. Angelopoulos y N. Panopoulos, "Smart Manufacturing and Tactile Internet Based on 5G in Industry 4.0: Challenges," Applications and New Trends, Electronics, 2021.

[2] L. Kang, W. Zhao, B. Qi y S. Banerjee, "Augmenting Self-Driving with Remote Control: Challenges and Directions," HotMobile '18: Proceedings of the 19th International Workshop on Mobile Computing Systems & Applications, 2018.

[3] P. Pérez, J. Ruiz, I. Benito y R. Lopez, "A parametric quality model to evaluate the performance of tele-operated driving services over 5G networks".

[4] 5GAA, "Tele-Operated Driving (ToD): Use Cases and Technical Requirements," 5GAA Automotive Association Technical Report, 2020.

[5] G. Fettweis y S. Alamouti, "5G: Personal mobile internet beyond what cellular did to telephony," IEEE Communications Magazine, 2014.

[6] ITU, "The Tactile Internet," ITU-T Technology Watch, 2014.

[7] 5G-Infrastructure-Association, "5G and e-Health," 5G-PPP White Paper, 2015.

[8] M. D. Luca y A. Mahnan, "Perceptual Limits of Visual-Haptic Simultaneity in Virtual Reality Interactions," 2019 IEEE World Haptics Conference (WHC), 2019.

[9] F. Hu, Y. Deng, H. Zhou, T. H. Jung, C.-B. Chae y A. H. Aghvami, "A Vision of XR-aided Teleoperation System Towards 5G/B5G," IEEE Communications Magazine, 2020.

[10] iNGENIOUS, "D6.1 Initial Planning for Testbeds," 2021.

[11] iNGENIOUS, "D3.4 Bio-haptic and XR-enabled IoT devices," 2022.

[12] G. Ganesh, A. Takagi, R. Osu, T. Yoshioka, M. Kawato y E. Burdet, "Two is better than one: Physical interactions improve motor performance in humans," Sci Rep, 2014.

[13] D. A. Abbink, T. Carlson, M. Mulder, J. C. F. d. Winter, F. Aminravan, T. L. Gibo y E. R. Boer, "A Topology of Shared Control Systems," IEEE Transactions on Human-Machine Systems, 2018.

[14] Y. Che, C. T. Sun y A. M. Okamura, "Avoiding Human-Robot Collisions using Haptic Communication," 2018 IEEE International Conference on Robotics and Automation (ICRA), 2018.

[15] iNGENIOUS, "D2.2 System and Architecture Integration (Initial)," 2021.

[16] R. Lozano, "Application of Haptic Gloves to Remotely Control 5G-Enabled Automated Robots," 2021.

16

The EFPF Approach to Manufacturing Applications Across Edge-cloud Architectures

Rute C. Sofia[1], Carlos Coutinho[2], Gabriele Scivoletto[3], Gianluca Insolvibile[3], Rohit A. Deshmukh[4], A. Schneider[4], Violeta Damjanovic-Behrendt[5], Fernando Gigante[6], Usman Wajid[7], Alexandros Nizamis[8], Dimosthenis Ioannidis[8], and Theofilos Mastos[9]

[1]fortiss Research Institute – associated with the Technical University of Munich, Germany
[2]Caixa Mágica Software, Portugal
[3]Nextworks, Italy
[4]Fraunhofer Institute for Applied Information Technology FIT, Germany
[5]Salzburg Research Institute, Austria
[6]AIDIMME, Spain
[7]Information Catalyst, UK
[8]Centre for Research and Technology Hellas (CERTH), Greece
[9]KLEEMANN HELLAS S.A., Kilkis Industrial Area, Greece
E-mail: sofia@fortiss.org; carlos.coutinho@caixamagica.pt; g.scivoletto@nextworks.it; g.insolvibile@nextworks.it; rohit.deshmukh@fit.fraunhofer.de; usmanwajid@gmail.com; alnizami@iti.gr; t.mastos@kleemannlifts.com; djoannid@iti.gr

Abstract

Manufacturing as a Service (MaaS) refers to a set of tools and processes that can assist the shared use of networked production facilities. In the core of this paradigm is a vision where manufacturing environments shall profit from an online set of tools and services that can be tailored to the requirements coming from the different manufacturers, thus reaching a higher degree of flexibility and an increase in production efficiency.

319   DOI: 10.1201/9781032632407-20

In the context of MaaS, the **Horizon 2020 European Connected Factory Platform for Agile Manufacturing (EFPF)** provides an operational instantiation of a large-scale MaaS across Europe, integrating a diverse set of services such as data analytics, factory connectors, and an interoperable Data Spine to proportionate a high level of automation across different shop-floors.

This chapter explains the EFPF MaaS concept, going over its architectural design, and giving insight into how developers and SMEs can profit from the EFPF open-source SDK to generate new products, and how these products can be integrated into the EFPF broad marketplace. The chapter gives insight also to the different pilots developed in the project, explaining challenges faced, and proposed solutions.

Keywords: MaaS, machine learning, IIoT, federated platform, SDK.

16.1 Introduction

In Europe, manufacturing is one of the key pillars of economical and societal development. While usually perceived to be solely limited to production, manufacturing businesses cross different areas and sectors, from agriculture, automotive, and construction, currently directly providing support for 32 million jobs in Europe[1]. While it shows a tremendous growth potential, manufacturing in Europe has seen a series of challenges, ranging from a shift in demand from goods to services; an increasing competition of emerging markets; lack of skills in different sectors, to comply with a technology-driven approach to manufacturing, required to make it grow to a sustainable level.

A key aspect to allow manufacturing to grow is to provide **Small and Medium Enterprises (SMEs)** with innovative tooling, to foment the development of innovative assets and services with a short time-to-market and to assist SMEs with broad dissemination coverage for the services developed. This aspect can be further developed, if SMEs can cooperate with research institutions, as this can assist in better understanding the novel directions to take.

Manufacturing as a Service (MaaS) therefore plays a key role in the future of manufacturing in Europe, in particular considering the development of SMEs. While there are multiple approaches to MaaS platforms, the key shared aspects relate with the capability to easily allow for new products to be

---

[1]https://www.iwkoeln.de/fileadmin/user_upload/Studien/IW-Studien/PDF/Studien_Manufacturing-in-Europe.pdf

generated and applied; to reach a high capability of customization to customer requests; and to ensure an adequate adaptation and integration of different tooling that can better support process and product efficiency. Backed up by edge- and cloud-based services, MaaS is currently reaching a mature stage, allowing for a true distributed manufacturing value-chain based on different sets of tools.

In this context, the current trends point to a combination of novel approaches, such as edge−cloud architectures [1], [2]; **Artificial Intelligence (AI)/Machine Learning (ML)**; semantic technologies; and **Industrial IoT (IIoT)** to sustain a MaaS distributed edge−cloud vision.

This chapter addresses the MaaS paradigm based on the **European connected factory platform for agile manufacturing (EFPF)**[2] concept and learnings, which integrate over 30 partners across the whole manufacturing value-chain (users, technology providers, consultants, and research institutes) from 11 European countries.

The key contributions of this chapter are:

- A presentation of an active MaaS concept, the EFPF architecture based on the implementation of advanced interoperability concept (Data Spine [3]) through innovative technologies.
- An overview of the EFPF SDK, which can be used by SMEs to compose and develop innovative applications that profit from the EFPF services and from the highly interoperable EFPF Data Spine.
- An overview of EFPF pilots deployed across Europe, describing challenges and solutions thereof.

16.2 Related Work

The European vision on Industry 4.0, the fourth industrial revolution, addresses the need to integrate a high degree of smart automation, where not just technology processes but also societal patterns are to be supported. Several related work has therefore been focusing on addressing the interoperability challenge in flexible, smart manufacturing. For instance, Datta et al. propose a secure and interoperable platform for lot-size-one manufacturing [4]. This platform is based on the EFPF collaboration tool, showing benefits in terms of interconnection of entities focusing on lot-size-one production.

Traditionally, the fastest step toward complete and integrated interoperable digitization is to rely on a cloud-based approach, as it provides more

---

[2] https://www.efpf.org/

flexibility in terms of product development, scaling, and product dissemination [5]. Cost-wise, cloud-based services become cheaper than investing on dedicated hardware. The use of cloud-based services is usually done based on an integrative perspective, where it is feasible to consider marketplace platforms to test and to try new suppliers, or eventually new customers based on a low-cost approach. This implies the development of highly interoperable and secure platforms, which on its turn require a vast support of different connectors, at different layers of the OSI stack [6].

The MaaS approach goes beyond cloud manufacturing platforms, in the sense that it addresses a collaborative, decentralized perspective integrating IIoT to boost new levels of process efficiency and productivity; sharing or community-oriented business models; and open-source software [7], [8]. Furthermore, a stronger involvement of all stakeholders, including the customer, in the overall manufacturing wholesale value-chain, is supported in the MaaS vision, by aiming at a higher degree of customization that is customer-driven [9]. This requires, as explained before, to integrate intelligence across the whole value-chain of manufacturing (across edge-cloud) and providing a distributed abstraction approach that can sustain the integration of the different manufacturing stakeholders, since the creation of materials, until the delivery of customized products on the market.

In this context, the work described in this chapter focuses on the initial steps that have been taken in the context of the European H2020 project EFPF, to provide an operational instantiation of a MaaS approach.

16.3 The EFPF Architecture

EFPF is a federated smart factory ecosystem that enables the federation of digital manufacturing platforms and interlinks different stakeholders of the digital manufacturing domain. The EFPF ecosystem enables users to utilize advanced interoperability solutions, implement innovative technologies, experiment with disruptive approaches, and develop custom solutions to maximize connectivity, interoperability, and efficiency across the supply chains.

16.3.1 The EFPF ecosystem as a federation of digital manufacturing platforms

The key components underpinning the EFPF federated platform ecosystem is illustrated in Figure 16.1. The EFPF ecosystem is formed by connecting a number of digital manufacturing platforms that provide ready to use

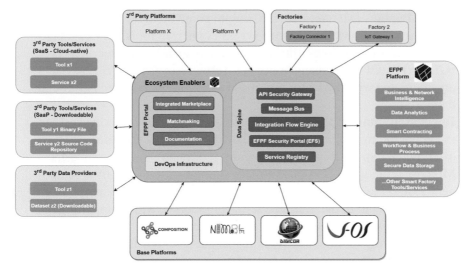

Figure 16.1 High-level architecture of the EFPF ecosystem.

and reusable functionalities. A set of central components called "ecosystem enablers" provide the core functionality that is needed to federate these platforms and enable interoperation among them. This ensures seamless access to the platforms' resources such as tools, services, and data, thereby enabling reusability and sustainability. The ecosystem enablers together with the tools and services of the connected platforms provide the necessary techniques and technologies to support the adoption and development of advanced manufacturing applications.

Some of the key components in the EFPF federated platform ecosystem include:

- **Data Spine [3]:** Corresponds to the core of the EFPF ecosystem that enables interconnection and interoperability. The Data Spine provides services such as single sign on; service registration and discovery; message brokering; and dataflow management and service composition. Being the interoperability backbone of the EFPF platform, one of the Data Spine's focuses is to bridge the interoperability gaps at the levels of identity providers, data models, protocols, and processes between the tools that it interconnects. The Data Spine supports both synchronous request-response as well as **asynchronous publish/subscribe (Pub/Sub)** communication patterns. The Data Spine's architecture and capabilities are explained further in the next section.

- **EFPF Portal**[3] [4]: Acts as the single point of entry for the EFPF ecosystem. It allows the users to access connected tools, services, platforms, and marketplaces through a unified **graphical user interface (GUI)**. The GUIs of many tools and services in the EFPF ecosystem are integrated with the EFPF portal and can be accessed directly through the portal.
- **Integrated marketplace** [4]: Provides an extensible framework to integrate multiple marketplaces, allowing users to access distributed offerings (from multiple marketplaces) through a unified interface. Moreover, the integrated marketplace framework consists of a component called "accountancy service" that tracks the user journeys from EFPF ecosystem to the interlinked marketplace(s), while supporting the sales-commission-based business models.
- **Matchmaking service:** Provides a federated search functionality that facilitates EFPF users to find the best suited suppliers from across different platforms and enables them to transact with them efficiently and effectively. Once a match of suitable partners is found, the matchmaking service enables users to form teams or consortia, to be able to jointly address specific business opportunities, and transact with them efficiently and effectively.
- **Factory connectors and IoT gateways**: Correspond to communication connectors deployed at the edge (e.g., MQTT Sparkplug connector) that collect data from the sensors and make it available to the cloud-native services such as the Data Spine. Some of the IoT gateways also consist of a middleware that provides some form of data processing functionalities, e.g., matchmaking between IoT data sources and services.
- **EFPF platform**: Provides unified access and interfaces to distributed smart factory tools and services. Examples of such tools and services include data analytics, predictive maintenance, track and trace, process design and execution, etc.
- **Base platforms**: Correspond to the four digital manufacturing platforms from the European Factories-of-Future (FoF-11-2016) cluster focused on supply chains and logistics, namely, COMPOSITION[4], DIGICOR[5], NIMBLE[6], and vf-OS[7]. The EFPF ecosystem is created by initially

---

[3] https://www.efpf.org/
[4] https://www.composition-project.eu/
[5] https://www.digicor-project.eu/
[6] https://www.nimble-project.org/
[7] https://www.vf-os.eu/

interlinking these base platforms. These platforms provide functionality that is complementary to each other with minimum overlap, and, hence, by interlinking them, the EFPF ecosystem is able to offer a comprehensive set of business functions.

- **Third-party platforms**: Correspond to the digital manufacturing platforms interlinked with the EFPF ecosystem that are provided by independent third parties. Each platform offers a range of tools and services that can be used by the users in the federation.
- **Third-party tools, services, and data:** Correspond to the individual tools, services, data APIs, etc., provided by independent third parties that do not belong to an existing platform.**Interoperable Data Spine:**

Figure 16.2 illustrates the EFPF Data Spine [3] as the central entity that enables the creation of the EFPF ecosystem by interlinking various platforms and enabling communication among them. The Data Spine follows a federation approach to interoperability, where the interoperability between a pair of services is established "on-demand," i.e., when required by a use case. There is no common data model or API imposed at the ecosystem level. This enables the creation of a modular, flexible, scalable, and extensible ecosystem.

The Data Spine consists of the following components that bridge the interoperability gaps among platform services at the levels of identity providers, data models, protocols, and processes and enables the creation of cross-platform applications in an easy and intuitive manner:

- **EFPF security portal (EFS)** federates the identity providers of the connected platforms and enables **single sign-on (SSO)** functionality in the ecosystem.
- **Integration flow engine (IFE)** provides a low-code development environment that can be used to create composite applications in the form of dataflows or "integration flows." The IFE provides a drag-and-drop style visual interface and built-in reusable components such as protocol connectors and data transformation processors that can be used to bridge the interoperability gaps among services.
- **EFPF message bus** enables asynchronous pub/sub-based communication in the EFPF ecosystem.
- **EFPF service registry** enables the lifecycle management and discovery of the service/API metadata that is needed for finding and consuming the services across the connected platforms.

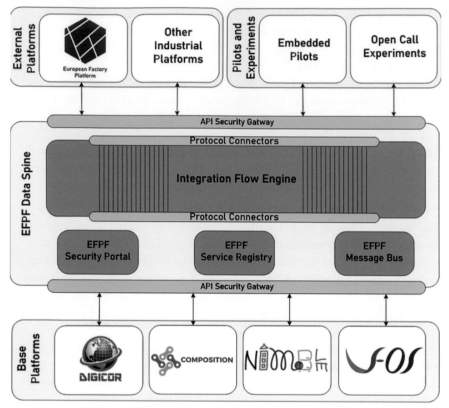

Figure 16.2 High-level architecture of the Data Spine [3].

- **API security gateway** acts as the policy enforcement point for the HTTP-based APIs exposed by the integration flows.

The Data Spine is realized through the implementation of several open-source components and the overall solution is made available as a permissive open-source solution for addressing interoperability challenges at diverse levels of the digital infrastructure. Overarching the interoperability features, holistic security, and privacy concepts are implemented to ensure transparent utilization of tools and services, as well as secure data exchange based on HTTP, MQTT, and AMQP protocols in the EFPF ecosystem.

The Data Spine was validated through the establishment of a platform federation that initially interlinked the tools, services, and user communities from the base platforms. Additional validations are carried out by adding external industrial platforms (from EFPF partners) in the federation.

Based on the interconnectivity and interoperability enabled by the Data Spine, the EFPF federation represents a vibrant digital ecosystem that brings together and interconnects the providers and consumers of smart factory tools, services, and interfaces. The tools and services in the EFPF ecosystem cover the complete lifecycle of production and logistic processes that take place in a modern industrial environment. Examples of the tools include, e.g., data gateways, distributed production planning and scheduling, distributed process design, production monitoring, real-time decision support, process optimization, risk management, and blockchain-based trust and message exchange.

16.4 EFPF SDK

The EFPF project aims to provide manufacturing businesses as an essential artifact, which is to have mechanisms to enable them to create their own applications, which can be best suited to the specific needs of the business, so that they do not require specialized companies (tied to EFPF) to make these applications. The objective is to enable the development of applications that can be done by small third parties or even developers from the manufacturing customer. This, on one hand, allows the customers to be less dependent on specialized companies for performing any development that involves EFPF, fostering an environment where the services of EFPF are made available in a centralized way so that they can be configured and applied to small high-value applications. On the other hand, this development environment also allows external third-party software development companies to use it for developing their own applications using the EFPF framework, where these developed applications can then be built and published in the EFPF marketplace, thus fostering a parallel business model that can bring them interesting revenue.

EFPF provides a range of tools included in its SDK[8] to help achieve the above goals. Several **Business Intelligence Applications (BI Apps)** were also developed to demonstrate its benefits to business as well as to highlight the SDK capabilities, which utilize different technologies provided by the EFPF SDK. Examples of these BI Apps are the **Shopfloor Intelligence BI App**, the **Lagrama Predictive Maintenance App**, and the **Spray Booth BI App**, which represent specific use cases that show users what they can achieve by using the SDK.

---

[8] https://www.efpf.org/sdk

The development environment is very rich, featuring best-of-breed solutions such as an SDK that centralizes the EFPF features and APIs so that they can be accessed, a full web-based IDE (based on Eclipse CHE, a project of the Eclipse foundation) to develop the applications, which is integrated with the SDK and with other EFPF-developed tools such as a Frontend Editor, which provides a simple way to produce the application's look and feel, the integration with WASP's Process Designer, which allows the users to define BPMN flows of the application behavior, and integrating the generating code back in the IDE. Other tools are also integrated such as the EFPF Engagement Hub, a portal that is aimed to promote the connection and interactivity between the developers, fostering open source and collaboration between them, as can be seen in Figure 16.3.

The EFPF SDK is a Javascript wrapper that comprises calls to the EFPF APIs, which then can be integrated in the IDE to make successful calls to the EFPF services as long as they are conformant with the corresponding protocols. The internal scripts have a flow that can be seen in Figure 16.4.

Moving along the SDK framework, the SDK Studio is a full-fledged integrated development environment (IDE), based on one of the most popular development platforms, Eclipse CHE, which allows having all the EFPF development environment in a Web-based platform, as can be seen in Figure 16.5.

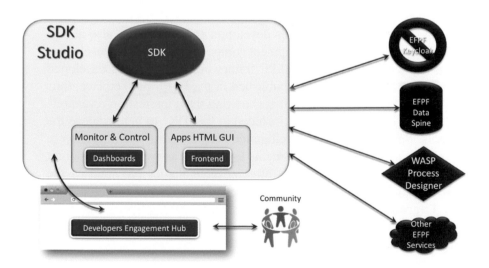

Figure 16.3   EFPF SDK architecture.

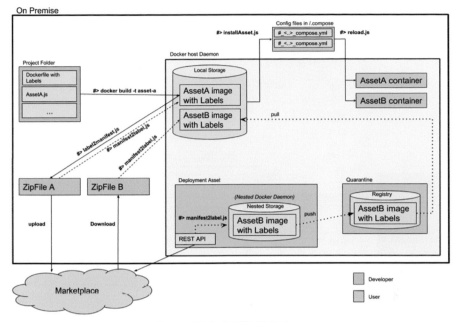

Figure 16.4 EFPF SDK flow.

The SDK Studio is able to develop applications in multiple languages and integrate with different technological stacks, and, of course, includes all the best features of the Eclipse IDE, such as the project development management, extensions, a complete editor with syntax highlighting, and many others. Despite the fact that the project uses Eclipse CHE, numerous customizations needed to be performed to integrate it with the EFPF environment, namely the SDK, the SDK Frontend, EFPF Keycloak, the WASP Process Designer, etc.

To enrich the look and feel of the developed applications, the EFPF SDK Frontend Editor is designed to support the development of custom applications initiated with the EFPF software development kit (SDK) based on the services provided by the EFPF platform. The Frontend's main functionality is to provide developers with a GUI editor for prototyping, to integrate and customize applications built with the SDK. Developers can combine all microservices based on implementations of the SDK integrated functionalities.

The frontend can be accessed by the SDK Studio interface using a plain browser. The solution is based on predefined templates that stand for

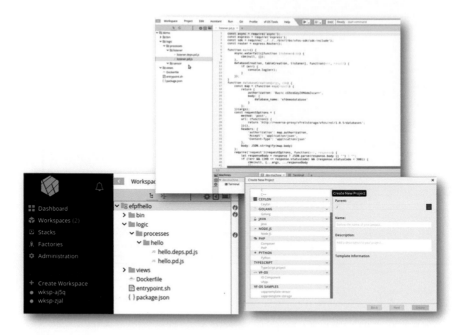

Figure 16.5   EFPF SDK Studio.

themselves (e.g., customized GUI elements) and can bind data sources from EFPF that are orchestrated by Application Development Studio. Application developers have a high degree of flexibility and power by combining the predefined templates and visual elements that can be used inline or nested. This approach results in a multitude of application designs.

The Frontend UI offers additional guidance and allows developers to speed up the process of rapid prototyping. Any design strategy is supported, and a broad range of applications can result from mixing single-page, multi-page, and progressive web application designs. The workflows are highly configurable translating business process models of the use-case scenarios into functional maintainable applications, as illustrated in Figure 16.6.

The main purpose of this web-based frontend is to get information from data-sources (e.g., databases, live sensor data, etc.) and display it in different components (e.g., tables, charts, etc.) in order to provide a better understanding of data, by using various visualizations elements. Each component presents specific data for each requested scenario. The Frontend Editor comprises numerous categories of components, such as horizontal/vertical tabs,

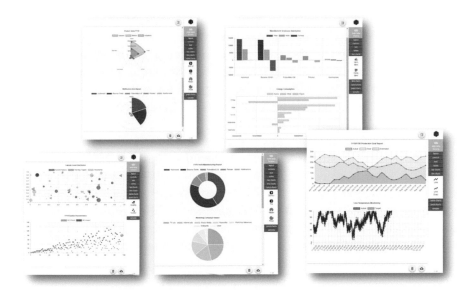

Figure 16.6 Frontend Editor architecture.

headers and footers, images, text labels and boxes, tables, and a variety of charts to display the proposed data.

To complement the set of tools available in the SDK framework, the EFPF Developer Engagement Hub has the purpose to define and develop a suite of tools that fit together and consist of a platform to support developer collaboration between developers, customers, and communities. It is a framework available from one single web-based platform, which not only supports the development of tools, but it also involves the development community, fosters their active contributions in the shape of tests, comments, suggestions, and new requests in the form of change requests in existing applications, e.g., to support other platforms, trends, needs, or extensions. It allows the community to download/reuse/fork the existing code from the Studio (if published) and actually use/test it on new conditions or scenarios. The outcomes of these tests will always come in the form of issues, reports, comments, or suggestions. It also promotes the usage and creation of standards, methodologies, and best practices. This framework includes mechanisms such as wikis, issue trackers, forums, and blogs. Other tools such as configuration management, business continuity, and business process design and management are initially conceived out of scope of this component and relevant to other components such as the SDK Studio.

This tool was developed on top of best-of-breed portal GitLab community edition (CE). Besides having all the standard features of GitLab, numerous developments were added to the base platform, such as allowing multiple level projects (useful for maintaining large projects) with multiple-level issue trackers as well, and the inclusion of a chatting tool for better collaboration between the developers, integration with the SDK Studio and many other features.

The methodology to develop apps using the EFPF SDK is very flexible, which can be shown in the prototypes developed within the scope of the project, where some were developed by developing a backend application, defining the application flow in the EFPF tool WASP Process Designer, then exporting the results of the flow definition to the EFPF SDK, and then defining a frontend for the application; others were performed defining a data source using the EFPF Data Spine AMQP tool and then displaying the resulting information on charts defined.

16.5 EFPF Selected Pilots

EFPF has addressed multiple scenarios in the context of Aerospace manufacturing[9], and out of the developed pilots, this chapter describes three specific pilots for different manufacturing environments, to provide an explanation on the interactions of different components across edge−cloud and on the value-add provided to manufacturing stakeholders via the EFPF tools.

16.5.1 Aerospace manufacturing pilot: environmental monitoring

This pilot aimed at addressing the need for highly customized solutions provided by small but innovative high-tech companies to commercial aircraft vendors. Currently, customer demands for specific features (e.g., novel cabin features) imply a fast answer with OEMs, e.g., Airbus, and high-tech SMEs' close cooperation. For this, it is relevant to be able to provide diversity in terms of production and supply network, which is often done based on a cluster centered on the OEM. EFPF has addressed the design for such needs and proposed implementation aspects for distinctive features, ranging from material parameter monitoring to bidding. The full description of the pilot is available in EFPF Deliverable D9.1 [10]. In this sub-section, two specific

---

[9] https://www.efpf.org/_files/ugd/26f25a_b498d53f78174f94b3077eaca42d34d3.pdf

technical scenarios are described: automated environmental monitoring and continuous monitoring of production machines.

The main aim of this use case is related to developing an interconnectable service that could capture environmental material data on a traditional shop-floor controlled by a manufacturing entity that does not integrate IT skills.

This use case has been developed together with two aerospace SMEs. The first, **Walter Otto Müller (WOM)**[10], aimed at controlling environmental aspects such as temperature and humidity in their manufacturing area, to ensure consistent quality and environmental conditions required for component tolerances. Aeronautics manufacturing handles strict specifications provided by large OEMs (e.g., Airbus, Boeing, etc.), including fine-grained requirements for the monitoring of varied materials in a component, e.g., paint. The second, **Innovint Aircraft Interior GmbH (IAI)**[11], aimed at monitoring the vacuum in vacuum-forming machines. Key aspects in this use case are related with adequately modeling and interconnecting the sensors that should be selected to perform the monitoring; how these could be digitized to visualize them in the EFPF user interface, and also how to allow for an automated result to be provided based on data extracted from multiple sensors, and a customized service deployment via the EFPF Data Spine.

The overall concept is illustrated in Figure 16.7. Different environmental sensors have been deployed in the shop-floors of WOM and IAI (IoT sensor device). The sensors on the shop-floor communicate (via wireless or wired interconnections) to a local IoT gateway (TSMatch) [12], [13]. The fortiss TSMatch gateway[12] provides a way to automate the detection and selection of sensors on a shop-floor (in the case of this pilot, environmental sensors). The raw data is processed via MQTT; semantic abstractions of the sensors are kept in TSMatch. A TSMatch application provides the user with a monitoring and notification application. This is therefore performed at a local level, within the shop-floor.

TSMatch results are sent via MQTT to the EFPF Data Spine. Therefore, to allow visualization of the data analytics supported by EFPF, the Symphony Factory Connector is used, to provide results (stored in the Data Spine) to the end-user anywhere.

The Symphony platform has been adopted in addition to TSMatch to provide a consistent edge/cloud distributed IIoT management service. To

---

[10] https://www.wom.gmbh/

[11] https://www.innovint.de/

[12] https://git.fortiss.org/iiot_external/tsmatch

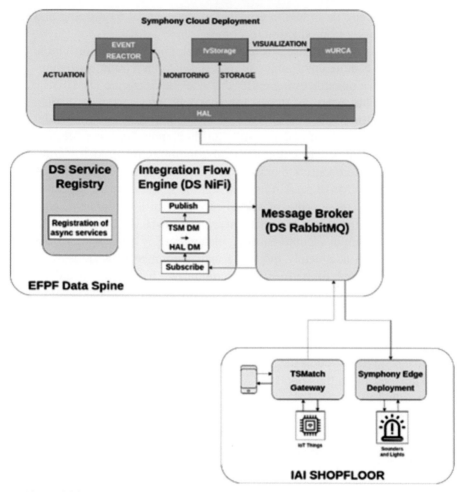

Figure 16.7   Interconnected components on the EFPF environmental monitoring pilot.

this purpose, two instances of Symphony have been deployed as illustrated in Figure 16.7. Sensors and actuators are managed by the edge instance of the platform, together with TSMatch, to provide low-latency functions (such as alerts requiring immediate action); historical storage, data analytics, and time-insensitive event reaction logic are provided by the cloud instance, together with a remote-control panel and visualization dashboard.

It is worth mentioning that the cloud instance of Symphony provides the digital twin models for some of the sensors and actuators in the shop-floor:

Figure 16.8 WOM settings for the control of temperature and humidity in a manufacturing area to ensure consistent quality and environmental conditions required for component tolerances.

the remote control panel reads values and performs actions using a cloud-based model of the devices, which is then synchronized with the actual state of the devices through the EFPF Data Spine, which is responsible for the edge-to-cloud communication and data model interoperability (as described in the previous sections).

The overall pilot requires the integration of sensors, which have been deployed based on embedded hardware as shown in Figures 16.8 and 16.9. The hardware has been installed in accordance with the strict requirements of aeronautics certification by the companies WOM and IAI.

Figure 16.9 shows some of the sensors installed in the pilot environment. The pressure sensor at the vacuum machine has been used to set up an AI/ML pipeline to remotely monitor the operational status of the machine itself and provide a predictive maintenance function. The pressure sensor at the vacuum machine has been used to set up an AI/ML pipeline to remotely monitor the operational status of the machine itself and provide a predictive maintenance function. The ML algorithm has been deployed as a service on the cloud instance of Symphony, again using the Data Spine as a message bus and data model interoperability tool. The continuous training of the model is performed in the cloud and fed by the data streams coming from the shop-floor. A user-friendly interface, built with the Symphony Visualization App, gives the user real-time feedback of the algorithm outputs (number of pump cycles and efficiency of the machine), together with a graphical plot of the sensor time series, as shown in Figures 16.10 and 16.11.

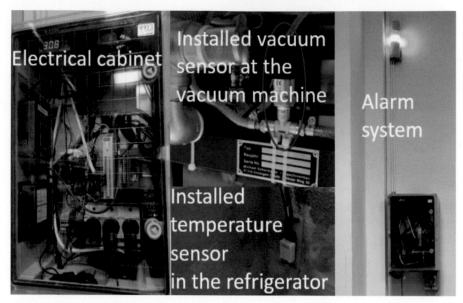

Figure 16.9   IAI settings for the remote monitoring of a vacuum forming machine to enable immediate actions when pressure values fall out of tolerance.

The setup of this pilot has clearly demonstrated the modularity and flexibility of the EFPF platform, which, on one side, allowed the seamless integration of edge-based tools, such as TSMatch, with an IIoT cloud platform, the Nextworks Symphony, providing data model interoperability; on the other side, it enabled edge–cloud communication between the two instances of Symphony, effectively decoupling low-level hardware interfacing, semantic data exchange, and high-level services provision.

The pilot further demonstrated how easily an effective solution can be deployed and applied to real-world scenarios, when the right tools and technologies are available.

16.5.2 Furniture manufacturing pilot: factory connectivity

The EFPF furniture manufacturing pilot[13] is represented by LAGRAMA as a furniture manufacturer SME based in Vinaròs, Spain, producing youth rooms, home offices, and specific home items such as lounges and wardrobes. Today's market requires permanent innovation in product development due

---

[13] https://www.efpf.org/_files/ugd/26f25a_753cd1c1db194c39b66c74957520a5f8.pdf

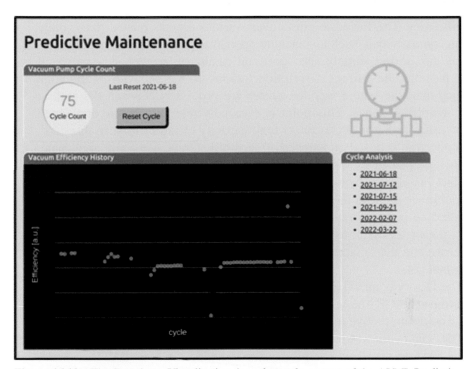

Figure 16.10 The Symphony Visualization App shows the output of the AI/ML Predictive Maintenance App.

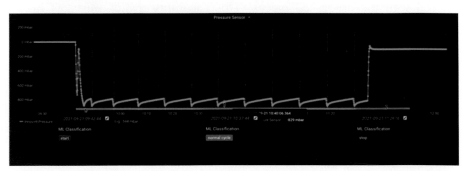

Figure 16.11 Symphony Visualization App displays the behavior of the remote pressure sensor.

to the changeability of the behavior of the new customers. This customization of the products implies dynamic changes in the production workflow where problems detected in machines and processes mean a reduction in the efficiency. The furniture pilot covers various aspects related to the daily production activities, such as machine operation, process definition and execution, monitoring, supply activities, and catalog management. Among all these features, the current description focuses on the behavior of the edge banding machine where wooden pieces are processed between the cutting and the drilling stages. This point is especially relevant; so any unplanned maintenance task comprises the overall capacity of the factory. In this case, the production is based on batches of parts of heterogeneous size and shape. Sensors are placed in selected motors in the machine and connected to an interface board on a factory connector, which monitors the measured values and publishes them to the Data Spine Message Broker. Data collected from the machine includes temperature, pressure, and electrical current. At this point, parameters such as the size of the datasets, the frequency of the data gathering, and the reliability of the prediction algorithms become extremely important [14].

The factory connectivity topic, represented by the edge banding machine operation at LAGRAMA, involves two main targets: the production improvement and the predictive maintenance.

The improvement of the efficiency of the edge banding machine of LAGRAMA to speed up the production reducing the overall time to serve the customer is the target of the production improvement objective. This has been achieved by displaying clear instructions to the operator about how to proceed with the processed pieces. This capability avoids mistakes in the classification process and detects any machine operation error. To this end, the barcode labels attached to the pieces that process the machine are scanned with a camera connected to the Industreweb Factory Connector, which queries an enterprise system to retrieve the information of the piece. Then, the instructions associated with the scanned piece are shown on a display to the worker. Figure 16.12 depicts the position of the elements involved in the solution around the edge banding machine.

The Edge Factory Connector allows the monitoring of the selected machine data by measuring KPIs, revealing opportunities for improvements in productivity and efficiency.

Reliable instructions and complete traceability of the manufactured pieces are provided by this deployment. The collected data is available to be used by other tools focused on other areas such as analytics and machine learning, risk evaluation, and reporting. This production optimization solution demonstrates an improvement in the overall production performance. From

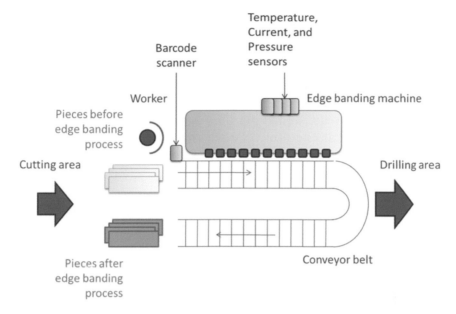

Figure 16.12 Basic layout representing the placement of devices in the machine.

Figure 16.13 Camera for pieces' label scanning and display showing the instructions to the operator.

a business perspective, the vision system provides time saving in the classification process and reduction of errors leading to benefits related to production costs, ensuring the quality level of the products. From the workers' perspective, the system supports the human tasks in the edge banding area, making the operators feel more confident during the handling of pieces. The overall solution for the production optimization increases the productivity of the workers at the edge banding stage of the production line [15].

The predictive maintenance target — which makes use of the sensors deployed in the machine — increases the machine availability by avoiding potential failures that take longer than the regular maintenance activities.

Data analytics applied to the industrial processes and equipment improves the manufacturing by reducing the machine downtimes and improving the quality of the deliveries. The data collected can be then processed by the analytics tools integrated in the component, as follows:

- The **anomaly detection service** is used to detect problems during the machine operation. This makes use of machine learning algorithms that take several months of machine operation to provide reliable information. The system also manages thresholds that represent the acceptable values of machine operation and are used to monitor the behavior of the line.
- The **Risk, Opportunity, Analysis, and Monitoring (ROAM)** transforms the data streams collected from the sensors into metrics. This provides a visualization to get insights about costs, risks, and opportunities. The tool sends warning emails to the users and manages recipes that can be adjusted to the production environment under consideration.
- The **Deep Learning Toolkit (DLT)** is another analytics tool that consumes the sensor data to predict machine failures. The collected data is labeled as right or wrong depending on thresholds and is processed through a neural network for training. The DLT brings real-time prediction of the machine operation on a short-term basis, keeping a confidence score that depends on the training process considering that, the more data is collected and processed, the more insights can be retrieved from the obtained results.
- The **Visual and Data Analytics Tool** provides the anomaly detection functionality with dashboard visualization. The EFPF Data Spine enables the integration with the pilot site and the EFPF Portal used by the end-users to access the different tools. This is depicted in Figure 16.14.

The factory data is sent to the Data Spine through the Factory Connector and is adhered to a raw/custom data model. The API of the Factory Connector together with the specification of this custom data model is registered to the service registry of the Data Spine. The API metadata of the data APIs from the registry are fetched to create iFlows, while the integration flow engine is used to transform the raw data into heterogeneous data models, as expected

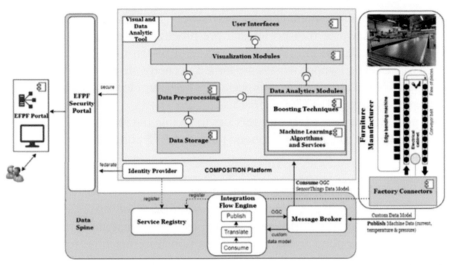

Figure 16.14 Overall architecture of the Visual and Data Analytics Tool and information flow [14].

by the tool. The data is then published to a topic through MQTT; so the tool can retrieve it to provide a graphical view through the visualization modules. The user interface is accessible from the EFPF portal ensuring the security by the use of the SSO capabilities provided by the platform [14].

The monitoring of the operation of the edge banding machine is particularly relevant when manufacturing in batches. Therefore, predictive maintenance enables LAGRAMA as furniture producer to prevent some parts of the machine from being damaged, leading to a decrease in productivity, losses, and bad reputation when deliveries are late. The machine learning model requires considerable time to be profoundly exploited. However, abnormal values can be detected outside the defined ranges according to the selected parameters. Getting warnings about the need for maintenance when any failure risk is detected in the machine operation provides a huge value from the business perspective.

16.5.3 Circular economy pilot — a waste to energy scenario

In this scenario, a circular supply chain loop has been enabled using the EFPF core infrastructure and tools [16]. Three companies participate in this scenario: (a) KLEEMANN, a global manufacturer of lift systems, escalators, moving walks, etc., which acts as a waste producer for this scenario; (b)

ELDIA, the largest waste management and recycling company in northern Greece that acts as waste transporter and pre-processor; and (c) MILOIL, an SME that produces Biodiesel, which acts as a transformer of the pre-processed wastes. The (wood) wastes are turned to energy that is finally used by KLEEMANN for its production processes. The latter closes the waste to energy loop, as illustrated in Figure 16.15.

EFPF provides various tools and services to enable the realization of the aforementioned circular economy scenario through EFPF portal interfaces, as described next.

16.5.3.1 Predictive maintenance services

Effective waste management, which is a core concept of this scenario, starts from waste reduction during production processes. Anomaly detection services have been applied to KLEEMANN's polishing machine in order to reduce defect parts and scrap metal wastes. The Visual Analytics tool from EFPF/CERTH has been used in this case [14]. The real-time anomaly detection is enabled from IoT vibration sensors. The data of sensors are pre-processed at the edge and, after that, are available to the Visual Analytics tool (cloud-based tool) through the EFPF Data Spine.

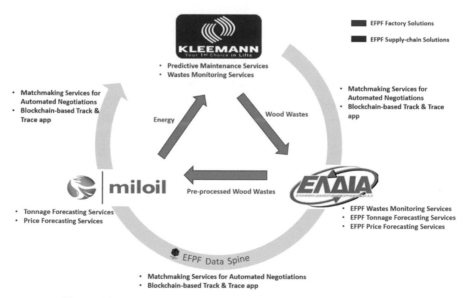

Figure 16.15   EFPF circular economy scenario and EFPF tools' usage.

Figure 16.16   Real-time anomaly detection for polishing machine.

16.5.3.2 Fill level sensors – IoT-based monitoring system

IoT fill level sensors have been installed in various bins and open top containers at KLEEMANN premises in order to enable the distance monitoring and the speedy delivery of waste management services. The fill level sensors functioned based on ultrasonic and IR sensors and their connectivity with EFPF ecosystem was enabled by setting up a LoRa network. A monitoring dashboard for various bins' fill level was realized through EFPF Data Spine and Visual Analytics tool interfaces. Furthermore, trend analysis services are provided in order to enable users to estimate the date that a bin should be emptied.

16.5.3.3 Online bidding process

Aiming to automate the negotiations among the participants in the circular supply chain scenario, an online bidding process tool was provided. This tool provides a virtual agent that represents each company. A semantic framework at the backend that is used to model companies, wastes, etc., enables the matchmaking of the agents. Moreover, the matchmaking capabilities of the solution enables the matching of a request with the best available offer based on best score algorithms.

16.5.3.4 Blockchain Track and Trace App

An application based on blockchain and smart contracts, shown in Figure 16.17, enables the secure handshake in wastes being exchanged and ensures the monitoring of the wastes in all the stages of the circular loop. The immutable transactions in the blockchain nodes provide full visibility and transparency in all stages of the scenario. The stage monitoring is available through EFPF web-based interfaces that provide the functionality to waste

Figure 16.17   Secure handshake based on Blockchain Track and Trace App.

producers to issue a digitally signed certification of its waste management process. The secure handshake among the participants that exchange wastes is enabled by a dedicated mobile app (both Android and iOS devices are supported).

16.5.3.5 Tonnage and price forecasting services

Visual Analytics tool provides services to companies ELDIA and MILOIL regarding the forecasting of future wastes tonnage and future prices of waste materials. The forecasting services are based on machine and deep learning techniques. The services enable the end-users to optimize their planning services and their waste collection processes.

16.6 Summary

This chapter describes the EFPF MaaS, which integrates over 30 partners across the whole manufacturing value-chain (users, technology providers, consultants, and research institutes) from 11 European countries and provides several tools that can assist a flexible and speedier digitization of manufacturing stakeholders. The chapter described the EFPF architecture and its main components, in particular, its SDK. Then, several pilots that have been developed together between research partners and SMEs have been described, explaining how the realization and support for data communication and processing across edge–cloud can be performed.

The developed tools and the learnings thereof have been applied in several pilots and open calls and are available to be experimented via thirds, via the EFPF marketplace.

Acknowledgements

This research was funded by the European Commission (European Union) within the H2020 DT-ICT-07-2018-2019 project "European Connected Factory Platform for Agile Manufacturing" (EFPF) under Grant Agreement No. 825075.

References

[1] Rauschecker, U., Meier, M., Muckenhirn, R., Yip, A. L. K., Jagadeesan, A. P., & Corney, J. (2011). Cloud-based manufacturing-as-a-service environment for customized products.

[2] Tao, F., Zhang, L., Venkatesh, V. C., Luo, Y., & Cheng, Y. (2011). Cloud manufacturing: a computing and service-oriented manufacturing model. *Proceedings of the Institution of Mechanical Engineers, Part B: Journal of Engineering Manufacture, 225*(10), 1969-1976.

[3] R. A. Deshmukh, D. Jayakody, A. Schneider, V. Damjanovic-Behrendt, Data Spine: A Federated Interoperability Enabler for Heterogeneous IoT Platform Ecosystems. *Sensors 2021, 21*, 4010. Special Issue "Industry 4.0 and Smart Manufacturing". https://doi.org/10.3390/s21124010.

[4] EFPF project deliverable "D3.11: EFPF Data Spine Realisation - I". June 2020. Available online: https://ec.europa.eu/research/particip ants/documents/downloadPublic?documentIds=080166e5d5ddfb6f&a ppId=PPGMS(accessedon22January2021).

[5] Datta, S. K. (2022, September). Secure, Interoperable, End-to-End Industry 4.0 Service Platform for Lot-Size-One Manufacturing. In *2022 IEEE 12th International Conference on Consumer Electronics (ICCE-Berlin)* (pp. 1-3). IEEE.

[6] Barik, B. K., Sahu, N., Ekka, A., Ekka, P., Padhan, S., Mishra, L., ... & Swain, L. (2021). Manufacturing Paradigms and Evolution. In *Current Advances in Mechanical Engineering* (pp. 705-714). Springer, Singapore.

[7] Haghnegahdar, L., Joshi, S. S., & Dahotre, N. B. (2022). From IoT-based cloud manufacturing approach to intelligent additive manufacturing: Industrial Internet of Things—An overview. *The International Journal of Advanced Manufacturing Technology*, 1-18.

[8] Ghomi, Einollah Jafarnejad, Amir Masoud Rahmani, and Nooruldeen Nasih Qader. "Cloud manufacturing: challenges, recent advances, open research issues, and future trends." *The International Journal of Advanced Manufacturing Technology* 102.9 (2019): 3613-3639.

[9] Kusiak, A. (2020). Service manufacturing= process-as-a-service+ manufacturing operations-as-a-service. *Journal of Intelligent Manufacturing, 31*(1), 1-2.

[10] Wang, X., Wang, Y., Tao, F., & Liu, A. (2021). New paradigm of data-driven smart customisation through digital twin. *Journal of manufacturing systems, 58*, 270-280.

[11] I. Martens (Ed.), EFPF Deliverable D.9.1 Implementation and Validation through Pilot-1, 2021. Available at: , xxxhttps://www.efpf.org/_fil es/ugd/26f25a_b498d53f78174f94b3077eaca42d34d3.pdf

[12] N. Bnouhanna, R. C. Sofia and A. Pretschner, "IoT Thing to Service Matching" 2021 IEEE International Conference on Pervasive Computing and Communications Workshops and other Affiliated Events (PerCom Workshops), 2021, pp. 418-419, vol 1, pp 418-419, DOI; 10.1109/PerComWorkshops51409.2021.9431128.

[13] E. Karabulut, N. Bnouhanna, R. C. Sofia, ML-based data classification and data aggregation on the edge. inProc. ACM CoNext2021, December 2021, Munich, Germany. Student poster. https://doi.org/10.1145/3488 658.3493786.

[14] Nizamis, A., Deshmukh, R. A., Vafeiadis, T., Gigante, F. Núñez, M. J., Schneider, A., Ioannidis, D., Tzovaras, D. (2022), Application of a Visual and Data Analytics Platform for Industry 4.0 enabled by the Interoperable Data Spine: A Real-world Paradigm for Anomaly Detection in the Furniture Domain. I-ESA'22 Interoperability for Enterprise Systems and Applications - Springer March 24, 2022.

[15] Bhullar, G., Osborne, S., Núñez Ariño, M. J., Del Agua Navarro, J., Gigante Valencia, F. Vision System Experimentation in Furniture Industrial Environment. Future Internet 2021, 13, 189. https://doi.org/10.339 0/fi13080189.

[16] Mastos, T. D., Nizamis, A., Terzi, S., Gkortzis, D., Papadopoulos, A., Tsagkalidis, N., ... & Tzovaras, D. (2021). Introducing an application of an industry 4.0 solution for circular supply chain management. *Journal of Cleaner Production*, *300*, 126886.

Part V

IoT Skills and Business Models

17

The EU-IoT Skills Framework for IoT Training and Career Development Processes

J. Soldatos

Netcompany-Intrasoft S.A, Luxembourg
E-mail: John.Soldatos@netcompany-intrasoft.com

Abstract

This chapter sheds light on the ever-important issue of IoT skills development, which is a key prerequisite for the successful development, deployment, and operation of IoT systems. It first reviews the wide array of different IoT skills that are typically required for the development, deployment, and operation of nontrivial IoT systems, including technical and non-technical skills. Accordingly, it introduces the IoT skills framework of the H2020 EU-IoT project, which provides a taxonomy of modern IoT skills, along with an approach for defining skills profiles, as well as related educational activities and learning paths. It also leverages the results of a skills survey to identify popular and high in-demand skills profiles. Finally, it uses the introduced framework to drive the specification of practical learning paths for these profiles.

Keywords: Internet of Things, skills, education, skills framework, courses, training, human resources, future of work, technical skills, social skills, soft skills, management skills.

351   DOI: 10.1201/9781032632407-22

17.1 Introduction

Recent studies have concluded that IoT skills are a catalyst for the accelerated adoption of IoT solutions and for the subsequent growth of the IoT market. This is because the IoT skills shortage is identified as one of the factors that hinder IoT deployment [1]. Figure 17.1 illustrates some of the most important factors that lead to the proclaimed skills shortage. These factors include:

- **The multi-facet nature of IoT skills**: Nontrivial IoT solutions integrate multiple technology solutions such as embedded systems, broadband networks, cloud computing, machine learning, and cybersecurity. Therefore, most IoT professionals are required to possess multiple skills from different technological areas. Furthermore, many IoT skills profiles ask for non-technical skills like business development, marketing, and collaboration skills.
- **The complexity of IoT solutions**: In recent years, IoT solutions have become more sophisticated. State-of-the-art IoT solutions comprise multiple technology infrastructures, which have diverse development and deployment requirements. To deal with this complexity, IoT teams must comprise professionals with multi-disciplinary profiles and different skillsets. The latter go beyond the basics of IoT systems and technologies.
- **Technology acceleration**: Digital technologies are evolving at a rapid pace, which results in a fast-changing IoT landscape. For instance, technologies like mixed reality (MR) and augmented reality (AR) were not in the IoT landscape a few years ago. In this dynamic IoT landscape, it is very difficult for skills development activities to keep up with the evolution of the state-of-the-art.
- **The skills shortage in related technologies**: IoT projects require skills in cutting-edge technological areas like machine learning (ML), artificial intelligence (AI), and cybersecurity. Each of these technology areas is experiencing its own skills shortage, which makes it very difficult to staff complex IoT projects.
- **The need for collaboration in IoT projects**: Successful IoT deployments require collaboration between different stakeholders. This asks for interdisciplinary and multi-disciplinary expertise, which can be hardly found in modern IoT teams.

In this landscape, most organizations are faced with significant skills gaps, which asks for frequent reskilling processes. In a recent survey of the World Economic Forum (WEF) [2] the participating companies pointed out

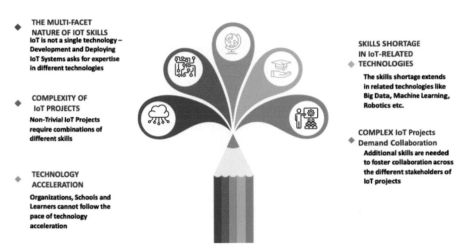

Figure 17.1 Factors contributing to the IoT skills shortage.

that they expected approximately 40% of their workers to undergo reskilling every six months. The same survey identifies the technical skills that are currently high in demand by companies, which include IoT. Moreover, the importance of non-technical skills like active learning and flexibility is stressed. Overall, employers acknowledge the need to intensify their investments in human skills development and are willing to undertake such investments. At the same time, policy makers are developing policies that foster digital skills development. For instance, the European Commission is currently implementing the ambitious European Skills Agenda [3], which is Europe's plan to help individuals and businesses to develop more and better skills. This skills agenda pays special emphasis on developing digital skills, including skills in areas like IoT, cloud computing, and AI.

To effectively plan their IoT upskilling and reskilling processes, organizations need to understand the various IoT skills and their interrelationships. Moreover, they must be able to map them to learning paths, training programs, and career development paths. This is also important for training and educating policy makers to develop effective reskilling and upskilling policies for both students and professionals. Therefore, there is a need for skills taxonomies that illustrate how diverse IoT skills are related to each, as well as how they can be bundled into coherent skills profiles.

In recent years, various educational organizations, consulting firms, and policy makers have identified skills that empower the development and operation of modern IoT systems. In several cases, they have also identified the interrelationships of these skills. Nevertheless, there is still a lack of an IoT skills framework that considers the latest developments in the IoT market and technologies. Considering this gap, this paper provides the following contributions:

- It introduces a novel framework for IoT skills, which considers recent advances in IoT technologies, as well as the need for complementing technical skills with social, business, and management skills. The framework has been developed in the scope of the EU-funded EU-IoT project, which provides resources and support services to the European IoT research community. It includes a taxonomy of IoT skills and can serve as a basis for defining skills profiles, education activities, and learning paths.
- It provides some concrete examples of IoT skills profiles, notably profiles that comprise skills that are high in demand in the IoT market. In this direction, the presented work leverages the results of an IoT skills survey that engaged over 100 professionals in the assessment of the relevant importance of various IoT skills. The survey was structured considering the introduced framework. Specifically, the participants were presented with lists of skills that were structured according to the framework.
- It illustrates some concrete examples of IoT skills profiles, along with learning paths that can be used to foster their development. Specifically, the suggested learning paths are associated with concrete courses in the training catalog of the EU-IoT project.

Note that the chapter consolidates and summarized findings that are already presented in the open-access whitepaper of the EU-IoT project [4]. These findings are included in this open-access book to boost the community's unlimited access to the EU-IoT project's results about IoT skills development.

The remainder of this chapter is structured as follows:

- Section 2, following this introductory section, provides an overview of research reports on IoT skills, including a review of relevant taxonomies. The section highlights the lack of a well-structured skills framework that considers the latest advances in IoT technologies.

- Section 3 introduces the EU-IoT skills framework as a multi-layer taxonomy. The framework considers the latest developments in IoT technologies, including developments in networking, IoT data analytics, machine learning IoT programming, and IoT security.
- Section 4 summarizes the results of a skills survey that was carried out with the active participation of more than 100 IoT professionals, who provided insights on the relevant importance of different IoT skills. A detailed presentation of the results of the survey is available in [4].
- Section 5 constructs some IoT profiles based on some skills that were identified as important in the skills survey. It also illustrates some indicative learning paths for the specified skills profiles.
- Section 6 is the final and concluding section of the chapter.

17.2 Related Work

IoT education and skills are catalysts for the adoption and growth of the IoT computing paradigm. At the same time, IoT skills are important for the development, deployment, and adoption of a range of related technologies such as AI and cyber physical production systems (CPPS). Moreover, industrial workers must develop IoT skills, to support the deployment and operation of Industrial IoT systems in their organizations in sectors like manufacturing, energy, oil and gas, mining, and healthcare. In general, IoT skills are important for most jobs and occupations of the future of work.

The future of work addresses a variety of industrial sectors, which require a broad range of IoT-related job profiles in various industries. Therefore, there is a need for identifying and properly structuring the various IoT skills in some IoT skills framework. To this end, many industrial, educational, and research actors have attempted to identify, document, and structure the rich set of modern IoT skills. The resulting classifications had different aims and objectives, such as employment, recruitment, education planning (e.g., [5]), curriculum development (e.g., [6]), industrial training (e.g., [7]), reskilling/upskilling, as well as policy development purposes [8] (e.g., industry/university collaboration [9]).

Several IoT skills reviews have focused on technical and technological skills. This is the case for reviews that aim at analyzing the technical skills required for developing and deploying IoT solutions. For instance, [10] outlines the importance of programming skills (e.g., Python, C, C#, Java Script) and knowledge of IoT protocols (e.g., Message Queuing Telemetry Transport (MQTT)) for IoT systems development and deployment. Furthermore, there are articles that structure technical skills in integrated IoT profiles like hardware designers, embedded firmware developers, backend developers, frontend developers, IoT application developers, automation, and systems integration engineers, as well as data scientists [11]. These roles include profiles that are more general than the scope of IoT applications (e.g., frontend/backend developers). However, IoT technical jobs and IoT profiles go often beyond hardware and software development. Specifically, they cover roles like IoT engineers, IoT architects, and IoT researchers [12].

Nevertheless, taking a purely technical view of IoT skills is not enough. This is evident in policy-related studies (e.g., [13]), including the European Skills Agenda [3]. These studies underline the merits and importance of complementary skills such as soft skills. The latter are considered prerequisites both for building IoT and automation systems and for alleviating the adverse effects of automation in employment. Typical examples of soft skills include problem-solving, creativity, communication, and persuasion.

Due to the importance of non-technical skills, various IoT and Industrial Internet of Things (IIoT) skills surveys suggest that thinking, social, and other soft skills are critical elements of IoT education or reskilling for industry professionals [14]. For instance, [15] illustrates skills for managerial positions. The authors identify skills like problem-solving, IoT usage, analytical capabilities, communications, lifelong learning, management skills, teamwork, openness for change, openness to digitization, openness to automation, and more. Additional non-technical skills are mentioned in [14]. They include self-awareness, self-organization, interpersonal and intercultural skills, social responsibility and accountability, leadership skills, people management, emotional intelligence, negotiation skills, entrepreneurship, and adaptability.

The above-listed reports and surveys on IoT skills do not provide any structured taxonomy of IoT skills. Moreover, they do not refer to some of the most recent IoT technologies in areas like analytics, embedded systems, and IoT networking. This is a significant gap for stakeholders like human resources professionals and policy makers, who need to understand the importance and interrelationships of various IoT-related skills prior to developing effective training programs and policies.

17.3 The Eu-IoT Skills Framework

17.3.1 Main principles

The EU-IoT framework has been developed based on the following principles:

- **Support for technical and non-technical skills**. The framework addresses technical and technological IoT skills, but also soft skills that relate to IoT professionals' roles.
- **Consideration of standards-based IoT stacks in the classification of IoT technical skills**. The framework structures the various technical IoT skills in-line with layered taxonomies of IoT technologies, such as the layers of standards-based IoT stacks like the stack of the IICF (industrial internet connectivity framework).
- **Classification of non-technical skills**. The framework structures the complementary non-technical skills into various categories such as legal, business, marketing, and social skills.
- **Extensibility**. The framework provides a way for structuring the various IoT-related skills. Interested parties can extend the framework with more skills while retaining its core structure.

17.3.2 Top-level categorization of IoT skills

The framework classifies IoT-related skills into four broad categories, as illustrated in Figure 17.2 and further detailed below:

- **IoT technical and technological skills**: This category comprises skills related to IoT technologies, including skills required to develop, deploy, and operate IoT systems. It provides broad coverage of the rich set of technologies that are currently associated with IoT systems.
- **Management, marketing, and regulatory skills**: This category comprises marketing and management skills that fall in the realm of IoT product and service development. It also includes regulatory-related skills such as general data privacy regulation (GDPR)-related skills and ethics-related skills.
- **IoT end-users and operator 4.0 skills**: This category consists of skills required for using and operating IoT systems in various sectors of the economy with an emphasis on industrial sectors.
- **Social and soft skills**: This comprises soft skills that are important for the development, deployment, operation, and use of IoT systems. It includes popular skills like teamwork, lifelong learning, and collaboration, which have clear relevance to IoT professionals as well.

Each of the four skills categories comprises a rich set of IoT skills, which are structured in subcategories. The structuring of the various skills provides a sound basis for understanding the types of skills needed for successfully

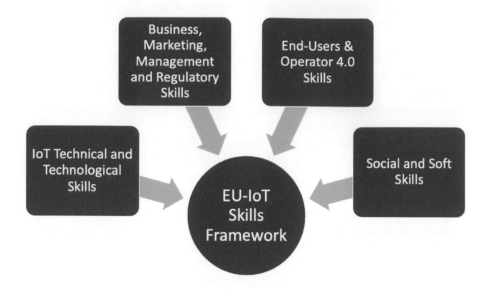

Figure 17.2   High-level taxonomy of the EU-IoT skills framework.

developing, deploying, operating, managing, and monetizing IoT systems. Hence, the various categories provide good coverage of the various types of IoT skills. Nevertheless, the listed skills provide by no means an exhaustive coverage of all the available IoT skills. As already outlined, interested parties can enhance the framework with more skills by expanding the list of skills that belong to the various (sub)categories.

17.3.3 The four categories of IoT skills

17.3.3.1 IoT technical and technological skills

The IoT technical and technological skills are further segmented into the following subcategories:

- **IoT devices skills**: This subcategory comprises skills associated with different types of internet-connected devices. Specifically, it includes skills associated with sensors, actuators, digital signal processing (DSP), field programmable gate arrays (FPGAs), the global positioning system (GPS), programmable logic controllers (PLC), wireless sensor networks (WSN), ad-hoc networks, radio frequency identification (RFID) devices and more. Each one of these skills corresponds to expertise regarding the structure, the computational capabilities, and the networking functionalities of these IoT devices.

- **Smart objects skills**: This subcategory complements device-level skills with additional skillsets that correspond to more complex and sophisticated smart devices such as cyber-physical systems and unmanned aerial vehicles (UAVs). These sophisticated devices are characterized as smart objects. The sophistication of smart objects asks for special skills in developing, deploying, and operating them.
- **Networks and connectivity**: This part of the IoT technical and technological skills focuses on networking and connectivity technologies that support IoT deployments. Our list of skills in this subcategory includes popular networking protocols and connectivity technologies such as Wi-Fi, bluetooth, and low power wide area network (LPWAN) technologies. It also comprises mobile networking technologies like 4G, long-term evolution (LTE), 5G and 6G networking technologies.
- **IoT protocols**: This subcategory comprises skills associated with IoT connectivity protocols such as MQTT, constrained application protocol (CoAP), and data distribution service (DDS). These skills are essential to the development and deployment of IoT systems since they abstract the transport of IoT data from the device to the applications that consume the data.
- **Cloud/edge/mobile computing**: Cloud computing, edge computing, and mobile computing-related skills are important to the development, deployment, and operation of nontrivial IoT systems, such as systems that integrate data and services from multiple distributed IoT devices. Hence this subcategory is devoted to cloud/edge/mobile computing-related skills.
- **IoT analytics**: This subcategory comprises skills that enable the analysis of IoT data using various technologies and techniques such as ML, deep learning (DL), and AI. A wide array of such skills is nowadays important for IoT systems development and deployment ranging from big data analytics to embedded machine learning and TinyML.
- **IoT security**: Cybersecurity is a critical element of the safe and reliable deployment of IoT systems. Thus, there is a need for security-related IoT skills, such as skills relating to security processes (e.g., risk assessment, pen testing) and to the secure operation of various types of IoT devices.
- **IoT software programming skills**: Most IoT systems comprise software components. Therefore, software development skills are important

for the development of IoT systems and applications. This subcategory includes the rich set of programming skills that enable the development of the software parts of IoT systems. These skills include for example programming in popular languages like Python, Java and Javascript, as well as in other specialized skills for programming of IoT devices, for example, robotics programming and Arduino programming.

- **IoT development methodologies**: Many IoT products and services are developed and deployed over scalable, distributed infrastructure by distributed development teams. Therefore, the establishment of state-of-the-art development infrastructures and the employment of proper development methodologies over them is very important for the deployment and operation of successful IoT services. Hence, this subcategory includes skills associated with mainstream development infrastructures and methodologies that are commonly used by developers and deployers of IoT systems. These infrastructures and methodologies include for example development and operations (DevOps), data operations (DataOps), and machine learning operations (MLOps) infrastructures.

- **IoT development and deployment tools**: This subcategory includes skills linked to the operation and use of IoT development and deployment tools, such as integrated development environments (IDEs) for IoT development.

These subcategories establish a useful taxonomy of IoT-related technical and technological skills, which can be extended with more skills under the specified skills groupings. The specification of these subcategories was partly driven by popular reference architectures that specify the technical building blocks of modern IoT systems. For instance, the devices, networking technologies, and connectivity protocols are building blocks of IoT systems specified in the scope of the industrial internet reference architecture (IIRA) [16] and the industrial internet connectivity framework (IICF) [17] of the industrial internet consortium (IIC). Nevertheless, skills related to the technical building blocks identified in these reference architectures have been enhanced with skills pertaining to cloud infrastructures, software engineering, and project management methodologies. The latter is not specific to IoT systems only, but rather applicable to a broader range of future internet systems. These broader skills are important for the development, deployment, and operation of cutting-edge IoT systems, which is the reason why they have been included in the taxonomy.

17.3.3.2 Business, marketing, management, and regulatory skills

This category of the EU-IoT skills framework underlines the importance of marketing, management, and regulatory skills for tasks like IoT project management and IoT product development. The category comprises skills clustered in two subcategories, namely:

- **Business, management, and marketing skills**: This is a broad category that comprises various business, management, and marketing skills for IoT products and services. For instance, it includes project management, product management, marketing, and financial management skills.
- **Legal and regulatory skills**: This subcategory includes the ever-important legal and regulatory skills that are required for developing, deploying, and operating enterprise-scale IoT products and services with commercial relevance. Such products must adhere to applicable laws and regulations such as the general data protection regulation (GDPR) regarding data management and data protection. Therefore, the subcategory includes skills associated with IoT ethics, GDPR, and other IoT/AI-related regulations.

The list of skills in this category is purposefully shorter than the list of technical IoT skills. This reflects the fact that the development and deployment of IoT systems require primarily technical skills, yet business, management, and regulatory skills are important as well. Like in the case of other categories it is possible to extend the taxonomy with more skills of business, management, and regulatory relevance.

17.3.3.3 IoT end-user and operator 4.0 skills

This category includes skills that should be possessed by the end users of modern IoT systems. It includes the following subcategories of skills:

- **Industrial automation skills**: IIoT systems are usually deployed to support, improve, and enhance industrial automation processes in sectors like manufacturing, energy, oil & gas, and mining. Therefore, this subcategory is devoted to industrial automation skills that end-users of IoT systems must possess to successfully adopt, use, and fully leverage IoT functionalities. Such industrial automation skills include for example skills associated with the use of legacy automation systems and technologies (e.g., PLC and supervisory control and data acquisition (SCADA)), as well as with popular industrial processes like quality control and production scheduling. It also includes skills linked to emerging digital tools for industrial automation like digital simulation and digital twins.

- **Asset management skills**: Asset management applications are found in almost all industrial sectors. They are deployed in all industries that manage physical assets such as in manufacturing, energy, and smart building applications. Therefore, end-users of IIoT applications for asset management must have relevant skills including asset programming, intelligent asset management, equipment maintenance, predictive maintenance, and more. The EU-IoT skills framework includes a special subcategory for these skills.
- **Visualization**: End-users of IIoT applications must understand and use visualizations of IoT data in industrial contexts. This subcategory is devoted to visualization skills, such as big data visualization, AR, MR, virtual reality (VR), and design of ergonomic user journeys.

Like in the case of the previous categories and subcategories, this list of identified skills for IoT end-users is representative rather than exhaustive. Interested parties (e.g., educators, human resources professionals, and policy makers) can extend the framework with more skills.

17.3.3.4 Social, management, and other soft skills

This category signifies the importance of soft skills for the development, deployment, and use of IoT systems. It comprises the following subcategories:

- **Thinking skills**, such as critical thinking, analytical thinking, and complex problem-solving.
- **Social skills**, such as teamwork, interpersonal skills, and professional ethics.
- **Personal skills**, such as lifelong learning, time management, people management, and emotional intelligence.

The relevance of soft skills for the development, deployment, and use of technology systems and applications goes beyond the scope of IoT systems and technologies. Their inclusion in the framework is aimed at ensuring that they are not ignored when developing or seeking for IoT talent.

17.3.4 Using the EU-IoT skills framework

17.3.4.1 End-user groups

The introduced framework is a useful tool for several stakeholder groups that engage in skills development processes, including:

- **IoT technology companies (e.g., IoT vendors and IoT solution integrators)**: These companies can use the framework as part of their hiring and skills development processes. It can serve as a guide for searching for the right talent, evaluating candidate workers based on their IoT knowledge and skills, as well as structuring training and skills development processes.
- **Users of IoT technology**: The framework can help companies that deploy and use IoT systems to properly shape the training and skills development processes of their digital transformation. The latter processes should put emphasis on developing or attracting professionals with the right IoT skills to ensure that their investments in IoT technology are effective and yield the best possible return on investment (ROI).
- **Policy makers**: Policy makers can consult our skills framework in the scope of their policy development processes, notably when developing educational and training policies. For example, they can use the framework to plan for training programs and effective educational policies that are relevant to modern IoT systems and address market needs.

17.3.4.2 Supporting training, hiring, and skills development processes

Some concrete examples of how to use the framework to support different types of training and skills development processes follow:

- **Training processes**: The framework can support the design and development of training programs that lead to the acquisition of certain key skills or even entire skills profiles. It can also help IoT professionals to select a portfolio of courses for developing or strengthening their IoT skills.
- **Hiring processes**: HR professionals can consult the framework when implementing hiring processes. Specifically, they can use it to identify the key skills required for specific positions. Moreover, it can help them cluster relevant skills and identify skills interrelationships. The latter is important when trying to hire or form a cohort of professionals that will staff some IoT-related department or project.
- **Skills development processes**: HR experts and individual IoT professionals can leverage the framework when designing skills development journeys. For instance, they can use it to cluster multiple related or complementary skills into skills profiles. Moreover, policy makers can

take advantage of the framework in their efforts to introduce new skills development programs that address proven skills gaps in the market.

- **Career development paths (CDP) specification**: Also, HR professionals can consult the framework when specifying and implementing CDPs for IoT roles. Specifically, the framework can help in the specification of meaningful CDPs, as well as their implementation through carefully selected collections of courses.

17.4 The Eu-IoT Skills Survey

17.4.1 Survey identity and methodological overview

In the scope of the H2020 EU-IoT project, we designed and executed an IoT skills survey that aimed at identifying the skills that are high in demand in the IoT market. The rationale behind the design and the implementation of the survey was to identify the IoT-related skills with the highest relevance in the IoT market. In this direction our methodology involved the following steps:

- **Designing the survey in-line with the EU-IoT framework**: The EU-IoT framework was used to structure questions about the IoT skills relevance and importance. Specifically, the survey was segmented into four subsurveys as per the four top-level skills categories of the EU-IoT framework. Hence, the four subsurveys concerned technical and technological skills, business and marketing skills, end-users, and operator 4.0 skills, as well as social and other soft skills. Each survey comprised lists of IoT-related skills. Participants were asked to grade the importance of each skill for the IoT market on a scale from 1 (very low) to 5 (very high). Hence, the importance of each skill was indicated by an importance score that was computed based on the total weighted average of the responses.
- **Collecting answers from relevant professionals**: IoT and HR professionals were invited to fill in the survey. The four different subsurveys were provided to different groups of relevant professionals with experience and expertise in IoT skills and IoT projects. For instance, the technical and technological skills subsurvey was answered by IoT professionals with relevant technical experience and expertise, as well as by HR professionals involved in IoT hiring processes. Likewise, the subsurvey on business, management, and marketing skills was answered by a different group that comprised professionals with expertise in IoT marketing and product management. Overall, as presented in Table 17.1, 70

Table 17.1 Number of respondents in the four subsurveys.

Subsurvey	Number of respondents
IoT technical and technological	70
Business, management, and marketing	37
End-users and operator 4.0 skills	40
Social and other soft skills	36

respondents answered the technical and technological skills subsurvey, 37 respondents answered the business and marketing skills subsurvey, 40 respondents answered the end-users and operator 4.0 skills subsurvey, and 36 respondents answered the social and other soft skills subsurvey. In total 183 respondents answered the four subsurveys. The participants come from different industries, including manufacturing, smart cities, energy, agriculture, and security. They also had various profiles and roles including project managers, technical project managers, engineers, data scientists, HR Professionals, developers, architects, researchers, product managers, and business development experts. All participants had jobs relevant to IoT and in most cases strong IoT knowledge and expertise.

- **Analyzing the results and identifying the most popular skills**: The results of each one of the subsurveys were analyzed to identify the popularity and importance of various IoT skills according to the opinions of the respondents. As already outlined, the relevant importance of each skill was ranked according to the weighted averages of the responses in the given scale. Skills falling within the same subcategory were directly comparable in terms of their importance and market relevance. For instance, the answers to the survey directly indicate the relevant importance of different device-level IoT skills and IoT analytics-related IoT skills. Skills falling in different subcategories of the same subsurvey (e.g., IoT networking vs. IoT devices skills) can only be indirectly compared.

17.4.2 Analysis of results and main findings

An exhaustive presentation of the results of the survey is beyond the scope of the book chapter. Interested readers are advised to consult [4], where the received responses and their analysis are described in detail. The following paragraphs illustrate and discuss the main findings of the analysis.

In general, the results of the survey indicate some of the most popular IoT skills according to the opinion of IoT professionals from different sectors.

The popularity of the skills is linked to the market demand for these skills, as the questions prompted the participants to rank the various skills according to their market demand and relevance.

17.4.2.1 Popularity of broadly applicable skills

One of the most prominent findings is that the most general and broadly applicable skills tend to be the most popular as well. The survey indicated that companies seek for professionals with a sound understanding of the basic skills due to their ubiquity and broad applicability. For instance, in machine learning and IoT analytics, the most fundamental skills (e.g., Big Data, ML, and Data Science) got higher ranks than more specialized and IoT-related analytics skills (e.g., TinyML) (see Figure 17.3). Similarly, as illustrated in Figure 17.4, MQTT skills were perceived as more important than other less general, sector-focused IoT protocols like OPC-UA which is primarily used in manufacturing and other industrial use cases.

Overall, the most popular skills were the ones that are broadly used in the scope of IoT systems and applications. This is because these skills enable professionals to engage in a wide range of IoT projects and activities.

17.4.2.2 Importance of specialized skills for sector-specific audiences

The survey unveiled that specialized skills are very important for specific segments and groups of IoT professionals. Specifically, the more specialized IoT

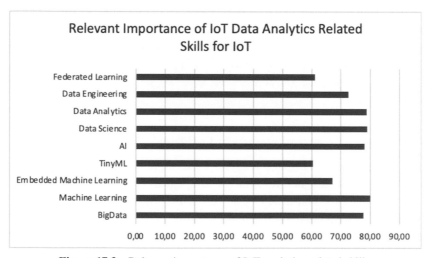

Figure 17.3   Relevant importance of IoT analytics-related skills.

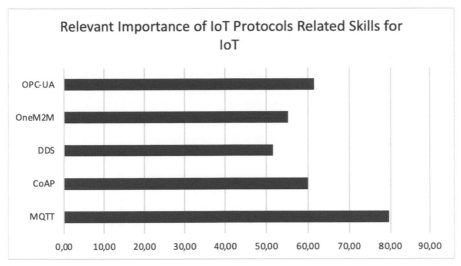

Figure 17.4 Relevant importance of IoT protocols-related skills.

skills are perceived as being very important for professionals within specific sectors. For instance, there are skills ranking very high within manufacturing (e.g., PLC and OPC-UA) and skills that rank very high within sectors that handle sensitive data (e.g., healthcare). This was evident in the segmentation of the responses according to the industry of focus of the respondents.

17.4.2.3 The importance of soft skills
Soft skills are a very important asset that complements IoT technical and technological skills. Several soft skills (e.g., lifelong learning skills) ranked very high in the overall standings of the skills that were included in the survey. Specifically, there are many skills that were graded over 70% (e.g., collaboration skills (Figure 17.5), time management skills, and people management skills) on the scale of the survey's importance. Successful IoT professionals cannot afford to ignore soft skills.

17.4.2.4 Skills clustering into skills profiles
The outcomes of the survey enable different approaches for clustering skills into skills profiles. Specifically, one can set criteria for the ranked skills to associate them with skills profiles. Such criteria may for example include the popularity of the skills and the need to combine skills from different (sub)categories of the framework. A set concrete and practical way to do this is presented in the following section.

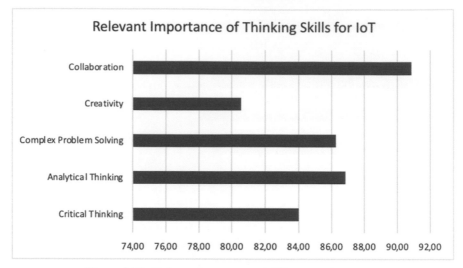

Figure 17.5   Relevant importance of different thinking skills.

17.5 From IoT Skills to Profiles and Learning Paths

17.5.1 Skills profiles and learning path construction methodology

To excel in the development, deployment, and operation of IoT systems and applications workers need more than IoT skills. For instance, IoT technical experts possess several of the previously presented skills from a single subcategory. As a prominent example, an IoT developer is likely to know more than one programming language to excel in the programming of the IoT Stack. However, it is also common for IoT professionals to possess technical skills from different subcategories of technical skills, such as programming skills and skills relating to IoT protocols like MQTT and CoAP. In most cases, IoT professionals match entire skills profiles that comprise multiple skills from different technological areas as well as non-technical skills (e.g., soft skills).

Clustering multiple IoT skills into skills profiles is very important for training and skills development processes. The latter is usually driven by the need to develop professionals that possess groups of relevant skills that enable them to undertake roles such as IoT software developer, IoT data engineer, IoT software engineer, IoT systems architect, embedded systems developer, and more. The EU-IoT skills framework can support the construction of skills profiles by facilitating interested stakeholders in selecting the skills to be clustered from a rich set of well-structured IoT skills. Using the framework stakeholders can easily identify available skills and how they relate to each other. Hence, they can structure relevant skills profiles that meet the needs of their organizations. There is a variety of different skills profiles such as hardware designers, embedded firmware developments, IoT networking experts, IoT solution integrators, IoT applications frontend developers, IoT data scientists, IoT automation engineers, and many more.

A skills profile can drive the specification of learning pathways (i.e., collections of courses and other didactic activities) that lead to the acquisition of the skills of a profile. These learning pathways can form the basis of entire training programs at academic or professional levels. The simplest form of learning pathway specifications involves the structuring of a set of courses within a training program.

The H2020 EU-IoT project provides three powerful tools that facilitate the construction of skills profiles and learning paths:

- **The EU-IoT skills framework**, which facilitates the construction of coherent skills profiles that comprise well-structured and complementary collections of courses.
- **The EU-IoT survey [4]**, which can drive the specification of skills profiles subject to criteria like the overall popularity of certain skills, their relevance to specific industries (e.g., manufacturing), as well as their complementarity. For instance, the most popular IoT analytics-related technical skills can be used to form an IoT data scientist skills profile. As another example, a collection of popular methodologies (e.g., DevOps), tools (e.g., NodeRed), programming languages (e.g., Python), and devices (e.g., sensors, WSN) related skills can serve as the basis for the specification of an IoT developer profile.
- **The EU-IoT training catalog [18]**, which provides a pool of training resources that can be used to specify training programs that lead to the key skills of a given skills profile. Specifically, with a skills profile at hand, interested stakeholders can consult the IoT training resources catalog to identify a concrete set of available courses that can be structured in a learning pathway for the given skills profile.

17.5.2 Examples of IoT learning paths

The following tables provide six concrete examples of skills profiles, along with the skills they comprise. They also provide an indicative set of courses that can support the development of the proper skills for each profile. The listed courses can be found in the Udemy training ecosystem and the EU-IoT

Table 17.2   Skills and learning path for the "IoT application developer" skills profile.

IoT skills profile: IoT application developer
Individual skills of the profile: Python, JavaScript, IoT & Cloud Computing, DevOps, Docker, Kubernetes, Sensors, WSN, Arduino, MQTT
Courses of the main learning path: 1. Practical iot concepts-devices, IoT protocols and servers DevOps 2. Introduction to IoT programming with JavaScript 3. Exploring AWS IoT 4. Project – 2022: CI/CD with Jenkins Ansible Kubernetes 5. Arduino for beginners – 2022 complete course
Other relevant courses: 1. Collaboration and emotional intelligence 2. I.T. project management for beginners: a step-by-step guide

Table 17.3   Skills and learning path for the "IoT data analytics expert" skills profile.

IoT skills profile: IoT data analytics expert
Individual skills of the profile: Data science, machine learning, TinyML, sensors, WSN
Courses of the main learning path: 1. Master machine learning and data science with Python 2. Intro to embedded machine learning 3. Sensors/actuators/data visualization with microcontrollers – IoT dashboard with Arduino
Other relevant courses: 1. Statistics for data science and business analysis 2. Collaboration and emotional intelligence

Table 17.4   Skills and learning path for the "IoT networking engineer" skills profile.

IoT skills profile: IoT network engineer
Individual skills of the profile: Sensors and IoT Devices, LPWAN, 4G/5G/6G, WiFi, Bluetooth, MQTT
Courses of the main learning path: 1. Internet of things (IoT) – demystified using three IoT devices 2. 5G Masterclass: architecture, NR RAN, core, and call flows 3. The ultimate WLAN and WiFi training course 4. The complete bluetooth/IoT design course for iOS
Other relevant courses: 1. Collaboration and emotional intelligence 2. I.T. Project management for beginners: a step-by-step guide

training resources catalog. Specifically, each of the contents of the table presents the following information for each one of the six skills profiles:

- **Individual skills of the profile**: This is the list of skills that an IoT professional must possess to qualify for roles associated with the skills

Table 17.5 Skills and learning path for the "embedded systems engineer" skills profile.

IoT skills profile: embedded systems engineer
Individual skills of the profile: Embedded systems, FPGA, printed circuit board (PCB) design, sensors, actuators, WSN
Courses of the main learning path: 1. Mastering microcontroller and embedded driver development 2. Learn the fundamentals of VHDL and FPGA development 3. Sensors/actuators/data visualization with microcontrollers – IoT dashboard with Arduino 4. Crash course electronics and PCB design
Other relevant courses: 1. Arduino: electronics circuit, PCB Design & IoT programming 2. Collaboration and emotional intelligence

Table 17.6 Skills and learning path for the "IoT project manager" skills profile.

IoT skills profile: IoT project manager
Individual skills of the profile: Project management, sensors, WSN, DevOps, agile development
Courses of the main learning path: 1. I.T. project management for beginners: a step-by-step guide 2. Agile PM 301 – mastering agile project management 3. Project – 2022: CI/CD with Jenkins Ansible Kubernetes 4. Sensors/actuators/data visualization with microcontrollers – IoT dashboard with Arduino
Other relevant courses: 1. Presentation skills: master confident presentations 2. Management skills – team leadership skills masterclass 2022 3. Collaboration and emotional intelligence

profile. The presented lists are indicative. It is possible to broaden the scope of a skills profile by including additional skills in the list. As already outlined, the development of skills profile could consider the results of our survey toward including both relevant and popular skills in the profile.

- **Courses of the learning path**: This field includes a list of courses that can help professionals learn the listed skills. The tables include courses from the EU-IoT training catalog and the Udemy training ecosystem [19]. These courses are considered mandatory for acquiring the skills that are mandated by the skills profile. There is a variety of equivalent or similar courses in the training catalog and other ecosystems (e.g., Coursera and EdX) that could help build similar learning paths. In principle, the development of a proper learning path can be a challenging

Table 17.7 Skills and learning path for the "IoT product manager" skills profile.

IoT skills profile: IoT product manager
Individual skills of the profile: Product management, sensors, WSN, cyber-physical systems
Courses of the main learning path: 1. Agile PM 301 – mastering agile project management   2. Great product manager: product management by a big tech's PM   3. Complete guide to build IoT things from scratch to market   4. Sensors/actuators/data visualization with microcontrollers – IoT dashboard with Arduino
Other relevant courses: 1. Presentation skills: master confident presentations   2. Management skills – team leadership skills masterclass 2022   3. Advanced product management: vision, strategy, and metrics

process that should seek the optimal complementarity and compatibility of the selected courses.

- **Other relevant courses**: This field includes additional courses that could strengthen the learning path for the skills profile at hand. These courses could be considered optional or "nice to have" for the target profile. Like in the case of mandatory courses, the tables include courses from the EU-IoT training catalog and the Udemy training ecosystem. However, there is a variety of equivalent or similar courses in the training catalog and in other ecosystems (e.g., Coursera and EdX) that could help to provide an alternative collection of optional courses in order to strengthen the learning path.

Overall, the tables provide a set of representative examples that aim at illustrating the process of specifying learning paths based on available catalogs of training resources. There is however much room for interested stakeholders to fine-tune the learning paths development process by scrutinizing the vast amount of training resources that are available in existing course platforms.

17.6 Conclusions

Nowadays, there is a proclaimed gap in skills for automation and the future of work [20]. Closing this skills gap is very important for adopting and leveraging cutting-edge technologies of the fourth industrial revolution in many economic sectors [21]. IoT skills are among the most important elements of the skills puzzle, as IoT technologies have a broad scope and are widely used in sectors like manufacturing, energy, healthcare, transport, retail, agriculture, and supply chain management [22]. State-of-the-art skills surveys identify some of the skills that are high in demand in the market. Nevertheless, they usually take a broad view that address many different digital technologies rather than focusing on the IoT skills and the IoT market. Motivated by this gap, this chapter has:

- Presented the findings of various skills surveys regarding the shortage of IoT skills.
- Introduced the EU-IoT skills framework as a structured taxonomy of IoT skills, including technical, management, and user-related skills, as well as the ever-important soft skills for IoT professionals. The framework can be extended with additional IoT skills.
- Summarized the findings of an IoT skills survey, which aimed at eliciting information about the IoT skills that are in the highest demand in the market.
- Illustrated how the skills survey and the EU-IoT framework can drive the clustering of individual IoT skills into wider IoT skills profiles.
- Provided concrete examples of learning paths for specific skills profiles based on courses and training resources of the EU-IoT training catalog [18].

Overall, this chapter has highlighted three tangible outcomes of the EU-IoT project (i.e., the skills framework, the survey, and the training resources catalog), which can be a great help to HR professionals and policy makers that plan, specify and execute skills development processes for the IoT computing paradigm.

Acknowledgements

This work has been carried out in the scope of the H2020 EU-IoT project (contract number 956671), which has been co-funded by the European Commission (EC) in the scope of its H2020 program. The author acknowledges valuable help and contributions from all partners of all projects.

References

[1] Feijao, Carolina, Isabel Flanagan, Christian Van Stolk, and Salil Gunashekar, The global digital skills gap: Current trends and future directions. Santa Monica, CA: RAND Corporation, 2021. https://www.rand.org/pubs/research_reports/RRA1533-1.html.

[2] The World Economic Forum, "The Future of Jobs Report 2020", October 2020.

[3] Communication from the Commission to the European Parliament, The Council, The European Economic and Social Committee and the Committee of the Regions, "New skills agenda for Europe: working together to strengthen human capital, employability and competitiveness" Brussels, 10.6.2016.

[4] John Soldatos. (2023). The EU-IoT Framework for Internet of Things Skills: Closing the Talent Gap (V1.0). Zenodo. https://doi.org/10.5281/zenodo.7544732

[5] Richert, A., Shehadeh, M., Plumanns, L., Groß, K., Schuster, K. and Jeschke, S., "Educating engineers for Industry 4.0: Virtual worlds and human-robot-teams: Empirical studies towards a new educational age", In IEEE Global Engineering Education Conference (EDUCON). Abu Dhabi, United Arab Emirates, 2016.

[6] Sackey, S. M. and Bester, A. 2016, "Industrial engineering curriculum in Industry 4.0 in a South African context", South African Journal of Industrial Engineering, 27(4), pp. 101-114.

[7] Piñol, T. C., Porta, S. A., Arevalo, M. C. R. and Minguella-Canela, J. "Study of the training needs of industrial companies in the Barcelona area and proposal of training courses and methodologies to enhance further competitiveness", Procedia Manufacturing, 13: pp. 1426-1431, 2017.

[8] van Deursen, A. J. A. M., van der Zeeuw, A., de Boer, P., Jansen, G., & van Rompay, T. (2021). Digital inequalities in the Internet of Things: differences in attitudes, material access, skills, and usage. Information, communication and society, 24(2), 258-276. https://doi.org/10.1080/1369118X.2019.1646777.

[9] Kumar, P. and Gupta, R. 2017, "The roadmap for enhancing university–industry research collaboration in India", Indian Journal of Public Administration, 63(2), pp. 196-227.

[10] Mary Shacklett, "Addressing the IoT Developer Skills Gap", IoT World Today, 16th September 2021, available at: https://www.iotworldtoday.com

[11] Adam Dunkels, "Technical Skills Needed for Professional IoT Projects", available at: https://www.thingsquare.com/blog/articles/developer-profiles-for-successful-iot-projects/,2019

[12] Shelby Hiter, Internet of Things Job Market: Build a Career in IoT 2022, December 1st, 2021, available at: https://www.datamation.com/careers/iot-job-market/

[13] M. Kritikos, "Digital Automation and the Future of Work", Scientific Foresight Unit (STOA), ISBN: 978-92-846-7281-3 doi: 10.2861/826116 QA-02-20-871-EN-N.

[14] W. Maisiri, H. Darwish & L. van Dyk, "An Investigation of Industry 4.0 Skills Requirements", South African Journal of Industrial Engineering November 2019 Vol 30(3) Special Edition, pp 90-105.

[15] Saniuk, S., Caganova, D. & Saniuk, A. Knowledge and Skills of Industrial Employees and Managerial Staff for the Industry 4.0 Implementation. Mobile Netw Appl (2021). https://doi.org/10.1007/s11036-021-01788-4.

[16] Industrial Internet Consortium, "The Industrial Internet Reference Architecture", Version 1.10, An Industry IoT Consortium Foundational Document, July 2022, available at: https://www.iiconsortium.org/iira/

[17] Rajive Joshi, Paul Didier, Christer Holmberg, Jaime Jimenez, Timothy Carey., "The Industrial Internet of Things Connectivity Framework", An Industry IoT Consortium, Foundational Document, 2022-06-08.

[18] The EU-IoT Training Catalogue, available at: https://www.ngiot.eu/archive-ngiot-training/(lastassessedJanuary2023).

[19] Udemy Training Platform, available at: www.udemy.com (last assessed January 2023).

[20] Daling, L. M., Schroder, S., Haberstroh, M. and Hees, F. "Challenges and requirements for employee qualification in the context of human-robot-collaboration", In IEEE Workshop on Advanced Robotics and its Social Impacts (ARSO). Genova, Italy, IEEE pp.85-90, 2018.

[21] "Skills for Industry - Curriculum Guidelines 4.0 Future-proof education and training for manufacturing in Europe", Luxembourg: Publications Office of the European Union, 2020, ISBN: 978-92-9202-823-7, doi:10.2826/097323

[22] John Soldatos, "A 360-Degree View of IoT Technologies", Artech House, ISBN: 9781630817527, December 2020.

18

Digital Business IoT Maturity Patterns from EU-IoT Ecosystem

Parwinder Singh, Michail Beliatis, Emilie Mathilde Jakobsen, and Mirko Presser

BTECH, Aarhus University, Denmark
E-mail: parwinder@btech.au.dk; mibel@btech.au.dk emiliemj@btech.au.dk; mirko.presser@btech.au.dk

Abstract

This paper presents the state-of-the-art novel and disruptive IoT business model practices, trends, and patterns in different industries studied under the EU-IoT project ecosystem. The patterns and best practices suggest an appropriate toolbox for stimulating a higher degree of innovation-driven thinking and exploitation. In addition, results from data collection, analysis, and architectural patterns, across 30 IoT use cases and surveys distributed over different domains, companies, and technologies, are presented. These results will act as guiding beacon and impact the future European IoT ecosystem. Beyond that, this will also exemplify best practices and technologies used to harness successful IoT solutions and relevant operation aspects in different domains. Essentially, this paper targets industry, innovators, IoT learners, and policy makers, offering inspiration and providing general guidelines on how novel technologies can be leveraged in the fast-changing landscape, thereby lowering the barriers for European stakeholders to adopt best practices that cover business-techno aspects for achieving success in the IoT area.

Keywords: IoT, business model evaluation, value network, EU-IoT, use cases, best practices, technology trends and patterns, DMAT.

377   DOI: 10.1201/9781032632407-23

18.1 Introduction

IoT is one of the most promising and revolutionary technology areas for future digital applications [1]. IoT is used for a wide range of domains such as industrial automation, healthcare, education, logistics, etc., and it spans from smart things [2], [3] to smart cities [1], [4] and smart industries [5–7]. IoT is predicted to change our lives as it comes with an enormous economic potential. The IoT architecture, which is applicable for all IoT solutions, generally consists of four layers: device, connectivity, cloud, and application [8]. The evolution of IoT is more than just technologies linked together as it involves entire ecosystems that consist of both technology and business constructs [8]. IoT ecosystems include many partners and stakeholders such as hardware makers, device manufactures, network service providers, cloud service providers, software vendors, standards bodies, regulators, industry groups, customers etc. [9]. This makes IoT domain a dynamic ecosystem, which is constantly improving, evolving, and bringing new business opportunities and challenges. Therefore, companies must develop and implement new business models that can help them to create, deliver, and capture the value produced by IoT [10], [11]. In addition, companies that succeed in developing and/or adapting their present BMs to the new technological potentials have extensive opportunities to innovate and to be highly competitive in market by generating values [12].

The success of businesses at present and in future relies heavily on the optimal utilization of technology [13]. Therefore, forces around the world, such as European Commission, are pushing hard for an evolution of the next-generation internet and relevant technologies. Key drivers of this evolution include IoT [14], [15], distributed edge computing, federated AI and analytics, augmented reality, tactile internet, data-centric services, blockchain [16], distributed architectures, scalability and interoperability [17], 5G and 6G networks, etc. However, to properly support and accelerate development of the evolution, there is a need of skills development in next-generation technologies and business models for optimal utilization of novel technologies. Therefore, it is necessary to create an understanding and alignment that enables industrial actors to adopt best practices for achieving success in the fast-changing IoT landscape. For this, EU embraces several initiatives that focus on the enhancement in the proliferation of new IoT solutions and creating ecosystem around them. EU-IoT project is one such initiative of EU that has vision to grow and consolidate the NG-IoT initiative and establish a competitive advantage by overcoming the current fragmentation of efforts to succeed in the IoT landscape.

18.2 Statement of Purpose

The purpose of this study is to explore and analyze different business models and technology patterns, values, trends, operational domains, and best practices that are enabled in IoT ecosystems in Europe by analyzing data based on 30 IoT use cases/success stories, for different industries. These use cases have been studied as part of the EU-IoT project, a coordination and support action under the H2020-EU program, grant agreement ID 956671. The EU-IoT project is also involved in the development of IoT business model innovation patterns and acceleration support oriented activities. These activities can help in accelerating the adoption of IoT-empowered solutions by lowering barriers in the IoT ecosystem and by supporting different stakeholders such as industry, innovators, learners, and policy makers. This will build and enhance required IoT skills and best practices ecosystem around different IoT business models. This is achieved by providing a toolbox that offers tools, templates, methods, and recommendations needed for practitioners to unlock successful IoT business model innovation. Hence, as illustrated in Figure 18.1, it all starts with the toolbox.

This toolbox offers (self-evaluation) tools, templates and methods that are combined with a set of recommendations on how to apply the toolbox, measure, and adopt best practices for IoT business model innovation. This targets industry stakeholders and addresses both innovators that are active users of IoT technologies already, but also the learners that are late bloomers in leveraging the innovation potential of digital technologies. The main objective of providing the toolbox is to effectively support industrial stakeholders and initiatives that foster the next-generation internet while stimulating innovation-driven thinking and exploitation. This will enable different stakeholders to leverage the best practices of IoT frontrunners to build the required skills and business models innovation in their domain of interest.

18.3 Methodology and Relevant Tools

The process of reporting on best practices and business model patterns for use cases has unfolded in three steps toward achieving the previously defined

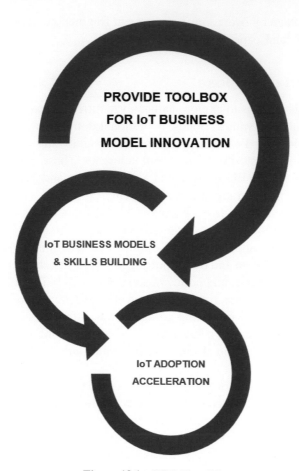

Figure 18.1   EU-IoT toolkit.

statement of purpose. The process that follows is composed of the steps that are illustrated in Figure 18.2.

Outcomes of the process include:

- Use case catalog of written success stories that introduce the explored IoT use cases. The catalog covers cases across 12 countries and 7 domains and in the scope of 18 different advanced technologies.
- Insights from analysis across all cases to identify and define archetypical factors for achieving success with IoT-empowered solutions (factors such as digital maturity levels on various dimensions, business model patterns (BMPs), and BM configurations for innovation).

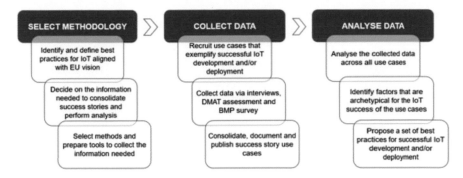

Figure 18.2 Process for reporting on best practices for IoT use cases.

- Overview that concludes upon analytical insights and sums up the identified best practices for IoT use cases, serving as a guide for successful IoT development and deployment.

18.3.1 Data collection and analysis methodologies

As mentioned earlier, this is the study of data that is collected across 30 IoT use cases and also contains findings of different surveys conducted at industry level as part of EU-IoT project. The methodology used here for collection and analysis of data relies on a range of methodological tools and techniques:

For the collection data, our research has employed a range of methodological tools. These constitute the scientific frame of reference for establishing an appropriate mechanism to gather information on best practices for IoT use cases, which includes interviews (semi-structured), digital maturity assessment tool [18], and business model pattern survey [19].

It should be noted that data collection has relied on self-assessment methodology, and results are therefore influenced heavily by the case companies' own self-perception.

For the analysis of data, our research has further employed a range of methodological techniques. These constitute the theoretical frame of reference for establishing a common understanding of the concepts that are essential in exploring best practices for IoT use cases. These techniques include digital maturity, BM patterns [20], and the configuration of BMs for innovation. The methodological tools and techniques are employed in symbiosis to explore the IoT use cases and produce the results that will be presented in the next section. The methodology is presented in a simplified overview in Figure 18.3.

18.3.2 Interviews

Information and insights on IoT use cases are derived from dialogue with the people that are/or have been severely involved in the use case. Hence, the

Interview

The interviews are conducted with one or more employees from each case company to represent both a technical and a business perspective. Results from interviews reflect the success story of individual IoT use cases and are presented in the use case catalogue.

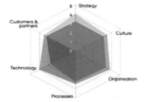

Digital Maturity Assessment

DMAT is an online assessment tool that measures and evaluates the digital maturity of a company through six dimensions. Results of it reflect the ability of case companies to digitally transform and adopt new technology.

Business Model Pattern Survey

The BMP survey provides a structured overview of the IoT applicable patterns used to shape the business models of the IoT use cases. Results from the survey reflects patterns that are archetypal for the successful leverage of IoT technology across the use cases.

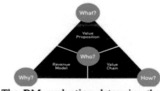

Business Model Evaluation

The BM evaluation determine the impact of an IoT solution on the configuration of the four business model dimensions. Result of the evaluation reflects the correlation between business model innovation and the IoT solutions developed and/or deployed by the use cases.

Figure 18.3 Methodological overview.

tool for data collection has been interviews based on a range of predefined questions to cover all relevant aspects and align the stories of the use cases. The methodology used for interviews was of semi-structured type. The interviews were conducted with one or more employees from each case company to ensure that their roles in developing and/or deploying the IoT solution represent both a technical and a business perspective.

18.3.3 Digital maturity assessment

The assessment of digital maturity is based on the research by Presser et al. [5], [18], and data collection was facilitated by the digital maturity assessment tool (DMAT). The term digital maturity refers to the measure of an organization's ability to create value through the implementation of digital solutions. Digital maturity is a key predictor of success for companies that initiate a digital transformation and high levels of digital maturity are often associated with having a competitive advantage. The DMAT assesses digital maturity along the dimensions of strategy, culture, organization, processes, technology, and/or customers and partners. The study takes an in-depth look at business dynamics and technological dynamics of relevance to IoT success in terms of digital maturity, BMPs, BM configuration for innovation, and technology trends. The quantitative results presented in Section 18.4 cannot be considered definitive but rather indicative for innovators and learners to achieve success in the IoT area.

Digital maturity self-assessment:
   The use case cluster has been assessed for the digital maturity of their companies by scaling themselves (on a scale from 1 to 10) based on relevant questions as illustrated in Figure 18.4, and the relevant points are given below:

- **Best practice comparison:** On a scale from 1 to 10, the case companies assess themselves to an average score of 7.87. It indicates that the case companies generally consider themselves close to being **perfectly digitally mature** and close to the digital top performer(s) in their respective sector.
- **Digital maturity of organization:** On a scale from 1 to 10, the case companies assess themselves to an average score of 7.70. It indicates that the case companies generally consider themselves to be at a **high level of digital maturity**. This result is consistent with the total average digital maturity score of 7.82, which indicates that the case companies possess a great amount of self-knowledge.

Self assessment

Best practice comparison

Digital maturity of organisation

Digital maturity of business model

Figure 18.4   Digital maturity self-assessment.

- **Digital maturity of BM:** On a scale from 1 to 10, the case companies assess themselves to an average score of 7.37. It indicates that the case companies generally consider themselves to have a **digitally mature BM**. This result, however, is lower than the self-defined digital maturity of the organization, indicating that the case companies acknowledge room for digital optimization in how value is created, delivered, and captured, in economic, social, cultural, or other contexts.

18.3.4 Business model patterns survey

The study of BMPs is based on the research by Weking et al. [19], and data collection was facilitated by a survey developed for the specific purpose of the EU-IoT project by the Interdisciplinary Centre for Digital Business Development, Aarhus University. The BMP survey is an online questionnaire that can be accessed via the online link. The patterns of a BM help us to understand the outline of the business. By using Weking et al.'s [19] taxonomy from 2020 to explore the BM patterns of our use case cluster, it is made very clear that they are all using the internet – or IT – as a fundamental source for building and innovating their BMs. The taxonomy depicts the super-patterns: **integration** that innovates its BM around new processes, **servitization** around new products, and **expertization** around a hybrid of products and processes.

18.3.5 Business model evaluation – innovation and configuration

The evaluation of BMs is based on the research by Gassmann et al. [21], and data collection was facilitated by the combination of the employed methodological tools. The concepts of BM innovation and BM configuration are explored with the theoretical framework of St. Gallen University [21], as shown in Figure 18.5, which depicts four dimensions that are the minimum requirements to define a BM. The four dimensions of a BM describe the rationale of how an organization creates, delivers, and captures value. This can be summarized as follows:

- WHO (customer) – Who are the target customers of the solution?
- WHAT (value proposition) – What does the company offer the customers? (Value design tool is the point of departure.)
- HOW (value chain) – How does the company, together with other partners, create this solution?
- WHY (revenue model) – How does the company create value in the form of revenue?

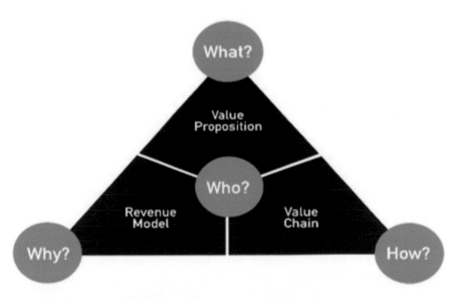

Figure 18.5 St. Gallen magic triangle.

Ultimately, the configuration of the dimensions is a plan for the successful operation of a business, and it provides the conceptual structure that supports the viability of the business. BM innovation is the process of reinventing or enhancing the BM by making simultaneous, and mutually supportive, changes to the dimensions.

18.4 Results and Analysis

This section will provide the results from data collection across the cluster of IoT use cases explored under the EU-IoT. The findings presented are gathered from the interviews conducted following semi-structured approach, and assessments of digital maturity dimensions, technology trends, and BM patterns using methods explained in Section 18.3.

18.4.1 Use case companies overview

The results cover a broad overview of the 30 IoT use cases, and background information on the case companies that have been selected as suitable units of analysis. To establish a complete picture of best practices for IoT use cases, data has been collected both qualitatively and quantitatively to ensure that the exploration considers both the individual specifics of the cases and the collective totality of the cluster. To make the data sources visible for the exploration as the foundation of our findings on best practices for IoT use cases, the case company details have been presented in Table 18.1. The people who represent the case companies are varying in gender, age, and professional role in the organization. All are, or have been, severely involved in the IoT use case, and all were volunteered interviewees. The cluster of case companies represent varying sizes measured on personnel numbers wherein 80% of the case companies can be defined as SMEs (i.e., having less than 250 employees), and the cluster thereby represents the backbone of European economy well, where 99% of all businesses are in the defined group of SMEs.

Some relevant information to consider in the exploration of best practices for IoT includes the timing of significant milestones achieved by the case company with regard to the use case. All the case companies covered in the cluster were founded between 1935 and 2019, with the average year of founding being 2006. Hence, majority of the case companies are founded in the most recent decade, with precisely 63% in the period 2010−2020. All the use cases covered in the cluster were initiated between 2007 and 2020, with the average year of founding being 2016. 80% of the IoT use cases were initiated in the period from 2015 and onwards. Only one of the 30 use cases was initiated before 2013.

Table 18.1   Data overview of case companies and related information.

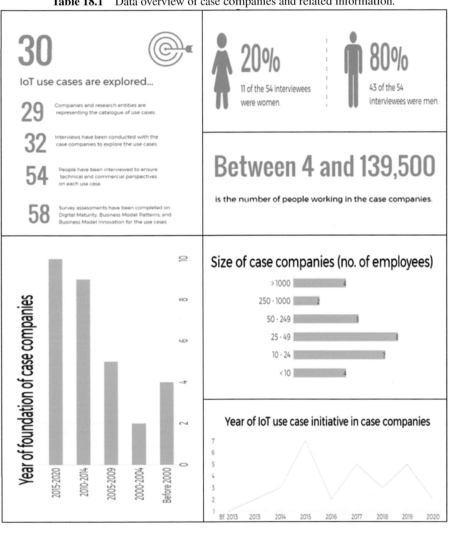

Table 18.1   (Continued.)

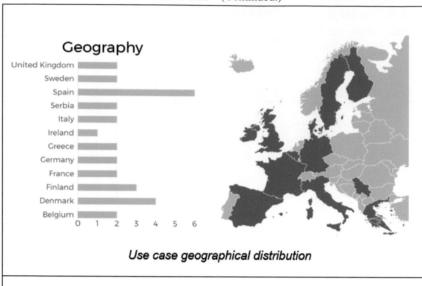

Geography

Use case geographical distribution

20 business

20 of the 30 IoT use cases proves best practice in business impact.

10 technology

20 of the 30 IoT use cases proves best practice in technology impact.

Note: In a business use case, the case company generates valuable impact by leveraging IoT technology in a solution, and in a technology use case, the case company generates valuable impact by offering IoT technology as a solution. Hence, Business use cases focus on IoT as value creation, and Technology use cases focus on IoT as value proposition.

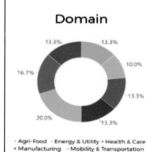

Domain

- Agri-Food · Energy & Utility · Health & Care
- Manufacturing · Mobility & Transportation
- Smart Cities & Communities · Other

The use cases are distributed across the six key domains. The seventh domain 'Other' covers cases in the areas of telecommunications, cyber security and cross-domain application.

Data insights:

- The data indicates that the corporate world has started to realize the value of developing and/or deploying IoT technology during the recent decade.

This reflects the increasing trend and overall growth in IoT solutions in the European landscape.

- None of the explored IoT use cases were initiated after 2020, which may indicate that a period of some years must occur after the initiation of an IoT initiative to mature it into a successful use case.
- Majority of best practice companies seems to be born digital and are founded on the basis of an IoT initiative, or adopts an IoT initiative within a short period of time after foundation.

18.4.2 Digital maturity

Digital maturity has been assessed to explore how successful IoT development and deployment interlinks with the digital maturity of a company. Based on an assessment of 30 use cases, the digital maturity patterns, studied for different companies, have been described in this section. It is found that the overall digital maturity score is 7.82 as highlighted in Figure 18.6 and the domain specific score is shown in Figure 18.8. The digital maturity (on a scale from 1 to 5) is mapped out on the six dimensions defined by the DMAT methodology, and the average distribution across the dimensions is illustrated in Figure 18.7. Across all case companies, **culture** is the most digitally mature dimension, and therefore likely to be a driver of digital competitive advantages.

Processes is the least digitally mature dimension and therefore likely to contain digital development areas. It has been observed that companies in the **manufacturing domain demonstrates the highest level of digital maturity**, whereas case companies in the energy & utility domain along with case companies in the **mobility & transportation domain demonstrates the lowest level of digital maturity**. In case of digital maturity across domains, the average distribution across the dimensions is illustrated in Figure 18.9. All domains are least digitally mature on the **processes** dimension.
Data insights:

- All domains are most digitally mature (DMAT score > 7) on the strategy, technology, and customers & partners dimensions. This means they are more digitally mature than the average for their respective sector and have exceptional abilities to digitally transform and to adopt new technology.

Digital Maturity

7.82

Figure 18.6 Digital maturity score across use case companies.

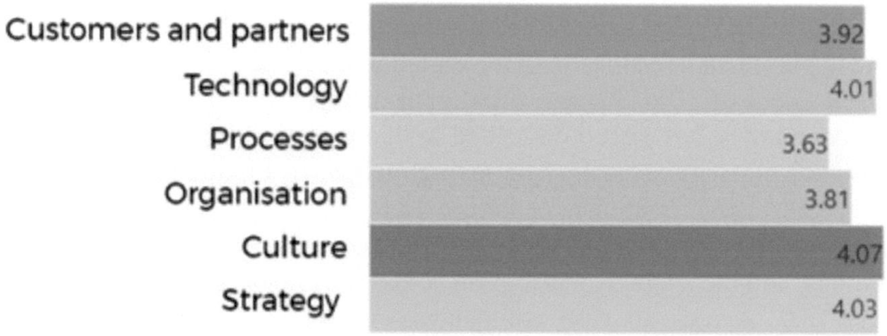

Customers and partners	3.92
Technology	4.01
Processes	3.63
Organisation	3.81
Culture	4.07
Strategy	4.03

Figure 18.7 Digital maturity dimensions distribution.

4.40 Agri-Food 3.81 Energy & Utility 4.40 Health & Care 4.69 Manufacturing 3.81 Mobility & Transportation 4.17 Smart Cities & Communities 4.41 Other

Figure 18.8 Digital maturity across domains.

- **Strategy** is likely to be the driver of digital competitive advantages for case companies in agri-food, mobility & transportation, and other, as this is the most digitally mature dimension of these domains.
- **Technology** is likely to be the driver of digital competitive advantages for case companies in health & care and smart cities & communities, as this is the most digitally mature dimension of these domains.

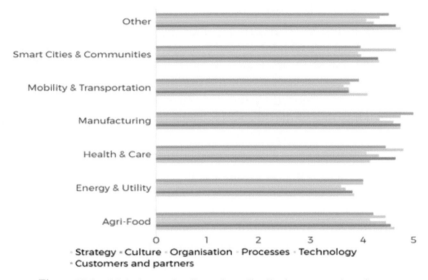

Figure 18.9 Digital maturity dimensions distribution across domains.

- **Customers & partners** is likely to be the driver of digital competitive advantages for case companies in manufacturing as this is the most digitally mature dimension of these domains. The same is true for energy & utility, although in combination with the technology dimension.
- **Culture** is the most digitally mature dimension on average across all domains. However, it does not apply to any isolated domain.
- The most digitally mature dimension differs across domains and includes strategy, technology, and customers & partners, indicating that these are the main drivers of digital competitive advantages.
- The data indicates that the digital capabilities of the use case cluster are vastly mature, which may be explicated by the origin of many of the case companies being born digital.
- The data indicates that **manufacturing** is the most digitally mature domain whereas **energy & utility** and the **mobility & transportation** are the least digitally maturity domains.
- **Processes** is the least digitally mature dimension across all domains, indicating that it is a digital development area for all companies regardless of domain.

18.4.3 Business model patterns

BMPs have been surveyed to explore how the BMs of use cases that successfully leverage IoT technology are shaped by IoT applicable patterns.

Figures 18.10 and 18.11 illustrate a distribution of the BM super and sub-patterns that have been archetypal for the IoT use case cluster. Majority of the use cases are characterized by the BM super patterns **servitization** and **expertization**. Only one of the 30 cases is characterized by the super pattern **integration**, and two cases cannot be characterized by any of the patterns suggested by the taxonomy.

- **Integration** implies that innovation initiatives made by the case company typically devote to new processes. This company strives to cover more activities in the value chain rather than specializing on a single step and/or selling directly to customers via online channels.
- **Servitization** implies that innovation initiatives made by the case company typically devote to new products or services. These companies strive to become a solution provider by offering new product support services instead of selling solely tangible products and/or integrating sensors into products.
- **Expertization** implies that innovation initiatives made by the case company typically devote to a combination of processes **and** products or services.

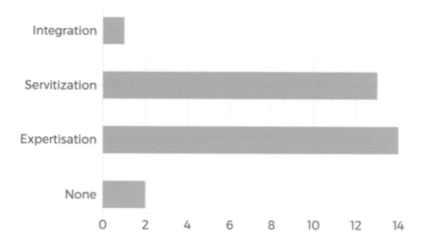

Figure 18.10   BM super patterns.

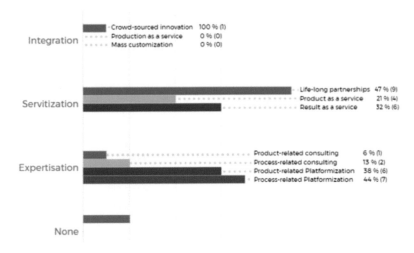

Figure 18.11 BM sub-patterns.

Table 18.2 Total distribution of business model patterns.

SUPER-PATTERN	SUB-PATTERN			
Integration 3 % (1)	Crowd-sourced innovation 4 % (1)	Production as a service		Mass customization
Servitization 43 % (13)	Life-long partnerships 32 % (9)	Product as a service 14 % (4)		Result as a service 21 % (6)
Expertization 47 % (14)	Product-related consulting 4 % (1)	Process-related consulting 7 % (2)	Product-related Platformization 21 % (6)	Process-relate Platformizatio 25 % (7)

*Note that two of the 30 use cases cannot be characterized by the patterns suggested by the taxonomy, and percentages are therefore calculated based on the remaining 28 cases.

These companies strive to apply internally built expertise and know-how in products, processes, or as a service. Table 18.2 is showing the BMP distribution in terms of super and sub-pattern classification. The results are showing that the **servitization** and **expertization** super patterns are trending in the industry. Under sub-patterns, **life-long** partnership is the highest choice of demand that the customer looks from the service provider of related product under servitization.

18.4.4 Business model innovation and configuration

BMs have been evaluated to explore how successful development and deployment of IoT solutions correlate with the configuration of the four BM dimensions and BM innovation. Figure 18.12 illustrates the total distribution of BM dimensions that have been subject to significant change, i.e., which specific dimension(s) in the case company BMs that were impacted by the development and/or deployment of the IoT solution.

Figure 18.13 shows the distribution of BM dimensions impacted per domain by the development and/or deployment of the IoT solution.

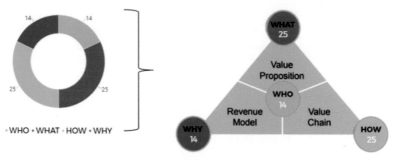

Figure 18.12   BM dimension distribution.

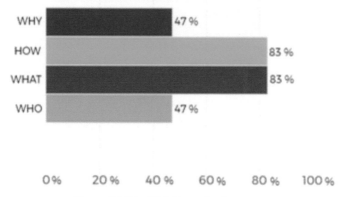

Figure 18.13   BM dimension impact.

Data insights:

- The **target customer** was impacted in 47% of the cases by the IoT development and/or deployment. Hence, the WHO of the BM has changed significantly for 14 of the 30 case companies.
- The **value proposition** was impacted in 83% of the cases by the IoT development and/or deployment. Hence, the WHAT of the BM has changed significantly for 25 of the 30 case companies. This means

the value proposition is typically the dominating subject of significant change in the domains agri-food, health & care, and smart cities & communities.

- The **value chain** was impacted in 83% of the cases by the IoT development and/or deployment. Hence, the HOW of the BM has changed significantly for 25 of the 30 case companies. The value chain is typically the dominating subject of significant change in the domains **manufacturing** and **other**.

- The **revenue model** was impacted in 47% of the cases by the IoT development and/or deployment. Hence, the WHY of the BM has changed significantly for 14 of the 30 case companies.

- The **four dimensions** are never equally impacted by the development and/or deployment of the IoT empowered solution. Only one or two dimensions can be simultaneously dominating subjects of significant change.

- The **WHO and WHY** dimension are rarely dominating subjects of significant change. These are either equally or less impacted than the **WHAT and WHY** dimensions.

To determine the correlation between BM innovation and the development and/or deployment of an IoT solution, we have explored the concept in alignment with the theory proposed by the University of St. Gallen [21], defining the occurrence of BM innovation with the occurrence of significant change in at least two of the four BM dimensions. The outcome of BMI is shown in Figure 18.14. Figure 18.15 illustrates the number of dimensions in the BM of the case companies that are impacted in specific domain by the development and/or deployment of the IoT solution. Figure 18.16 illustrates the number of dimensions in the BM of the case companies that are impacted

90 %

of the use case companies were subject to Business Model Innovation as an outcome of IoT development and/or deployment.

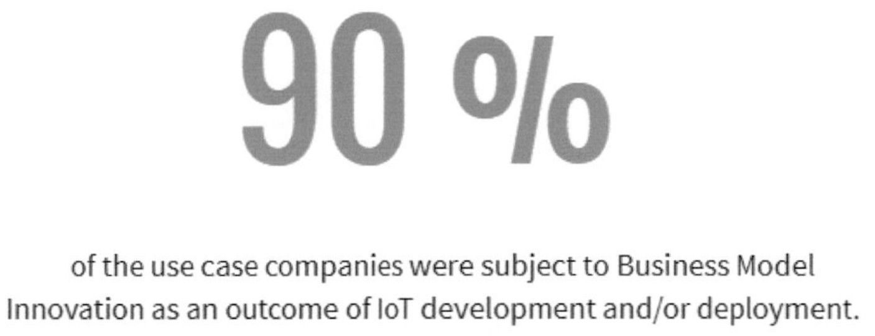

Figure 18.14   BMI outcome.

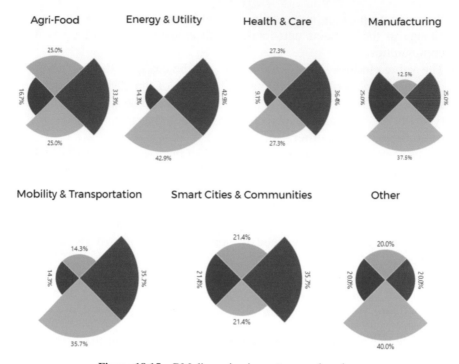

Figure 18.15   BM dimension impact across domains.

by the development and/or deployment of the IoT solution – distributed across domains. Figure 18.17 illustrates all the BM configurations of the case companies, i.e., the combination of BM dimensions that are impacted by the development and/or deployment of the IoT solution. The BM dimension combinations WHO-WHAT-HOW-WHY, WHAT-HOW-WHY, and WHAT-HOW are the most popular configurations that are subjected to significant change, as an outcome of the case companies' IoT development and deployment.

Data insights:

- Almost half (43.4%) of the case companies were impacted on two BM dimensions, and almost a fourth (23.4 %) were impacted on three BM dimensions and equivalent (23.4 %) on all four BM dimensions.
- All case companies were impacted on at least one BM dimension.
- The case companies were, on average, impacted on 2.65 dimensions. This indicates that the best practices for IoT typically include significant change in two or three BM dimensions.

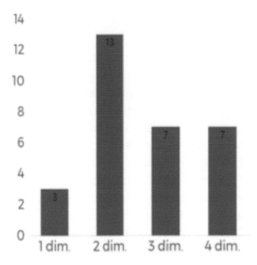

Figure 18.16 BMI-BM dimensions impacted per case.

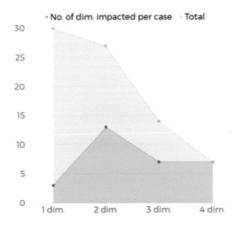

Figure 18.17 BMI – number of BM dimensions accumulated impact.

- **90% of the case companies** were impacted on more than one BM dimension and are therefore cases of BM innovation.
- The case companies across all domains were on average impacted on 2.25−3.00 dimensions. This indicates that the **best practices for IoT**

− no matter what domain the company operates in − typically include significant change in two or three BM dimensions.

- As an outcome of development and/or deployment of the IoT empowered solution, companies in the domains **manufacturing** and **mobility & transportation** are more likely to see impact on two BM dimensions, whereas companies in the domains agri-food and health & care are more likely to see impact on three BM dimensions.

- The data indicates that successful BMs in the IoT area are impacted on their **value proposition** and/or value chain by the development and deployment of IoT solutions. Hence, the single BM dimensions that are most often subject to significant change are WHAT and WHO.

- The data indicates that the combinations of BM dimensions that are most often subjected to significant change include: WHAT-HOW, WHAT-HOW-WHY, and WHAT-HOW-WHY-WHO. These configurations seem archetypical for achieving success in the IoT area.

- The data indicates that **BM innovation** − with 90% probability − is an outcome of best practice of IoT development and/or deployment.

Figures 18.18–18.20 have illustrated all the BM configurations of the case companies − both per case, the actual accumulated total of the cluster, and the potential accumulated total of the cluster, which are summarized as follows:

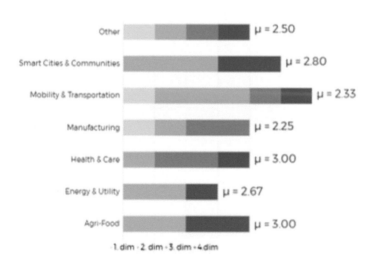

Figure 18.18   BMI across domains.

Figure 18.19   BM Config-Dimension combination per case.

- All illustrated two-dimensional BM configurations are applied in 37% or more of all the potential BMI cases.
- All illustrated three-dimensional BM configurations are applied in 30% or more of all the potential BMI cases.
- The four-dimensional BM configurations are applied in 26% of all the potential BMI cases.
- The BM dimension combination **WHAT-HOW** was among the most popular configurations for significant change (applied in 26% of all the potential BMI cases).
- This specific combination was applied in 54% of the potential two-dimensional BMI cases, and it is part of the **BM configuration in 74 %** of all the potential BMI cases.
- The BM dimension combination WHAT-WHY was not among the most popular configurations for significant change (applied in 4% of all the potential BMI cases).
- This specific combination was applied only in 8% of the potential two-dimensional BMI cases, but it is, however, part of the BM configuration in 48% of all the potential BMI cases.

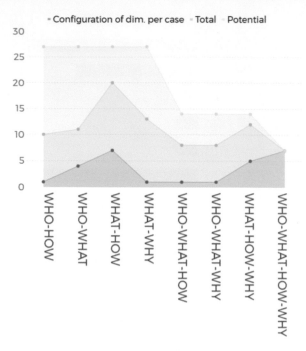

Figure 18.20   BM configuration – BM dimensions combination accumulated.
*Note that three of the use case cluster's 30 BMs are not subjected to BMI. Potential
calculations are therefore based on the remaining 27 BMI cases.

- The BM dimension combination **WHAT-HOW-WHY** was among the most popular configurations for significant change (applied in 19% of all the potential BMI cases).
- This specific combination was applied in 36% of the potential three-dimensional BMI cases, and it is part of the BM configuration in 44% of all the potential BMI cases.

*Note that configurations not mentioned constitute less than 40% of the total accumulated BMI cases.

18.4.5 Technology trends

Technology trends that characterize IoT use cases have been explored to conclude whether the application of specific technologies is repetitive for achieving success in the IoT area. In the setting of digital business, both IT and IoT can play a role, as highlighted in Figure 18.21, which is constitutive,

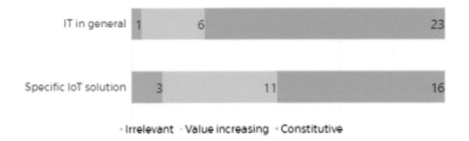

IT in general 1   6   23

Specific IoT solution 3   11   16

· Irrelevant · Value increasing · Constitutive

Figure 18.21   Role of IT and IoT.

value increasing via IoT solution development or deployment or irrelevant for the general BM of the organization. Figure 18.22 shows technology trends applied in the context of case companies.

Data insights:

- To 90% of the case companies, the **specific IoT solution** developed and/or deployed adds value to the overall BM of the company. To more than half (53.3%), the IoT solution even matures into having a constitutive role, causing IoT to drive the selection of patterns that depict the overall BM of the company.
- **IT as a general phenomenon** is value increasing for the business of almost all the case companies explored and constitutive to 76.7% of them. This indicates that the value potential of business directly relies on the integration of IT-driven BM patterns for three-fourth of the companies.
- The data indicates that IT as a general phenomenon often plays a constitutive role in the BM of companies that successfully develop and/or deploy IoT solutions. Hence, the best practice seems to rest upon the **digital underpinning**.
- The data further indicates that the specific IoT solution being developed and/or deployed should at least assume a value-increasing role for the overall BM of the company to foster future success.
- The data indicates that key technological trends include **sensors and/or cameras**, **artificial intelligence**, **digital twins**, **machine learning**, and **open software and/or hardware**. These constitute the archetypical technologies that presently seem repetitive for achieving success in the IoT area.

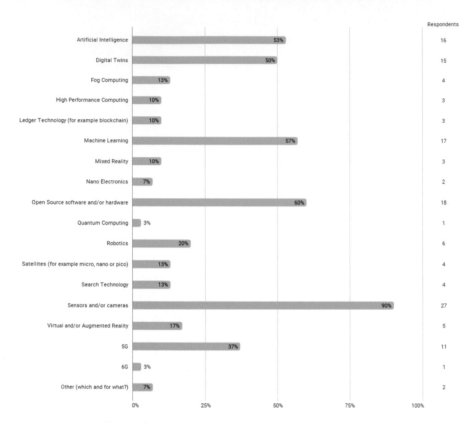

Figure 18.22   Technologies applied base case companies.

- Other technologies applied include **addictive manufacturing**, **LoRa**, and **software-defined networking (SDN)** technology.
- **Sensors and/or cameras** is the utmost adopted and widespread technology, with 90% of the IoT use case cluster applying it in their case companies.
- **Artificial intelligence**, **digital twins**, **machine learning**, and **open software and/or hardware** are also common technologies that are applied in half or more of the case companies.
- **6G**, **quantum computing**, and **nano electronics** are the technologies that are least applied in the case companies.

18.4.6 Relevant skill areas and patterns

This section highlights the trends of skills in the IoT area (Figures 18.23, 18.24) based on relevant survey conducted with various random professionals across industries as part of the EU-IoT project study.

Data insights:

- **All IoT skill areas are important**. However, **IoT data and related data analytics** skills and modern computing (cloud/edge/mobile) seem to be the most important in modern times.
- **IT sector is the most prevalent** area where these skills are used and known.
- At resource level, **engineers are the most interested and expected to be skilled** in these areas.

18.5 Conclusion

This study has presented the analysis for 30 IoT use cases carried out as part of the EU-IoT project with an objective to explore and analyze different business models and technology patterns, values, trends, operational domains, and best practices that are enabled in the IoT ecosystem. The data has been collected across Europe from different domain companies that varied in size and scale of operations. In order to fulfill the objective, various business modeling tools have been used, which includes interviews, surveys, DMAT, St. Gallen's magic triangle, and BMP survey. This study also presented the background of

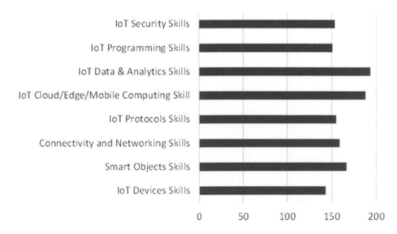

Figure 18.23 IoT skill areas importance.

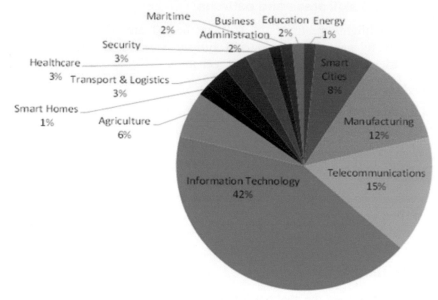

Figure 18.24   Skills survey sector distribution.

those tools and how they have been used in relevant context. There are a lot of data collected for 30 use cases and each use case is then analyzed individually and in an aggregate manner to derive the impact in terms of digital maturity, business model patterns, business model innovation, and configuration aspects. In addition, the applied technology trend in all the cases has also been presented. Finally, for practitioners/recruiters, the required skill patterns are also presented, which are mapped to relevant IoT skill areas based on the surveys conducted with various professionals across industry. Beyond that, it tells what kind of business models patterns (integration, expertization, and servitization) are used in IoT ecosystems and what the role of the underlying ecosystem is. The data indicates that **IT as a general phenomenon often plays a constitutive role** in the BM of companies that successfully develop and/or deploy IoT solutions. Hence, the best practice seems to rest upon digital underpinning. The data further indicates that the **specific IoT solution** being developed and/or deployed should at least assume a **value-increasing role for the overall BM** of the company to foster future success. The data also indicates that **key technological trends** include sensors and/or cameras, Artificial intelligence, digital twins, machine learning, and open software and/or hardware. These constitute the archetypical technologies that presently seem **repetitive for achieving success in the IoT area**.

Acknowledgements

The data and results shown in this study have been collected and evaluated as part of the EU-IoT project through a coordination and support action under the Grant Agreement ID 956671 of H2020-EU program.

References

[1] R. Nicolescu, M. Huth, P. Radanliev, and D. De Roure, "Mapping the Values of IoT," J. Inf. Technol., vol. 33, no. 4, pp. 345–360, Dec. 2018, doi: 10.1057/s41265-018-0054-1.

[2] M. J. Beliatis, N. Lohacharoenvanich, M. Presser, and A. Aagaard, "Internet of Things for a sustainable food packaging ecosystem insights from a business perspective," in 2019 Global IoT Summ IEEE, 2019.

[3] K. Acharya, M. J. Beliatis, and M. Presser, "AUR, A Unit to Relate: Regulating Air Conditioning Use with IoT to address social disparity within urban Indian homes," 2019 Glob. IoT Summit IEEE, 2019.

[4] G. Reggio, M. Leotta, M. Cerioli, R. Spalazzese, and F. Alkhabbas, "What are IoT systems for real? An experts' survey on software engineering aspects," Internet Things, vol. 12, p. 100313, Dec. 2020, doi: 10.1016/j.iot.2020.100313.

[5] M. J. Beliatis, K. Jensen, L. Ellegaard, A. Aagaard, and M. Presser, "Next Generation Industrial IoT Digitalization for Traceability in Metal Manufacturing Industry: A Case Study of Industry 4.0," Electronics, vol. 10, no. 5, 2021, doi: 10.3390/electronics10050628.

[6] N. Rasmussen and M. J. Beliatis, "IoT based Digitalization and Servitization of Construction Equipment in Concrete Industry," 2019 Glob. IoT Summit IEEE, 2019.

[7] O. F. Grooss, M. Presser, and T. Tambo, "Surround yourself with your betters: Recommendations for adopting Industry 4.0 technologies in SMEs," Digit. Bus., vol. 2, no. 2, p. 100046, 2022, doi: 10.1016/j.digbus.2022.100046.

[8] M. Presser, Q. Zhang, A. Bechmann, and M. J. Beliatis, "The Internet of Things as Driver for Digital Business Model Innovation," in Digital Business Models: Driving Transformation and Innovation, A. Aagaard, Ed. Cham: Springer International Publishing, 2019, pp. 27–55. doi: 10.1007/978-3-319-96902-2_2.

[9] S. Kar, B. Chakravorty, S. Sinha, and M. P. Gupta, "Analysis of Stakeholders Within IoT Ecosystem," in Digital India: Reflections and Practice, A. K. Kar, S. Sinha, and M. P. Gupta, Eds. Cham: Springer International Publishing, 2018, pp. 251–276. doi: 10.1007/978-3-319-78378-9_15.

[10] A. Aagaard, Ed., Digital Business Models: Driving Transformation and Innovation. Cham: Springer International Publishing, 2019. doi: 10.1007/978-3-319-96902-2.

[11] A. Aagaard, M. Presser, M. Beliatis, H. Mansour, and S. Nagy, "A Tool for Internet of Things Digital Business Model Innovation," in 2018 IEEE Globecom Workshops (GC Wkshps), Dec. 2018, pp. 1–6. doi: 10.1109/GLOCOMW.2018.8644517.

[12] D. Langley, J. Doorn, I. Ng, S. Stieglitz, A. Lazovik, and A. Boonstra, "The Internet of Everything: Smart things and their impact on business models," J. Bus. Res., vol. 122, Jan. 2020, doi: 10.1016/j.jbusres.2019.12.035.

[13] O. F. Grooss, M. Presser, and T. Tambo, "Balancing Digital Maturity and Operational Performance - Progressing in a Low-digital SME Manufacturing Setting," Procedia Comput. Sci., vol. 200, pp. 495–504, 2022, doi: 10.1016/j.procs.2022.01.247.

[14] T. Iggena et al., "IoTCrawler: Challenges and Solutions for Searching the Internet of Things," Sensors, vol. 21, no. 5, p. 1559, Feb. 2021, doi: 10.3390/s21051559.

[15] A. F. Skarmeta, J. Santa, M. J. Beliatis, M. Presser, and et al., "IoTCrawler: Browsing the Internet of Things," GIoT 2018 Proc. IEEE Commun. Soc., 2018.

[16] P. Singh et al., "Blockchain for Economy of Scale in Wind Industry: A Demo Case," in Internet of Things, vol. 13533, A. González-Vidal, A. Mohamed Abdelgawad, E. Sabir, S. Ziegler, and L. Ladid, Eds. Cham: Springer International Publishing, 2022, pp. 175–186. doi: 10.1007/978-3-031-20936-9_14.

[17] P. Singh, K. S. Acharya, M. J. Beliatis, and M. Presser, "Semantic Search System For Real Time Occupancy," in 2021 IEEE International Conference on Internet of Things and Intelligence Systems (IoTaIS), 2021, pp. 49–55. doi: 10.1109/IoTaIS53735.2021.9628719.

[18] A. Aagaard, M. Presser, T. Collins, M. Beliatis, A. Skou, and E. Jakobsen, "The Role of Digital Maturity Assessment in Technology Interventions with Industrial Internet Playground," Electronics, vol. 10, p. 1134, May 2021, doi: 10.3390/electronics10101134.

[19] J. Weking, M. Stöcker, M. Kowalkiewicz, M. Böhm, and H. Krc-mar, "Leveraging industry 4.0 – A business model pattern framework," Int. J. Prod. Econ., vol. 225, p. 107588, Jul. 2020, doi: 10.1016/j.ijpe.2019.107588.

[20] C. A. de Souza, J. N. Correa, M. M. Oliveira, A. Aagaard, and M. Presser, "IoT Driven Business Model Innovation and Sustainability: a literature review and a case Study in Brazil," in 2019 Global IoT Summit (GIoTS), Aarhus, Denmark, Jun. 2019, pp. 1–6. doi: 10.1109/GIOTS.2019.8766371.

[21] O. Gassmann, K. Frankenberger, and M. Csik, "The St.Gallen Business Model Navigator," 2013. https://www.alexandria.unisg.ch/224941/ (accessed Jan. 06, 2023).

Index

About the Editors

Rute C. Sofia (Ph.D. 2004) is the Industrial IoT Head at fortiss - research institute of the Free State of Bavaria for software intensive services and systems. She is also an Invited Associate Professor of University Lusófona de Humanidades e Tecnologias, and an Associate Researcher at ISTAR, Instituto Universitário de Lisboa. Rute's research background has been developed in an industrial and academic context. She was a co-founder of the COPELABS research unit, and the COPELABS scientific director (2013-2017), where she was a Senior Researcher (2010-2019). She co-founded the Portuguese startup Senception Lda (2013-2019), a startup focused on personal communication platforms. Her current research interests are: network architectures and protocols; IoT; Edge computing; in-network computing; network mining. Rute has published over 70 peer-reviewed articles in her fields of expertise and 9 patents. She is an ACM Europe Councilor, an ACM Senior member, and an IEEE Senior Member. She was an IEEE ComSoc N2Women Awards co-chair (2020-2021). She is also a member of the Expert Group of the Networld ETP.

John Soldatos (http://gr.linkedin.com/in/johnsoldatos) holds a Ph.D. in Electrical & Computer Engineering from the National Technical University of Athens (2000), is an Honorary Research Fellow at the University of Glasgow, UK (2014-present), and an Innovation Delivery Specialist with Netcompany-Intrasoft. He has significant experience in working closely with large multi-national industries as R&D consultant and delivery specialist, while being scientific advisor to high-tech startup enterprises. Dr. Soldatos is an expert in Internet-of-Things (IoT) technologies and applications. He has played a leading role in the successful delivery of more than seventy projects, for both private and public sector organizations, including complex integrated projects. He is co-founder of the open source platform OpenIoT. He has published more than 200 articles in international journals and conference proceedings. He has co-edited and co-authored seven edited volumes (books) on IoT and Artificial Intelligence (AI) related topics.